Building the
Atlantic World

OTHER FOREIGN POLICY RESEARCH INSTITUTE BOOKS:

PROTRACTED CONFLICT

A FORWARD STRATEGY FOR AMERICA

A FOREIGN POLICY RESEARCH INSTITUTE BOOK

BUILDING THE

ATLANTIC WORLD

BY ROBERT STRAUSZ-HUPÉ, JAMES E. DOUGHERTY
AND WILLIAM R. KINTNER

With Stefan T. Possony, Robert L. Pfaltzgraff, Jr.,
Richard B. Foster and Francis P. Hoeber

HARPER & ROW, PUBLISHERS
NEW YORK, EVANSTON, AND LONDON

TO A. W. S.

WHO DESERVES WELL OF HIS COUNTRY

AND

THE ATLANTIC COMMUNITY

CONTENTS

PREFACE

The overarching problem confronting the United States in the second half of the twentieth century is the creation of a more stable international order. If the United States is to master this task against the contention of communist leadership, it must enlist the support of likeminded peoples. Since the peoples of the West are joined by kindred values and institutions, the United States turns logically to them as partners in the great undertaking. The North Atlantic Community possesses human and material resources which, in their totality, far exceed those of its adversaries. Yet the mere existence of superiority is not sufficient to face down the challenge of tyranny confronting the values of the West. It is the thesis of this study that the peoples of the West, if they are to assure their own future, as well as to continue to foster the development of new societies in Asia and Africa, must achieve a greater measure of Atlantic unity.

From its foundation in 1955, the Foreign Policy Research Institute has been preoccupied with the quest for Atlantic unity. The Institute initiated the Conference on North Atlantic Community which was held, September, 1957, in Bruges, Belgium, under the joint auspices of the University of Pennsylvania and the College of Europe. This meeting, organized under this Institute's supervision, brought together more than one hundred leading Americans and Europeans to discuss the intellectual and cultural basis of the Atlantic Community. The Bruges Conference was a major attempt to explore the fundamental cultural and intellectual problems of Atlantic cooperation. From this Conference issued the idea of an Atlantic Institute as a means for promoting scholarly and cultural exchange within the Atlantic Community and developing study programs relating to political, economic and social problems of common Atlantic concern. The Atlantic Institute began its work in Paris under the direction of the Honorable Henry Cabot Lodge in 1961.

In 1959, the United States Senate Foreign Relations Committee contracted with the Institute to prepare a study on "United States Policy Toward Western Europe." This study, which, along with twelve others on various aspects of American foreign policy, was published by the Government Printing Office in 1961, centered upon the military, politico-diplomatic and economic aspects of American policy toward Western Europe during the decade of the sixties.

The problems of cooperation among the peoples of the Atlantic ocean basin are inextricably linked to those posed by the global confrontation between the free and open societies of the West and the communist powers. In May, 1959, *Protracted Conflict,* published under the imprimatur of the Institute, examined the principles guiding the communist conflict management and the techniques and strategies of the Cold War. An Institute sequel to this book, *A Forward Strategy for America,* proposed broad policies for the United States and its principal allies to insure the eventual triumph of the open societies.

The North Atlantic Treaty Organization, the primary instrument of Western security, has become a familiar and important part of the configuration of international relations. NATO's future, however, like life itself, is by no means assured. Much has already been achieved by the existence of NATO. But the Western Alliance, if it is to endure, must continue to serve the purpose for which it was founded, namely, to provide for the security of the North Atlantic area. If it fails in this task, it is not likely to inspire the continued support of those countries which are its members. April, 1969, will mark the twentieth anniversary of the formation of NATO, the year in which the members will review their adherence to the treaty. It is because of their abiding belief that the strengthening of the West—economically, politically and spiritually, as well as militarily— is the key to American and Free World security that members of the Foreign Policy Research Institute have collaborated in this study. It is their hope that *Building the Atlantic World* may clarify the task of adapting NATO to the needs of the next decade.

The writing of this book was completed several weeks before President de Gaulle's celebrated January 14, 1963 press conference and the subsequent French veto of the British entry into the Common Market. We addressed our critique to the political forces, the economic pressures and conflicting military concepts that helped to promote this rupture in the Western ranks. We believe that our analysis has been substantiated in large measure by these events. We also hold that the political concepts set forth in this book provide a basis for restoring harmony within the Grand Alliance. Whether that Grand Alliance will be transformed into a durable political community will depend on the willingness of its members to transcend their parochial interests and to display a "decent respect" toward one another's legitimate aspirations. At the end of the book we have added a postscript which sets forth our interpretation of the crisis in January, 1963, and the kind of steps that might be taken on both sides of the Atlantic to heal the breach which has been opened by the French suspension of the Brussels negotiations. In a few places in the book we have taken brief note, for the sake of completeness, of this development without, however, otherwise modifying the text.

The research for this study has been generously supported by a grant from the A. W. Mellon Educational and Charitable Trust. We wish to express our gratitude to this Trust for supporting our effort, particularly to Adolph Schmidt, whose intuitive recognition of the pressing needs for greater transatlantic cooperation has been a stimulating inspiration to this work. We are also grateful to the Relm Foundation, whose support enabled us to secure assistance in the writing of the chapter on the economics of the Atlantic world.

As many other studies completed by the Foreign Policy Research Institute, the present work was enriched by the advice of experienced persons in public and private life. The authors consulted with research organizations, academic institutions, U.S. Government agencies, and officials of Allied governments, and benefited from participation in numerous conferences on both sides of the Atlantic world.

The key ideas of this book were discussed in meetings of the Associates of the Foreign Policy Research Institute and the Institute Staff. A special indebtedness must be acknowledged to the following Associates for their invaluable critique and comment: Dr. Norman D. Palmer, Professor of Political Science, University of Pennsylvania; Dr. Froelich G. Rainey, Professor of Anthropology, University of

Pennsylvania, and Director of the University Museum; Dr. Arthur P. Whitaker, Professor of History, University of Pennsylvania, and Director of the Institute's study of Argentine Nationalism; Dr. Roy F. Nichols, Vice-Provost, Dean of the Graduate School of Arts and Sciences, and Professor of History, University of Pennsylvania; Dr. William Y. Elliott, Professor of Government, Harvard University, and adviser to the Department of State; Dr. James R. Schlesinger, Professor of Economics, University of Virginia; and Dr. Hans Kohn, Professor Emeritus of History, College of the City of New York. Dr. Kohn, one of the great pioneers in the field of Atlantic Civilization Studies, has taken an exceptional personal interest in this project, and his influence is perceptible on many pages of the book.

The three principal authors are alone responsible for the integration of the materials and ideas on which they have drawn. The four associate authors are responsible for the initial drafting of several of the chapters. Dr. Stefan T. Possony, Director of International Studies at the Hoover Institution, Stanford University, associated with this Institute since its foundation in 1955, was a co-author of *A Forward Strategy for America* and a principal contributor to *Protracted Conflict*. Dr. Possony is one of the country's foremost authorities on political-military strategy, and his contributions to this book have been invaluable. Mr. Robert L. Pfaltzgraff, Jr., a staff member of the Institute, and in 1960–61 an instructor of Political Science at the University of Pennsylvania, is currently engaged in research for his doctoral dissertation in the United States and Great Britain. Under a Penfield Fellowship from the University of Pennsylvania he is examining the development of British attitudes and policy toward the European Economic Community. Mr. Richard B. Foster, the Director of the Defense Analysis Center of Stanford Research Institute, has brought to this study his deep familiarity with the strategic and technological aspects of North Atlantic defense. Mr. Francis P. Hoeber, Stanford Research Institute, is the author of several authoritative studies on the comparative economic potential of the Soviet Union, Communist China, Western Europe and the United States. The personal participation of Messrs. Foster and Hoeber in this study in no way implies endorsement of the findings of the book by the Stanford Research Institute.

In the drafting of certain chapters, the following contributed most significantly: Chapter 1, "The Meaning of the Atlantic Community,"

Mr. Robert L. Pfaltzgraff, Jr.; Chapter 3, "The Defense of Atlantic Frontiers," Dr. Stefan T. Possony and Mr. Richard B. Foster; Chapter 4, "The Economic Base of Atlantic Power," Mr. Francis P. Hoeber with the assistance of Mr. Herbert K. Folpe, a research assistant of the Foreign Policy Research Institute. A number of friends contributed ideas and suggestions in the formulation of this chapter, most importantly, Dr. Virgil Salera of Alameda State College, Dr. James Schlesinger, Dr. Stefan T. Possony, Mr. William Dale, who is currently with the International Monetary Fund, and Mr. Sperry Lea, National Planning Association. Mr. Robert L. Pfaltzgraff, Jr., Stuart L. Hannon and Vladimir Petrov contributed to Chapter 6, "The Grand Design and Its Opponents: A Western Response"; Tai Sung An, research assistant of the Foreign Policy Research Institute, and Stefan T. Possony submitted memoranda which were helpful in the preparation of Chapter 7, "Institutions for the Future Atlantic Community."

The authors wish to express their thanks also to Miss Diane Kressler, Dr. J. Roffe Wike II and Dr. Gerhard Mally for research which assisted them in the writing of this book.

They are grateful, too, to Mr. Robert C. Herber, Managing Editor of *Orbis*, the Institute's quarterly journal of world affairs, and administrative officer of the Foreign Policy Research Institute, for his comments on the manuscript and his administrative assistance throughout the course of the study. Prior to publication of this book, parts of Chapter 3 and nearly all of Chapter 5 were published in article form in the Summer and Fall, 1962, issues of *Orbis*. The authors are particularly indebted to Miss Diane Kressler, Mrs. Carole Nein, Mrs. Margaret Capotrio, Mrs. Patricia Martin, Miss Kay Christiansen and Miss Kay Kintner, who typed and proofread the several working drafts of each chapter as well as the final manuscript.

Others whom the authors wish to thank for their advice, cooperation and assistance are: Mr. Raymond Albright; Major General Stanton Babcock (Ret.); Brigadier General Donald Bennett, USA, of the NATO Standing Group; Dr. Kurt Birrenbach, Deputy (CDU) of the Bundestag of the German Federal Republic; Dr. Alvin J. Cottrell, Institute for Defense Analyses; General Pierre Gallois; Mr. Livingston Hartley, U.S. Citizens' Commission for the Atlantic Convention; Mr. James Huntley of the Atlantic Institute; the Honorable Henry Cabot Lodge, Director General of the Atlantic Institute; Colonel Ferdinand Otto Miksche; Brigadier General Robert C. Richardson, III, USAF; Dr. Timothy Stanley, Council on Foreign Relations; Dr. Dirk Stikker, Secretary General of the North Atlantic Treaty Organization; Mr. Irwin Tobin, Office of European Regional Affairs, U.S. Department of State; Mr. Pierre Uri of the Atlantic Institute; and Dean Francis O. Wilcox of the School of Advanced International Studies, the Johns Hopkins University. The principal authors are, of course, responsible for the specific views advanced in this book.

ROBERT STRAUSZ-HUPÉ
JAMES E. DOUGHERTY
WILLIAM R. KINTNER

"The existence of a community is a
state of mind—a conviction that goals
and values are widely shared, that effective
communication is possible, that mutual
trust is reasonably assured."

J. W. FULBRIGHT

CHAPTER **1** THE MEANING OF THE

ATLANTIC COMMUNITY

To the future historian, the unity and vitality of the North Atlantic Community, evoked by the challenges of our time, may well appear to be the outstanding event of the twentieth century. Between 1930 and 1950, Western civilization was psychologically unprepared for the sudden and unexpected assault launched by its alienated members. It was in danger of succumbing first to fascist, then to communist, aggression. The idea of free men and free minds in an open society, which is the essence of the North Atlantic civilization, defies the rote of history. The conception of freedom as the birthright of every man, product of the nonhistorical optimism of the eighteenth century, has illuminated only a brief moment in the procession of the ages. It happens that this moment is still ours. To wrest from it an enduring order is not a task that can be accomplished haphazardly while doing "business as usual." Our society—so new and so complex and still so untried—can survive and advance only if its members are united in common effort, conscious of what they hold in common.

From the days when the first European settlements had taken precarious root on American shores, the conflicts among the European powers reverberated across the Atlantic. Together with their origin, the Europeans on both sides of the Atlantic shared their history. At times, the common burden chafed. Throughout much of its history the United States sought to steer clear in peacetime from undertakings which might have led to its political involvement in Europe. Yet the pull of countervailing sentiments as well as strategic logic drew the United States into the world political arena—and

1

drew it the more irresistibly the more American wealth and power increased. The very rise of the United States altered the world balance of power.

Twice in this century the United States has chosen to intervene in wars which had their origins in Europe. Heeding Canning's call of more than a century ago, the United States sought to redress the balance of power in the Old World. In two world wars the United States chose intervention as the sole alternative to the domination of Europe by hostile forces. American policymakers, complex as might have been their motivation, acted as if impelled by strategic necessity: the power capable of dominating the vast Eurasian land mass would gain such a decisive strategic advantage over its opponents that global control might be within its grasp.

After World War II, the United States, for a brief moment, thought of repeating the withdrawal of the twenties and again cutting its overseas commitments. Winston Churchill's famous speech at Fulton, Missouri, in 1946, warning of the dangers of communist expansion and urging a strengthening of the Anglo-American alliance, failed to alarm the American public. Americans, by and large, in their desire to be left alone in the aftermath of victory, grasped neither the new threat posed by communist expansion, nor did they perceive the extent to which war had eroded British power. It was the inability of Britain to protect Greece and Turkey from communist encroachments that led to President Truman's decision in 1947 to underwrite the security of these countries. The communist-led revolt in Greece, followed by the communist coup in Czechoslovakia and the Soviet attempt in 1948 to force the Western powers out of Berlin, spoke louder than Mr. Churchill's somber rhetoric. The United States had expended its blood and treasure to defeat Nazi Germany and insure the freedom of Western Europe. Yet victory in World War II had been paid for by a swath of chaos and destruction across Europe. First, American policy addressed itself to the economic recovery of Western Europe. The Marshall Plan set Western Europe upon the road to an economic prosperity which was to surpass the most optimistic expectations of donor and recipients alike. The flow of American aid helped revive the enormous productive energies of Western Europe. It did not fill the vacuum of power. Shortly after the inauguration of the Marshall Plan, the United States, in a momentous departure from its long-cherished policy of avoiding "entangling" alliances, forged a coalition of North Atlantic countries and pledged itself to maintain permanently its military force in Continental Europe.

The creation of the Atlantic Alliance could not fail to elicit from the communists angry cries of protest. They portrayed NATO as a tool of Western "aggression," as the principal weapon of "capitalist" countries in their strategy to destroy communism and to stem the tide of "national liberation" sweeping Asia, Africa and Latin America. The thrust of communist propaganda points to communist strategic objectives: The repeated Soviet threats to Berlin and the exploitation of unrest in the underdeveloped areas are designed to divide the United States and its European allies and, ultimately, break up NATO. Upon the dissolution of the Atlantic Alliance, the United States would stand alone against the combined resources and manpower of Communist Eurasia.

The North Atlantic area possesses human and material resources that, by a wide margin, exceed those of the communist bloc. Barring the most extraordinary developments such as a catastrophic lapse of statesmanship and erosion of the will to self-preservation, the North Atlantic peoples can maintain this lead for the foreseeable future, if not for another century. Within the North Atlantic area remains the world's greatest reservoir of skilled manpower. It surpasses by far the rest of the globe in industrial productivity. Even in combined population, the countries of NATO dwarf the Soviet Union and its East European satellites. In short, although the United States cannot look with indifference upon the loss of any region of the world to the Sino-Soviet bloc, Western Europe is the one center outside the United States which, in the most literal sense, is vital to the United States—as vital indeed as almost any place inside the territorial limits of the United States.

The story of West European economic growth and cultural efflorescence during the last decade mocks the philosophic pessimism which, for nearly a century, bewailed the decadence and decline of Europe. Not only does it refute the "inevitabilities" of communist theory; it also confirms the pragmatic insights of American experience: the Europeans have managed to marry private industrial expansion to general social improvement. In retrospect, it can be seen that no amount of individual national initiative could have worked the miracle of the fifties had it not been for the collective courage to experiment with varied and novel forms of political, military and economic unification. It is the results of these experiments which contain an answer—at least a tentative one—to the most pressing question of the age: how to adapt the nation-state system to the industrial-scientific revolution. Western Europe's renewed economic vigor and resurgent political imagination make it the most tempting of the prizes sought by the communists. For the communists, Western Europe is a standing ideological challenge—and the decisive stake in the struggle for world power. Western Europe has grown rich; her very wealth has created new problems and dangers. But the thrust of federative achievement in Europe and the durability of the Atlantic Alliance give new impetus to an idea which has persisted for centuries—the basic unity of the Western world and its civilization.

I

Common interests draw the North Atlantic peoples together. But beyond the need to pool resources to meet common dangers are the more enduring bonds of a common civilization—of shared values, compatible political institutions, and a network of communications and exchanges of scientific, social, political, economic and artistic ideas—which have enriched the lives of peoples on both sides of the Atlantic from the earliest days to the present. The North Atlantic Community transcends both in time and purpose the challenges of totalitarianism, old and new, to the West. It does not exist solely by virtue of the creation of NATO in 1949, however important that Alliance may be to the security of its members. It is the product of centuries of contacts and exchanges, of the adaptation of European civilization to the environment of the New World.

It is commonplace to speak of America's discovery of Europe in the twentieth century. To be sure, in the nineteenth century, the United States bent its energies singlemindedly to the building of a civilization in the New World. Yet, even in the midst of the absorbing tasks of continental expansion and empire, Americans did not lose sight of the basic unity of the North Atlantic area. One of the earliest American historians, Alexander Hill Everett, wrote in 1827: "As respects the United States, their history sufficiently proves, if theory were wanting, that it is not in their power to separate themselves entirely from the great political system of Christendom, with which they are naturally connected by community of origin." Everett recognized the debt of the United States to Europe for its political and cultural heritage. "In the United States," he wrote,

we have brought, as we suppose, the forms of government to still greater perfection, have cleared away many abuses, avoided many errors, and introduced great improvements in the details of administration; but we are still proud and happy to look to Great Britain as the source from which we have drawn all our political institutions, with the alterations necessary to accommodate them to our situation and habits; and some of the most valuable—as the *habeas corpus* act and trial by jury—without any alteration at all. The American Constitution, as was justly remarked by the illustrious Fox, is that of England improved by the results of the experience of a thousand years.[1]*

Almost from the very first European explorations of the New World, the North Atlantic peoples have been engaged in an exchange of ideas, institutions, commerce and populations. Since the first European settlements, an Atlantic Community has existed, for the adventurers who first crossed the Atlantic and set foot on the shores of the Western Hemisphere brought with them European customs, ideas and products, and took back with them samples of life in the New World. Although Europeans ventured to all corners of the globe and established settlements, nowhere did they succeed so thoroughly, with the exception of Australia and New Zealand, in transplanting European civilization as in the Western Hemisphere.

The settlers brought from Europe a heritage which, even after adaptation to a new environment, was preserved and enriched. The colonists drew heavily upon Europe for the ideas from which they developed their political, economic and social systems, for even in the seventeenth and eighteenth centuries newspapers, books, travel and correspondence linked the peoples on the rim of the North Atlantic basin. Raw materials moved eastward to be processed in Europe, and manufactures from the Old World filled shops in the colonies. In the nineteenth century, Europeans such as Cobden and de Tocqueville crossed the Atlantic to observe the emergence of political systems and social orders which embodied ideas and values brought from Europe and tested in the New World. Americans journeyed to Europe to see at first hand the birthplace of the civilization which they acknowledged as their own.

---

* Superior numbers refer to Notes, beginning on page 347.

Of all the world's great civilizations, none has placed such great emphasis upon education as the West. Leading writers, poets, painters, sculptors and musicians have crossed and recrossed the Atlantic, widening the exchange of ideas and styles. Americans in considerable numbers have always journeyed to Europe to complete their education; now large contingents of students from the Old World attend American educational institutions and carry back to their native lands not only the learning but also American "know-how" and the American "way of life." From the eighteenth century to the present, American artists and writers have gone to study and to work to London, Paris, Florence and Rome. For generations, American philosophers studied in the Germany of Kant, Hegel and Fichte. In the nineteenth century, American educators, including Sylvanus Thayer, Horace Mann and Henry Barnard, studied the educational systems of Prussia and Switzerland. The earliest American universities were patterned after Oxford and Cambridge, and at the end of the nineteenth century graduate education in the United States came heavily under the influence of German universities. American men of letters, from Washington Irving to Ernest Hemingway, have found inspiration for their writings in European settings and ideas. Henry James, a leading nineteenth-century American novelist, spent much of his time in Britain; T. S. Eliot, probably the most influential poet of the twentieth century, was American born and bred, but has lived most of his adult life in Britain; Gertrude Stein, one of the most original among the American poets and writers of the times and an influential connoisseur of art, lived in Paris for most of her life. Hemingway, one of our most popular novelists, was, until the last years of his life, an expatriate in Europe. James Whistler and Mary Cassatt, two of the most significant American painters of the late nineteenth and early twentieth centuries, were closely identified, respectively, with Britain and France. Only during the twentieth century have European intellectuals and artists, in considerable numbers, sought refuge in the United States. Some of Europe's most creative and productive minds have become closely identified with the United States at the peaks of their careers. Thus American art, letters and science have been exposed to the influence of Thomas Mann, Béla Bartók, Ludwig van der Rohe, Walter Gropius, Edward Teller and Albert Einstein, to mention but a few. From the physical sciences and medicine to the social sciences and humanities, Europe and North America have jointly enriched Western civilization.

The United States was not alone in establishing transatlantic links with Europe. Nowhere is the cultural unity of the North Atlantic area more apparent even to the casual observer than in Canada. Throughout its history, English- and French-speaking Canadians have lived side by side, each group the carrier of the culture of its respective motherland to the New World. The traveler to Canada readily sees a blend of European and American influences adapted to a distinctive Canadian environment. Canada, like the United States of America, was founded in diversity. Its continuing ties with Great Britain and the cultural and linguistic affinity of many of its people with France, combined with Canada's historic friendship with the United States, provide one of the strongest links joining the American and the European components of the North Atlantic community. Like its neighbor to the south, Canada is still in the process of amalgamating and synthesizing its European heritage.

The southern reaches of the Western Hemisphere represent, to some degree, a continuation of Europe. The language, culture and appearance of the centers of Latin America are predominantly European. Spanish, Portuguese or, as in the case of Haiti, French are spoken as the national languages. In the colonial period Latin America looked to Europe for authority and ideas. By the early nineteenth century the ideas of the Enlightenment and the French Revolution helped to stir the revolt of the Creoles against the *peninsulares* in Spanish America.

Independence from Europe did not mean the dissolution of all cultural and economic ties with Europe. Trade and commerce necessitated contacts with Europe, and by the end of the nineteenth century Great Britain had become the leading investor in Latin America. Immigrants from other European nations enriched the culture and economy of Latin America. But the nations of Latin America followed a course which differed markedly from that of the United States and Western Europe. Representative government, as practiced in the North Atlantic area, did not take root. Democratic constitutions provided a façade for the subordination of the nation to the will of a ruling elite or a dictator. Moreover, no Latin American country reached the stage of economic maturity of the United States and Western Europe. In its broadest sense, the Atlantic Community includes Latin America, but clearly the problems which confront this region differentiate it from the industrially more advanced nations of the North Atlantic area.

The North Atlantic Community has always been a *civilization de dialogue*. A continuing exchange of ideas between Europeans and North Americans has influenced strongly the life of peoples on both sides of the Atlantic. If Europe provided the initial impetus to the growth of the Atlantic Community by colonizing the New World, the colonists themselves gave to Europeans a powerful stimulus in government, social organization, technology, literature and art. The pluralism and diversity which are perhaps the most important characteristics of Western civilization offered free scope to the creativity of peoples sharing similar basic values and thus provided ideal conditions for the cumulative enrichment of the political, economic, social and intellectual life of the entire North Atlantic area.

Nowhere was the interaction between Europeans and Americans more apparent than in the development of political institutions on both continents. The framers of the American Constitution drew heavily upon the philosophies of Locke and Montesquieu. Modern Canadian political institutions are deeply beholden to British parliamentary experience as well as the lessons of federalism, a principle suited to the governing of far-flung territories such as those of North America. In its government and political thought the United States embodied the most advanced ideas of eighteenth-century Europe, and life in the New World as perceived by Voltaire, Rousseau and others exercised a great influence upon the writings and ideas of the Enlightenment. The Enlightenment, in turn, shaped the minds of Americans, such as Franklin and Jefferson, and faith in progress and human improvement, born of the eighteenth century, has permeated the American mind even to the present day.

Europe, in time, was to remold its political systems and to utilize the methods tested on the Western shores of the Atlantic. European intellectual and political leaders often shared with Americans their aspirations for liberty and saw in the New World the practical application of their political theories. To Americans and Europeans alike, the establishment of a new social order on the Western shores of the North Atlantic marked the beginning of a new and revolutionary epoch in which the social orders of other areas of the Atlantic Community were destined also to undergo transformations. The

American example furnished for Europeans a model to be emulated by revolutionaries or to be opposed by proponents of the old order. According to John Adams, as well as later students of history, the American Revolution was no less influential than the writings of Voltaire, Diderot and Rousseau in igniting the French Revolution and in bringing widespread changes in the status quo elsewhere in the Atlantic Community. Seeing in America Europe's future, James Bryce, in *The American Commonwealth*, wrote that "America has in some respect anticipated European nations. She is walking before them along a path which they may probably follow."

The growth of representative political institutions antedated the Industrial Revolution. Yet economic transformation hastened the democratization of social orders in the Atlantic Community. It may well be that there is a close relationship between the skills of political organization perfected in the North Atlantic area and the judicious use of the region's bountiful economic resources as well as the achievement of the world's highest average living standards. The North Atlantic peoples, bent upon the perfection of local and national self-government, provided the political stability which safeguarded their economic development. In modern times, other regions of the globe have not been endowed with this felicitous combination.

Perhaps the most tangible link between peoples of the North Atlantic area has been the movement of population. In the century between the end of the Napoleonic Wars in 1815 and the outbreak of World War I, at least thirty million immigrants crossed the Atlantic from Europe to the New World. In succeeding waves, they came first from Northern and Western Europe and then from Europe's Southern and Eastern reaches to work in American factories, farms and mines. They provided the manpower and skills without which the United States could not have risen to its pre-eminent world position in the twentieth century. It was the entire North Atlantic area which contributed to the economic growth of the United States and all other countries of the Western Hemisphere. Conversely, in the early years of the twentieth century, the foreign-born in the United States sent overseas annually close to $250 million. These remittances helped improve living standards in many European communities.

This movement of ideas, people and commerce strengthened a civilization rooted in the critical spirit and political concepts of ancient Greece, in the secular laws and principles of organization bequeathed by Rome, in the Judaic idea of one God, the Creator of man, and in the Christian concept of faith, divine justice and spiritual equality. To these ideas of the Atlantic Community can be traced much of Western technology and science, painting and sculpture, political theory and government, philosophy and religion. From this heritage has sprung the political and social ferment which in succeeding ages has rocked Western civilization, and still convulses its structure today. It is this tradition—in truth, a revolutionary tradition—which provides the basis for the dynamism and creativity of our civilization. Its spread across the globe has stirred the ancient civilizations of Africa and Asia and sparked the revolutions now sweeping the underdeveloped world.

Hellenism, the Judaeo-Christian religions and the Roman law stand at the cradle of North Atlantic civilization. But Greco-Roman civilization was rooted in the lands ringing the Mediterranean. The faith of the Hebrew prophets and the authors of the Gospels drew upon the cults and the imagery of the Middle East. An integral part of Christian theology derives from the Neoplatonists of Alexandria and from Saint Augustine, who was Bishop of Hippo in eastern Algeria, and thus from North Africa. These traditions were to become the property of Western civilization, but they also gave birth to ideas whose appeal was to become universal.

They flourished, long before the North Atlantic civilization was born, in many non-Mediterranean countries. Even today they live on in several lands outside the North Atlantic area. Russia and Armenia were once Christian; Ethiopia is one of the oldest Christian countries on earth. Hellenism lived on in Byzantium and the Islamic world at a time when West Europeans knew little or nothing about its philosophical and aesthetic heritage. When the West foundered in barbarism, Rome lived on in Constantinople, the second Rome. Yet it was among the European peoples that out of these roots grew a new and dynamic civilization, that European civilization which embraced the Judaeo-Christian concept of man's individual relationship to God, the Greek idea of reason triumphant over superstition and magic, and Roman practicality in administration and law. It is from the synthesis of these three traditions that issued the Carolingian Renaissance of the eighth century, the Scholasticism of the thirteenth century, the Humanism of the fifteenth century. That synthesis dissolved in the long and devastating civil wars of the sixteenth and seventeenth centuries which are called the Religious Wars.

From the crucible of ideological and systemic conflict arose a new civilization which, although it was based upon the preceding one and absorbed it, was fundamentally new and different from all other civilizations, past and contemporary. From the seventeenth century onward, this new civilization flourished in the littorals of the North Atlantic, on the shores of an open sea with its vast horizons, luring men to new, globe-encompassing spiritual and social adventures. In the making of the North Atlantic civilization many peoples, above all the Dutch, the English, the Anglo-Americans, the Germans and the French, took a leading part.

A new spirit of scientific inquiry, starting with Copernicus, Kepler and Galileo, and culminating in Newton, advanced rapidly the discovery of nature. It reaffirmed the Greek tradition of intellectual curiosity. It blazed the trail toward an unprecedented understanding of the laws governing nature and placed in the hands of man an ever surer command of the potential forces latent in nature. The new science differed from all preceding science: it formed an all-encompassing world image and stressed the practical applicability of natural laws. The insights of pure science were translated speedily into practical devices that alleviated human drudgery and suffering. Bacon censured Aristotle because "he had been incapable of doing anything for the welfare of mankind." In the *New Atlantis* he wrote: "The end of our foundation is a knowledge of causes and secret motions of things, and the enlarging of the bounds of human empire, to the effecting of all things possible." In his *Discours sur la Méthode,* Descartes declared that the place of scholastic philosophy should be taken by "a practical philosophy through which, by understanding the force and action [of natural phenomena] as well as we understand the diverse trades of our artisans, we could employ them in like manner for all their proper purposes, and thereby become the very masters and possessors of nature." In the seventeenth century, the Royal Society of London for the Promotion of Natural Knowledge became the center of experimental research in Western Europe and a model for other countries.[2] Its roster included such renowned names as Voltaire in France, Benjamin Franklin in North America and James Watt in England. They and their fellow philosophers were apostles of the new spirit of technological innovation, of rational faith in progress and of empirical verification. This same spirit fathered the Industrial Revolution. From the cornucopia of industrialism flowed those innumerable devices, from the steam engine to electronic calculating machines and lifesaving drugs, which were to raise average living standards for men everywhere. Within a hundred years, average life expectancy has doubled; so has the world's population.

The second *idée force* which molded North Atlantic civilization is derived from the Roman tradition, although it rejected its authoritarian spirit: the insistence upon the rule and impartial majesty of law—a rational and universally applicable law, before which all men are equal.

Western legal thought rests upon Roman foundations. Yet it is enlivened by an un-Roman concern with the legal protection of individual liberty against governmental authority, whether exercised by a monarch or by the people; with the limitation of the powers of government; and with vigilant defense against possible abuses of power and authority. It is only within the last century, however, that these ideas have gained currency in most countries of the Atlantic Community. Their spread and hardy resistance to new tyrannies have been wrought from the trials, errors and sacrifices of the Atlantic peoples.

In the North Atlantic area law came ultimately to occupy a position above that of monarch and executive, as well as of party and legislature. In nearly all countries of the North Atlantic, an independent judiciary now administers the rule of law. Freedom of legal systems from political or religious control was unknown before the rise of modern Western civilization.

The third legacy of the ancient world to modern Western civilization is respect for individual freedom based upon a latitude of tolerance, of freedom of conscience and of thought on a scale unprecedented in the history of mankind. Descartes, Milton and Locke proclaimed in their writings the right of man to think for himself. A spirit of tolerance nourished the growth of a pluralistic society—a system of political, economic and legal balances—which accommodated not only the public, but also a great variety of private sectors of social life. The right to diversity, in turn, was codified in a body of laws protecting freedom of thought, press and assembly, and safeguarding the individual citizen against arbitrary arrest. The vigorous affirmation of the right to local self-government countered trends toward the excessive concentration of authority in the hands of the state.

From the Western religious and humanistic traditions sprang a value system in which man as an individual ranks high. Respect for the sanctity of human life, the right to an inviolate personal life, and freedom of speech, conscience, opinion, belief, religion and association are values which have been most fully developed and practiced in the Atlantic Community. Gaps exist between the value goals of modern Western civilization and the degree of their attainment. Nowhere have these ideals been fully realized; yet the peoples of the North Atlantic area have gone further in thought and deed toward making them part of their everyday lives than any other people before them. The incongruities between the goals and the practice of modern Western civilization should be ascribed—at least in part—to its newness, to the fact that two centuries count but for a short segment in the span of history.

Implicit in the values of North Atlantic peoples is a recognition of the dual principle of individual liberty and the common good. From respect for the dignity of the individual flows a sense of social responsibility for the protection of the weak and disinherited. A new social consciousness regarded a steady, progressive amelioration of living conditions as a duty upon society; triggered the rapid mitigation of the barbaric penal laws still prevailing in Europe in the eighteenth century; and led to a general refinement of mores.

These three developments—the spirit of rational science and its permeating influence throughout all spheres of life; the spirit of individual liberty and its realization in a body of laws safeguarding the individual against oppression by government or privilege; the spirit of consideration for every fellow man—form the basis of North Atlantic civilization. The three constitute a whole, closely interwoven and inseparable. They balance each other. The spirit of individual liberty is on guard against the perversion of the spirit of rational science into the soulless idolatry of efficiency under the writ of technocratic dictatorship. The spirit of consideration for every fellow man sets limits to, and balances, the spirit of rational science and the spirit of government by law.

Out of the Puritan and Glorious Revolutions emerged our modern

Western civilization with new and broadened principles and a universal appeal to diverse peoples throughout the world. From the eighteenth-century Enlightenment and the French Revolution came an emphasis on intellectual freedom and republican government which was to strike the imagination and to stir the hearts of countless peoples.

During the nineteenth century modern Western civilization seemed destined to spread over the whole globe. Its principles— respect for individual liberty and initiative, freedom of thought, tolerance, open-minded search for truth, parliamentary representation and an independent judiciary—found followers in diverse countries spiritually or geographically remote from the North Atlantic Community.

This picture changed with the coming of World War I. The rise to power of Lenin in the midst of the chaos into which the great war plunged Russia, the least westernized European country, marked the first disdainful and open rejection of the philosophical principles of modern Atlantic civilization. In the Central European frontierlands of the North Atlantic civilization, the moral and political disorder which the war left in its wake spawned fascism. Fascism not only imitated Lenin's methods, but shared his conviction that modern Western civilization was doomed and that the twentieth century would be the century of totalitarianism.

The Atlantic Community is not definable primarily in geographic terms, for its limits cannot be fixed arbitrarily. Its boundaries have undergone many changes. In 1940 the frontiers of this Community were pushed back to the English Channel, and most of Europe lay in the grip of the dictatorships of Hitler, Mussolini and Stalin, all of whom waged war against the fundamental values of the West. Despite the existence of the Iron Curtain today, the Atlantic Community cannot concede that the center of Germany marks its eastern frontier, for there are peoples in Eastern Europe who have fought and died for values cherished in the West and who, given the opportunity freely to do so, would choose them again. Although the Atlantic Community includes much of Europe and the Western Hemisphere, its historic core has been the countries which border the North Atlantic.

The meaning of the Atlantic Community lies in the extension of human liberty and equality, in government under law and in representative political institutions. Countries having once departed from the Atlantic Community rejoin it, as Germany, turned totalitarian from 1933 to 1945, has done. In some countries of the North Atlantic area democratic institutions are deep-rooted; in others their substance is fragile. Closer integration with the more democratic countries will help those latter countries and their more precarious political systems to evolve representative institutions of their own.

The development of the Atlantic Community is not directed against other nations or civilizations and even less to the maintenance of imperial control or influence over other peoples. It is not a Holy Alliance of the *beati possidentes*. It represents an effort to transform principles into reality, both within the North Atlantic area and in the world at large. But however ennobling the values of the West, our civilization could hardly survive without the power needed to protect both the North Atlantic area and peoples elsewhere desirous of preserving their freedom. Americans are not alone in postulating the relationship between North Atlantic unity and North Atlantic security. Europeans, including the great French historian, Michelet, in his *La France devant l'Europe*, written in 1871, warned the Germans who had vanquished France to visualize the unity of the Western world. Michelet, like Marx before him, saw in Russia the greatest threat to the West. With considerable foresight, he viewed the modernization of Russia and the emancipation of its serfs as a means of strengthening autocratic government, making possible the emergence of a "socialist tyrant," of a Tsar who would be a "Messiah of the Serfs, a barbarous Messiah, terrible to Europe." To meet this danger, he urged unity for the common defense of the West.

I call here to a European congress . . . the English, the French, the Belgians, the Dutch, the Swiss, I call the Germans. I call here the two worlds. I solemnly call upon young America. Let her justify our hope, let her be deaf to all the petty interests, free of all petty rancours, devoted to the great general interest of all human progress, closely associated with the civilized West, with the cause of liberty which she has supported so recently and which she has made so gloriously victorious.

Two years later, another French historian, Henri Martin, called for the unity of Europe in a federation founded on individual liberty to safeguard the West against Russia. In Russia, he declared, the

state, "*l'association moscovite* . . . rests on a community personi-
fied in one man who can arbitrarily dispose of all liberties, all
property and all families." Europe disunited, he suggested, would
be conquered by Russia, leaving "America, our daughter . . . alone
[to] preserve all the higher elements of human civilization. . . .
Then there will be only two powers left on earth which will divide
it up as between the light and the darkness. All moral life will then
take its refuge in the other [Western] hemisphere." Europe and
America together, he declared, could safeguard the West.

Many others on both sides of the Atlantic—Alexis de Tocqueville,
John Hay, Henry Adams, Lord Bryce, Admiral Mahan, Thorstein
Veblen, Sir Norman Angell—saw that an "Atlantic System," if it did
not already exist, had to be created. An editorial in the *New Republic*, on the eve of American entry into World War I, declared that
"What we must fight for is a common interest of the western world,
for the integrity of the Atlantic Powers. We must recognize that we
are in fact one great community and act as a member of it . . . by
showing that we are ready now . . . to defend the western world,
[to lay] the cornerstone of federation."

Writing in 1917, Norman Angell, the famous English Quaker,
suggested an idea which, had it been adopted, might have changed
the course of history.

The survival of the Western democracies, in so far as that is a matter
of the effective use of their force, depends upon their capacity to use it
as a unity, during the War and after. That unity we have not attained,
even for the purposes of the War, because we have refused to recognize
its necessary conditions—a kind and degree of democratic internationalism
to which current political ideas and feelings are hostile; an internationalism which is not necessary to the enemy, but is to us. . . .

He can in some measure ignore it. We cannot. His unity, in so far as it
rests upon moral factors, can be based upon the old nationalistic conceptions; our unity depends upon a revision of them, an enlargement into an
internationalism. . . .

The greatest obstacles to a permanent association of nations by which
the security of each shall be made to rest upon the strength of the whole
are disbelief in its feasibility and our subjection to the traditions of
national sovereignty and independence. Were it generally believed in and
desired, it would be not only feasible but inevitable. . . .

Return to the old relationships after the War will sooner or later doom
the democratic nations, however powerful each may be individually, to

subjugation in detail by a group, inferior in power but superior in material unity—a unity which autocracy achieves at the cost of freedom and human worth.[3]

In 1938, while Nazi armies were poised to overrun Europe, Clarence Streit proposed a new form of democratic unity, with an Atlantic union government, citizenship, defense force, currency, postal and communications system, and a customs-free economy. During the Second World War Walter Lippmann also urged the United States to "consolidate the strategic and diplomatic connections already existing, of the Atlantic Community." Then, these solutions seemed too drastic to be adopted by North Atlantic governments or to be greeted enthusiastically by popular opinion.

II

Despite the movement of ideas, commerce and population within the North Atlantic area, differences have persisted between the United States and Europe from the earliest settlements in the New World to the present day. They exist as well among the European nations themselves and are sometimes as pronounced as those between the United States and Europe. Even within the United States, however, sectional differences cleave a nation of continental dimensions. The Middle West, for example, sometimes displays toward the Eastern seaboard an attitude resembling that shown occasionally by the United States as a whole toward Europe.

Differences, real or perceived, have given rise to the ideas which Europeans and Americans hold of each other's political, social and economic orders. It is difficult, if not impossible, to reduce the infinite variety of American views to a common notion about things European. In the same way, Europeans hold diverse views about America—and, for that matter, about themselves. The parentage of America is certain: she is the child of Europe, but she has repudiated no small part of her European heritage. If there is a popular American image of Europe, it has been shaped by the countervailing forces of repulsion and attraction. Because millions of immigrants came from Europe in search of a new political, social and economic order, Europe has represented to generations of Americans a past which they rejected in favor of a new way of life. For all the contacts which have existed historically within the North Atlantic area, there remains the residue of an American psychological alienation from

Europe, from a caste-ridden society that reserved its opportunities to the privileged few. America kept her promise. A highly mobile and egalitarian society bent upon economic progress developed the world's highest average standards of living. For a while, Europe seemed unable to rival the American achievement. Yet, from the catharsis of wars and revolutions, a new Europe has risen. The Europe which immigrants left in the nineteenth century is not the Europe of today.

Paradoxically, the more vigorously America affirmed her political independence and cultural otherness, the more strongly her European heritage reasserted itself. Today, the European presence is more evident than ever before. Its tokens, some significant and some quaint, are the increase in the sale of European automobiles, the interest in European films, the growth in foreign travel and the expansion of American companies and investment abroad, especially since the inception of the Common Market. Some European artifacts exert a certain snob appeal. Undoubtedly, this phenomenon is characteristic of our "affluent society." European products are, by general American standards, more unique, more elegant, more sophisticated, and add up to a more varied and enjoyable way of life. But the acquisition of European products and cultural patterns by larger numbers of the American upper- and middle-income groups is not without its drawbacks. Americans may consume or adopt the objects, manners and ideas of Europe without understanding Europe or European life. They seek in things European a vehicle of spiritual emigration, a romantic escape from distasteful aspects of their own lives. They do not care, lest the engaging image fades, to weigh soberly the reality of European life and its problems, its similarities with and its differences from life in the United States.

In part, at least, because of cherished stereotypes, the United States, throughout much of its history, looked askance upon political collaboration with Europe, except in periods of grave threat to its own security. Much of the American unwillingness to draw closer to the Europeans derives from the demonology of European colonialism and imperialism. Large numbers of Americans have viewed European empires in terms of that British Empire of the eighteenth century from which the United States seceded. The United States had never been involved, except relatively briefly and against its inclination, in the administration of alien peoples. To generations of Americans, including most policymakers, European empire simply meant the domination of worthy, simple, native peoples in Africa and Asia by European aristocrats, military groups and colonial bureaucrats. This notion has been as firmly rooted in the American mind as its corollary, namely, Europe as the fountainhead of authoritarianism and decadence. Seldom, if ever, were these empires seen in geopolitical terms or in the context of an international balance of power. Instead, the United States identified its own struggle for independence with the anticolonial movements in Africa and Asia, despite the fact that the thirteen colonies of 1783 were culturally and, notably, technologically England's equal, a phenomenon which has no counterpart in the history of the emancipation of the Afro-Asian states from European rule.

The American image notwithstanding, European colonial powers have made great contributions to the development of the newly emerging states of Africa and Asia. These states themselves are the creation of the European powers, for without the forces of nationalism unleashed by Europe, the dominant political configurations of these areas—particularly Africa—might still be based largely upon tribalism rather than upon Western-type political systems. The differences between the European and American approaches to political problems such as colonialism are less apparent than imagined. Some Europeans, notably the Scandinavians, have voiced even greater support to movements for independence in Africa and Asia than has the United States. Some Europeans, and Canadians as well, have suggested that the United States is, in fact, a colonial power, imposing its rule upon sundry Pacific islands for strategic, and upon Puerto Rico for economic purposes. Americans need not rise to defend their stewardship in the Pacific Ocean and the Caribbean Sea. In turn, they might concede that Britain and France, by word and deed, are as committed to decolonization as are they themselves.

American political leaders of both parties helped to perpetuate the preconceptions about European colonialism which embittered our relations with our principal NATO allies. They assert that the American mission must be to "win over" the countries of Asia and Africa. These, we are told, are the peoples who are our principal friends and partners in the building of a new world. It is they who articulate most clearly that "world opinion" to which the United

States must appeal. Such a policy may have considerable attraction to those impressed by numbers and size, and to political leaders who have been accustomed to cater to a diversity of whims in order to win elections. A deep distrust of European colonialism has made us uncomfortable in our dealings with European nations while reinforcing a penchant for closer relations with the former colonial areas—because such closer relations not only accrue to mutual benefit but also implicitly censure colonial wickedness.

Just as American images of Europe influence the formulation of American policy, so do the European images of the United States play a significant role in the policies adopted by the nations of Europe. Basic to the European image of the United States is the idea of a gauche, brash and perhaps crude youth, lacking in culture and worshiping technology and gadgetry—in the words of Oswald Spengler, "a boundless field and a population of trappers, drifting from town to town in a dollar-hunt, unscrupulous and dissolute."

The change in power relationships has given Europeans added cause for concern about the United States. So long as Europeans considered themselves to be the masters of their own destinies, they could view with equanimity the caricature of the United States as an awkward and immature dolt. But now that Europe's power vis-à-vis that of the United States and the Soviet Union has diminished, alleged American immaturity in world affairs becomes a matter of no little concern to Europeans. Moreover, such an image of the United States alleviates a feeling of European inferiority in power by allowing Europeans to look down on Americans as uncouth, uncultivated or naïve. Some Europeans, as, for example, groups within the Conservative Party in Britain, have derived satisfaction from the idea that Europe's proper role in the postwar world was to lead and educate the new colossus in the practice of international leadership.

In yet another respect changes in power relationships have influenced European attitudes toward the United States. The devolution of European empires and the consequent rise of new states have contributed to the feeling of physical inferiority in Europe. The United States, by its attitudes and policies, has not alleviated this sentiment, nor has it endeared itself to some of its NATO allies. Not a few Europeans have detected a note of hypocrisy in American attitudes toward colonialism, for in some areas where the United States favored national self-determination its business interests made inroads into markets previously dominated by the Europeans. Not a few Europeans attributed to Americans such ulterior motives, especially after the Anglo-French intervention in Egypt in 1956. The stand of the United States was said to have been prompted by concern with the American stake in the oil resources of the Middle East, rather than by more elevated considerations of international legality.

Western Europe has had to adjust not only to an altered power status in the world, but also to the spectacle of peoples recently governed by Europeans participating in international affairs as independent states. For the most part, the transition to independence has been smooth, and cordial relations between the new states and their former rulers have developed. But European powers, still confronted by knotty colonial problems or the hostility of former colonies, are apt to view the failure of the United States to side with them as a failure of the United States to live up to its commitments to the Atlantic Alliance as a whole.

Even on matters of foreign policy, however, European reactions to the United States have been by no means wholly critical. On many issues, intellectuals as well as trade union leaders, socialists as well as conservatives, have supported the United States. On the Suez question, for example, the bulk of the Labour Party in Britain opposed the Conservative Government, while openly supporting the policy of the United States against Britain and France. André Malraux, French novelist, archaeologist, art historian, Resistance member and twice minister, declared at the fiftieth anniversary dinner of the French Institute of New York, on May 15, 1962: "For culture, for an Atlantic civilization, for the freedom of the mind, I offer a toast to the only nation that has waged war but not worshiped it, that has won the greatest power in the world but not sought it, that has wrought the greatest weapon of death but not wished to wield it; and may it inspire men with dreams worthy of its action."[4]

For some groups in Europe, however, the United States presents a disquieting image. Not a few European intellectuals, for example, can take little comfort in what they rashly conceive to be the status of their American counterpart—a member of a society in which individuality is dwarfed by mass production and culture itself has been put in the tender care of Madison Avenue salesmanship. Quantity appears to replace quality, refinement in detail seems to give way to boldness in contour; brightness and glamour replace charm; efficiency is preferable to style; and, ultimately, the technician replaces the intellectual. In Europe itself, where intellectuals held, until quite recently, a status comparable to that of the clergy in earlier centuries, the influence of the "American way of life" appears now to threaten a once secure position. This is one explanation, though not the only one, for the ease with which some European intellectuals have glided into communism or neutralism.

Yet never before in their history have the United States and Western Europe resembled each other as much as they do today. They share problems which are posed by democratization and industrialization, the very forces which have created new opportunities for all. The United States was first to face these problems. Now it is Europe's turn. World War II altered fundamentally the structure of European society. The age of mass consumption has come to Europe. The economic and social problems of the "affluent society," which have faced for a decade or so the United States, are beginning to confront the nations of Western Europe. Since World War II the breakdown of the class structure, the extension of educational opportunities and the rise in living standards have revolutionized Western European society. The European Economic Community, together with other novel forms of political and economic cooperation, is stimulating new taste and patterns of consumption similar to those of the American public. The West European democracies have shown that they can create, despite their relatively small and heavily populated territories, standards of living for their citizens approaching those of the United States. Thus, in essentials, most of the countries of Western Europe have grown closer to each other and to the United States in the last generation.

The United States is not *ein Land ohne Kultur*, as Europeans once wrote, a backward country lacking the refinements of higher civilization. The life of educated groups in the United States is in many ways like that of similar classes in Europe. American intellectual life thrives, despite (or because of) the existence of a society based upon mass consumption. Never in history have the cultural achievements of Western civilization been within the grasp of such large numbers of people as today in the United States. Moreover, many Europeans enjoy American films, music and sports as much as Americans themselves. These changes and their implications will not be registered immediately in public consciousness. "Changes in national thought occur not by mutation but by evolution. Old ideas do not suddenly become obsolete; rather they gradually become irrelevant. And in all societies people are slow to discover the irrelevance of their traditional vocabulary."[5] Whatever Europe is, it is not a center of stagnation, authoritarianism, colonial domination and decadence, nor is it just a museum and a romantic retreat for sophisticated, jaded Americans. It would be tragic if Americans and Europeans allowed the distorted and unattractive images of one another conjured up by past history and misconceptions about it to prevent them from understanding their similarities and affinities and devising new political arrangements firmly based upon a consensus of common values, interests and aspirations.

III

The rise of communism and its bid for technological supremacy, the decline of Western Europe as the center of world power, and the birth of new states and new patterns of world trade have created grave problems for the nations of the North Atlantic Community. Increasingly, solutions to these problems lie beyond the grasp of individual nations, even the strongest among them. In Europe and, to a lesser extent, in the North Atlantic area, the idea of supra-nationalism has captured many minds and challenged the idea of the nation-state as the basic unit of the international order. The quest for unity in Western Europe and in the Atlantic Community can be viewed as a pragmatic attempt to deal with "functional" problems, economic and military, by adapting the forms of Western representative government to the exigencies of contemporary international life. Complex procedures of voting and decision-making, applied by intergovernmental and supranational commissions and committees, provide for the representation of many diverse groups and interests within the member states. These institutional devices of Western integration not only serve the welfare and security of the North Atlantic people, but elaborate also models of political and economic collaboration which might furnish guidance to the newly emerging states, among which only few can lay claim to more than nominal sovereignty and can afford the heavy burden of statehood.

One of the most felicitous North Atlantic contributions to the art of government is the American development of the federative idea. Federalism, the governing of a vast region under conditions of diversity and local autonomy, provided a novel means of organizing society in the New World and may hold the key to effective government elsewhere, in Afro-Asian areas as well as in the North Atlantic area as a whole.

Since the end of World War II we have witnessed the rise of a variety of consultative, cooperative and supranational institutions whose purpose is to enable the member states to do together the many things—political, economic and military—which they cannot do so well by themselves or cannot do at all. In Europe, a new kind of organizational structure—specialized or functional—has made its appearance during the last decade. Embodying certain features of the federative principle, its *raison d'être* derives from a function such as production rather than from geography, which thus far has been the principal attribute of federal states. Many new organizational devices are being tried—and, on the whole, tried successfully —in Western Europe and in the North Atlantic Community. In the few years since World War II, the West has taken steps toward unification which seemed impossible a generation ago. There exists in the North Atlantic area an organic unity which surpasses that of all other regions. Communist unity has been forged in the crucible of conquest and coercion. On paper, the Union of Soviet Socialist Republics is a federation; in fact, the so-called autonomous republics are the mere puppets of communist imperialism. European supranationalism and Western unity in defense have each provided perspectives within which the peoples of the North Atlantic Community have begun to look beyond the nation-state. As yet, agreement on a grand design for North Atlantic unity is lacking. Its outlines, however, can be discerned in the many organizations which have begun to link the European and North Atlantic peoples.

Large as has been the contribution of the American experience to the development of federalism, it need not necessarily be taken as the sure and only guide toward Atlantic unity. Were it not for unique geographic features and the smallness of its territory, the Swiss Confederation should be acclaimed as the classic example of the species. The British Commonwealth, despite or because of its high degree of informality, represents one of the happiest adaptations of the federal concept in history. Moreover, the successful history of American federalism cannot be read without reservations: notwithstanding the immense prestige of the federal idea, the United States has been moving increasingly toward a centralization which tends to curb local autonomy and the autonomy of the states. The history of mankind, the fashionable optimism of our day notwithstanding, is not the history of the unbroken progress of mankind. In the past, federations grew, did for their members what none of them could have done singly—and broke up. In fact, the federal idea is one of the oldest ideas of political organization. It informed the Holy Roman Empire, the Hapsburg Empire and, for a brief period, the German Empire, Scandinavia, the United Kingdom, the Netherlands, France, Spain and Italy. Each knew a federal epoch. After some time, each abandoned the federal concept. If the federative idea is to preside over the making of an Atlantic Community and if its realization is to endure, then the makers of the Atlantic Community will have to bring to their task political insights more profound and techniques more ingenious than were vouchsafed to their predecessors on the road to federalism. While seeking to transcend the nation-state system they must come to terms with the concept of the nation-state in its modern setting rather than oppose or ignore it.

The national state exists. So does the pressing need for its integration into larger units. The problem should be viewed as one of dialectical interrelationships rather than irreconcilable opposites. To be sure, nationalism has proven a significant obstacle to the evolution of NATO and other supranational organizations within the Atlantic area. Yet national freedom and national self-determination stand high on the list of the values which the collective defense of the West proposes to insure. Thus, the proponents of the federal concept must show that it is compatible with national freedom, and that, under modern conditions, the best way to insure national freedom is precisely the federal arrangements which they envisage.

It is at this point—the point of intersection between the pull of national loyalties and the inexorable movement toward supranational units—that Western civilization meets its supreme test. A generation ago, the nation-state system and Western dominance both seemed impregnable. Since then, the systemic revolution has undermined the nation-state as the primary force on the world's political stage and simultaneously has triggered the overthrow of the Western empires, and set in motion the masses of the colonial, the "underdeveloped," world. World War II and the concurrent development of weapons of mass annihilation tremendously accelerated both manifestations of *the* world revolution, for systemic revolution and the rising of the masses are but the two sides of the same coin. The patent inability of the nation-state—even the biggest nation-state—to safeguard the lives and property of its citizens has engendered a crisis of confidence in national sovereignty, its worth and its rights, especially the right to call upon average men and women to give their lives in its defense. In this as in every preceding revolution of modern times, the tremors are being recorded most sensitively by one particular segment of society, namely the intelligentsia.

The fact is that the intellectuals everywhere are deserting in droves from the idea of the nation-state and, because nation-state, colonial empire and war were so closely linked in history, the idea of Western civilization as a good worth living and dying for. Hence the receptivity of so many intellectuals to the appeal of pacifism—now read: ban-the-bomb unilateralism—of world government to be established here and now and irrespective of who will run it and what ideas about man should inform it; of nationalism as long as it is not Western; and, last but not least, of communism, which has incorporated all anti-Western appeals and slogans into its sophisticated arsenal of propaganda weapons. Hence also the growing reluctance to use force in the defense of legitimate national interests and of the legitimate interests of the West as a whole. Hence the case of bad conscience that grips a not inconsiderable number of intellectuals when any issue arises in the West's relationship to the ex-colonial peoples, to whom, in expiation of the West's sins, is attributed a wisdom and a love of peace beyond all understanding.

The psychosis of the disaffected intellectual segment seeps into the rest of the citizenry. It is so easy to reject a proposition in the national interest or, for that matter, of international justice by toting up the statistics of hypothetical megaton damage—without, of course, adverting to the fact that analogous statistics apply to the potential aggressor and deter him from testing the hypothesis. Once the costs of the use of force are no longer felt to stand in any plausible relation to freedom and justice, nothing is any longer worth fighting for. Then nothing remains but the hope of accommodation on any issue that might call for the use of force—though virtually all vital issues in world politics are pregnant with the potential use of force—or a greater and brighter hope, namely, that the potential aggressor now sees things as we do, is about to mellow and will join us in peaceful labors in the vineyards of human happiness.

That nothing in history and in the conduct of particular aggressors justifies this hope is a matter that need not detain us at this point of the discussion. What matters is that the "Struggle for the Minds of Men," which is viewed by the Western publics as a competition over the ideological orientation of the so-called uncommitted peoples, is, in fact, a struggle for the mind of the West itself. The issue is clear: The West must regain confidence in its basic values and the courage to defend them *at any price*. Indeed, the nation-state can no longer arouse that sense of community which nourishes great purpose and steels the will to great achievement. The disaffected intellectual—and all intellectuals are disaffected to varying degrees —is right in his rejection of the prevailing international system, although his conclusions as to what should be done to improve it might be wrong and even deleterious to the public's best interest— and his own. The design of a Western Community, successor to the system of nation-states, provides a challenge to creative imagination and, last but not least, an alternative to the febrile utopias that now engage some of the most intelligent, frustrated and confused Western minds.

That the alternative is a practical one might make it unpalatable to those intellectuals who have embraced the idea of world government under law precisely because it is a utopia and hence satisfies the longing for the unattainable. But once the political leadership of the Western countries has staked out the objectives and the greatness of the challenge stands out for all to see, the task, because it is a great and challenging one, should engage the minds and kindle the enthusiasm of all those who search for a noble and satisfying cause. Here, however, it is necessary to enter a caveat: Even the widest agreement on the fact that the making of the Atlantic Community is an appealing alternative to defeatism as well as to utopianism does not vouchsafe, as a matter of course, the successful execution of the grand design.

It would be pleasant, indeed, could the Atlantic Community be built by ever closer cultural cooperation and by ever freer economic exchanges—in brief, by those ameliorative peaceable processes which appeal so strongly to Western humanitarianism. Yet every step on the road toward the making of the Atlantic Community is beset with danger. In the last resort, the threat of communism is the threat of naked power, and the communists, fully aware of the implications of Atlantic unity to *their* grand design, will use any means to thwart the closer union of the Western peoples. The Soviet intellectual elite condones the exercise of power in the service of the communist cause. If the corresponding Western elites shrink back from the use of force when clearly challenged by force, then even the most fervent agreement on the making of the Atlantic Community will stand for naught.

In the words of the Secretary of State, Mr. Rusk, "We seek not the victory of one nation over another or of one people over another, but a world-wide victory for freedom."[6] If it is the world-wide victory of freedom that the Atlantic peoples seek, then the practical applications of this magnificent concept must be spelled out lest it be allowed to fade into the penumbra of magnificent yet meaningless generalities. Just as the framers of the Atlantic Charter faced the specific problem of Nazi aggression, so now the immediate threat to the survival and spread of freedom is the Soviet drive for world hegemony. The one bastion that today guards what is left of world-wide freedom is the military arm of the Atlantic Community, namely NATO. To defend the residual world freedom and to recapture ground lost, the Atlantic Community must grapple with and master the problem of Soviet expansion. The solution of this problem calls for many policies and programs; none of them will prove effective if it is not backed by instruments of force formidable enough to command the respect of the Soviets.

It would be well not to exaggerate the economic benefits that are likely to flow from an Atlantic federation or to expect that political federation must follow forthwith the creation of an Atlantic market. In fact, the execution of even the boldest scheme for Atlantic economic integration is unlikely to restore the freedom of trade achieved under the informal and highly effective system of the nineteenth century. As a matter of fact, it can be argued that free trade and federal union are not necessarily contingent upon one another and that Atlantic economic partnership can be forged quite effectively without any further advance toward political unity. What primarily gives meaning to the contemporary striving toward federal and confederal arrangements is the need for common political and military defense. Nevertheless, under contemporary, revolutionary conditions, international commerce cannot be insulated from the forces impinging upon the present political and military balance of power. Nor is it conceivable that in the absence of a high degree of political unity the economic resources of the Atlantic Community could be pooled in the economic development of the rest of the world or in such vast undertakings as, for example, the development of space technology.

The West's search for unity has been spurred by several forces— the inability of individual nation-states to provide separately for the safety and welfare of their populations amidst dynamic technological change, and the growing threat to the North Atlantic peoples and the remainder of the Free World from an expansionist Sino-Soviet bloc. Yet only a consensus on values can keep together for any length of time what expediency has joined together. The North Atlantic peoples have developed to a greater degree than any others a common moral outlook. The lack of such a common fund of beliefs and norms is at the root of the failure of the United Nations to transform itself into an effective institution—effective enough to begin to accomplish the principal purpose inscribed in its Charter. The legal, social and political systems of the Atlantic nations are either closely similar to, or at least compatible with, one another. Thus the foundations exist upon which intergovernmental and supranational institutions can be built and strengthened. Other regions may also develop in time that moral and legal consensus which would permit them to become united from within. Be that as it may, it is first in the Atlantic Community that new forms of federative organizations are likely to evolve.

The North Atlantic peoples should not and cannot aspire to that monolithic unity which mocks the federative pretensions of the communist state system. The idea of Leviathan negates the Western idea of diversity in unity. Yet "diversity in unity" implies a balance —and the will and wit to maintain it. The peoples of the North Atlantic are still far from realizing fully the values and interests which bind them together. Until they understand more clearly the degree to which their destinies are linked, the North Atlantic countries will continue to suffer crises in leadership, economic rivalries and difficulties in concerting political actions and making strategic assessments. In the last resort, the fortunes of the Atlantic Community are in the hands of an experiment in education; in this respect the making of Atlantic unity differs but little from the making of any other democratic institution.

Modern Western civilization is beset, as have been all great civilizations before it, by grave problems and dangers. Some of these dangers are common to all historic epochs; others are novel, for they are inherent in the unique character of the North Atlantic civilization, its technological progress and its global spread. Modern Western civilization, with its unprecedented mobility of ideas, men and things, has brought dynamic change to the entire globe. All mankind passes through the throes of a permanent scientific and social revolution. It has been suggested that modern civilization thrives on a process of "creative destruction." The frontiers of exploration are inexorably pushed forward. Unending is the quest for truth and for the development of new potentialities.

Many have been the prophets of the decline and disintegration of modern Western civilization, and for many years it has been fashionable to speak of the eclipse of the West. To some measure, however, the growing awareness of the perils to Western civilization signifies a healthy reaction against the Western democracies' penchant for complacency in peacetime. The peoples of the West have managed more than once to confound the prophets of doom. The vigor of the West revealed itself in the struggle against the fascist powers. Today, it is sometimes difficult to recall how weak the North Atlantic countries thought themselves in 1940 and how irresistible seemed the advance of totalitarianism. Since 1945, by and large, the devolution of the Western empires has proceeded in a peaceful and orderly way, with a legacy of goodwill for the former rulers. Such change has no precedents in the history of empires. The supreme efforts of the Western democracies in war and their bounding vigor in the years since World War II attest to the vitality of the North Atlantic civilization. Indeed, if Western civilization seemed on the wane in the decades between the two world wars, internal events within the Atlantic world since 1945 have reversed this trend.

Now, the task of Western diplomacy is to deter the communists from repeating the mistakes made by the German, Italian and Japanese leaders in initiating World War II. In short, one goal of the North Atlantic countries is to refute the communist doctrine which postulates the inevitability of Western "capitalist" disintegration. Only by affirming their unity based upon common spiritual and moral values can the North Atlantic peoples dissuade the communists from harboring the illusion of the "decline of the West" which proved the undoing, but not without great bloodshed and destruction, of the fascist leaders.

The moral and intellectual values of modern Western civilization were developed by the North Atlantic peoples. In principle, however, these values are the potential possession of all peoples. Modern Western civilization has a universal appeal. The common denominator of its values is the liberty of every individual everywhere—if not today, then, potentially at least, tomorrow. Thus, North Atlantic civilization resumes the tradition of its precursors, of Christianity, of Hellenism and of the universal citizenship and law of the Roman Empire.

The communists and not a few of the non-Western peoples of the Free World have engaged in eclectic raids upon the West's storehouse of technological achievements, while rejecting Western political, moral and spiritual values. As yet, we know little about the moral, political and social conditions of technological progress—except that it issued from the West's spirit of free inquiry. Yet the history of modern science and technology is still in the making. It is not certain that the structure reared by Western science and technology will stand after its nonmaterial foundations have crumbled. Certainly, Western civilization is not just science and technology, nor, for that matter, social organization. It is a manner of living, a habit of being civilized which is acquired and kept by cultivating a sense of moderation—of live and let live. It is precisely this sense of moderation which makes civilized life possible.

The way of life—the routine, so to speak—of Western civilization is characterized by three distinct though related social attitudes. The first is the recognition of the legitimacy of, and the necessity for, opposition as a constructive force in the interplay of politics and the development of thought. In the view of the North Atlantic civilization, a society is the more highly developed the more effectively it absorbs, on the basis of equality and freedom, various ethnic groups and religious faiths, social classes and cultural traditions, and the more readily it welcomes a variety of individual experiences. The second is the closely related commitment to the open society, with its unhindered and unceasing exchange of ideas and the constant movement of persons and goods. The third is the acceptance of the mandate of social improvement, as, for example, the integration of a discontented proletariat into industrial society, or, in more recent times, the removal of domestic racial inequality—and the performance of these tasks under the rule of law.

Today, Western civilization faces two major problems, each no less difficult than those with which it has already grappled. The peoples of the North Atlantic area must, on the one hand, transcend that self-centered particularism which mars their own community and, on the other hand, assist their former dependencies in the transition to freedom and equality, easing the new nations' access to the mainstreams of modern life. No other civilization has set out upon so formidable a task; no other civilization has gone further on the way toward achieving successfully the transformation of one state-system into another one and toward the voluntary dissolution of empires. The West did not invent imperialism and colonialism. They are common to all civilizations; but only the Western peoples have set themselves the goal of creating those very conditions which made the emancipation of the peoples under their rule possible and, sooner or later, inevitable. The iniquities of Western colonialism are many. But its redemption lies in the revulsion of conscience which spread throughout the publics of the Western colonial powers themselves, deliberately inculcated an anticolonialist attitude in the dependent peoples, enforced reforms and speeded policies of emancipation. Not so surprisingly, the devolution of empire has created as many problems as it has solved. The settlement of what remains of the colonial issue and the ferment of new nationalisms call for the closest collaboration of all North Atlantic countries. In the last resort, they alone can assure liberty to the less developed countries; for it is they who have advanced furthest toward the realization of an open society and are powerful enough to defend the approaches against the twin threats of anarchy and tyranny.

Modern Western civilization can claim, far more justly than communism, to have unleashed, and to live by, a "permanent revolution." In a civilization whose very genius lies in its unlimited capacity for creative change no one generation can afford to rest on its achievements. Hans Barth wrote:

The history of the Western world . . . shows that which must be considered its unalienable heritage cannot be regarded by each generation as an automatic possession, to be passed on unimpaired and without a struggle to coming generations. This heritage must be defended ever anew, because it is a treasure that can be retained only as long as men are ready to make sacrifices. For this possession represents the very basis of life itself, in default of which life would not be worth living.

The continued vitality and growth of the North Atlantic Community are not only in the interests of its own peoples; they are also the last best hope of mankind. The revolutions which convulse the world today spring from the seeds planted everywhere by Western civilization. The North Atlantic peoples do not seek to press other peoples into a utopian mold. Their blueprint for world order is implicit in their own institutions: the universalization of the open society in which human aspirations are increasingly fulfilled. That so permissive a scheme for world order can be taken for Western imperialism in a new guise bespeaks a profound misunderstanding of the hopes and fears of the Western peoples—if not naïve susceptibility to communist propaganda. The spirit of the Atlantic Community is positive, not negative, as are, because they seek to squeeze life into the Procrustean bed of theory, all political utopias. The Atlantic Community, by strengthening its own cultural consciousness and affirming its own values, can help all those who, inspired by the Western traditions of liberty, seek some measure of this liberty for themselves. Thus the North Atlantic peoples will open a new chapter not only in ordering relationships among themselves but also in relating themselves to the other civilizations on this shrinking globe.

CHAPTER **2** THE POLITICAL HISTORY OF NATO

A whole generation has grown to maturity that knows —whatever it does know—of the end of World War II only what it has learned from the accounts of its elders. It is no longer easy to recapture the mood of the late 1940's. The Western nations had disarmed; Western Europe had hardly begun to mend its economic fabric; and the Red Army stood in Central Europe poised, so it seemed, to debouch into a Western military void. No one can say with certainty how real was the Soviet menace in 1949. But, although Soviet intentions could not be assessed, Soviet military capabilities and the general outward thrust of Soviet policy made the menace appear real enough to the statesmen of the West.

Hence the first purpose for which NATO was formed was to provide the Atlantic nations with security against the threat of Soviet military attack. There can be little room for argument on this score. It is good to raise a reminder from time to time of this original purpose of the Alliance: NATO was established to fend off the dangers of a Soviet thrust westward to the English Channel.

Since 1949, NATO's military strength has been improved steadily, not because the statesmen of the West have been plotting aggression against the Soviets, but simply in response to the sustained efforts of the Soviets to expand their military might. The total military potential of the Soviet bloc, relative to that of the West, is greater now than it was in 1949, when the United States enjoyed an atomic monopoly. Today as then, it is the commitment contained in the North Atlantic Treaty, and little else, which renders a Soviet attack improbable.

Some may argue that the presence of a resentful China to the rear is sufficient to deter a Soviet attack on Western Europe. The Sino-

34

Soviet relationship, to be sure, is fraught with formidable stresses and strains—the same stresses and strains which, to some degree or another, assail all relationships within the communist bloc. But no amount of Chinese antagonism to Soviet claims to primacy in the communist world can remove the threat to Europe posed by the very real military capabilities of the Soviets. Several years must pass before China can boast of nuclear plenty. Meanwhile, the possible economic, scientific, technological, political and strategic gains to be made by a takeover of Western Europe greatly outweigh the possible dangers posed to the Soviets by China. Indeed, a U.S.S.R. that was in control of all Europe would be in a much better position to assert leadership over China.

The West's military problem—the problem posed by Soviet capabilities—remains as grave as ever. Yet its gravity does not guarantee the permanence of the Alliance. The impermanence of military alliances irrespective of the dictates of military logic has been an ever-recurring phenomenon of history from the days of ancient Greece to the epoch of the Napoleonic Wars on to the period between the two world wars. Today, the same question must be asked: Can a purely military alliance hold together indefinitely without making significant progress toward closer political unity? In peacetime, an external threat, however grave, evokes but intermittent and marginal public response. It may harden public attitudes. But a posture of defensive readiness is bound to become rather tiresome with the passage of time. Fear may indeed contribute much toward the haphazard growth of a sense of common interest. The history of nationalism is also the history of the alien *bête noire,* and all nationalisms thrive to a greater or lesser extent on xenophobia. But fear and hatred alone are never sufficient to create and sustain a genuine consciousness of community. Fear, even when justified by objective facts, nevertheless arises from the collective unconscious. It is essentially an emotional, instinctive reaction. Beyond fear, the rational awareness of political community grows from the recognition of a common positive task.[1] A community, if it is not to brood neurotically over its mere physical survival but to flourish healthily, must draw its strength from a creative promise rather than from the presence of some great danger or challenge outside itself. Men form a community insofar as they embrace an inner spiritual principle which enables them to master their own destiny, to perform worthy deeds and to attain in various ways a more perfect level of human existence.

The question is often asked whether the Atlantic Community would collapse if the Soviet menace were to disappear tomorrow. The hypothesis, admittedly, is abstruse. For many years to come, the West is bound to look apprehensively upon the Soviet Union as an ideologically hostile rival. But as a logical exercise, the hypothesis of a sudden end to the Leninist empire can serve a useful purpose in helping us to test our attitude toward NATO, and toward the more comprehensive notion of the Atlantic Community. Certainly, the fellowship of a military alliance, although it might not dissolve entirely, would be radically altered. But if the disappearance of the common danger would drain the *élan vital* from the Atlantic Community, then no real Atlantic Community yet exists. Those who are charged with the responsibility for carrying the Alliance forward to its next stage of development cannot afford to forget that, in the concrete order of international politics, there is a very definite relationship between the existence of NATO and the nature of the communist threat. If there really is an ideological schism within the communist bloc, its causes must be traced at least in part to the creation and maintenance of the Atlantic Alliance. NATO has wrenched history out of the course plotted for it by Marx, Lenin and Stalin. The present schism within the bloc consists largely of a dispute over the question, "Where do we go from here?" It is not so much an indigenous process of "evolution" within communist society as the external resistance to communist expansion—the thwarting of the dialectic by NATO's strength—that has brought about strains and rifts within the communist bloc. Should NATO disintegrate, it is very likely that the communists would reconcile their ideological differences and, encouraged by the prospect of easy pickings, join ranks in militant solidarity.

The need for a positive political purpose was recognized by the architects of NATO when they drafted Article II of the Treaty: "The Parties will contribute toward the further development of peaceful and friendly international relations by strengthening their free institutions, by bringing about a better understanding of the principles upon which these institutions are founded, and by promoting conditions of stability and well-being." The statement, to be sure, was a cautious one. Although Article II goes on to call for the elimination of conflict in international economic policies and the encouragement of economic collaboration among the members, it contains no hint of anything even remotely approaching political integration. The Treaty went no further than to require the parties to consult together whenever, in the opinion of any one of them, the territorial integrity, political independence or security of any of the members should be threatened.[2]

It is highly doubtful that in 1949 a single member government would have been willing to subscribe to the concept of closer political unity, even as the expression of a distant policy goal. For that, the vestiges of traditional nationalist feeling were still too strong. The British had not been able, in spite of two world wars, to divest themselves entirely of nostalgia for the days of "splendid isolation." True, they were more attracted to the idea of the Atlantic Community than to the "Idea of Europe"; but at the same time they felt themselves bound to the Commonwealth—an allegiance which, combined with their immemorial aversion to formal pledges and written constitutions, made them wary of proposals for political integration. Nor would the United States Senate have ratified an instrument which implied any commitment, however vague, that impinged upon national constitutional prerogatives.[3] Europeans on the Continent were scarcely more conscious of a wider community of interest. French diplomacy had not yet embarked upon the course toward a Franco-German *rapprochement,* and the French public had not yet discerned in European integration a guarantee of security against a resurgent, independent Germany. The enslavement and then the liberation of Europe still evoked vivid memories. The smaller European countries could not be expected to contemplate enthusiastically the dilution of their sovereignty in a broader institutional arrangement in which the larger powers, including Germany, would have preponderant weight.

Western Europe itself, though less heterogeneous than the Atlantic Community as a whole, was unable to agree on the principles which should underlie regional unification. "Depending upon the basis of definition chosen—geographic, strategic, political, economic, cultural or spiritual—the concept of European unity linked different groups of countries for different purposes."[4] It is not surprising, then, that the wider differences in political structure and processes within the Atlantic Community (as, for example, between the United States

and Portugal), as well as the great disparity of international interests and policies (as, for example, between even Great Britain and
the United States) deterred the NATO partners from setting their
sights at closer political unity.

NATO, therefore, was established not as a supranational or federal organization, but as a defensive league of states and lacking
any organs of central government. Each member guarded its
sovereign prerogatives. In theory, precise distinctions can be drawn
between federations, supranational organizations, confederations and
mere alliances. In real life, which is always imprecise, the controversy over the differences between these types of associations is
apt soon to reach a point of diminishing returns. But, in the present
context, at least a rough distinction between a confederation and
an alliance helps to fix the actual scope and limits of NATO. A
confederation, although it does not impinge on the sovereignty of
its members, does possess a central government (possibly including
legislative, executive and judicial organs) of expressly delegated
powers.[5] Members of a confederation, unlike those of most federations, reserve the right to withdraw from the compact if they wish
to do so. But while they remain in it they are obligated to carry out
the decisions of the central organs, so long as these act within the
scope of their defined powers. Moreover, although the members of a
confederation usually vote as equal states, they can be considered
legally bound to follow specified decisions which are taken by
simple majorities.[6]

NATO was set up as an alliance, not a confederation. It is an intergovernmental group whose members undertake to consult, to coordinate and to cooperate. Whatever controls NATO exercises over
its members, it exercises them with the approval of its members. The
NATO bodies such as the Secretariat and the Council can facilitate
communications among governments, approve reports, render opinions, make recommendations and address requests. But NATO, as a
strictly intergovernmental body, cannot lay down binding policy
guidelines, nor can it issue authoritative directives, not even in the
crucial area of military defense, which is the *raison d'être* of the Alliance. Each member government, in effect, retains a veto. The parties,
it is true, declare that an attack upon one shall be deemed an attack
upon all. But each state remains the final judge of what action, including the use of armed force, it shall undertake in support of its

treaty obligations. The architects of NATO hoped that intensive joint planning among the members (e.g., standardization of equipment, joint training exercises, combined deployment, joint war exercises, mutual exchange of intelligence, close cooperation in the planning of national defense policies and intensive political consultation) would generate centripetal forces sufficient to offset the centrifugal tendencies which invariably plague alliances in times of crisis. But in the final analysis, significant policies within NATO can be developed only through the process of diplomatic negotiation. Article IX of the Treaty, which sets up the North Atlantic Council, defines neither powers nor procedures. The Council can take decisions only by unanimous consent.[7]

The ever closer teamwork and growing military strength of the Atlantic Alliance during the 1950's were great political achievements, which should not be underestimated. Never before had so many free states entered into arrangements for such intimate exchanges of view, such regular and continuous coordination of military polices. The Treaty provides that the Council "shall be so organized as to be able to meet promptly at any time." As a matter of fact, the Council, complying with directives laid down at the Lisbon meeting, can be said to have been in almost permanent session since 1952. During the following five years, which were "building years" for NATO, the Council held more than five hundred meetings and created nearly a score of principal committees.[8] Much was accomplished:

By 1957 NATO was able to claim that in seven years its forces for the defense of Europe had increased four- or five-fold and that they were infinitely more effective as regards fire-power, combat value and common planning. A common infrastructure had been set up of airfields, communications and pipelines without which a modern army cannot function: as one illustration, the number of airfields for jet aircraft was increased from twenty to one hundred and fifty. Considerable progress had been made—though many believed not enough—in the joint planning of defense production and in the standardization of equipment; furthermore, by means of the "Annual Review," agreement was reached between all the allies on the reconciliation of their defense programs with their national resources and on the equitable sharing of the cost of the common defense. The joint expenditure on defense of the NATO countries had risen from 20 billion dollars in 1950 to 60 billions in 1957.[9]

Some might regard such an evaluation as slightly sanguine. Nevertheless, the important progress made by NATO toward the defense of Europe during the mid-1950's cannot be gainsaid. NATO developed and, more important, applied the concept of balanced collective forces, with specialized national contributions under a single Supreme Allied Commander aided by an international staff. NATO facilitated consultation among its members on such matters as the reunification of Germany at the time of the Berlin Conference of 1954; the preparation of Western diplomatic positions for Four-Power disarmament negotiations and for the Geneva Summit Meeting of 1955; and other general problems of East-West relations. Perhaps most significantly, NATO eased Germany's return to the Western fold. The Berlin Conference of 1954 had made it clear that the reunification of Germany was out of the question in the prevailing climate of the Cold War. Shortly thereafter, amidst national frustration over the war in Indochina and apprehensions over France's ability to stand up to a resurgent Germany without close British support, the French Parliament defeated the European Defense Community (EDC) and thus closed the door on a purely European solution of the problem of the integration of Germany into a Western system of defense. It was NATO that provided an environment in which the independence and the rearmament of West Germany could be brought about within the framework of the controls of the Western European Union, thereby permitting the Federal Republic to make a major contribution in forces and territory to the defense of Western Europe. These were indeed historic achievements. Meanwhile, there was a steady improvement in organizational machinery. In 1955, M. Paul-Henri Spaak observed that NATO Council discussions decreasingly resembled formal international meetings and were becoming more like cabinet deliberations.[10]

The growing intimacy of the Council smoothed the path of Allied diplomatic cooperation. Yet serious problems of coalition diplomacy remained. Generally speaking, the members' record of agreement on matters affecting the territorial heart of the Alliance, Western Europe, was good. But, with embarrassing frequency, they found themselves unable to coordinate their policies in areas of the world outside the explicitly defined NATO theater. In Malaya, Indochina and Korea, for example, the one Western nation which considered its interests to be most directly at stake took up the fight against communist expansion, while its major allies extended mostly limited support, or abstained from giving any assistance, or tried to act as a brake upon the initiative of the embattled party. The British felt that the magnitude of the American effort in Korea detracted from the task of building NATO and might trigger a general war. The British, thanks to a fortuitous combination of circumstances and an astute counterguerrilla strategy, were able to eliminate the communist threat to the Malayan Peninsula; but the British and the Americans were reluctant to come to the overt military aid of the beleaguered French in their unpopular colonial war in Indochina. When the United States finally advocated joint Allied intervention in the spring of 1954, the British rejected the suggestion on the grounds that it would jeopardize the pending Geneva negotiations for a settlement in Southeast Asia. Each of the three major powers had its reasons for wishing to preserve its position in the Far East or in Southeast Asia against communist encroachment. NATO had a stake in the outcome of the military encounters with communism in those regions. But NATO made no serious effort to develop unified policies corresponding to its interests. Admittedly, there were complex political, military and ideological reasons for this failure— the failure of coalition diplomacy. These reasons perhaps made the failure understandable, but they did not render its consequences any the less dangerous.

The inability of the leading European nations of the Atlantic Alliance to devise common policies to protect their relatively remote interests in the Far East and Southeast Asia during the period 1949– 1954 emboldened the Soviet Union to intensify its harassing and penetrative maneuvers in more sensitive regions on NATO's southern flank. The Soviets had reason to believe that the United States, Great Britain and France would find it difficult to coordinate their actions against the rising tide of anti-Western nationalism within the Arab world. Anti-Western sentiment had been gathering force for a long time; it required only the proper combination of arms, propaganda and diplomatic support to raise it to a critical pitch. During the early 1950's the United States had given the Egyptians a certain amount of diplomatic support in their efforts to bring about the withdrawal of Great Britain from Suez and the Nile Valley.[11] In North Africa, where the French were embroiled with the Al-

gerian nationalist guerrillas, the United States had struck an anticolonialist pose, much to the chagrin of the policymakers in Paris.
Not a few Europeans suspected that the American attitudes and
policies had been dictated largely by "oil politics" rather than anticolonial sentiment. Soviet strategists could hardly be blamed for
thinking that the clashing interests within the capitalist camp were
about to erupt, as foretold in Stalin's last thesis, in open "imperialist"
conflict, nor for surmising that a challenge, hurled down in the
Middle East, would throw the West into disarray.

There is no need to recount the melancholy story of the Suez
crisis, of the Soviet role in it, and of how Britain, France and the
United States met that crisis.[12] No useful purpose can be served
now by trying to fix blame. Suffice to recall that the Suez episode
found the United States and the Soviet Union aligned against
Great Britain and France, and that NATO faced its gravest political
crisis. Confused and paralyzed, the Alliance could not even contemplate steps to take advantage of the Soviet empire's most serious
"time of troubles" to date—the nationalist outbursts in Eastern
Europe.

Transatlantic distrust had reached a peak. American officials
acted as though they had been deceived by their counterparts in
London and Paris. The British and French felt that they had been
let down shamefully by their American allies. Sir Geoffrey Crowther,
the former editor of the *Economist* and a staunch friend of the
United States, asked whether the official attitude of the Department
of State meant that

the alliance will be expected to work in matters that the United States
deems important, but not in matters that Britain and France deem important, and even perhaps vital to their existence? If that is the American
attitude . . . then it is hard to see how there can be an effective alliance.
. . . I am not trying to say that the State Department must always dance
to a Franco-British tune. It is obvious that the strongest member of the
alliance must have the biggest say in determining its policies. . . . But it
is also in the logic of alliance that the permanent and vital national interests of the weaker partners become permanent and vital interests of the
United States.[13]

The crisis of confidence which confronted NATO at the time of
Suez and Hungary compelled the statesmen of the Alliance to take
a long, hard look at the question of political coordination. The

military preparations of Britain and France for intervention in Egypt had not been discussed in the North Atlantic Council. NATO was saved not by pondered statesmanship, but by a fortuitous development: the Alliance might well have disintegrated had it not been for the explosion set off by Soviet policy in Hungary. When the Committee of Three[14] delivered its report on nonmilitary cooperation at the Council meeting in December, 1956, the member governments were in a chastened enough mood to pay attention to its recommendations.

The "Three Wise Men" argued that the health of NATO depended first and foremost on the wholehearted acceptance by all its members of the political commitment to collective defense. "An alliance in which the members ignore each other's interests or engage in political or economic conflict, or harbor suspicions of each other, cannot be effective either for deterrence or defense."[15] Security, said the Three, is far more than a military matter. "The strengthening of political consultation and economic cooperation, the development of resources, progress in education and understanding, all these can be as important, or even more important, for the protection of the security of a nation, or an alliance, as the building of a battleship or the equipping of an army."[16] Such cooperation could not be brought about overnight or by fiat, but only by creating over the years the necessary habits, traditions and precedents. The Three concluded that the long-term aim of NATO must be "the development of an Atlantic Community whose roots are deeper even than the necessity for common defense. This implies nothing less than the permanent association of the free Atlantic peoples for the promotion of their greater unity and the protection and the advancement of the interests which, as free democracies, they have in common."[17]

The most important recommendation of the "Three Wise Men" was to strengthen political cooperation within NATO without weakening the ties of NATO members with other friendly countries or with other international organizations, especially the United Nations. They did not, however, suggest any significant modification of NATO's political structure, and in this sense the report was less helpful than it might have been. The desired objective was to be reached primarily through more intensive consultation within the established framework. The Three pointed out that consultation among the members of an alliance means much more than mere exchanges of information:

It means more than letting the NATO Council know about national decisions that have already been taken; or trying to enlist support for those decisions. It means the discussion of problems collectively, in the early stages of policy formation, and before national positions become fixed. At best, this will result in collective decisions on matters of common interest affecting the Alliance. At the least, it will insure that no action is taken by one member without a knowledge of the views of the others.[18]

Specifically, member governments were urged to inform the Council of any development significantly affecting the Alliance, not as a mere formality but as a preliminary to effective political consultation. Both individual member governments and the Secretary General were enjoined to raise within the Council any question which was of common NATO interest and not a purely domestic concern. Member governments were expected to desist from committing themselves to policies or making major pronouncements, on matters affecting allies, without adequate advance consultation, except in cases where circumstances made consultation demonstrably impossible. In developing national policies, members were urged to take the interests and views of other governments into account. Once a consensus had been reached within the Council, it should be reflected in the formation of national policies. If a government failed to comply with understandings reached in the Council, it should offer an explanation to the Council.

All the Committee's proposals were approved by the Council. The United States enthusiastically supported the appeal for more intensive consultation within NATO. At the Heads of Government Conference in December, 1957, the United States announced that its permanent representative to the Council would be kept fully informed of any national policies which might impinge upon the interests of NATO or its members and would be invited, when sojourning in the United States, to participate in meetings of the Cabinet and the National Security Council.[19] The consultative process hit its stride markedly in succeeding years. For example, according to the testimony of Secretary General Spaak, the United States during the year prior to September, 1958, did not send the Soviet Union a single diplomatic note on the proposed summit conference without first submitting it to the NATO Council.[20]

At the start, the Western governments had not been agreed on the desirability of a second venture into summit diplomacy after the barren results of the first. The United States was unenthusiastic about the proposal for a second summit meeting. But after the launching of the first sputnik inflated Soviet prestige, yearning for a high-level talk grew apace in Britain and elsewhere throughout the West. The United States, once it had bowed to the rising pressures for another round of summitry, managed to obtain its allies' agreement on the need for advance diplomatic spadework in order to enhance the chances of the meeting's success, and upon the inclusion in the agenda of the right of Eastern European peoples to choose their own governments.[21] This latter demand signified NATO's willingness to undertake a modest diplomatic initiative against the Soviet bloc, even at the risk of dimming the prospects for a summit gathering. Most Western statesmen conceded that if the Soviets refused adamantly to discuss one of the fundamental sources of postwar tension in Europe another trek to the summit was pointless.

During the years 1957–1962, the NATO governments encountered the least of their difficulties in their efforts to achieve a minimal unity of policy on those security issues which arose out of NATO's immediate strategic confrontation with the Soviet Union. They cooperated most smoothly on European military defense, international arms negotiations and the closely related problems of Germany and Berlin. Opinions differed widely, to be sure, over the best methods of achieving the objectives of the Alliance, the timing and phasing of moves, and the details of the tactical plans to be pursued. But generally speaking, during those five years the members of NATO stood together in matters touching their common commitment to the defense of Europe. They remained steadfast in their determination to resist outright Soviet military aggression. The Atlantic partners were, for all intents and purposes, of one mind in rejecting various communist proposals for disengagement, such as the thinning out of forces or the denuclearization of Central Europe. They agreed, sometimes in the face of vigorous domestic opposition, that these proposals, if accepted, would jeopardize the success of NATO's forward defense strategy and lead to an asymmetrical change in the situation, i.e., a relative deterioration of Western Europe's security posture. At the same time, they did not falter in their quest for *effective* arms control agreements. At least up to 1961, the United States, Britain and France were fairly successful in coordinating their positions for comprehensive disarmament negotiations with the Soviets (but not for test ban negotiations).

Throughout the last five years, the Western powers have not lost sight of the fact that the most crucial political question in East-West relations is still that of the future of Germany. The Western Allies, despite persistent rumors and suspicions that they were on the verge of weakening in their resolve, maintained a reassuringly firm and consistent position when it came to actual negotiations on the German question.[22] Perhaps the United States, Britain and France have not pressed for a German settlement as vigorously as the German Federal Republic would have liked, but the Big Three have not deviated from their determination to permit German reunification only on the basis of free all-German elections. Actually, the Western Allies have been less concerned with bringing about German unity than with keeping the Federal Republic in NATO and in the integrative institutions which emerged in Western Europe during the 1950's. At least up until the present time, however, a majority of the West German population has been willing to accept, if not in word then at least in fact, this order of priorities.

The Western Allies, aware that the continued freedom and viability of West Berlin is essential to the health and self-confidence of NATO, have closed ranks whenever the Soviets have increased their pressure upon the former German capital.[23] Disagreements undoubtedly have appeared from time to time about the most effective means of dealing with the latest Berlin crisis. The Americans and the British have differed over the desirability of adopting hard-and-fast advance plans for handling various contingent situations as soon as they arise instead of waiting to consult after the crisis has developed. The French have differed sharply with their major allies over the desirability of Soviet-Western negotiations on Berlin.[24] On occasion, Western statesmen have succumbed to the temptation to play a lone diplomatic hand by suggesting the creation of a free, neutral city, entrusting Berlin to the United Nations and internationalizing the access routes. But meanwhile, preparations have gone forward to impress the Soviets with the Allies' resolution to meet force with force and thus to deter the Soviets from a quick grab at West Berlin. Premier Khrushchev's deadlines have come and gone, but the overt military challenge which many Western analysts have frequently feared since 1959 has not materialized. Instead, the unexpected happened—the Berlin wall was built. In a non-military move, the Soviets unilaterally altered the status of Berlin, or perhaps merely ratified in concrete an assumption which had been gradually growing on both sides of the Iron Curtain but which no one cared to make explicit, namely, that Berlin's chances of becoming the capital of a reunified Germany within the foreseeable future had been reduced to almost zero. The Berlin wall was, in a sense, a testimony to NATO's apparent willingness to meet a test of military strength if such a test were thrust upon it. At the same time, it was a taunting reminder that the leading nations of the Atlantic Alliance have not yet overcome the political weaknesses inherent in alliance diplomacy, and that they are not yet able to cope with the full spectrum of political weapons which are available to the Soviets.

The members of NATO would do well to "examine their consciences" periodically and take stock of the manner in which they have risen to the external challenge, fulfilled their mutual obligations and coordinated their policies for the achievement of the common purpose which they profess. Even in their direct dealings with the Sino-Soviet bloc, their record of teamwork is far from perfect. The U.S. and Britain, hoping to halt the spread of nuclear weapons, have engaged in test ban negotiations with the Soviets over the strenuous objections of the French. British leaders came close at times to violating the spirit of the Alliance by seeking to act as intermediary between the United States and the U.S.S.R., proposing compromise solutions—and this apparently without prior consultation with Washington. American policymakers caviled at Prime Minister Macmillan's suggestion, made during his trip to Moscow in the spring of 1959, for a politically agreed quota of on-site inspections, instead of a quota determined by scientific criteria, as a means of breaking the impasse in the test ban negotiations. The different approaches to summit diplomacy,[25] the Anglo-American "agreement to differ" on the question of admitting Red China to the United Nations, and the dispute between Washington and London early in 1962 over the British sale of jet planes to the Peking regime did not bespeak an Anglo-American team spirit. These frictions pointed to a serious lack of those agreed principles which should guide the dealings of Western governments with the Sino-Soviet bloc during periods of temporary *détente* in the Cold War. The Western powers were not at all united on their assessment of whether "peaceful coexistence" is possible and, if so, on what or whose terms.

Internal Alliance relationships, too, have been marred only too frequently by nettlesome misunderstandings and exhausting disputes. Despite the unanimous assent to the recommendations of the Three Wise Men in 1956, NATO governments have not always lived up to their obligations to consult and coordinate policies. The famous White Paper on Defense of April, 1957, in which Great Britain announced that for economic reasons she intended to shift from a conventional to a nuclear strategy, caused considerable dismay within European NATO circles. The British cuts had been planned unilaterally without prior consultation either in NATO or within WEU, to which Britain had given a pledge in 1954 not to reduce her Continental commitments except with the approval of a majority of the members.[26] Furthermore, to proceed in the direction of their new nuclear strategy, the British required from the United States a form of technical assistance which seemed to make of Britain a privileged ally of the United States. This was one of the factors which eventually spurred French determination to join the nuclear club.[27]

The preferred position which Great Britain enjoys apparently without the prior concurrence of the whole Alliance gave rise to some bickering over questions of national prestige. After the advent of President de Gaulle to power he sought to win for France a place as a Great Power—a power equivalent at least to Britain. President de Gaulle insisted that France be counted in on disarmament talks lest the three nuclear powers reach agreements at French expense. De Gaulle hastened preparations already under way to establish at great cost a national nuclear force which would enable him to acquire both a negative veto and a positive directing voice in any nuclear decisions which might affect French security. But even after the first successful test in the Sahara, the United States did not relax its policy governing the transmission of nuclear data. The French resented Washington's refusal to share with one of its major allies nuclear secrets which were in the possession of the Soviet Union. But this was not de Gaulle's only grievance. He insisted that France receive greater consideration in the nomination of NATO ground, air and naval commanders. At the same time he rejected the principle of military integration, which he interpreted to mean subordinating national defense arrangements to NATO control without receiving in return any guarantees sufficient to safeguard France's vital interests in Africa as well as in Europe.[28] The French Government countered NATO military integration by three unilateral actions: (1) It refused to integrate French fighter planes into the Alliance's air defense system. (2) It withdrew from CINC-SOUTH (the Allied Naval Forces in the Mediterranean) a number of French units which had previously been assigned to NATO command in the event of war. (3) In the absence of a satisfactory agreement on the sharing of control, it refused to allow the establishment of IRBM bases and the continuation of storage of atomic weapons on French soil. The latter decision compelled the NATO Commander in Chief to redeploy more than two hundred American fighter bombers from French airfields to other bases.

De Gaulle, in letters to President Eisenhower and Prime Minister Macmillan in September, 1958, called for the creation of a closer working relationship among the three leading members of NATO.[29] The United States received the proposal for the so-called "tripartite directorate" unfavorably, the Department of State taking the position that the excepted nations would feel they were being relegated to second-class membership, with adverse repercussions upon the Alliance. The French rejoined that the Continental members already labored under a sense of inferiority vis-à-vis Great Britain, the special confidant of the United States. The French appeared to be more interested in developing a common strategy among the three NATO members who bore the greatest strategic responsibilities *outside* the European territory of NATO, than in acquiring a privileged voice in the determination of intra-European NATO policy. "France," wrote René Pleven, "the only continental member of NATO which today has defense responsibilities of comparable magnitude to the British, would also like to have the means of making her voice heard."[30] He caviled at the term "tripartite directorate" and denied that France was seeking arrangements which would obviously arouse opposition within the organization.

What France was trying to do was simply to get the United States to realize how important it is that the nations of the West stand together against the Soviet challenge and that they be so organized that they cannot be taken by surprise whenever and wherever that challenge is presented. The French thesis is that the surprises which the Soviet Union is adept at producing in all parts of the world may at any moment directly affect the territories of the French Community; and that in view of this it would be both logical and useful to allow France to participate in the formulation of global defense plans. . . . It wants permanent cooperation with the United States and Great Britain along these lines, whether through NATO or otherwise.[31]

President de Gaulle proved unable, during the four years after 1958, to acquire the kind of voice which he wanted in the making of Western policy. His disappointment in this respect undoubtedly goes far toward explaining his subsequent opposition to Britain's entry into the Common Market.

Apart from France, NATO has been plagued by a number of "intramural" tensions involving other members. On balance some of these tensions may have been fraught with less significance for the well-being of NATO, but the feelings which they have generated have not necessarily been less intensive. For at least three years, the Cyprus dispute embittered the relations of Greece with Great Britain and Turkey, until the good offices of Secretary General Spaak helped to pave the way for a settlement. For a number of years Great Britain conducted a running feud with Iceland over fishing rights in the waters around Iceland. The British and the West Germans engaged in prolonged haggling over the issue of financing the maintenance of British troops in Germany. For several years after the Rome Treaty went into effect, practically all the NATO leaders were deeply concerned with preventing the permanent formation of two hostile trading blocs in Europe. In recent years, American officials have devoted a great deal of effort to persuading the Europeans, especially the West Germans, that they should share more equitably the burdens of international security and economic development. Not all governments thus dunned responded graciously. Perhaps some of these conflicts, viewed in retrospect, do not seem too serious now that they have been resolved or at least are no longer topics of heated public controversy. But they certainly seemed nearly as important in the years when they were fraying the tempers of NATO diplomats as do those issues which today rend the Alliance.

Such concrete problems as determining the political status of

Cyprus, settling the dispute over Icelandic fishing rights or working out satisfactory arrangements for troop supports might be exasperating. But they are not unmanageable. They lend themselves to relatively precise definition; they are susceptible to eventual resolution by diplomacy on a mutually acceptable basis. It is much more difficult to come to grips with problems which arise, not from clear-cut differences of national interest, but rather out of deeply rooted hatreds and suspicions—debris of victory and defeat. The Western Alliance, unfortunately, has had more than its share of such thorny problems. Among these, one of the most persistent and potentially most dangerous stems from the undercurrent of mistrust toward Germany which runs through the Atlantic Community.

In the early years of their membership in NATO, the Germans were often accused of failing to make their full military contribution to the Alliance. But more recently, under the impact of a mounting Soviet propaganda campaign,[32] many in the West have begun to express fears of a resurgent German militarism which would seek to "drag" NATO into a revanchist war for the reunification of the country and the recovery of the lost territories beyond the Oder-Neisse. Actually, although adherence to the Western pact has done little if anything to advance the cause of reunification, Chancellor Adenauer has remained unswervingly loyal to NATO. Indeed, as spokesman of the NATO country in the most exposed position, he has been the most ardent champion of military and political integration. Furthermore, under the provisions of the Western European pact, the Federal Republic has been subject during the last decade to more international arms control than any other country in the world.[33] Nevertheless, the slightest hint that the United States might make nuclear weapons available to the West German army has invariably aroused strident opposition in such persistently anti-German quarters as the British Labour Party.

Many Germans are apprehensive over the prospect that their country might someday be converted into an atomic battlefield. They are not at all sure that nuclear weapons should be stationed permanently on the soil of the Federal Republic, regardless of who controls them. Their fear is exploited by those of their countrymen who would gamble on some form of neutralization and "denuclearization" as the most likely roads to national unity. The West, when its attention is attracted to this segment of West German opinion, is often led to suspect the Federal Republic of preparing to disengage itself from NATO and to carry on direct bilateral negotiations with Moscow over the future of the divided country. Yet neither Chancellor Adenauer nor Willy Brandt, the opposition leader, has ever sought to dominate the Alliance militarily or to abandon it politically. The majority of the West German people, and the two largest political parties, appear friendlier to NATO in the sixties than when the Federal Republic was first admitted more than seven years ago.[34] There are good reasons to conclude that the Federal Republic is firmly oriented toward the Western Alliance: (1) The Franco-German *rapprochement* remains in force; in fact, with the signing of the Treaty of Cooperation in early 1963, the ties between the two countries had become too close for some. (2) The Germans have never agitated for a withdrawal of foreign forces in favor of national defense autonomy. (3) West German businessmen have been just as enthusiastic as their counterparts in neighboring countries over the promises of economic unification. (4) Chancellor Adenauer probably did as much as any other West European leader to forestall open economic warfare between the Common Market and the European Free Trade Association and to find a diplomatic route for British entry into the EEC. In sum, the Federal Republic of 1962 bore little resemblance to the Weimar Republic of 1922 or 1932. Bonn's negotiations with Spain in 1960 for military supply depots and air training facilities, and the direct talks of Ambassador Kroll with Soviet leaders at the Kremlin at the height of the Berlin diplomatic crisis in late 1961, may have reflected a certain ineptness in gauging the psychological impact of these moves on other Allied capitals,[35] but it was farfetched to raise, as did certain Western journalists, the specters of the Hitler-Franco friendship and the Rapallo Pact.

If the Germans find that, no matter what they do, they can never live down their Nazi past and be accepted fully as members in good standing of the Atlantic Community, they might be sorely tempted to move in other directions. Mistrust breeds mistrust. Since 1958, the Germans have come to suspect the British of being willing to negotiate a "shady deal" with the Soviets over Berlin or over the whole question of Germany's future. Many Germans have been resentful of reports that not a few Frenchmen, unable to erase from their minds the history of Europe from 1870 to 1945, are not really willing to see Europe plunged into war for the sake of defending—of all places—Berlin. Some Germans have wondered about French motives for trying to "bundle" the Federal Republic into the Coal and Steel Community and the Common Market, and undoubtedly they have asked themselves whether the United States, Great Britain and France (along with the Soviets) do not secretly rejoice at the prospect of a Germany irrevocably and permanently divided.

These mutual doubts and recriminations are typical of the divisive forces that, in recent years, have assailed NATO from within. There have been recurring alarms that France is on the verge of collapse, civil war or fascism; that the Scandinavian members are being tempted to sever connections with NATO and create a neutral Nordic bloc;[36] and that the rise of militant pacifism in Great Britain might jeopardize the continued U.S. reliance on British bases.[37] Some Americans have wondered whether the British, looking wistfully for a *rapprochement* with the Soviets, have lost their traditional sense of political realism. For the three years prior to August, 1961, the British looked upon the Common Market as a threat to their economic well-being—almost as a Franco-German plot; the French, on the other hand, scarcely disguised their conviction that the British were out to dilute the Common Market and blunt the force of its drive toward closer Franco-German political cooperation. The French, furthermore, have often accused their two major allies of being unsympathetic to what they were trying to accomplish in Algeria, and of trying to prevent them from gaining admittance as full-fledged members of the nuclear club. Finally, prior to the latest Berlin crisis, many West Europeans were apprehensive over the prospect that the United States intended to straighten out its balance-of-payments deficit by reducing its commitment to the local defense of Europe in favor of heavier reliance upon the intercontinental missile deterrent. The decision of the Eisenhower Administration in December, 1960, to withdraw military dependents seemed to lend substance to these apprehensions. Some Europeans in recent years have oscillated unstably between fear that the United States *would not*, at the "moment of truth," defend them with nuclear weapons and, at other times, fear that it *would*. Their dilemma may have been exaggerated, but to the extent that it exists it must be traced, at least in part, to a disquieting lack of faith in the quality of American leadership under grave stress.

When problems have arisen that touch the very heart of the Alliance, it has generally been possible to discuss them frankly in the Council. Sooner or later, the more serious and concrete difficulties have been liquidated through some kind of institutionalized action. But the manner in which the NATO partners have dealt—or, more accurately, have failed to deal—with their policy differences on questions originating in their relations with the non-Western regions of the world has left much to be desired. Despite the good intentions which the Council members expressed in adopting the Report of the Three in December, 1956, the process of disimperialism and the efforts of the Western powers to provide for the stability and security of either independent states or still dependent territories in Asia, Africa and Latin America has too often found NATO to be a house divided. In view of the Soviet disposition to look upon the decolonized zones and other underdeveloped regions as the vulnerable strategic rear of the Western state system in which a strategy of outflanking and attrition can be most safely executed, the inability of the Atlantic nations to coordinate their foreign policies toward the non-NATO areas must be chalked up as the most abysmal failure of the Alliance—perhaps the one which, in the final analysis, will prove its undoing.

Algeria furnishes a good case in point. Speaking in strict legal terms, Algeria was really a NATO problem. Article VI of the Treaty specifically mentioned the Algerian Department of France as forming part of the area to be defended against armed attack (irrespective of its source). Indeed, the Western Mediterranean Command of NATO originally had its headquarters in Algiers. But psychologically and politically, so far as a large segment of Western opinion was concerned, Algeria long stood outside NATO, in spite of the fact that the struggle there had the most serious implications for the internal political health of France. Indeed, for divisive effects upon French society, the Algerian crisis must be ranked with the Dreyfus Case and the schisms of the Pétain era. In the last-stand effort to vindicate its honor after the inglorious loss of Indochina, the French government siphoned off virtually all its forces from the NATO central front and dispatched them to North Africa. When de Gaulle came to power in 1958, he came as the liquidator of the nation's dilemma. His brand of prestige nationalism, which has usually been interpreted as hostile to NATO and cool to the idea of West European political integration, must be understood in terms of his compelling desire to revivify a nation which not many years ago looked very much like Lenin's "weakest link in the chain" of the Western state system.

President de Gaulle frequently lectured his allies on the crucial importance of France's stand in Algeria for the future defense of Europe's southern flank and for the securing of sub-Saharan Africa against communist penetration. De Gaulle, we must presume, saw what should be obvious to any strategist: Were Europe to lose all control over the Mediterranean's southern littoral, the West's strategic position in the world would be gravely weakened—far more gravely than by de Gaulle's pointed snubs to NATO. Strategic realities provided a rational basis for French impatience at the apparent inability of most Americans to see the Algerian struggle in any terms other than those of anticolonialism.

French dismay reached its peak when the United States abstained in the General Assembly vote of December 13, 1958, on a resolution to recognize the right of the Algerian people to independence. The climate of Franco-American relations began to improve somewhat toward the end of 1959, after President Eisenhower endorsed de Gaulle's offer of three eventual political choices for Algeria. All through 1960 and 1961, as strident opposition to the French President's aims mounted among the Algerian *colons,* the United States Government seemed to become increasingly sympathetic toward de Gaulle's purpose in North Africa. Meanwhile, de Gaulle's Algerian policies posed the most delicate questions of Alliance diplomacy. The French President needed the cooperation of his allies—at least in the form of "benevolent neutrality"—in order to achieve his objectives in Algeria; but, determined to uphold French "grandeur," he could not openly request their assistance. To "save appearances," it was essential that the solution should spring from the genius of France alone. At times, NATO had to serve as a convenient whipping boy on whom the muscles of national self-assertiveness could be exercised, while popular support was built up inside France for an Algerian settlement which few observers in 1958 thought feasible. But, to the dismay of those who wished to see the Alliance strengthened, the Evian Accord did not pave the way for a more pro-NATO attitude on the part of the French President.

In spite of the painful lessons learned at Suez, the NATO countries at one time or another have fallen out among themselves in every region of the world. The determination of the United States to maintain, in the face of Chinese communist threats, the status quo in the Taiwan Straits area has failed to evoke support in Western Europe. The United States and Great Britain, it is true, did manage to achieve an unusual degree of success in coordinating their policies in the Middle East during the critical summer of 1958, but even then they did not see fit to give to the North Atlantic Council advance notification of their joint military intervention in Lebanon and Jordan. (France showed her pique by refusing to countenance a proposed "summit" meeting at the United Nations.) Beginning in 1960, Portugal's official indignation began to mount steadily at the refusal of the NATO allies to furnish diplomatic support in the United Nations on the Angola question; Premier Salazar hinted that his country, possessor of the important Azores base, might withdraw from NATO unless greater Allied cooperation on colonial problems were forthcoming.[38] French, Belgians, Portuguese and other Europeans were highly displeased by the direction of United States policy in the Congo crisis, and their displeasure has had enduring repercussions within the Alliance. (See Chapter 5.) At the height of the Laotian crisis in the spring of 1961, the Quai d'Orsay displayed marked coolness toward suggestions by the Kennedy Administration that the United States might intervene to halt communist penetration in Southeast Asia.[39] The United States, in the midst of the West Irian crisis in early 1962, withdrew landing rights for Dutch planes bound for Indonesia. Such policy attitudes hardly bespeak alliance-mindedness. *It seems to be almost a diplomatic rule of thumb that, outside the NATO area, the troubles of each one of the Allies are his own business. What is more, each government often appears determined to keep it that way; it welcomes support from Allied capitals but brooks no foreign "meddling," be it even in the form of advice.*

The absence of Alliance solidarity on issues arising outside the precisely defined scope of the NATO Treaty was brought home to the United States, rather painfully, in the case of Cuba. After the ill-starred "invasion" at Cochinos Bay in April, 1961, Britons were not reluctant to remind Americans ironically that Cuba was their Suez. The United States, humiliated and confused by the debacle, found its allies looking on with an air of condescending detachment.[40] It seemed that here at last was an appropriate occasion for the Europeans to demonstrate their pent-up resentments against certain features of U.S. Alliance diplomacy, or the lack thereof, during the last decade. In February, 1962, the Director of the Policy Planning Council of the Department of State, Walt W. Rostow, in a follow-up to the Punta del Este Conference (at which it was agreed that the communist regime in Havana should be excluded from the affairs of the OAS), went to Paris for the purpose of asking the Atlantic allies to cut off all their strategic trade and to reduce their general trade with Cuba. The State Department's request met with a distinctly lukewarm reception. One European official was quoted as saying that "if the issue of NATO solidarity comes up, we will certainly have something to say about that."[41] An American correspondent in Paris commented as follows:

The fact of the matter is that no agreement has ever been reached on just how much and when consultation should be held within the North Atlantic Treaty Organization. The United States has argued that its worldwide responsibilities prevent it from placing many of the issues with which it is confronted before other nations concerned primarily with the specific Atlantic area covered by the alliance.

A question being increasingly heard in Western Europe is: What does the alliance mean to the United States? Behind the question lies the conviction that Washington has not played fair by its allies on a number of problems that are vital in the capitals concerned.[42]

Even though the conversion of Cuba into a forward Soviet base represented the most dangerous incursion into the North Atlantic area ever carried out by the communist bloc, the United States encountered considerable difficulty in trying to persuade its allies that they should refrain from carrying goods to Cuba, thereby freeing Soviet bloc shipping for the large-scale delivery of arms to the Castro regime. (More than half of Cuba's total foreign trade in mid-1962 depended upon the shipping companies of NATO countries.) The shipowners of a few allied countries, such as Turkey and West Germany, voluntarily acceded to the American requests. But Britain, Greece, Norway and other allies were reluctant to apply any pressures against their own shippers so long as they continued to maintain diplomatic relations with Havana. The United States finally felt compelled to order the closing of its ports to ships engaged in Cuban trade and to all ships of any country if any of its registered vessels carried war material to Cuba. Regrettably, the United States was not able to secure the cooperation of its allies without threatening sanctions against their shippers.

The U.S. decision on October 22, 1962, to "quarantine" Cuba for the purpose of halting the Soviets' offensive missile build-up came as somewhat of a surprise to the European allies. Not until hours before President Kennedy's address to the American people on a matter of great "national urgency" did former U.S. Secretary of State Dean Acheson arrive in Paris for explanatory talks with NATO representatives. The Allies, however, responded to the U.S. initiative with alacrity, and moved to give full diplomatic support to the leader of the Alliance in a major strategic confrontation with the Soviet Union. President de Gaulle noted that he had been "informed" rather than "consulted." There was a general realization, however, that the rapid nature of the Soviet build-up had necessitated a unilateral move by the United States. The Washington correspondent of the *New Statesman* made this observation: "A handful of officials—15 at most—were involved in the minute-to-minute decisions during the fortnight of crisis. They were able to act swiftly, flexibly and effectively in a way that simply would not have been possible with extensive consultation."[43] The West European press for the most part applauded the firm stand taken by President Kennedy in the face of accumulated Soviet provocations in the Western Hemisphere, and the image of the United States as leader of the coalition improved markedly.

Several days after the institution of the blockade, many Europeans experienced a brief sensation of alarm when Premier Khrushchev offered to withdraw Soviet missiles from Cuba provided that the United States would dismantle medium-range missile bases in Turkey. NATO diplomats in Paris were quick to brand the offer as dangerous to Western security and to the morale of the Allies. The United States, well aware that it could not afford to order the summary liquidation of a NATO base (in the same cavalier fashion in which the Soviets appeared willing to deal with Cuba), categorically rejected Khrushchev's offer. The decision of the U.S.S.R. on October 29 to accede to U.S. demands without any apparent *quid pro quo* was hailed in Allied capitals as a significant diplomatic victory for the United States. The Cuban crisis, more than any other previous development, compelled the Atlantic allies to recognize the fact that, in the current protracted conflict, they were becoming increasingly dependent upon one another for the preservation of vital national interests outside the area of NATO Europe.

Many of the differences of opinion and conflicts of political interest which have plagued NATO are deeply rooted in international reality and cannot be lightly glossed over. The anticolonialist tradition plays a powerful emotional part in the formulation of American foreign policy, whereas the Europeans are readier to dwell on the positive rather than the negative results of modern Western imperialism. Europeans are often irritated by the tone of moral superiority adopted by Americans who are archsensitive to "colonialist" motives in Asia and Africa but oblivious of their own willingness to pursue interventionist policies for the sake of Western Hemispheric security. Some of the differences may be attributable to misunderstandings which will subside as the flow of communications improves. Others are, no doubt, founded in the unchangeable facts of political geography. (The United States, e.g., as a Pacific power, is bound to remain more concerned over the defense of the Taiwan Straits than the British, who have liquidated all their strategic responsibilities in the Far East except those directly related to their residual commercial interests.)

In any alliance of fifteen nations, difficulty in coordinating policies is to be expected. But in the usual course of events, complete unanimity on all issues is not required. The smaller allies, as George Liska has pointed out, are realistic in their estimate of the role which they ought to play in consultations:

> They wish to be consulted in a way which would give a decent semblance of reality to their standing as partners and to the representative character of the major ally's diplomacy. Only when they are directly involved do lesser allies demand the right of veto as well as that of remonstrance. On the other hand, the major ally wishes to be consulted chiefly in order to have the opportunity to authorize or veto action, or to be able to disassociate himself from the inception, implementation and consequences of a lesser ally's conduct.[44]

Liska draws a useful distinction between *ad hoc* consultation on issues of special concern to a particular ally and a more stable pattern of frequent and intimate consultation, not necessarily among all the members of the Alliance, but at least among the major ones. He is of the opinion that in a healthy alliance the defense of "vital interests" by individual allies, although it may not always command full allied backing, will not as a general rule lead to the suspension of the alliance. After comparing the relative merits of a limited-liability alliance with an alliance of global competence, he concludes that the argument for a total alliance is both cogent and appealing "when the particular alliance, like NATO, is the chief safeguard of a beleaguered civilization. Without a leader, an alliance system lacks a head; without an inner core of solidarity, it has no heart."[45]

None of the policy divergences which have cropped up among the Atlantic nations prior to late 1962 could be said to be of catastrophic proportions when measured against the total strength of the Alliance. They have not prevented the Alliance, in periods of crisis, from achieving its central purpose, i.e., common defense. Indeed, to a certain extent they have constituted part of the buoyancy of a free, pluralist coalition. The Atlantic nations, subscribing to a liberal dialectic of history which holds that sounder political decisions can be expected to emerge from the clash of open argument than from the imposition of uniform doctrine, have understandably shied away from the formation of a "NATO party line" covering all international issues. But family quarrels among allies should not be carried to the point of exhausting energies, weakening the fabric of mutual trust, blurring judgments and distracting attention from the positive common tasks waiting to be done. Certainly the last decade has witnessed some intra-NATO conflicts which transcended the bounds of healthy give-and-take. These disagreements have sapped the power of Western diplomacy. They have placed an unnecessary additional strain upon the resources of American policymakers, who have often had to pursue straddling policies for inordinately long periods of time. They have reinforced incipient tendencies toward neutralist policies among offended parties. They have enmeshed Western policymakers in time-consuming attempts at conciliation, thus preventing the Allies from devoting a larger portion of their efforts toward the development of constructive initiatives in international policy. Worst of all, they have deprived NATO of an abiding feeling of permanence and solidarity.

To be sure, at the most critical junctures, the leaders of the Atlantic nations have been able to speak with eloquent language and to operate with the appropriate devices of dynamic group diplomacy. They have managed to quiet misgivings, iron out ruffled feelings and compose, at least temporarily, troubled minds. But there is a widespread uneasiness throughout the West—a feeling that the response of the Alliance as a whole to the full range of challenges posed by the Sino-Soviet bloc has been sporadic and inconsistent, fluctuating according to the weight and direction of communist initiatives. The policy differences persisting among NATO members have been of sufficient magnitude to make the perennial Soviet game of *divide et impera* seem well worth playing.

Although NATO was formed mainly to turn back the threat of Soviet communism, recent years have witnessed a growing awareness of the positive creative social goals to which the Atlantic Community is committed. These goals are both internal and external. *Internally,* the Atlantic nations are concerned with fostering steady economic growth and freer trade;[46] the rational resolution of social problems such as racial tensions, industrial relations, education and urbanization; the perfection of democratic political institutions and processes; and a general rise of the cultural and social *niveau* of the Western peoples as a whole. *Externally,* the Western nations have begun to make progress toward the following long-range objectives: the establishment of a firm link between their own community of high productivity and the vast community of need comprising the free countries of Latin America, Africa and Asia; social reform and economic modernization in the underdeveloped lands; the political education and evolution of the new states within a framework of respect for their local cultural patterns; and the molding of an international order in which the dangers of violent change will be steadily minimized and universally valid concepts of human liberty under a rule of law will prevail.

Within recent years, much more attention has been devoted within Western political and intellectual circles to the positive economic purposes of the Atlantic Community than to its positive political, social and cultural purposes, whether internal or external. It would be unfortunate if the Atlantic Community should come to be looked upon, in the words of Edmund Burke, "as nothing better than a partnership agreement in a trade of pepper and coffee, calico or tobacco . . . a partnership in things subservient only to the gross animal existence of a temporary and perishable nature," when it really should be understood as "a partnership in all science, a partnership in all art, a partnership in every virtue and in all perfection."

It will require consummate skill on the part of Western statesmen to express these positive goals of the Atlantic Community in such a way as to inspire in their own people the will to greatness, and at the same time to attract rather than alienate the non-Atlantic world.

Secretary of State Dean Rusk described these objectives in a passage which bears quotation at length:

We want . . . a world of peace and progress under law. And I would lay particular stress on the word "progress." For there can be no greater error than to regard peace as a permanent ratification of an unacceptable *status quo*. Peace in such terms would be quickly shattered by the explosive forces of change. The object of peace is not to bring change to an end: It is to provide peoples the opportunity to achieve essential change without war.

We seek, in short, not a static but a dynamic peace. We hope for a world in which frontiers will mark national identity and not national self-assertion; in which peoples can peacefully revise their own institutions to meet their own national needs; in which nations differing in their internal forms of organization will dwell together in mutual self-respect and freely exchange goods and persons and ideas; in which competition among national states will lose its cutting edge as nations work together in the common interest of mankind; in which the dignity of the individual will be securely established on the basis of social justice, civic freedom and international order.

We seek, above all, a world of free choice in which a great diversity of nations, each faithful to its own traditions and its own genius, will learn to respect the ground rules of human survival. We do not wish to make the world over in our own image—and we will not accept that the world be made over in the image of any society or dogmatic creed. Against the world of coercion, we affirm the world of choice. We believe that the revolution of human liberty will never come to an end.[47]

Since World War II, the historic phenomenon known as Western colonialism has undergone "four-fifths liquidation." From the grant of independence to the Philippines in 1946 to the debut of Ruanda and Burundi in 1962, more than thirty governments have been brought to birth under Western auspices in a transformation much more amazing than the original building of European empires in Asia and Africa. Serious problems may yet arise over British Borneo, Angola, the mixed settlements in East Africa, the Persian Gulf sheikdoms or, for that matter, Algeria and the other new independent states of West and Central Africa. But as the process of orderly disimperialism proceeds, the leading NATO powers should find it less difficult to coordinate their policies toward the non-Atlantic areas of the world, and to approach those areas as a regional grouping with fairly well-defined and intelligible political and economic interests which coincide in large measure with the interests of the new states. The United States has always been reluctant to help its European allies maintain colonial positions. The coordination of policies designed to assist the weaker nations to remain independent should prove to be a different matter, both within NATO and among the nonaligned countries as well.[48]

It remains to be seen whether the new states of the world can be convinced that they have greater reason to fear the rising imperialism of the Soviets than the setting imperialism of the West. Perhaps with the passage of years the peoples of the erstwhile colonial territories will realize increasingly that the political ideals which informed their drive toward self-determination are traceable to no other source than Western culture itself. Perhaps they will come to see that this culture is so saturated with the notion of human liberty that the imperialism exported by the West contained within itself the seeds of its own dissolution—seeds which were disseminated through the channels of Western education. There was economic exploitation, to be sure, as well as economic development, but in the final reckoning the ideas of equality, national independence and freedom of opportunity turned out to be stronger than any purely economic motivations. The new states have challenged the West to grant them freedom, sometimes in polite encounters, sometimes in brutal struggles, and in all cases they have won. Not infrequently, their victories came earlier rather than later because their efforts to achieve national independence found support among influential segments of Western society.

Today, these states are confronted by the threat of a different imperialism, managed by a monolithic apparatus which is more adept than the pluralist West ever was in the sciences of international social engineering. The Leninists, equipped with the latest devices of technology, can control a whole modern industrial nation more efficiently than a British colonial administrator could a Sudanese village thirty years ago. Should any of the new states be absorbed into the Sino-Soviet bloc, the prospect of regaining independence will be slim indeed. Liberation through a costly military struggle with large-scale intervention by the West might be conceivable. But it is out of the question that a band of indigenous patriots, bent upon carrying out a second movement of national liberation, could by themselves throw off the communist yoke. Certainly such local patriots would never be able to appeal to any dynamic liberal tradition in the cultural background of Russia and China. The fate of Hungary and Tibet stands in striking contrast to that of Kenya and Algeria, not to mention Tanganyika and Guinea.

The question, then, is whether the young states of Asia and Africa, as well as the older republics of Latin America, can be brought to appreciate an important political truth of the twentieth century: namely, that in emerging from the tutelage of the Western imperial powers, they have gained the dignity of independence not only for the first time but probably for the last time, too. If they can, be brought to such an awareness, they will be wary of their relations with the Sino-Soviet bloc; they will refrain from experimenting with trial membership in the bloc; and the neutralism which they profess will come to mean more and more that they simply wish to be left at peace with their work of development, and less and less that they are morally indifferent to the outcome of the world ideological struggle.

CHAPTER **3** THE DEFENSE OF

ATLANTIC FRONTIERS

Ever since Hiroshima, the changed nature of strategy has been the subject of a lively debate in every major capital of the world. Within NATO the debate has frequently turned acrimonious, for Washington, London, Paris and Bonn have not been talking about the same problem. To London and, to a lesser degree, Washington the central issue is to deter war. But continental Germany and France are more concerned with the protection of their land and their peoples in the event war should come. There is still no consensus as to how best to deter war. But a great strategic gulf exists between those who believe that military operations would be futile if war should occur and those who, beyond the intricate dialectic of deterrence, seek assurance that their homeland will be defended against aggressors. The dichotomy between these two views cannot readily be resolved. The designers of NATO strategy, however, must take these two views into account and seek to reconcile them, or else face mounting political strains within the Alliance.

Following the October, 1962, Cuban missile crisis, many well-meaning men again persuaded themselves and their countrymen that a completely disarmed world is possible. To those who acclaim confidently the incipient obsolescence of military power it may seem rude to suggest that the survival of Western civilization has never been more dependent than it is today upon possession of the right kind and number of armed forces.

For several years the military problem of assuring the security of the countries of Western Europe embraced by the North Atlantic

Alliance appeared to be insoluble. But recent advances in offensive and defensive weapons technology have eased some of the difficulties confronting military planners for NATO. As things stand now, as well as for the foreseeable future, the security of NATO in which Europe is organically linked to that of the United States, is a far more manageable military problem than the defense of Fortress America. Upon the long-term solution of the NATO problem hinges the existence of the Atlantic Community.

The most direct, significant and heart-rending confrontation between communism and freedom cleaves Europe along the Iron Curtain. The line of division between the captured peoples of Eastern Europe and their more fortunate neighbors to the west stretches from the Baltic to the Dardanelles. If the Soviet system is to "mellow" and if the peoples now under communist domination are ever to rejoin an orderly community of nations, the attractions and pressures generated by a revitalized and democratic Western Europe will be the instrumental source of such change. For Western Europe is still the bearer of those great political and spiritual ideas which arose in Greece and Palestine several thousand years ago. Rarely have greater dangers beset Western civilization than today. Never has the logic of its defense been so difficult to understand.

Paradoxically, these ideals which the West defends so apathetically still hold the major threat to communist totalitarianism. Let us begin with what should be obvious: European economic growth and political integration contradict vigorously the communist ideological belief that *communism is in alliance with the inescapable and predictable workings of history.* Yet upon the belief in the absolute force of the historical dialectic rests the psuedo-religious edifice of communism.

The dynamic political integration and economic growth of Western Europe do more than block the communist challenge. They threaten the fundamental ideological base of communist rule. If communism is ever to hold securely its East European conquests and Russia itself, the Soviets must seek to destroy free Europe, whether by military force or by other means. The growth of a genuine Atlantic Community opens prospects even more displeasing for the Kremlin. Hence, as long as NATO Europe remains militarily vulnerable, the Soviets may be tempted to use force to shatter Western Europe's economic prosperity and political unity. Conversely, if

NATO's military strength removes this temptation, the long-sought transformation of Soviet communism is most likely to occur.

Global Strategic Perspectives

There has been an increasing flood of speculation about the changing nature of NATO Europe's security problems. Hardly anyone outside the ranks of the militant pacifists and unilateralists disputes the indivisible connection between the defense of Western Europe and the United States' own security. Yet when it comes to examining the problems of European defense in the context of the global confrontation between the U.S.-led coalition on the one hand and the immense but geographically cohesive Sino-Soviet bloc on the other, the area of agreement shrinks and the margin of conjecture widens.

Never before in history has a power assumed the widespread geographical security commitments now shouldered by the United States. The northern security arc stretches from Japan across Alaska and North America to Greenland, Iceland, Scandinavia, the Elbe and the Turkish Straits. All along that arc, United States commitments are underwritten by bases manned by American forces. Furthermore, along the southern borders of the communist bloc the U.S. has entered several security alliances and, in addition, pledged itself to the defense of various places not covered by bilateral base or force agreements. This net of multilateral and unilateral obligations stretches from Turkey, Iran and Pakistan to Southeast Asia, the Philippines and Taiwan. It extends all the way to the northern arc junction point—the American base in Okinawa. On the southern arc are located only a small number of American bases, and American forces are few. Nevertheless, American security involvement in the gray area from Turkey to Hong Kong is just as real as that along the arc that separates the protagonists across the poles.

In this age of missiles and jet aircraft, the compact territory of Eurasia between the Oder and the Bering Sea offers communist strategists the advantage of interior lines. Because American security commitments are so large and so ubiquitous, the ramparts of the Free World are nowhere defended at maximum strength. Because American forces are spread so thin, and because along so many sectors of the front the communists enjoy a local superiority, either in troop numbers or weapons systems or both, American defenses are vulnerable. Furthermore, the United States has generally conceded the strategic—and, perhaps, even the tactical—initiative to the communist bloc. The corollary of conceding the military initiative to an aggressive protagonist would be logically the maintenance of a position of superior strength along the perimeter of defense, for in such an asymmetrical situation mere parity of military forces provides no guarantee of stability. But given the present array of forces, the United States finds it difficult, if not impossible, to achieve a safe margin of superiority.

Another factor now enters the global strategic equation: the present and potential power of Communist China in the Far East. China's economic difficulties do not portend the collapse of the militant Chinese communist regime. Furthermore, current developments make it likely that the military arsenal of Communist China will, before the end of the sixties, include both nuclear weapons and perhaps short and medium range missile systems. In Southeast Asia and in the Far East, as the November, 1962, border war between Red China and India demonstrated, there is no conceivable counter to China's growing military power except that which the United States might provide. Consequently, it is likely that U.S. involvements in Asia will necessitate additional deployments of forces to the Pacific area. If a shift in the balance of military power were to compel the United States to increase its military forces in the Japanese-Korean sector, Taiwan, Southeast Asia, and perhaps in South Asia, the United States would have to choose between two alternatives: either to augment greatly its allocation of resources to military security or consider the withdrawal of forces now assigned to the European region. Obviously, if the United States chooses to maintain its forces at their present levels and wishes to check the future aggression of Communist China, a much smaller portion of its strength will be available for the defense of Europe. The shape of things to come, calling for the adjustment in U.S. force deployments, is clearly visible now. In any case, it would be less than prudent to count on fortuitous developments which would arrest the growth of Chinese communist power. Similarly, the United States cannot expect to be delivered miraculously from the threats to itself and its allies in the Middle East and Africa, where the almost total lack of effective Free World strength invites the intrusion of the Soviet Union, so skilled at fishing in troubled waters.

F. O. Miksche has described this threat succinctly:

On the "encirclement front"—in the Middle East and Africa—the chief threat to Europe is implicit in the ambivalent policies pursued by many of the underdeveloped states who hold out their hands simultaneously to East and West. In the process, some of them will inevitably end up in Moscow's well laid snares. Thus, the threat of Europe's slow encirclement along its flanks is much more immediate than is the danger of frontal aggression by the Soviet Union. It follows that the *sine qua non* of Western defense must be to put a stop to the "seesaw" policies of Europe's former dependencies. Will it be possible to do this without resort to military measures?[1]

Whether the danger of Soviet frontal assault in Western Europe is greater than the envelopment threat via the Middle East and Africa is really immaterial.

What matters, as these global considerations reveal, is that the cloth of Western defense is cut too short, and that pulling it up or down or sideways will not help to cover all the exposed parts of the West's military anatomy. This embarrassing problem allows for one, and only one, rational solution: the increase of the over-all strength of the NATO Alliance by the most economic and equitable means. Discrepancies in burden sharing characterize the Western alliance.* As of 1962 the total defense effort of the Common Market countries *plus* the United Kingdom was less than a quarter of that put forth by the United States. There are fewer men under arms in Western Europe relative to population than in either the United States or the Soviet bloc. The problem can be solved provided two conditions are met: namely, that (1) the European NATO partners increase their own defense efforts; and (2) the United States pursues policies which will persuade them to do so.

NATO was formed in 1949 primarily to protect Western Europe against a land invasion launched by the Soviet Union. In the meantime the strategic picture has changed not only in Western Europe but also throughout the entire world. Now the crucial problem is not so much what the United States can do to help the Europeans in their own defense, as what Europe can do to increase total West-

* See Chapter 4, "The Economic Base of Atlantic Power," for a discussion of the economic issues involved in "burden sharing."

ern strength and thus to relieve the United States of some of its onerous burdens and free its hands for dealing with mounting dangers elsewhere, including the Western Hemisphere. A primary task facing the Western Alliance over the next decade is to assure the military resurgence of Western Europe.

The resurgence of Western European military power, however, now calls for a reorientation of United States policy. Since the end of the Korean War United States strategy has reflected a preoccupation with the question of central war, namely an intercontinental nuclear exchange between the Soviet Union and the United States. Consequently, we have tended to give less attention to the problems of local military confrontation around the perimeter of the Sino-Soviet bloc. We have treated the defense of these areas, even including our vital NATO commitments in Western Europe, as if they were tactical, peripheral military problems.

If we but looked at West European security from the vantage point of either Moscow, Paris or London, our perspective would change. The Soviet Union views NATO Europe as the most tempting and valuable prize of the East-West conflict. Western Europe possesses the resources which the Soviet Union might seize and exploit to catch up with and surpass the United States economically and technologically. The Soviets have deployed in Eastern Europe a large arsenal of surface-to-surface missiles which could be used in a disarming strike against NATO forces and U.S. nuclear retaliatory capabilities stationed in the West European area. The abortive 1962 Soviet attempt to deploy comparable medium-range missiles in Cuba should have brought home to the American people the hazards of such an exposed position. U.S. strategists tend to describe weapons systems as either strategic or tactical according to the range of the weapons. Intercontinental missiles are thus strategic, whereas weapons possessing ranges even as great as 1,500–2,000 miles are regarded as tactical. It would be more logical to classify weapons according to the objective to be obtained by their employment. In this sense, Soviet surface-to-surface missiles zeroed in on targets in Western Europe have exactly the same strategic mission as ICBM's zeroed in on targets in the United States. Certainly, they are strategic to the French, British, Germans or Italians located on the receiving end of such missiles.

Divergent views as to what is strategic or tactical have important implications to the world-wide power equation between the United States and the U.S.S.R. The United States currently enjoys an advantage over the Soviet Union with respect to intercontinental weapons for the so-called central war. But the Western Alliance is at a critical disadvantage with respect to the local defense of Western Europe and other areas around the Sino-Soviet periphery. Consequently, the Soviets are able to keep Western Europe a hostage for U.S. behavior elsewhere. This situation, too frequently ignored in the United States, is the root cause of many of the foreign policy problems confronting Washington.

NATO Today

In the current debate over the optimum defense policy for Europe, all responsible parties are seeking to improve the safety of the international environment against the occurrence of war. A serious disagreement exists, however, over the best way of deterring attack against the NATO area. One school of thought favors a reduction in the U.S. reliance on nuclear weapons to discourage local aggression. This school of thought, motivated perhaps by considerations of arms control, would emphasize larger conventional forces, downgrade the role of tactical nuclear weapons, and depend heavily upon the threat of strategic nuclear retaliation to prevent Soviet military penetrations which could not be contained by conventional means. A second school, to which the authors belong, believes that a strategy based upon conventional forces backed by the threat of strategic nuclear retaliation is vulnerable to criticism on two principal counts: (1) A conventional build-up may very well be misinterpreted by the Soviets to mean that the West is reluctant to employ nuclear weapons in the defense of Europe. In this case, the likelihood of war would increase because the Soviets might be tempted to take a gamble which they would not take if they expected a nuclear response (if not immediately then at least in the early phases of the conflict). (2) In the event that such a Soviet attack could not be turned back by conventional means, the United States and its allies would have virtually no option except to unleash all-out nuclear war. The authors of this book advocate a defensive posture which would be adequate across the full spectrum of possible Soviet challenges. They especially are convinced that a tactical nuclear capability ought to be retained, both to decrease the probability of an attack and to raise the chances that, if an attack occurs, it can be dealt with short of a strategic retaliatory response.

NATO Europe is a military hodgepodge, its national forces ill equipped for modern war. Its only significant nuclear forces are jealously controlled by the United States. The air defenses of NATO are inadequate and missile defenses do not exist. A mixed manned-aircraft, surface-to-air missile defense cannot assure the comprehensive air defense of Western Europe. The declining effectiveness of the manned interceptor and the increasing effectiveness of the surface-to-air missile have rendered obsolete the air defense arrangements which purport to guard Western Europe. Modern air defense should consist primarily of missiles and only secondly of manned interceptors. In the critical central front the Soviet Union is proceeding to establish a missile-air defense system utilizing nuclear warheads which will render manned aircraft operations over satellite territory highly unprofitable, unless the defenses can be wiped out.

While the West is still casting about for sources of troops or trying to make up its mind as to whether certain categories of NATO troops (or indeed any at all) should be equipped with nuclear weapons, the Soviets maintain a rounded military posture, including nuclear-armed ground forces which incorporate a high percentage of superior armored units. The critical situation of Western Europe is compounded by Soviet possession of a family of surface-to-surface missiles with ranges of 100 to 2,500 miles, covering all Europe. The shorter-range surface-to-surface missiles pose a threat which NATO cannot presently counter. The Soviets possess these weapons in far greater numbers than the West. The significance of Soviet surface-to-surface weapons depends upon the nature of the targets they can destroy. Studies indicate that Soviet missiles of medium range could, with their high accuracy and controlled yields —controlled with respect to both explosive force and radiation— disarm NATO and cancel out its retaliatory capabilities without inflicting catastrophic civilian casualties or excessive collateral damage on European industries.

In sum, the Soviets deploy more troops in the crucial central front, have far stronger back-up reserves and, for good measure, enjoy superiority in MRBM's, manned aircraft and mobile surface-to-surface missiles. Hence they are in a position, if they so choose, to create military situations which NATO could handle only with extreme difficulty.

As long as the Soviets are inhibited from launching a direct attack against the United States or its NATO allies, they may try to paralyze and fragment NATO through intermittent probes that fall below the "threshold" of an obvious threat to United States survival. The Soviets will seek either to raise this threshold through an adroit game of psychological conditioning or to lower NATO's nuclear capabilities via negotiations for nuclear-free zones in Central Europe.

Small-scale ground probes designed for political-psychological exploitation may yet occur. Berlin is an ideal locus for such a strategy of bedevilment. The major danger of a ground invasion, however, lies in a total war situation—after, rather than before, a disarming strike. It is, to say the least, unlikely that in a global war Europe would be allowed to remain a military sanctuary. Upon the defeat of the NATO forces, however, Western Europe might offer the Soviets an alternate base of operations which the U.S. would be loath to destroy, for the liquidation of the Soviet forces could entail the annihilation of the hostage European population.

The Soviet Union, as a result of intensive efforts to create its differentiated nuclear capability, may one day be able to initiate military action against NATO along a wide spectrum, including, but not limited to, a "clean" disarming strike against NATO's European-based retaliatory capabilities combined with a ground attack employing tactical nuclear weapons or with a "conventional" land-air attack. The last type of attack, in which the Soviets would refrain from the initial use of nuclear weapons, would presuppose the political or military isolation (via disengagement schemes) of the United States—which, we must presume, is the principal objective of Soviet coexistence strategy.

The inadequacy of the existing and projected military posture of the Atlantic Alliance is fraught with increasingly ominous implications. That NATO falls short of being an effective sword-and-shield of the West, practically no one denies. All the principal members of the Alliance are agreed upon the need for a change. But the direction in which NATO strategy should be changed and the measures that should be adopted to put changes into effect remain matters of dispute. There are two main schools in contention. One asserts that the main danger confronting NATO arises from the Soviet capability to launch a massive conventional assault against the West. Those who share this opinion urge a local defense of NATO based largely on stronger conventional forces and the downgrading, if not elimination, of tactical atomic weapons from the Western arsenal.[2] The opposing school sees marginal utility in conventional forces but regards the comprehensive incorporation of nuclear weapons into NATO forces as indispensable to the survival of the Alliance. Between these poles of contention a variety of conventional-atomic combinations has been proposed. The issues are vital. Unless a strategy can be designed that will commit the European peoples far more deeply to their own defense, NATO may one day fall prey to an adroit campaign of Soviet nuclear blackmail laced with calculated military probes.

Heeding the criticisms leveled at the "new look" and "massive retaliation" policies of the Eisenhower Administration for their real or fancied shortcomings, the Kennedy Administration has introduced major modifications in United States military doctrine.

The strategic problem which has perhaps concerned the Kennedy Administration more deeply than all others is the fact that each possible employment of force carries with it to some unknown degree the chance of "escalation" into thermonuclear war. Fundamental to President Kennedy's military policy is the determination to control the employment of force in order to rule out, insofar as is humanly possible, the chance of expanding—"escalating"—a conflict through miscalculation. A statement of President Kennedy presented to the Congress in March, 1961, read as follows:

Our defense posture must be designed to reduce the danger of irrational or unpremeditated general war—the danger of unnecessary escalation of a small war into a large one, or of miscalculation or misinterpretation of an incident or enemy intentions.[3]

Inherent in the Kennedy Administration's military philosophy is the idea of the "pause," first publicly expressed by General Norstad. To reduce the danger of irrational and unpremeditated general war in Western Europe, the Soviets are to be given the opportunity to terminate the conflict before NATO initiates a more destructive form of warfare. While it must be conceded that the Soviets, too, may fear the prospect of escalation, the first initiative to stop fighting or to "escalate" is forfeited in advance to the Soviet Union. Under these circumstances, a pause might conceivably result in the collapse of the Western will to fight, particularly if the United States and the other NATO countries were unwilling to provide themselves in advance with an "all-level" deterrence. Unless the Soviets confined themselves to a limited attack, launched to test the Western will, the enforcement of a conventional pause beyond a very few days would require a greater build-up of NATO ground forces than the Allies have hitherto been willing to contemplate seriously.

The implementation of President Kennedy's philosophy led to a shift from main reliance on nuclear weapons to a greater reliance on conventional forces. Henceforth the U.S. attempted to persuade its NATO allies to: (a) build up conventional forces so as to reduce dependence on atomic response; (b) arrest or reduce proliferation of national atomic capabilities; (c) withdraw atomic weapons from forward areas or "lock" them so local commanders could never use them unless physically released by political authorities; (d) rely on SAC and sea-based forces outside any possible limited war area for atomic firepower if and where necessary; (e) plan on maximum political consultation before releasing atomic weapons, even where conventional resistance is proving inadequate; (f) trust the U.S. to provide the strategic deterrent and tactical atomic systems to deal with the threat to NATO; (g) change basic NATO strategy directives in consonance with these concepts.

The well-publicized U.S. emphasis on conventional forces for the defense of Europe engendered international repercussions, particularly since European forces are mostly conventional anyway. In Western Europe, it loosed a stream of severely critical comments. Subsequently, Administration spokesmen, particularly Secretary of Defense McNamara, acknowledged publicly that strategies could not be changed precipitately and that for a long time, if not indefinitely, the military security of the Free World will be largely dependent upon nuclear weapons, which the United States might be compelled to introduce if Soviet aggression could not be contained by nonnuclear means.*

* Defense Secretary Robert S. McNamara, at a September, 1962, news conference held in Washington after his return from an inspection of American forces near the East German border, said that U.S. and West German planes, armed with tactical A-weapons, are on runway alert there. His unusual stress

Despite the United States' efforts to emphasize conventional weapons in Western Europe, NATO has too few forces to pursue a balanced nuclear-conventional strategy. To be sure, the 1961 Berlin situation galvanized the United States into stepping up its own conventional capability; but the example prompted only one country in Europe to emulate it—West Germany. Thus, in high strategy, as in so many other areas, *plus ça change, plus c'est la même chose.* The Kennedy Administration, however much it dislikes the fact, has remained largely dependent upon a nuclear capability for the defense of the NATO area.

Arrayed against NATO, large communist air-missile surface forces, operating under an integrated command, stand in Eastern Europe. Here and now, the NATO forces cannot match them. Except for the U.S. component, NATO forces are too weak to engage successfully Soviet armies equipped with nuclear weapons. Furthermore, the paralysis engendered by the Western European paucity of intermediate missiles damps support for any conventional build-up. As matters now stand, the cities of Western Europe are hostages to U.S. good behavior. This unpleasant fact neutralizes much of the decisive advantage the U.S. enjoys in the intercontinental strategic balance. The net global effect of the existing imbalance of tactical missiles in Europe is to degrade our avowed selective retaliatory strategy to a species of finite deterrence. Yet the fact that the Soviets may have found a reasonably cheap method of putting a strategic stranglehold on the United States is blithely dismissed by many American strategists.

The American effort to sell NATO a flexible military philosophy has been largely unsuccessful. Our NATO allies, as of the end of 1962, had refused to change the original NATO strategic guidance and directives calling for use of atomic weapons, if necessary, from the onset; they had augmented, instead of reducing, national efforts to create independent strategic capabilities as evidence of their attitude toward U.S. promises and "will" to use under all circumstances; and, not so surprisingly, though they welcomed promises of consul-

---

on nuclear power caused reporters to ask if this had special significance. "No," he replied, "I was just being factual. Our policy, which is sometimes misunderstood, is to use whatever weapons are necessary to preserve our vital interests. Quite clearly, we consider access to Berlin a vital interest." Washington *Post*, September 29, 1962, p. 1.

tation before use of atomic weapons, they expressed concern that delay in the use would result in acceptance of local loss in preference to "escalating." At the same time, our Allies opposed vociferously hints that atomic weapons stocks in forward areas might be reduced, and questioned the worth and purpose of mechanical "lock" devices—the so-called "permissive links." Most of them reacted guardedly to statements criticizing the worth of such national strategic efforts as the British V-Force and French *force de frappe;* and, lastly, they failed to respond to repeated calls for a conventional build-up. Indeed, some NATO nations are actually planning major reductions.

It is, of course, an easy and a tempting pastime to lecture the European NATO states on the virtues of augmented forces, but such appeals will not put one additional soldier in the field. The Europeans are aware of the fact that NATO forces, unless armed as well as their Soviet opposites, have little chance of winning either a purely conventional engagement or a tactical nuclear war, and that they might as well save themselves the trouble of creating a second-best establishment. The greater military flexibility which the Kennedy Administration is justifiably seeking requires both *more* forces in NATO and *more* modern weapons—nuclear and conventional—for them.

As long as these military deficiencies exist in Western Europe, NATO has but one possible reply against all major forms of Soviet attack: immediate or delayed retaliation with long-range nuclear weapons. The American strategic capability is the capstone of Western security. In fact, the ability to invoke it against a major Soviet attack represents the one and only deterrent—at least for the immediate future—to the Soviet employment of force.

United States home-based nuclear power is organically linked to the defense of Western Europe.[4] Hence the United States seeks to convince its NATO allies as well as the U.S.S.R. that its American-based long-range retaliatory power is ample, securely protected, controllable and resolutely committed to the defense of Europe. But it is at least arguable whether the United States, in its quest for a centralized, indivisible nuclear deterrent, is forfeiting some of the very flexibility which it professes to be seeking. One may ask whether a nuclear force based largely on the oceans and in the United States can by itself fend off indefinitely a Soviet move against the West's most vulnerable position in Europe—West Berlin.

The strategy to which the United States and its West European allies are now wedded drains their political initiative. To regain the freedom of political maneuver, the NATO Alliance must resolve a number of thorny military issues. It must first devise a military doctrine that is logical, understandable and acceptable to the political and military leaders of all the major NATO countries. Collectively and individually, the NATO countries will then have to pursue national defense policies compatible with the agreed-upon military doctrine. Subsequently, military technology will have to be exploited vigorously on both sides of the Atlantic to insure that the weapons exist, or can be developed, that will mesh the agreed strategic concepts. Concurrently, appropriate forces, utilizing the weapons produced by a cooperative NATO technological effort, will have to be raised, trained and deployed. Common tactics for the employment of these weapons should be devised and "gamed" so that the NATO troops can fight together most effectively.

The divided sea and air-ground battle concepts of World War II are now obsolete. The new tactic must serve an integrated force in which naval, air, missile and ground units are combined. It goes without saying that the organizational structure of all national components, as well as the international military headquarters established for the control of larger units, will have to be organized in a manner fully compatible with the technological and tactical doctrines on which consensus is reached. With respect to NATO organization much more attention must be given to strengthening the command arrangements and the force components of the Northern Region (Norway and Denmark) and the Southern Region (Italy, Greece and Turkey). In fact, most of the discussions concerning NATO appear to concentrate on the problems confronting the Central Front; the problems of the Northern and Southern fronts are almost totally ignored in the current strategic literature.

Soviet Strategy and Assets

At the Twenty-second Congress of the CPSU, October, 1961, Minister of Defense Malinovsky set forth the communist doctrine of war as follows:

The character of modern war . . . lies at the basis of Soviet military doctrine. One of the important theses of this doctrine is that a world war, if it should nevertheless be unleashed by the imperialist aggressors, will inescapably assume the character of a nuclear-rocket war, that is, a war in which the main striking force will be nuclear weapons, and the main means of delivering these weapons to their targets will be rockets.

The Presidium of the Central Committee of the party and the Soviet Government have demanded and do demand of us that we devote special attention to the initial period of a possible war. *The importance of this period lies in the fact that the very first mass nuclear strikes are capable, to a vast extent, of predetermining the whole subsequent course of the war* and could lead to such losses in the rear and among the troops as would put the people and the country in an exceptionally difficult position.[5]

Mindful of the current "objective balance" of forces, the Soviet leaders fear thermonuclear war. This fear, though rarely publicly expressed, runs deep. Communist fear of thermonuclear war—manifest in the 1962 Cuban missile crisis—reflects a realistic recognition of existing American strategic power. The Soviets' dread of war is tempered by their knowledge of democracy's ingrained aversion to destructive conflict and, especially, to the initiation of wars. It is highly unlikely, the Soviets believe, that the United States can be provoked into launching a thermonuclear attack. Consequently, barring the debatable dangers of "accidental war," a thermonuclear war is probable only if the Soviets choose to bring it about, or if they commit a strategic miscalculation which brings in escalation. In view of their basically cautious traditional military doctrine, it seems that the Soviet leaders would deliberately launch a nuclear attack only if they were certain that they could emerge from the war relatively unscathed and vastly superior to their foes.

The Twenty-second Party Congress discussed, at considerable length, military doctrine as laid down by Khrushchev in January, 1961, and its amplification supplied by Malinovsky in his address to the Party Congress. Subsequently, a simplified version of what might be dubbed the Khrushchev-Malinovsky doctrine appeared in *Red Star* (*Krasnaya Zvezda*), notably the issues of December 14, December 18, 1961, and January 10, 1962. The articles explained the fivefold organization of the Soviet armed forces into strategic rocket troops, ground forces, air forces, air and missile defense forces and naval forces. They hinted vaguely at a future rocket space force.[6] Unambiguously, they acclaimed the strategic rocket troops as the main arms of Soviet might.

Red Star of December 14, 1961, stated that in the ground forces "the main forces are the rocket groups and units of operational-tactical significance equipped with nuclear and other types of ammunition, and capable of reaching targets up to hundreds of kilometers." Furthermore, it is "now beyond doubt that the nuclear rockets have become the main weapon *of the ground forces*" (italics added). Then the writer dwelt on the fact that old tactics and the old operational art have become "senseless." The analytical discussion here turned specifically to the inadvisibility of concentrating large bodies of troops, lest they be destroyed by nuclear weapons, before an attack.

In an article published in *Communist Armed Forces* (*Kommunist Vooruzhennykh Sil*), No. 6, 1962, the writer asserts that a future world war will be "above all a nuclear missile war," in which "the rocket troops for strategic purposes will assume the first place." However, final victory will be dependent upon the coordination and cooperation among all forces and weapons systems. Rockets have replaced artillery; hence the need for armor. Presumably armored units are best equipped to survive a nuclear surprise attack.

The Soviet ground forces, too, are designed to include a capability for engaging in nuclear combat. In fact this is their most distinctive characteristic, irrespective of whatever other features they bear. Perhaps for the purpose of confusing the West as to their military thinking, the Soviets frequently deride the possibility of tactical atomic warfare, especially in a "limited war." Yet they themselves have given full consideration to the doctrinal problems, the kinds of weapons to be employed and the associated troop organization required for such conflict. This is not to suggest that the Soviets have fastened upon tactical atomic warfare as their preferred strategy for an attack upon NATO. Yet, regardless of their *intentions*, they are definitely acquiring a tactical atomic *capability*. Undoubtedly, they realize that circumstances might arise in which a tactical atomic attack on Western Europe would appear to represent a feasible alternative, and that tactical atomic warfare could certainly play an important role in future general war. Western analysts cannot entirely discount the possibility that Soviet tactical nuclear capabilities exercise, in crisis situations, a deterrent effect upon Western responses. If the U.S.S.R. develops a substantial superiority over the NATO forces in this dimension, it will create an imbalance fraught with dangerous consequences.

The Chief Marshal of Soviet Artillery described in great detail the variety of Soviet tactical atomic weapons and the kinds of targets against which they might be used:

When talking about rockets of operational or tactical importance it is necessary first of all to note the circumstances, that units of regimental level and higher are armed with these rockets and at the present time [these weapons] are the strength of ground forces. Rockets of operational-tactical meaning are assumed to be nuclear and other rockets with a range from several tens to several hundreds of kilometers. Such a wide bracket of ranges of rockets for this purpose is fully substantiated when the wide circle of military tasks is taken into account, which is decided by them [the rockets].[7]

According to an article in *Voynnii Vestnik,* the Soviet ground forces' journal, atomic weapons are the most important means of defeating the enemy. It should not be inferred from this that the Soviets regard nuclear weapons as the answer to every situation. Conventional weapons systems are not replaced by but rather supplement and extend nuclear firepower; sometimes they substitute for it. The existence and employment of nuclear weapons, however, will profoundly affect other weapons and the entire organizational structure. The Soviets, for example, emphasize armored troop carriers as essential to exploitation of a tactical atomic attack.[8]

The Soviet doctrine for tactical atomic war stresses speedy and timely maneuvers. "The factor of time," write A. Kazaryan and D. Reznik, "especially in modern warfare, saturated by rocket-nuclear weapons, has an exceptionally important meaning."[9] The critical time factor influences all Soviet preparations for a future atomic war. This has led to the development and tactical use of faster means of transportation, i.e., tanks, armored personnel carriers, armored cars and helicopters. As early as 1956, the Soviets began to meet the problems inherent in atomic warfare by the organization of rocket forces and by giving an increased role to armored forces and to airborne troops. The Soviets differentiate between the employment of strategic and tactical atomic weapons in the context of a general war. They may be contemplating use of tactical nuclear weapons in conjunction with a "disarming strike" on Western Europe, exploited by a quick seizure of terrain by the Red Army.

The Soviet tactical atomic warfare doctrine calls for closing with the enemy and maintaining close proximity with his forces. Close proximity with the enemy lessens the chances of counter atomic attacks. The Soviets anticipate that frequent gaps in their own lines and those of the enemy will be a typical condition in a future atomic battle. Currently, Soviet development of doctrine, Soviet organization, weapons and training for tactical atomic warfare surpass those of Western armies with the exception of U.S. forces in Germany. Consequently, if forces so designed were to attack a NATO force which is not similarly armed, organized or trained, they would best it. This dismal prospect cannot be wished away.

Certain conclusions can be drawn concerning Soviet military doctrine, strategy and posture. First, the Soviets view military force as the essential backstop of diplomacy. Even in the nuclear age they continue to adhere to the Clausewitzian dictum that war is a continuation of politics by other means. Second, they conceive of war, should their diplomacy ever lead to war, as a total conflict of long duration which they must be prepared to wage to its ultimate conclusion. They are keenly aware of the great significance of striking or warding off the first nuclear blow. Their doctrine calls for nuclear strikes on population centers as well as on military forces. Soviet military thought tends to invalidate the popular U.S. concept of "accidental" nuclear war and the possibilities of conducting a no-cities strategy. It must be recognized, however, that there has been much genuine doctrinal ferment and uncertainty in the Soviet Union growing out of the implications of modern weaponry for strategy and force structure. The Soviet marshals, just as much as Western strategists, are in a real quandary on many issues: implications of dual capability for size of forces and how to fight a war; character of strategic forces and how far to go down the road from purely deterrent to pre-emption-capable first-strike forces; and the offense-defense mix. Consequently, we should be chary of imputing to them more perfection of planning and execution, more unity between doctrine and force structure, than may really be the case.

Facing the Future

It matters very little whether the Soviets today have few ICBM's and many MRBM's. What matters is that war will not come unless the Soviets have possessed themselves of considerable—or rather superior—forces and large numbers of nuclear weapons of all kinds.

It is against *this* contingency that the Alliance must remain prepared.

Since it will take many years before the European nations can be prepared for modern war, the foundation of the future security of the Atlantic world must be laid today. It is crucially important to pursue a strategy and maintain a force posture which will deter whatever conflicts the Soviets may be tempted to initiate against NATO. Hence NATO has no choice other than to move toward a strategy based on military-technological superiority. The Western world envisages hopefully an evolution within the communist system. Such a change for the better will never occur as long as the Kremlin leaders believe that their strategy of world revolution might succeed. The pursuit of a NATO strategy of supremacy is contingent upon a more equitable utilization of resources and effort within the NATO Alliance. There are numerous thorny issues which have to be dealt with on a continuing basis within NATO. In the nuclear age, atomic firepower has become fundamental to all military strategy. However, nuclear warheads must be teamed with other forces in both the attack and defense. Behind the combat forces, NATO needs effective logistics systems, communications structures, civil defense and early warnings systems.

We do not propose to examine in this chapter the full agenda of military problems confronting NATO, created by existing deficiencies in the Alliance and the changing character of the Soviet military threat. We will not, for example, discuss the vital mission of assuring control of the North Atlantic Ocean. But focusing our attention on Western Europe, we will set forth some criteria for the design of NATO's future military posture, whose core must be built on a wide array of nuclear weapons. Without forces armed with nuclear weapons the flexibility of response so assiduously sought by the Kennedy Administration will never be obtained. Since this issue is so crucial, let us examine the pros and cons of the various schemes for nuclear sharing within the Alliance as well as the impact of arms control negotiations on United States nuclear policy.

The United States, because of flaws in its strategic thought, has not sought the technical contributions which modern Europe can give to Western defense. To achieve a common integrated and technologically up-to-date defense system, the NATO Alliance must progress beyond the concept of stable deterrence. A genuine deterrent must rest on substantial superiority. Then, if deterrence should fail, NATO would possess capabilities suitable to win a military conflict. Only a dynamic technological program, designed to stay ahead of the growing armaments of the Soviet Union, will keep the Alliance together and in good health. In addition to technological preeminence, NATO must achieve a comparable integration of tactics and strategy—or, in other words, operational unification. The organizational-operational problem encompasses the following aspects: (1) choosing the best organization for the various weapon-force systems; (2) combining weapon-force systems operationally; (3) coordinating the distinct theaters within Europe; and (4) coordinating the effort of Europe with that of the United States—the conduct of a theater war within the context of a global war.

In redesigning NATO's military strategy certain other problems must first be solved. Among these are: (1) how to develop a doctrine for atomic warfare both for limited, localized conflict in Europe and as part of a general war posture (this doctrine must be sound militarily and, at the same time, acceptable to our allies); (2) how to obtain a political consensus on control of NATO's military forces at any level of employment; (3) how to build up necessary "threshold" forces. The military problems of NATO can be approached only if, at the outset of the discussion, political problems are bracketed out temporarily. However distasteful it may be to discuss coldly the contingencies of war, such discussion is essential to strategic analysis. If a deterrent force is to be credible, it must be operationally sound. Despite the Soviet bloc threat in nuclear weapons and superior ground forces and the features of European geography as well as high population density, NATO's first task is to protect the peoples of Western Europe physically. This task requires determination of what kind and how many forces and weapons are to be deployed in what organizational setting. Once we know this answer and then have settled on a common doctrine, we can allot each member state a quota of troop strength and weapons production. Then a proper organization can be designed.

In terms of missions, the strategic requirements of NATO include forces for offensive, defensive, ground battle and anti-occupation action. The offensive mission calls for more than strategic nuclear forces. NATO should possess the capability, in the event that deterrence fails and war breaks out, to penetrate into East Germany and thus to assist those large numbers of East Germans who will join eagerly in the battle against the Soviets. Our own nuclear counter-force strikes into the satellite regions should be calculated to end the war quickly and with least possible damage to the captive peoples, who potentially are our allies. NATO must possess adequate defenses against air and missile attack, not merely for the purpose of protecting the larger cities and other strategic targets, but also (and perhaps predominantly) to protect NATO forces, including the ground forces. The ground capability must be great enough to check minor probes as well as contain a major Soviet thrust launched in conjunction with a missile strike. NATO must also be able to reconquer any territory lost in the initial invasion. Such a capability should be reinforced with ground-support aircraft, missiles with ranges of several hundred miles and perhaps airborne forces. Elimination of all manned aircraft from the NATO arsenal would weaken NATO's defense against invasion. The anti-occupation mission aims at preventing an invader from holding and digesting his conquest. Such a capability might be developed by creating a citizens' force, which if occupation appears imminent could arm itself with appropriate weapons. As part of defense, protection against a wide range of nuclear hazards would have to be devised. Such protection would be provided by our own forces within Europe, by the utilization of relatively "clean" nuclear arms and, of course, by the availability of shelters and other civil defense provisions, not only for the civilian population, but also for the troops manning missile sites and air bases.

To fulfill those missions, what should be the right proportion between NATO's ground forces, air forces, anti-air and missile forces, naval forces and, possibly at a later date, strategic nuclear forces?

This question cannot be answered intelligently unless we first solve the problem of integrating air-missile-ground forces. The increasing effectiveness of missiles has rendered obsolete the concept of separate air forces and armies conducting a coordinated battle. The Soviet Union has wisely adopted operational unification of its varied combat forces. What NATO requires are air-missile-ground combat forces conducting their operations in accordance with an integrated military doctrine.

The question is no longer whether we should field conventional or nuclear divisions. *The problem is to design a type of ground com-*

bat unit which is responsive to the requirements of modern war. Such a unit must necessarily consist of a mix of conventional and nuclear arms. In any case, it must be equipped and organized for the real battles which could be fought, rather than for a variety of political and psychological maneuvers with military forces, under-taken before the military battle is joined.

The most crucial question facing NATO is the incorporation of nuclear weapons into the Alliance structure. Unless an operational deterrent force acceptable to all members of the Alliance is de-veloped, progress toward a real military capability will falter. A primary concept for employment of nuclear weapons should be that each sovereign nation, barring the formation of a West European nuclear force,* can use them, not for aggression but in its own de-

* To aid the reader in distinguishing among the various types of deterrents which are discussed in this and in succeeding chapters, the following definitions are offered: (a) A *national deterrent* is one that is owned and controlled by a single country. The separate nuclear forces of the U.S., Britain and France fall into this category. (b) A *NATO deterrent* is a combined nuclear force formed by national contributions from the nuclear members of the Alliance. In recent years, it has been taken for granted that a NATO deterrent would have to remain primarily under the control of the United States unless other control arrangements which circumvented the problem of "fifteen fingers on the trigger" could be worked out and approved by the North Atlantic Council. The con-cept of a NATO deterrent does not necessarily imply that the Western nuclear powers would place all of their nuclear weapons under NATO. The U.S., for example, would contribute to the NATO force along with Britain and France, but the U.S. would probably keep most of its strategic nuclear weapons outside of NATO arrangements. But if the Alliance should at some future time be transformed into an Atlantic Confederation, it is conceivable that all of the West's nuclear power might be organized under joint control. (c) A *European deterrent* is one that is formed by pooling the nuclear weapons of the European powers (i.e., at the present time, Britain and France) and placing them under joint European control. Although West Germany does not have an independent national deterrent to contribute, it might be possible for her to participate in the financing, technological development and political-military planning of such a deterrent. If the U.S. should assist in the creation of such a European deterrent, it would expect it to be coordinated closely with the American deterrent through the framework of NATO. It will be shown in Chapter 5 that the Western European Union (WEU) constitutes one plausible channel through which a European deterrent might be created. Formed originally by pooling the forces of Britain and France, such a deterrent would be under the operational control of the members of WEU—Britain, France, West Germany, Italy and the Benelux countries. (d) The term *multilateral deterrent* refers to any amalga-mated nuclear force to which two or more nations contribute components and in which the weapons systems are placed under joint planning and operational control. Hence, this term might properly be applied either to a NATO deterrent

fense, in its own air space and on its own soil. These weapons must be of a kind and so deployed that they can be brought to bear tactically if and when the Soviets launch a major assault into friendly territory. The concept for the use of *strategic* weapons would be governed by another doctrine.

A New Design for NATO

A new and comprehensive strategy, genuinely acceptable to all of NATO's European members, must utilize NATO's military power to deter the Soviet Union from aggressive action and, if deterrence fails, defeat the communist forces in war. The most realistic way to deter war in Europe is to convince the U.S.S.R. that it can be prevented from obtaining a specific, even quite limited, objective and that this can be done with means appropriate to the circumstances.

There appear to be three possible military choices open to NATO. One is to continue with more or less the existing strategy and force posture. In short, NATO would continue to field relatively weak shield forces and would continue to rely for its defense primarily upon a U.S. second-strike strategy. According to official U.S. statements made in June, 1962, the United States did—or might—possess the means to conduct a counterforce strategy.[10] The counterforce doctrine envisages attacks on armed forces, the military support structure and the military command and communication centers. A counterforce strategy calls for employment of protected weapons wherewith to wage discriminatingly a controlled nuclear war. Within six months after espousing counterforce, however, Washington appeared to be moving toward a doctrine of strategic stability reminiscent of finite deterrence. Yet, since the best way to deter war is to be able to wage it successfully, it seems inconceivable that the Administration will permanently abandon its once active interest in a counterforce strategy based on military superiority.

---

or to a European deterrent. President Kennedy used the term *multilateral deterrent* in referring to the Polaris submarine force envisaged in the Nassau Pact of December, 1962. Whether or not it is feasible to create a "mixed manning" force, in which the weapons systems would be manned by composite crews recruited from the nationals of various NATO members, and from which it would be impossible for the individual member to withdraw its national components, was a much-debated point in the early months of 1963.

The possession of an adequate civil defense and a comprehensive air-missile defense system would ease the conduct of a controlled, counterforce strategy. The creation of an effective air defense and missile defense system in Western Europe employing advanced technologies which are already available in the United States is feasible within the limits of the state of the art and economic resources. Such a defense can largely neutralize the capabilities of the Soviet family of surface-to-surface missiles deployed throughout Western Europe. Furthermore, if the Soviets initiate a conflict against Western Europe and the United States, the NATO air and missile defense establishment-to-be will destroy a larger portion of the Soviet over-all forces (which are, from the Soviet point of view, strategic) than could air-missile defenses located in the United States.

Another corollary of controlled war is the availability of communication, which will permit advising the enemy concerning certain actions. The United States appears to be searching for a command-control-communications structure which will permit a controlled, counterforce strategy. Whether it will, in fact, achieve the capability for such a strategy remains to be seen. At the same time, the United States has advocated a build-up of forces for NATO Europe which would improve the flexibility of NATO's response. But, under the dispensation of current official thought, this flexibility is not to support a pure counterforce strategy. Its purpose is to reduce the possibilities of a localized conflict in Europe escalating into global thermonuclear war.

One possible solution for NATO's problem would be to create a military machine which would permit NATO to meet Soviet forces "across the board." NATO, were it armed with forces which could match the full conventional or nuclear panoply of Soviet military might, could repel any one of a wide variety of aggressions without having to resort to the use of nuclear weapons, except at a relatively high threshold. A substantial increase in NATO ground forces, far greater than that now being considered, would be required to support such a strategy. It calls for precisely that major increase in ground forces and supporting units which, heretofore, NATO has been unwilling to provide. This reluctance to deliver additional ground forces has been defended by the hoary argument that the United States and its European allies can never match the unlimited reservoir of communist manpower. However, it should be evident that, collectively, the NATO countries possess both a manpower and an economic potential vastly superior to those of the Soviet Union and its satellites. If every NATO government would maintain armed services proportionately as strong as neutral Sweden and Switzerland, NATO could create the required forces for an "across-the-board" strategy. If, however, the past performance of most NATO governments is any indication of their future intent, it is highly unlikely that they will do so.

If one takes into account the trend of Soviet military thought and the actual Soviet military posture, a purely conventional defense of Europe would appear to be an exercise in futility. Admittedly there is no proof that a tactical nuclear war could be waged in Europe without either the U.S. or the Soviet strategic forces becoming engaged. The Soviets may thus be deterred from attacking Europe because U.S. strategic forces pose a threat to their homeland. A third alternative, i.e., the middle between the extremes of primary reliance on conventional means and exclusive reliance on a strategic deterrent, appears to rest on the solid foundation of military logic. Of course, U.S. strategic forces must cap NATO's tactical atomic capability.

The sought-for increase of dual capability forces in Europe, i.e., forces possessing both a conventional and a nuclear arsenal, can be justified only if NATO's strategy is keyed to tactical atomic warfare. This alternative, too, calls for an increase in existing NATO ground forces. It would require the development of a doctrine for tactical atomic warfare and the modernization of NATO forces so that they could participate actively in a nuclear conflict. The absence of an agreed doctrine of tactical nuclear warfare and the lack of forces prepared to fight a nuclear war are perhaps the greatest deficiencies in NATO's military planning.

On November 21, 1960, General Norstad proposed a cure to the ailments of Western strategy generally compatible with the third alternative mentioned above.[11] His prescription was as follows: All forces of the Allied Command in Europe must be organized, equipped, trained and deployed so as to be able to react promptly and efficiently with conventional weapons, when such weapons are adequate to the military situation, and atomic weapons, when the use of such weapons is necessary. It seems clear that General Norstad did not believe that NATO can or should prepare to wage a full-scale conventional war in Europe.

It should be a primary task of the NATO Council to define cases of self-defense which will require automatic employment of nuclear weapons. NATO must convey to the Kremlin its intentions and plans with the utmost clarity. The greatest danger of Soviet aggression or a war of miscalculation lies precisely in ambiguous responses. In short, "agonizing hesitation" is the greatest enemy of a real deterrent. Only automaticity in accordance with politically determined rules will make the NATO deterrent credible and the defense of NATO against major invasion possible. Not only is this important psychologically; NATO exercises have revealed that nuclear weapons are most useful when employed against the initial assault of an aggressor.

The fundamental engagement principle, both for surface-to-air missile and ground defense, must be that hostile crafts or troops, as soon as they launch major aggression against NATO territory, encounter an immediate reaction by lower-yield nuclear weapons. Such *automaticity* renders credible NATO's deterrent posture. If there is no such automaticity, deterrence is subject to doubt, and doubtful deterrence is no defense at all. It is much wiser to make it clear to the Soviets from the start that any substantial penetration will trigger a nuclear response than to create an atmosphere of indecision which may invite attack and eventually bring on nuclear firings anyway. Automaticity should be paired with a set of safeguards against aggressive operations from our side, since restraints upon unwarranted or precipitate unilateral action are legitimate and desirable. But the problem of preventing unilateral actions by members of the Alliance has been given too high a priority in NATO discussions. The logically prior problem, i.e., that of making deterrence credible, is infinitely more important. After all, the West is confronted not by the resurgence of aggressive totalitarianism in its own ranks, but by the dangers of Soviet aggression. In these matters it is only prudent to set straight the priorities of danger.

The military doctrine for the defense of the NATO Alliance, conceived within the framework of a strategically sound and a politically reasonable grand strategy, must answer these questions: What should be the extent of NATO's commitment to a nuclear strategy? Should NATO's nuclear posture be graduated or discontinuous? The following approach is suggested: (1) In the years ahead, the United States could create the maximum deterrent to war *by helping the Europeans acquire an integrated nuclear capability.*

(2) While making it clear to all concerned, including the U.S.S.R., that the defense of NATO is based firmly on the intended use of nuclear weapons against large-scale attack, the United States should collaborate with its European allies in developing a system of lesser responses to more limited tests.

Thus far, NATO has not fully incorporated modern weapons systems into its forces. With some exceptions, NATO forces in Europe are not designed to fight the Soviet armed forces on a basis of equality, let alone superiority. A truly effective deterrent strategy calls for symmetry among the kinds of forces maintained by the respective protagonists in Europe. As John Strachey expressed it:

> Nothing less than at least an approximate symmetry of power at *every level,* conventional, tactical nuclear, thermonuclear, is indispensable to the stability of the balance: for if either side lets itself become markedly inferior, at any level, it will be faced with the dilemma of "escalating" to the next level above or surrender.[12]

This observation cannot be gainsaid despite the fact that strategic confrontations are always asymmetrical, with each side enjoying intrinsic advantages. It would be the height of folly, however, for one side to omit from its arrangements an ingredient that would counter an operational capability of the other. Accordingly, nuclear weapons in superior strength should be available in NATO Europe at various levels: battlefield tactical weapons, weapons for defense against missiles, intermediate-range weapons for support of the surface battle and strategic weapons. To these requirements should be added flexibility in the warhead stockpile, i.e., an adequate supply of nuclear warheads of varying yields, operational characteristics and battlefield effects.

Influential voices appear inclined to deny the necessity or desirability of tactical atomic weapons or intermediate-range land-based mobile missiles in the hands of NATO. The communiqué of the December, 1962, Nassau Conference between President Kennedy and Prime Minister Macmillan, for example, did not mention land-based missiles. Airborne missiles were mentioned and dismissed, and the Polaris system was called the "Key to Defense."[13] Those who would like to see all land-based atomic weapons removed from NATO's arsenal favor a NATO armed solely with conventional forces, backed by the seaborne Polaris missile with nuclear warheads and, ultimately, by the United States Strategic Air Command. On strictly quantitative grounds, however, Polaris missiles cannot replace tactical atomic weapons. The U.S. Polaris offer can be interpreted as a maneuver, nonetheless, to substitute Polaris for tactical atomic weapons so that, subsequently, "provocative" land-based systems can be withdrawn from Western Europe.

Even as staunch a proponent of increased conventional forces for NATO as John Strachey, while asserting that the introduction of tactical nuclear weapons into NATO to compensate for NATO's deficiency in ground forces was a wholly unsuccessful move, is under no illusion that they could now be abandoned. "Once the Russians have possessed themselves of such weapons," Strachey contends, "it is manifestly impossible to ask NATO troops to face them with conventional weapons alone. One might as well ask them to throw away their automatic rifles and resume the pike."[14]

The Soviet possession of a family of surface-to-surface intermediate-range missiles, capable of delivering nuclear warheads, threatens continuously the exposed target systems of Western Europe. These weapons exist in large numbers; there are indications, particularly since the deployment of Soviet missiles into Cuba, that many of them are mobile. With such weapons, the Soviets can launch an almost instantaneous nuclear-disarming strike on NATO. Again, this capability can best be offset by the existence in Western Europe of a comparable system of mobile land-based intermediate-range missiles.[15]

Let us assume that NATO made the decision (which it has not yet made) to develop an effective air and defense system as well as a defense system against incoming missiles. At the present state of the defensive art, nuclear warheads would be required to create a viable, integrated NATO-wide, air-missile defense system.

A moderate number of low-yield, highly mobile, short-range atomic weapons on the soil of certain European countries could strengthen their security against invasion. Since these weapons do not necessarily cause widespread destruction, or excessive contamination, they would constitute a credible deterrent. Their use would be preferable to the loss of national independence. They would increase both the cost and risk calculations which the Soviets would have to make prior to an attempted invasion. Their very presence in Europe would deprive the Soviets of one of their most awesome advantages—the ability to mass large numbers of men for attack.

Fear of escalation is a two-way street. *If the Soviets fear, just as much as we, that a tactical atomic war will flare into thermonuclear war, then a tactical nuclear force in Europe should serve to render any kind of planned attack in that region less "thinkable."*

Only the extension of symmetry throughout the range of nuclear weapons systems can increase progressively the deterrence of warfare in Europe. Symmetry means that a capability of one side is offset by a counter possessed by the other. It does not mean that both have identical weapons; one side may be offensively armed, the other defensively. In addition to technological symmetry, NATO requires quantitative superiority. Consequently, a range of nuclear weapons —battlefield, tactical, intermediate-range missile and air and missile defense weapons—must be deployed in Europe if NATO is to achieve symmetry with existing Soviet military capabilities.

Symmetry between the Soviet Union and the NATO Alliance signifies the availability of United States strategic power at all times. The arch of the Western deterrent system rests upon United States power. Whether any part of strategic U.S. nuclear power should be based in Europe, or be responsive to NATO's political direction, as distinguished from prior consultation regarding its possible employment in Europe, is a politically complicated question—one that will be dealt with later.* But if total symmetry did exist, the onus of escalation at any stage of the conflict would be placed on the Soviet Union.

The opponents of nuclear symmetry argue that the first use of a tactical nuclear weapon would lead automatically to a full-scale thermonuclear exchange. Their much publicized obsession with the inevitability of escalation has engendered strong doubts throughout NATO Europe as to whether the United States will use atomic weapons if lesser means fail to repel a major local act of aggression. If, in addition to symmetry, NATO enjoyed superiority, Soviet escalation would not take place. John Strachey raises his voice in warning: "It seems foolish loudly to proclaim that total disaster is certain if the first tactical nuclear is detonated. If we convince our opponents of that we might regret it one day."[16]

Strachey, nevertheless, recognizes that there is some danger of escalation, and he seeks to hold it to the lowest possible level. He

* See Chapter 5, "A Political Framework for Nuclear Partnership."

argues that the provision of the necessary conventional forces will reduce the necessity for employing tactical atomic weapons to hold the line in every situation. As he puts it, "Once we take the first major step in escalation from the conventional level to the tactical nuclear weapon, we have immensely increased the danger of going all the way to thermonuclear exchange."[17] Approximate symmetry in ground forces affords *one* protection against this danger. Another is to confine the initial use of nuclear weapons against an invading force within the defender's own territory. Qualitative and quantitative superiority is a third.

Can the divergencies within NATO be reconciled? The basis of a consensus exists. (1) NATO must possess conventional means to handle local probes and thus minimize the need in "tests of strength" to "escalate" into tactical nuclear weapons. (2) NATO will use atomic weapons as soon as a major attack starts unless the attack is strictly conventional—a purely hypothetical case. (This has been NATO policy all along.) However, NATO should avoid strategic policies which lead to genocidal retaliation and prepare itself to conduct a counterforce strategy against invading forces. (3) NATO, to make this policy credible, will maintain the necessary atomic-equipped forces and weapons in the hands of troops in the forward areas. The forward deployment of nuclear weapons will underscore the decision to use tactical atomic weapons to defend Europe far more convincingly than portentous statements on the might of SAC or NATO Polaris forces.

In addition to inhibiting the Soviets from exploiting gaps at the lower end of the military scale the more ominous danger—a disarming strike against United States and European-based nuclear weapons—must be deterred. Actual Soviet aggression, as distinguished from politically exploitable threats, will be spearheaded or paced by nuclear strikes to enhance the chances of victory. Low-key attacks which invite a United States nuclear counter would be both costly and risky from the Soviet point of view. Consequently, NATO should not overinsure itself against the least likely Soviet option at the neglect of a total nuclear posture required to block *all* Soviet aggressive options. With these considerations in mind, it is now possible to examine the role of nuclear weapons in the defense of Europe.

Not all ground units need be equipped with nuclear weapons.

Front line units may be supported by higher-echelon rear units armed with nuclear devices. We should not close our eyes, for political reasons, to the fact that, at the main front, most of the combat units will be German. Hence, in view of Soviet doctrine and preparations for tactical atomic warfare, the Germans, if they are not to have and hold nuclear weapons, must be able to count on the nuclear support of non-German units. If such support in the shape of nuclear battlefield weapons is not forthcoming, the Germans will either not fight or, if they fight, will be speedily defeated. An alliance cannot be built on a policy which denies the key element of modern weapons to a particular front—to be more exact, to the decisive front.

There are ways of dealing with the political issue of nuclear weapons in Germany. With respect to ground forces the forward lines could partially be defended by ground demolitions. Of course, nuclear demolitions could not be extended offensively beyond the border. Units in the border regions could use very short-range tactical weapons. The longer-range weapons should be held by units deployed farther back. A possible arrangement to safeguard against the unauthorized and unprovoked use of nuclear weapons would be to entrust the forward nuclear defense to troops from nations other than the host country. Another solution might provide for the stationing in the forward area of high-ranking officers from various nations. Their task would be to insure on-the-spot mutual supervision. In other words, it should not be beyond the ingenuity of NATO statesmen to devise some sort of an inspection arrangement. If inspection is deemed feasible in a hostile country, it surely should be feasible in a friendly one. A final solution might be to entrust the nuclear defense of the forward area exclusively to longer-range weapons; but thus to forgo battlefield weapons would be unsound militarily and would hence weaken the credibility of the deterrent —which does not mean that longer-range weapons are not needed in supporting roles.

If the defense is properly organized, atomic weapons should confer an advantage on the defense over the offense in land battle. This is essentially true, provided, of course, the requisite technology is available. The attacker, in order to advance, will have to expose himself. On the other hand, a completely immobile defense could be blasted out. Yet the inherent advantage of the defense could be gained if adequate technical, engineering and organizational preparations are made. It should be added that this proposition may not always hold true in case of invasion if, for example, the invader achieves a high degree of surprise, or moves in through the air. The point that needs stressing, however, is that the nuclear arming of Europe for defense enhances the chances of peace rather than increases the risks of war. As President Kennedy so forcibly demonstrated in the Cuban crisis, modern weaponry insures the success of diplomacy.

As far as air and missile defense is concerned, a proper defense of the European continent can be secured only by a European command, and not by any one national establishment. Within that command, each nation should fire those ground-to-air rockets which are in its territory. But, for geographical reasons, the defense of some targets will have to be entrusted to units located in other nations. If the defense is entirely based upon rockets of reasonably moderate range, there is little danger that these weapons would be used for a wanton attack on enemy territory. The situation differs with respect to longer-range rockets that might be necessary for antimissile operations. We must remember that Nike-Zeus, for example, is armed with a nuclear warhead of considerable size, since a lesser charge would impair its effectiveness. The lethality of this or comparable missiles could be improved and the nuclear radiation hazard reduced if the U.S. pushed the development of the neutron bomb for its antimissile warheads. It is impossible to gainsay the overwhelming importance of ground-to-air rockets and their necessary dispersal across national boundaries. Hence the Alliance cannot serve its purpose if it is not based on mutual trust which permits military deployments in accordance with missions rather than national boundaries.

Low-yield nuclear weapons in the hands of well-trained active and reserve formations could make it extremely difficult for an invading army to operate with efficiency. This is a point of considerable political significance: the capability of conducting an effective atomic defense can help to restore a sense of confidence and viability to a small state. The development of such a capability, admittedly, poses several problems requiring careful study. National units would have to be skillfully trained and tightly disciplined in the handling of fractional-kiloton weapons. Local populations, for their own peace of mind, would require assurance that amidst the chaos of invasion these weapons would not fall into the hands of unauthorized or irresponsible elements, and that there were rational strategies for using them to hamper the enemy's military operations without causing excessive suffering to the nation's own people. Furthermore, if such weapons were to serve any deterrent purpose, they would have to be deployed in advance in such a manner as to permit their timely use against oncoming forces. This requirement poses technical questions of command and control, albeit of a lower order of magnitude than those raised by larger nuclear weapons. The citizen army concept, which U.S. military authorities reject out of hand (perhaps because they mistakenly equate it with U.S. Reserve or National Guard organizations), might yet be assigned a vital role in creating the forces needed against ground attack. In the event the defense fails, the citizens' army could be given the anti-occupation mission. In considering this fallback mission, however, care would have to be exercised against conveying a defeatist outlook either to the Allies or to the Soviets. The various kinds of modern weaponry suitable to resistance operations (small atomic weapons, chemical weapons, high explosives, small arms, etc.) require a much more detailed analysis than could be attempted here. It should be recognized, however, that by utilizing the experience of the smaller countries which rely on the citizen army system (e.g., Switzerland, Sweden and Israel), NATO can improve its position against the contingency of ground attack and thereby make such an attack extremely unattractive and unlikely. The Swiss have already voted, in principle, to reserve the right to arm their citizen forces with nuclear weapons. Frederick M. Stern, one of the leading proponents of further utilization of this system in NATO, wrote in 1960: "Large effective reserve forces standing ready at any time can be created at a fraction of the cost of conventional-type forces, and in a way that eliminates all political and psychological fears." The type that fulfills these demands is the "citizen army."[18]

A thorough look should be taken at the size and kind of forces required by the NATO Alliance and the manpower resources of the Alliance members. How many professional front-line units are needed? What kind and scale of reserve forces? What specialized forces, such as antimissile and Polaris submarine crews? What kind of burden sharing would alleviate existing inequities as to length of service in the armed forces of the various members of the Alliance? One of the paradoxes of NATO's military situation today is that in actual number of men under arms NATO matches the Soviet Union, but this manpower, recruited, trained and assigned by different defense ministries, is not efficiently utilized by the NATO powers as a whole.

With respect to strategic forces, the question is whether each nation needs, or is entitled to possess, a small nuclear capability which it can use according to its sovereign decisions, with no strings attached. If this capability is relatively small, its possessor, let us say France, hardly will break ranks and launch an aggressive war. The idea that a small nuclear power will provoke war by an attack of desperation and thus engage the Alliance is most unlikely.

The specter of future Algerian OAS-type organizations arising in some European countries and taking over part or all of the military force is frequently raised. Often the purpose is to generate distrust of the good sense, loyalty and discipline of the men who compose Western military forces. The birth of the extremist OAS organization in Algeria has been frequently ascribed to certain peculiar tendencies in the French national character. The problem is far deeper. Most member nations of NATO found it convenient to wash their hands of the French problems in Algeria rather than help France to achieve a constructive solution for the Algerian revolt. The Algerian case has implications for NATO's future. Frustrated revolutionist, irredentist and extremist political movements, if they were to arise in NATO's midst, might well capture some military support. On the other hand, a broad political consensus within NATO as to how to deal with the real threats confronting the Alliance will be supported by stable, disciplined and democratically oriented armed forces.

But even if hotheads were to launch a nuclear war out of pique, the operation would recoil upon the unruly member if the other members of the Alliance were to disassociate themselves immediately from the aggressive act. Admittedly, the sovereign possession of a nuclear capability allows a nation to invoke the *casus belli* in case of attack without reference to what its treaty partners will decide. Since the national interests of the United States and of other countries differ, it is really asking too much of the United States to act always in accordance with the national interests of other peoples, its best friends included. This is the heart of the matter: Unless the political framework of the Atlantic Community undergoes substantial alterations, we cannot argue convincingly that our allies are not entitled to act in accordance with their own national interests. We have the choice of moving toward Atlantic unity and an integrated nuclear force or to facilitate a collective nuclear force to those of our allies who wish it. If we do not come down on the side of one or the other alternative, we cannot expect our allies to stay in the Alliance—or, if they stay, to be trustworthy.[19]

There is another, a middle or stopgap, solution: the European nations could band together and either add forces to SAC or create a European SAC themselves. Under such an arrangement no national unit could act on its own volition, or even on the will of its government, but would be assigned to a supranational force, whether it be a European or an all-NATO one. The need to establish such an added deterrent capability is not pressing today, whereas the early acquisition by the major NATO nations of defensive and tactical nuclear weapons is an urgent matter. But if the current trends of Soviet technology and armaments persist, it might be desirable in the future for the European members of NATO to contribute their share to the Free World's strategic resources. Moreover, it may not be prudent policy to exclude the main members of the Alliance from the responsible management of the main weapons systems. They, too, have to learn the facts of strategic warfare. They will not grow up strategically unless they have nuclear capabilities and, therefore, the trained personnel who can tell the political leaders what they need to know about modern war. If our allies remain ignorant of nuclear war, we cannot expect them to cooperate with us in strategic operations.

Graduated Response and the Pause

If, within the guidelines of a sound doctrine for tactical atomic war, the optimal balance between nuclear and conventional forces is attained, aggression could be deterred or defeated without resorting to nuclear weapons except in response to massive conventional or nuclear attack. The West's range of choice could thus be preserved; precipitate and possibly catastrophic escalation could be avoided. To prevent escalation, NATO needs a force structure which would prevent an opponent from gaining any military advantage through escalation and insure his defeat if he were to raise the level of violence. Genuine deterrence, flexibility, and the prevention of escalation, of course, are predicated on the provision of the requisite combined strength which NATO has been hitherto unwilling to field. Choice is not a function of vocal wishing. Flexibility of defense and, hence, flexibility of *policy* are a function of available forces.

To the extent that we can join with the Europeans in devising means of defense that offer the greatest chance of deterring war, to that same extent will we revitalize NATO. *A strategy looking to the nuclear defense of Europe should therefore be conceived as a means to insure the defense of both the U.S. and Europe.* Since both the Soviet Union and the NATO allies are facing the same problems of military technical renovation, they both must design forces to fight in a nuclear environment without a major break between the final employment of conventional means and the first employment of nuclear weapons.

Surface forces, however, must be properly equipped and organized to achieve superiority for the defense. The nature and speed of action of nuclear warfare preclude post-H hour distribution of weapons or deployment of delivery systems. NATO cannot ignore this central fact. If NATO fails to reorganize, train and deploy forces to make the best use of atomic firepower, it will derive little military value from the fact that some atomic weapons have been scattered in the area of combat.

NATO, endowed with the proper combination of nuclear and conventional forces, would regain the power to make any war a poor bargain for the Soviet Union. By blocking each likely avenue of attack, the defense reduces, so far as is humanly possible, the chances of any attack. In particular, the potential high effectiveness of air and missile defense is such that the attacker will have to devote his efforts to penetrating defense rather than attacking targets. In the present contest, deterrence requires a visible military posture which assures friend and potential enemy alike that military aggression in any degree and anywhere will be met rapidly by forces sufficiently strong to render it unprofitable. The closing of all exploitable gaps in Europe will make all kinds of war, either conventional or nuclear, less likely to occur there and elsewhere.

As an added deterrent factor, the United States and NATO should inform the Soviet Union that in the event of any aggression they would abandon the declaratory policy of the "peaceful liberation" of the satellites and provide the peoples of Eastern Europe military assistance to regain their independence. An explicit willingness to free the peoples of Eastern Europe from their communist masters would place severe restraint on Soviet strategy.

NATO's strategy has been called a deterrent strategy. Implicit in nuclear deterrence is the assumption that in the atomic age physical survival is the overriding preoccupation of states; and that the states possessing nuclear arms so deploy their atomic capabilities as to assure their longevity. States are assumed to act "rationally"; the stark requirements of survival are assumed to blanket out "extraneous" ideological or emotional considerations. That deterrence hinges upon the commonsense, rational reaction of statesmen to the threat of nuclear disaster becomes obvious to anyone who has sampled the growing literature on this topic.

Many skeptics, however, repudiate the idea of deterrence because they either question the existence of the military conditions underlying the doctrine or, while acknowledging these conditions, deny that the danger of mutual annihilation restrains *all* statesmen of the world. The heart of deterrence, of course, is credibility. To be deterred, the potential aggressor must credit the opponent with the means and the resolve to employ military forces in order to make aggression unprofitable. *Forces vastly superior to those of an aggressor are of no advantage unless the aggressor believes his adversary has the will and ability to use them.* During most of the 1930's, France and Britain possessed superior military strength; but Hitler discounted their will and ability to use their forces singly or collectively.

Herman Kahn has classified deterrence according to the nature of the threat: (1) deterrence of direct attack; (2) deterrence of extreme provocation; and (3) deterrence of moderate provocation or limited aggression. A deterrent force, to be effective, must be able to deal with these three threats.[20]

Kremlin tactics in Berlin since 1958 fell under the rubric of moderate provocation or aggression. The Kremlin avoids extreme provocation such as the outright seizure of West Berlin, which would trigger strategic retaliation, but has chosen a series of moderate provocations to nibble away gradually at the Western position and the morale of the Berlin population. This raises the question of the need for a deterrent against moderate provocation or aggression. Can such a deterrent be devised?

Some observers feel that nonmilitary deterrents have not been adequately explored or utilized in regard to the Berlin crisis. There has been almost no effort to notify the opponent, in advance, of the consequences of his moves. For example, a strong statement on possible Western countermeasures made by the President of the United States in the weeks immediately preceding the sealing off of Berlin might have acted as a deterrent. Measures might have ranged from knocking down the barricades at check points to the application of economic sanctions. Probably the belief held by some Western statesmen that any action involving the use of force might "escalate" into a thermonuclear war has made them reluctant to plan timely and firm ripostes.

The Soviets, aware of the influence of the "automatic escalation school," are seeking to demonstrate through a carefully calculated series of "crises" that the main element of American power, namely, the threat of nuclear retaliation, has been neutralized and that, therefore, the United States can no longer be counted upon to defend Europe.

Deterrence is a declaratory policy addressed to the psychology and rationality of the opponent. The opponent must be aware of the fact that he is confronted by a comprehensive spectrum of available weapons and other political and economic counters. The spectrum of retaliation that keeps the opponent inhibited must bracket massive attack as well as peripheral probes and even forestall political warfare actions such as the building of the Berlin wall.

Whatever the merits of a deterrence strategy, its effectiveness is directly dependent upon the success with which the deterrent posture can withstand specific operational testing. A posture that could not meet any test would be worthless. One that could cope with the full range of enemy actions would not be tested. The Soviet Union did test our deterrent posture by moving missiles into Cuba. President Kennedy's actions impelling Khrushchev's decision to withdraw the missiles did much to restore the credibility of the U.S. strategic deterrent. It should be obvious that the Soviets did not "escalate" in Cuba because the United States possessed a substantial strategic superiority and an overwhelming local conventional advantage, both of which President Kennedy was willing to employ.

The status of the local deterrent in Western Europe is less certain. Most European NATO forces are conventional. Upon this fact centers the discussion about NATO's inadequacies. At the main points of contact, West Germany, Greece and Turkey, stand considerable conventional forces, but unfortunately, with the exception of American units in Germany, no nuclear forces. If NATO is to possess a real deterrent, such questions as the role of conventional forces, exact meaning of a "pause" and the proper response to frontier incidents must be answered. Frontier incidents in which hand grenades and submachine guns are fired are often discussed as though they were serious strategic problems. A frontier incident may be either a genuine flare-up or a mere subsidiary and carefully controlled maneuver in the Cold War. If the Soviets want to attack NATO, they are unlikely to initiate the war through a frontier incident. If they use these incidents as a distracting cover operation, we should be far less concerned about them than about the attack which will follow in due course.

Similarly, in the minds of some experts, the problem of the "pause" looms far more important than it really is. Certainly, if a "pause" can be forced, this would give us great tactical advantages on which we should seek to cash in. But the question is: How much effort in men, money and material do we want to invest in this sort of "last try"? If we were to expend a considerable part of our strength on gaining a few hours or days of grace, what other parts of our strength would we elect to reduce? If the Soviets decide in earnest on an attack upon Western Europe, the "pause" will be of little service to NATO. (If we "pause" without being able to blunt the Soviet attack, we will presumably consult with our allies as to the next move.) The choice will be limited either to initiating the use of nuclear weapons or to accepting tactical defeat. Unfortunately, many Europeans are convinced—and the Soviets would be—that, having "paused," we will cut our losses rather than risk the danger of escalation into a general nuclear war. Hence delaying prompt counteraction could do us immeasurable harm.

The notion that the Soviets would send a sizable "armed probe" into Europe and thus alert our retaliatory force seems fanciful. But let us assume an attempt by East Germany against West Germany, or of Hungary against Yugoslavia, or some other operation which is either unwanted by the Kremlin or launched as an oversized Cold

War maneuver. We should be able to ascertain the true nature of such an attack and, with the NATO forces now on hand, achieve the desired "pause." Most likely, if the Soviets attack Europe in earnest, they will attack with all their forces, using nuclear weapons. If the Soviets take the risk of attacking, which involves the risk of escalation, they will do so only if they think they are ready to go all the way. In this case, there is no advantage for them to risk a nuclear first strike upon their forces and targets,[21] and it is infinitely less risky for the Soviets to destroy *our* strike forces in the first place.

The argument that a "pause" could prevent an incident from getting out of hand makes sense only if East German and other satellite battalions cross "accidentally" into our line in a proxy war. But if the Soviets were to decide on such a proxy conflict, they would do so only if and when they felt certain that they could prevent "escalation." The various schemes for "options" and "pauses" are vitiated by the high probability that the Soviets, if they were to strike, would simultaneously attack at the front and in the rear, and would try, as a first step, to destroy all those of our weapons systems which could pose a real threat. Europe would be turned forthwith into a battlefield in depth.

Viewing the matter thus, the deterrent will not be credible unless NATO provides for the automatic employment of nuclear weapons in defensive configurations under circumstances stipulated in advance by the appropriate political authorities. *Credibility, as long as it is predicated upon delayed decision-making in Washington, shrinks to a fifty-fifty probability: Either Washington makes the decision to use nuclear weapons or it does not.*

General Norstad's qualifying phrase—"except in certain well-defined cases of direct self-defense"—provides the key principle for the automatic employment of nuclear weapons in case of attack.[22] Without adoption and implementation of this fundamental condition, the credibility of the NATO deterrent will gradually decline to a dangerously low level.

The Problem of Nuclear Sharing

Opinions range widely as to whether the European members of NATO should share in the possession, planning and operational control of a nuclear arsenal. The matter is of the utmost importance.

According to Walter Lippmann, "The critical issue within the alliance comes from a rebellion against the American monopoly of nuclear power."[23]

The first step toward nuclear sharing in NATO occurred when the Heads of Government, meeting at Paris in December, 1957, announced a NATO decision to "establish stocks of nuclear warheads which will be readily available for the defense of the Alliance, in case of need."[24]

After numerous meetings on the issue, at the NATO Conference of Foreign and Defense Ministers in Athens in May of 1962, the United States sought to placate European desires for greater participation in the nuclear protection of the NATO area. A plan, first put forward by Secretary of State Christian Herter at Oslo in 1958, was resubmitted and accepted. The United States committed a number of Polaris submarines to NATO, although such vessels were to be operated not by mixed NATO, but by American, crews. A procedure was agreed upon whereby the tight grip of the United States on nuclear weapons data would be loosened and the United States and her NATO allies would consult on the location, size, power and uses of American nuclear forces in Europe and elsewhere, such as the Formosa Straits. In short, we offered to share with our European allies the decision on issues which are of relatively little direct concern to them and which they might prefer to leave to us.

In addition to this inexplicable gesture, we graciously offered our European allies little which they did not already know or possess. The American-commanded Polaris submarines (ideal weapons for certain purposes) form a *strategic* weapons system. The Europeans, so the contemporary American argument goes, should not need such a system since the United States possesses all the strategic strength required. But at Athens not a word was said about giving the European NATO countries the *tactical* air and missile defense and IRBM nuclear weapons which NATO does need in order to re-establish in Europe military symmetry vis-à-vis the Soviets. Likewise these weapons were passed over in silence by the communiqué following the December 1962 Kennedy-Macmillan Nassau discussions.

Before examining the prevailing views regarding the possession and control of nuclear weapons, as well as the nuclear posture of NATO, we must first explore the implications of a widely endorsed strategic concept which, at its core, contains the notion of Nuclear Fortress America. Those who advocate the concept of Central War, namely, that nuclear weapons should be the exclusive monopoly of the two major protagonists in the struggle, i.e., the United States and the Soviet Union, urge a policy which, upon closer examination, benefits neither the United States nor Western Europe. Paradoxically, the strategic meaning of this policy is far more ominous for America than for Europe. For under this policy the United States will bear the brunt of any nuclear war and suffer by far the greatest damage and destruction.

The second consequence of an evolution toward Nuclear Fortress America will be the freezing of NATO as an alliance of unequals. The resentment toward a United States effort to monopolize NATO strategy and policy will grow in Western Europe and ultimately destroy the Alliance.

United States nuclear policies have up to now stifled European technological advance; hence the United States carries an unequal burden in the common defense. The U.S. will have to devote an excessive share of its energies to military research and development as long as it spurns the creative scientific and technological contributions which Western Europe can make to the common task.

Europe's resentment will frustrate our stated objective—the creation of a more coherent, stronger alliance. A free community signifies shared power; if one member seeks to monopolize power, the sense of community withers. Oddly enough, the sharing of power is fundamental to the American system. The American Constitution was designed both to diffuse and share power among various political entities. The sharing of power begets responsibilities. The opposite course, namely the monopoly of power indispensable to security, begets irresponsibility. These trends are already evident in France. De Gaulle today is controlling his resentment toward the United States atomic monopoly because he is a responsible man. De Gaulle's successor, who may be armed with nuclear weapons, might lack de Gaulle's sense of political responsibility.

In short, the United States nuclear policy—at least until the beginning of 1963—was a monopolistic policy, running diametrically counter to our efforts to form a more perfect Atlantic Union. Partnership demands a responsible sharing of power. Over the long run we Americans have recognized that monopolies, whether political or economic, manage to defeat the purpose for which they were

created. The American monopoly of nuclear power bids fair to
defeat the purpose of the United States and, for good measure, to
wreck the Atlantic Community. It is time we abandoned this disruptive policy and recognized the sharing of nuclear power to be
essential to the creation of a powerful Atlantic Community.

The *raison d'être* of the national nuclear deterrents that already
exist in Britain and France is more a political than a military one.
Before examining the arguments against national deterrents in
Europe, it will be useful to look at the reasons which seem to favor
the acquisition of independent nuclear capabilities. These must be
adequately understood before the Atlantic Community can formulate realistic policies for more mature "nuclear sharing" arrangements than most of those hitherto put forth.

Robert Osgood has compiled a most helpful summary of the
reasons usually advanced *pro:*

(a) to obtain a more credible and reliable deterrent to military incursions
that the United States might not counter with American-controlled nuclear weapons; (b) to gain greater protection against "nuclear blackmail"—
that is, against various forms of Soviet pressure backed by the threat of
nuclear attack or a conventional conflict entailing the risk of nuclear war;
(c) to contribute to the West's combined deterrent posture by supplement-
ing America's nuclear striking force; (d) to support political and military
courses of action, including those outside the NATO area, that the United
States might not be willing to back at the risk of her own military involvement; (e) to enhance bargaining power and influence vis-à-vis the United
States and other allies in matters of foreign policy, military strategy and
disarmament; (f) to enjoy the most impressive military attribute of national
autonomy and prestige and avoid dependence upon another nation's control of this fateful weapon; (g) to rationalize economies in other military
expenditures, and especially in mobilized manpower, by offering the public military strength at a tolerable cost; (h) to avoid being left out of an
expanding nuclear club.[25]

The case against national nuclear deterrents has been argued
exhaustively—and sometimes with considerable vehemence and bit-
terness.[26] It is said that the efforts to create such deterrents, even
with United States assistance, cannot but drain the resources, economic and technological, of any but the largest powers. Concentration upon nuclear policy is likely to divert attention away from
needed conventional forces.

Each case of proliferation creates additional pressure for still other countries to seek to acquire nuclear capabilities, which in turn supposedly would heighten the danger of accidental occurrences, strategic miscalculations and other events that might serve as catalysts of large-scale nuclear war. A common variant of this "expansion pressure" theory is that, were the United States to help its European allies to develop nuclear capabilities, the Soviet Union will be forced to give nuclear weapons to the East European satellites and to Communist China. Politically speaking, however, the analogy is invalid. It is generally agreed that the United States can trust its European allies farther than the Soviet Union can its partners to the east and west. Moreover, if Communist China can acquire nuclear capabilities of its own, it is practically certain to do so regardless of what policies of restraint a West European state such as West Germany, e.g., may choose to pursue. Not a few strategic analysts within the West are of the opinion that the diffusion of nuclear weapons to other nations would compound the problems of arms control and reduce further whatever chances of reaching some kind of international arms agreement may exist. Not so surprisingly, the arguments about control are more often made by established nuclear powers—*beati possidentes*—and especially by the United States, than by the would-be possessors of national deterrents.

The United States–European cleavage concerning NATO's nuclear policy can scarcely be mistaken for an element of Western strength. Before suggesting how to overcome this cleavage, the various proposals regarding the policies which NATO and the U.S. *within* NATO should pursue with regard to nuclear weapons must be examined.

Albert Wohlstetter's celebrated *Foreign Affairs* article, "Nuclear Sharing: NATO and the N plus 1 Country," listed four main policy alternatives for the European nations in NATO: (1) the rejection of nuclear weapons, of the American guarantee and of all association with nuclear powers; (2) the development of national strike forces; (3) a jointly controlled NATO force; and (4) reliance on the United States guarantee. Wohlstetter did not explore the possibility of a "European" deterrent. Nor, because of limitations of space, did he deal with nonnuclear warfare or with tactical nuclear weapons except to show their connection with his main argument.

But the fact is that most discussions of nuclear sharing virtually ignore the question of battlefield nuclear weapons, the use of atomic warheads in air and missile defense, as well as the value of intermediate-range missiles. Because of their importance one might consider a NATO nuclear force equipped with tactical and intermediate-range weapons as a category distinct from a NATO force equipped with strategic weapons such as the Polaris.

The first policy, i.e., repudiation of nuclear weapons, receives support only from those who see the danger of war with the Soviet Union as a consequence of the arms race and not of communist ambitions. Repudiation of nuclear weapons, let alone total disarmament or submission, would not necessarily diminish the Soviet motive for attack. A nonnuclear defense as a substitute for any reliance on nuclear weapons could be overwhelmed by Soviet nuclear aggression. Fortunately, unilateral nuclear disarmers are still a minority in the West, although as far as the forces of the European members of NATO are concerned an unwanted situation of potential nuclear disarmament exists.

The second policy, i.e., developing national nuclear strike forces, is based on the belief that no nation will assume the risks of annihilation to defend another. At the same time, a lesser power can deter a major one if it possesses effective retaliatory strength. Therefore if nuclear weapons are diffused, the proponents of this policy assert, the likelihood of thermonuclear war will be reduced.

The most compelling case against additional national deterrents, however, rests on purely military calculations: Can a British or a French national deterrent really deter? Albert Wohlstetter argued that a small nuclear power, wielding a few instruments of retaliation, might have deterred a large nuclear power a few years ago, before the distinction between a first- and second-strike capability was fully understood. Later, according to Wohlstetter, it became clear that missiles or bombers in exposed positions above the ground would not be enough; a nuclear force, to be an effective deterrent, must enjoy a substantial degree of invulnerability. It must be dispersed or immobile, protected against blast, and secured against the disruption of command and control systems. Wohlstetter noted that:

In the last year or two, it has become somewhat better understood that, even for the United States, getting a responsible deterrent to Russian attack is far from easy. It is vital and feasible, but hard. Yet the United

States has incomparable advantages of distance, size and industrial strength.[27]

The economic costs and the technical difficulties involved in building a protected or mobile nuclear force appear, however, to be considerably lower in 1963 than when Wohlstetter wrote his "N plus 1 Country" article. Yet if Great Britain and France *individually* cannot achieve invulnerability for the nuclear forces they possess or are likely to acquire, of what use, then, will be the forces which the Europeans create?

"The least that can be said," wrote Raymond Aron, "is that a European incapacity (for building a genuine deterrent strike force) has yet to be proved, and that a deterrent force which is not quite up to the latest scientific discoveries is not thereby deprived of psychological-military value."[28]

A European government that has it within its power independently to pull the trigger on a few dozen nuclear weapons brandishes a "triggering deterrent" which might theoretically plunge the world into general nuclear war. In other words, the threat of escalation, which numbs the great majority of American strategists, greatly amplifies the potential "punch" of an English or a French deterrent. (In actuality, very few Americans fear the irresponsible use of a British nuclear force; it is the French force and the possibility of a future German force which cause concern.)

Can anyone realistically contemplate the prospect of a Soviet strike on France *alone,* which bypasses American missiles elsewhere in Europe and stops just short of American installations in Britain? Some strategists might argue that France has rendered herself peculiarly susceptible to such an attack by keeping her soil clear of American nuclear installations, but despite this circumstance a hyperactive imagination is required to postulate a discriminatory Soviet first strike upon French territory. Such a contingency is a pure strategic abstraction, unrelated to realities.

No matter how piqued Washington might be at the intransigence of a de Gaulle, it is highly unlikely that the United States would stand idly by and watch the Soviets dig a hole in the West where France once stood. Even if France in a fit of national petulance should someday march out of NATO, no one who feels himself part of Western culture could survive the annihilation of France with political, psychological or moral equanimity. But even beyond these considerations there are technical factors which greatly complicate the problem. It is very easy to say, as some analysts do, that the United States will never allow its strategic nuclear responses to depend upon the decisions of a foreign military force over which it could not exercise effective control. But regardless of how efficiently the United States would have centralized and disciplined the command and control system of its deterrent, it could not help developing a severe case of nerves while Soviet missiles were hurtling over Western Europe. The Soviets, in order to avert misunderstandings, might have to "tip off" Washington in advance to the effect that they intended no more mischief than to demolish France. At this point, the strategic model collapses under the weight of its political absurdity. The Cuban missile affair serves only to demonstrate that the concept of the *force de frappe*, which has its origins in political motivations, cannot be easily laid to rest by the mathematical games of strategists.

We may safely assume that not all policymakers, whether in Moscow or Paris, have shut their minds to the primacy of politics over military strategy. Political rather than strategic factors prompt de Gaulle to exploit the national nuclear deterrent as a lever against the Soviet bloc and within the Western Alliance. It is quite true, as Osgood points out, that "the hypothetical credibility of a threat of suicide is not a sound basis for an ally's pursuit of military and political independence." But the Europeans who have supported the idea of national deterrents are by no means hypnotized by a strategy which culminates in suicide; they are not motivated in formulating government policy by any collective death instinct. On the contrary, they seem convinced that there are vital positive political purposes to be achieved along the path which they have chosen.

The underlying motives for a national strike force are political. As Lord Home told Parliament in March, 1963, "If we have not the will to defend our country with the most modern weapons, we ought not to claim to be a great power." Sovereignty is based on up-to-date military capability. Countries justifying their desires for national forces argue that a strike force will give them greater control over their own self-defense. Arguments against nuclear strike forces are proposals for unilateral disarmament by others. Even were an ally to cast his "veto" on the use of the NATO strike force, in order to avoid a nuclear exchange, there is no absolute assurance that the U.S. would not use SAC. Presumably, SAC would not be part of the NATO force. Thus, the veto would not necessarily assure NATO members control over the decision to avoid nuclear war. The key question is whether NATO would be more willing to make a collective decision for nuclear war than would the U.S. unilaterally. In other words, would a NATO force with more than one finger on the trigger improve on the U.S. guarantee?

For some years to come a NATO nuclear strike force, particularly one designed to do almost the same task assigned to SAC, seems superfluous. But the military function of a nuclear force, whose threefold mission would be to provide battlefield tactical nuclear support to ground forces, insure an effective air and antimissile defense system, and provide intermediate-range missiles to interdict hostile lines of communication, would differ sharply from that of strategic retaliation. Prior to 1970, it is true, no national nuclear strike force or even a combined NATO strategic strike force could add very much to the over-all strategic nuclear equation between the United States and the Soviet Union. On the other hand, battle-field tactical and intermediate-range nuclear armed missiles located in Europe and under the control of the European nations of NATO can alone provide that symmetry of forces which appears mandatory in the light of our previous analysis. NATO need not wait until 1970 to obtain such weapons. Unfortunately, the logical requirement to provide nuclear weapons in these categories has been almost totally ignored by the U.S. in the current debate over nuclear sharing in NATO.*

Wohlstetter, writing in 1961, supported the fourth policy, namely, NATO reliance on the United States. This policy contains within it the seeds of a potential "Nuclear Fortress America." From the perspective of RAND analysts immersed for many years in the study of Central War a good case can be made for this policy. The Soviets have solid reason to doubt their ability to isolate Europe, i.e., to attack Europe without attacking the United States. The United States would find it difficult to distinguish between an attack on Europe and the first wave of a wider attack which would involve

---

* Subsequently, in Chapter 5, "A Political Framework for Nuclear Partnership," the creation of such a force under the control of WEU is discussed.

the United States. Furthermore, the United States is not only treaty-bound to defend NATO members in the event of an attack on them, but would find its own vital interests seriously jeopardized if the Soviets were to take over Western Europe, or even West Germany, with all its industrial capacity.

The Soviets, however, are more likely to take their guidance from an evaluation of the concrete, "objective" situation than from a subjective appraisal of United States intentions. Despite trends toward nuclear concentration in North America, as long as United States nuclear forces are dispersed throughout NATO the Soviet planners cannot be certain that either the United States or Western Europe can be knocked out separately.

Throughout 1962, President Kennedy and President de Gaulle joined in an oblique debate over nuclear weapons; both failed to make the essential points. President Kennedy, irrespective of the merit of his policies, stood on firm ground when he argued that so long as the United States bears the main responsibility for the defense of the West it will participate in Western diplomacy and even guide it as it can. Many commentators pointed out that France's voice was louder than her real power justified, not to speak of her slim contribution to NATO. Little purpose is served by dwelling on France's shortcomings. More important is the fact that United States policies appear to inhibit the strengthening of France as a military power. The United States shoulders most of the burdens for Western defense, but it does so in part because it has pursued policies which increase the weight of its own military burdens. It would be much wiser to search for ways through which United States allies can be strengthened militarily. If our allies grow stronger, they can relieve us of some of the burdens which we carry now unnecessarily and at great risk to our own security.

Admittedly, if national strike forces were to remain separate, they would undermine coordination. These forces might enable key allies to invoke the *casus belli*. We might as well recognize the fact that nations still make decisions in accord with their presumed national interests. The NATO nations, unless they believe their genuine national interests are best served and even enhanced within the Alliance framework, will be inclined to follow the dictates of their own security. Raymond Aron, who opposes national nuclear capabilities, has argued cogently for a European deterrent force:

It does not seem to me, at first sight, that the existing balance of power or the precariousness of peace would be much altered by the subdivision of the Atlantic deterrent into two strike forces, one American, one European, closely linked with each other. Furthermore, if one day eastern Europe were to be evacuated by the Red Army and western Europe by American forces as part of a general settlement of the German and European problems, would it not be desirable, from the point of view of American interests, to be able to fall back on a European deterrent force capable of filling the gap left by the departure of close to half a million GI's?[29]

France, of course, has long held out for her own nuclear deterrent. Due to the initial rigidity of the McMahon Act provisions, the United States was unable to supply either materials or technical assistance. As a result, the French embarked long ago on a program of nuclear development which has yielded some results.[30] The French atomic program, whose size and potential effectiveness has been underestimated in the United States, has raised the morale of what may be called our "forgotten ally." Nor can we overlook the fact that the French atomic program is an integral part of the French scientific and technological renaissance. According to de Gaulle's Minister of Defense, Pierre Messmer, "French military programs are an irreplaceable part of scientific, technical, and industrial progress."[31]

France has been continuously and, in the opinion of many observers, justifiably vexed over what she calls the "Anglo-Saxon" hegemony within NATO. That the United States has favored Great Britain in the past in European problems is not a matter of dispute. As the sole formal West European victor in the Second World War, the United Kingdom has retained a status in American eyes to which France seems unable to lay claim. The 1958 version of the McMahon Act authorized the disclosure of information to allies who had acquired a nuclear capability—a provision which the United States seems to ignore studiously when it comes to the French.

The United States has been reluctant to disclose to an ally advance weapons information for fear that such assistance might be mistaken by its potential adversary and the suspicious neutralists as a gift of these weapons themselves. While it is paradoxical that the United States should deny to an ally information that its potential adversary possesses, the French Government has never requested explicitly such information.

The Impact of Arms Negotiations on NATO Posture and Strategy

Considerations other than those of the McMahon Act appear, however, to influence U.S. policy regarding nuclear sharing in NATO. There has been a fear that nuclear "proliferation" will diminish any possible chances for disarmament. The mere mention of the possibility that American atomic information might be conveyed to our allies has been sufficient to elicit from the Soviets the pious warning that nuclear diffusion will doom disarmament. Whether or not the Soviets really want disarmament remains problematical.

"Soviet leaders," states Richard B. Foster,

pursue their strategy of conflict vigorously and with increasing confidence. They show neither the overwhelming fear of nuclear war which might justify attempted bluffs on the part of the United States nor a willingness to negotiate seriously on the reduction of dangers of nuclear war. On the other hand, they do not display that mad pugnacity of a Hitler which might impel them toward a pre-emptive war. They appear, however, to feel that the recent technological, diplomatic and military advances of world communism give them unusual freedom of maneuver.[32]

Having analyzed the pronouncements of Premier Khrushchev in his significant speech of January 6, 1961, and in an earlier statement to the Moscow Congress of Communist Leaders in November, 1960, Charles Burton Marshall concludes as follows:

A pervading idea [in these documents] is the totality of the claim on the future asserted by Communists. The law underlying their conception of what is rightful and what is not is taken as law of history. It is conceived of as ordaining the universal triumph of Communist interests and purposes.

Those interests and purposes accordingly are asserted to have an exclusive access to legitimacy, and all other interests and purposes are regarded as deviant and illegitimate. Peace means an ordering of affairs furthering Communist ascendancy. Peaceful coexistence means, besides an absence of general war, essentially a situation clear of impediments to Communist expansion. . . . Disarmament is regarded as a weapon in the striving for Communist triumph. On our side the purpose and the hope may be to achieve agreements walling off military factors from issues in contention. That purpose and that hope are not reciprocated. Disarmament is to be an effective factor in inflicting defeat on us.[33]

In his celebrated speech of January 6, 1961, Khrushchev candidly stated: "The fight for disarmament is an active fight against imperialism, for narrowing its war potential." Foster writes:

The Soviet Union has apparently made the arms control issue an integral element of its overall cold war strategy and has chosen general and complete disarmament (GCD) as a major instrument of political and propaganda warfare. The conflict environment, however, seems to preclude the negotiation of a mutually acceptable disarmament agreement at this time or in the foreseeable future. On the other hand, the risks in the present situation are so severe that neither the attempts to mitigate them by unilateral action nor the diplomatic dialogue between the antagonists can be permitted to lapse.[34]

Nonetheless, since only a strong Western position will advance genuine negotiations, NATO's main concern should be to ascertain how nuclear weapons can contribute best to over-all Western strength. In a world in which the propaganda content of arms control negotiations may be paramount, a coherent guiding policy for NATO nations participating in these negotiations is indispensable.

Presently, however, there is a wide chasm between Atlantic Community defense planning and the conduct of disarmament negotiations with the Soviets. General and Complete Disarmament, as endorsed in principle by both the United States and the Soviet Union, if it could ever be achieved, would mean the end of the NATO Alliance which we are committed to maintain. At the present stage of history, universal disarmament appears to be an impossible goal, for both political and technical reasons. Implicit in GCD is either the elimination of all nuclear weapons or the creation of a nuclear weapons monopoly within the United Nations. But can the United Nations be converted into an effective world federation while deep ideological and political hostilities remain? The degree of ideological and political consensus required on a global scale for GCD does not yet exist.

There is scant evidence that the Soviets will take GCD seriously before they have accomplished their international objectives. It is politically naïve to suppose that, in an ideologically divided world, they will dismantle forces. Furthermore, are they as afraid of accidental war as the West? They ridicule the "bourgeois" theory that war issues from causes such as those that lead haphazardly to automobile accidents. They have repeatedly asserted that they will be the last to "test." So far as we know, there were no demonstrations of Soviet scientists, intellectuals, students or mothers against the breach of the test ban moratorium. But when the United States followed suit by testing, the pacifist protest in the West was vehement. Beyond the imperceptible efforts of a few marching mothers (from the West) in Moscow and the abortive efforts of a handful of Western scientists to unfurl a homemade banner in Moscow, the pacifist reaction was confined almost exclusively to noncommunist territory.

The Western powers, in the interests of their own self-preservation, should begin at least to ask more searching questions about what a GCD world would be like. The transition to GCD may very well be more dangerous and destabilizing than the maintenance of existing nuclear weapons systems, kept safely under controls.

The achievement of a stable arms balance seems more feasible politically but far more difficult technically. How is the balance to be achieved? Even if we solve all the numerous problems involved,* we face the risk of not knowing when the balance has been achieved, or of keeping the balance once it has been achieved in an era of rapidly changing military technology. Despite its theoretical attractiveness, the quest for a stable arms balance can exert a drag effect on the development of defense capabilities and has actually done so in the United States and could do so for NATO.

In the aftermath of the crisis created by the U.S. discovery of Soviet medium-range missiles in Cuba, speculation centered on a strategic bargain resulting from the exchanges between President Kennedy and Premier Khrushchev. In his news conference of November 20, 1962, President Kennedy twice said, "This is a very

---

* Among the problems to be solved in a quest for "arms stability" in Europe are the conventional-nuclear ratio, the need for flexibility of response and the danger of overemphasizing conventional capabilities at the expense of nuclear defenses. (We do not want to make the European region a safe area for communist aggression.) What kind of Soviet-Western agreements, formal or informal, on the level and deployment of certain types of armaments in Europe are feasible? Schemes include: (a) demilitarized zones; (b) disengagement of Soviet and United States forces from Central Europe; (c) elimination of certain categories of weapons, especially nuclears and the means of their delivery; (d) limitations of the size of forces and armaments deployed by both sides within an agreed Central European zone; (e) increased flow of communication and intelligence without armaments limitation.

climactic period." A few hours prior to the President's press conference, Secretary of State Rusk told the Foreign Policy Association
in New York, "I suspect that we are on the edge of perhaps unprecedented events that could affect the peace of the whole world."[35]

Both the President and the Secretary of State appeared to hint at
the possibility of some nuclear disengagement scheme in Central
Europe. In the wake of his failure to overthrow the strategic balance
by one bold stroke, Khrushchev quickly changed roles from a
Machiavellian deceiver to the kindly peasant leader who placed the
salvation of humanity above parochial communist ambitions. The
possibility of an understanding which the United States might reach
with Khrushchev seemed fraught with a fundamental change of
strategy, i.e., the U.S. would place less reliance on tactical nuclear
weapons and greater reliance on conventional forces to hold the line
between NATO and the Warsaw Pact. In short, for a Khrushchev
pledge not to try another Cuba, the United States would reduce its
nuclear capabilities in Europe. The knotty problem of inspection
would not arise, since presumably the reductions would be made
voluntarily by the United States.

In view of the Soviet record in disarmament negotiations, it seems
highly unlikely that the U.S.S.R. would agree to formal stabilizing
arrangements in Western and Central-East Europe unless NATO
could be weakened thereby. The Soviet position in East and Central
Europe rests upon the presence of military power which has never
been politically ratified either by the Western powers or by the
"host" countries. How long would the Ulbricht regime last without
Soviet military support? Would the Soviets accept the principle of
full international inspection in Eastern Europe though not in the
U.S.S.R. itself? Would they be willing to link the creation of a
nuclear-free zone and United States–Soviet troop disengagement to
complete elimination of the Iron Curtain? On the other hand, the
United States would be foolhardy to accept any such scheme unless
verified by inspection procedures which would involve dismantling
the Iron Curtain.

Even though GCD is impossible, and stable balance at reduced
armaments levels in Europe is a very remote possibility, there is
nevertheless an arms problem within the NATO area. As in any
military situation, certain dangers, proximate or remote, exist. Consistent efforts should be made to reduce these dangers, especially

those which worry the European NATO allies. An arms control policy for NATO should be designed to give greater satisfaction to our NATO allies than to the U.S.S.R. If the opposite proves to be the case, it means that we have for all practical purposes abandoned the Atlantic Alliance. The purpose of NATO arms control policy should not be to pursue an elusive thing called "stable arms balance," but rather to reduce the dangers inherent in the present nuclear situation by undertaking unilateral moves to improve both the political and technical aspects of command and control of nuclear weapons in order to achieve the following objectives: to establish safeguards against the outbreak of war if an accidental nuclear detonation should occur; to prevent the outbreak of unwanted full-scale nuclear war by catalysis (i.e., by the action of a third country which draws the U.S. and the U.S.S.R. into a nuclear war against their will); to prevent war by strategic miscalculation; to be prepared to limit damage if war occurs.

A problem to which far too much attention has been given is the initiation of nuclear war as a result of the orders of a psychotic personality such as Hitler. One most unpleasant fact about the thermonuclear age is that very little can be done to defend oneself against a well-armed and totally nihilistic enemy. A nihilistic enemy equipped with large numbers of missiles armed with thermonuclear warheads can destroy either Europe or the United States. By the appropriate design of our own military posture we can place restraints on potential enemies which will induce them to act reasonably rather than nihilistically. We should not overlook the fact that military strength in optimum configurations can influence and restrain the psychopath. Furthermore it is difficult to see how a psychotic leader of a hostile country could obtain the consent of all his colleagues and his chief military subordinates to launch his country upon a completely nihilistic course of action. Hitler, for example, issued orders to carry out a "scorched earth" policy in Germany in the closing days of the Second World War. His subordinates sabotaged his orders.

The foregoing dangers are real. Some of them may be mitigated by unilateral United States and NATO actions. Some people hope that they can be eliminated through meaningful agreements reached with the Soviet Union. In searching for such agreements via negotiations, however, the leaders of NATO must never forget that *détente* is a function of a changed political climate, not a function of obsolescence of or alterations in defense capabilities. Consequently, NATO arms policy, at this juncture in history, should have as its purposes *the enhancement of strategic flexibility, the promotion of safety and the strengthening of the total deterrent to war.* It would be tragic if NATO arms control policy should actually turn out to be an excuse for relaxing the West's defenses and thus an incentive to Soviet aggression.

While the possibility of significant arms relaxation in Europe is not in the cards at the present time, the conditions for such a development might conceivably arise in Europe during the next decade. NATO policy should be designed to leave the path open for this contingency, without failing to maintain an up-to-date military defensive posture in the meantime. Under no circumstances should the mere hope of *détente* be allowed to condition the pace at which the modernization of NATO defenses occurs. Modernization, rather than arms control, should be the first item on NATO's present agenda.

Technological Partnership for Defense

That tremendous technological advances are altering the security needs of the Atlantic world is obvious. So is the fact that Soviet technology is harnessed to the military power of the Soviet Union. Soviet leaders are deeply aware that technological superiority weighs heavily on the scales of a military or a political conflict.[36]

Major General G. I. Pokrovsky, nuclear physicist and an expert on explosives, missiles and rockets, wrote in 1956:

The level of development of military technology depends directly on the level of economic and technological development . . . and has, in recent times, come to depend in large measure directly upon the level of development of science and upon the intensity and purposefulness of the scientific research work which is conducted in any given country. Thus, military technology is one of the fundamental lines connecting military affairs with the development of the economy and of science.[37]

The United States, too, strives with all its might to bend its scientific and technological resources to the service of national power. Dr. Jerome B. Wiesner, President Kennedy's Director of the Office of Science and Technology, informed the Congress in July, 1962, that the United States Government would put more money into research and development in the fiscal year 1963 than it spent "in the entire interval from the American Revolution through and including World War II."

This commitment is fraught with enormous domestic as well as international consequences. Scientists are rapidly changing patterns within nations as well as the structure of international relations. In the United States expanding industrial complexes cluster around great universities, research centers and laboratories.

As for tomorrow, James Reston discerns these perspectives:

> One can almost plot America's economic development in the future by locating the Nobel Prize winners in the natural sciences. There are seventeen of them in California, eleven in New York, five in Massachusetts, two in New Jersey and seven in the Middle West.[38]

What is now true of the United States will be equally true of Europe. Europe's future economic and industrial growth as well as strategy will be largely dictated by the extent of transatlantic cooperation on the advanced frontiers of science and technology. Europeans, increasingly aware of the political and economic prizes associated with the acquisition of advanced technology, fear technological subordination to both the United States and the Soviet Union.

Our NATO allies possess industrial resources and pools of skilled scientists and engineers, the potential of which could determine the outcome of the West's competition with communism.

Scientific cooperation between the United States and all the nations of Western Europe is even more necessary today than it has ever been. An integrated effort to mobilize the technological resources of Western Europe and pool them with those of the United States is, however, still largely nonexistent.

An embryonic United States effort to stimulate European weapons developments began in the fall of 1953 with the establishment of the program now known as the Mutual Weapons Development Program (MWDP). Its purpose was to provide United States financial, and, to the extent possible, technical assistance to highly promising weapons development projects of our North Atlantic Treaty allies, and other friendly nations. The program, which has not been vigorously implemented, includes support of technical centers needed by our North Atlantic Treaty military commands.[39]

Although progress has been made in many areas, as of 1963, Europe still lagged far behind in advanced military technology. Opinions differ as to how long it will take Europe to catch up—either unaided or with U.S. assistance. Raymond Aron asserts that "It is certain that the western European states together have the financial and technical means for producing thermonuclear bombs and medium-range ballistic missiles (the qualification due to the relatively short distances separating launching sites from eventual targets)."[40]

Whether Western Europe achieves these goals remains to be seen. For the long pull, Europe must increase its technological educational effort by a factor of two or three. In addition, more attention must be paid to establishing modern laboratories and other research resources. Technological education was introduced in Europe after the Napoleonic Wars. It was by the systematic training of technicians that France, Germany and other countries launched their campaign to "catch up" and surpass British industry. Today's Soviet challenge to the West has been motivated by a similar aim. The Kremlin knows that the dialectic of history will bring victory to communism only if the Soviet Union can acquire the skills and provide the capital and other resources to achieve a massive technological superiority over the West.

The Soviet objective—to achieve clear-cut technological superiority over the West—has been pursued relentlessly under centralized direction. The expansion and improvement of Soviet military technology must command our special attention. The Soviet challenge to Western science is reinforced by a huge and effective organization of scientific research, development and education.

If present trends prevail, the West could fall behind the Soviet Union—unless the United States undertakes a free exchange of technical information with its principal allies. Technology cannot be a major source of strength to a coalition when the senior member withholds knowledge that may be essential to the defense of all members.

Technology in general—and this point stands out in especially bold relief in military matters—must serve the common cause of freedom through cooperative venture. If the U.S. continues to withhold its technological treasures from its allies—and especially from the technologically advanced ones—it may end up poorly armed as well as alone in the power struggle.[41]

Two questions are before the United States: Do we wish NATO Europe to become a center of modern military power? If we do, will we, in our own strategic interests, help our allies to build a modern military technology?

Methods by which the peoples of the West can strengthen their scientific potential have been under study for the past several years. Of particular importance is the study undertaken by the Science Committee of the North Atlantic Treaty Organization.[42]

The Committee's report stressed the need to restore to Western scientific culture its traditional freedom of movement between nations and regions. The report made it quite clear that the Western nations have little choice but to devote to science those resources which match its importance to their own security and to the development of their institutions.

The key idea which engaged the discussions of the Study Group set up by the NATO Science Committee was the establishment in Europe of an International Institute of Science and Technology as a cooperative center of research and advanced education in the sciences and technology.[43] In the United States, institutions like the Massachusetts Institute of Technology and the California Institute of Technology have had a tremendous influence on the development of science and technology. Western Europe as a whole could easily muster the required talent and equipment to found an International Institute comparable to the Massachusetts Institute of Science and Technology in size, scope and quality.

The fullest possible collaboration between North America and Western Europe in the fields of nuclear weapons, propulsion systems, missiles, electronics and space would make a vital, a crucial, contribution to the collective defense of the Atlantic world. Many useful peaceful applications will flow from this effort. In 1959 the Foreign Policy Research Institute prepared a study on United States foreign policy for Western Europe for the Senate Committee on Foreign Relations. Among other things the Institute concluded that the United States should help to *"provide key NATO allies of the United States with an independent nuclear capability which will enable them to meet local threats on their own."*[44]

It is not essential that all the technologies under development in the United States or in the Soviet Union be duplicated in Europe. Preferably, there should be an integrated American-European plan for research and development and for the location of production units. As things stand, the technological gap between the United States and the U.S.S.R. on the one hand, and Europe on the other, is becoming broader rather than narrower, and the gradual development of space as a military sphere will unbalance the situation even further. This dangerous gap must be closed. The task is nothing less than winning the technological race in all significant military areas, explosives as well as delivery means and support systems, for use in ground, sea, air, missile and space combat.

The nuclear arming of NATO Europe calls for research and development programs designed to devise those nuclear weapons which are most suitable for utilization on the European continent. European forces should be armed with nuclear weapons of very high efficiency, in order to keep the weapons small and mobile. If Europe is to be armed atomically, it must be armed on a rather large scale, and possess warheads for different carrier systems. This requires either additional production facilities in Europe or top production in our plants, a subject scarcely discussed between U.S. and Allied officials.

For Americans, it is inconsistent to welcome transatlantic cooperation in space while decrying such cooperation in nuclear technology. In fact, the two technologies are interrelated. "Problems of space propulsion," wrote J. S. Parker, Space Executive of the General Electric Company, "are accelerating interest in and knowledge about new sources of electric power: fuel cells, plasma power, photoelectric power, thermionic conversion, and advanced types of atomic reactors."[45]

Both a space program and a nuclear development program in Europe will be costly. Yet sound investment in these fields will buy both increased security and accelerated economic progress. Contrariwise, nations resigned to let others exploit these, the newest and most exciting technologies, condemn themselves to a secondary industrial and economic status—and to permanent insecurity.

Burden sharing in the fullest sense—the sharing of skills, manpower, funds and materials—will distribute the costs among the peoples of the Atlantic world and, at the same time, spread among them the benefits of the common endeavor.* Technological partner-

---

* See Chapter 4, "The Economic Base of Atlantic Power," for a discussion of the concrete problems of burden sharing.

ship across the Atlantic would be one of the principal means for establishing a community of achievement, for community means "doing great things together." Such a partnership would not only strengthen the physical security of the West; it would also restore the confidence of the Western peoples—a confidence which has been gravely shaken—that their culture is still the very heart of modern civilization.

It is difficult to see how these problems can be mastered except by joint over-all planning. A common plan would have to start from *a total NATO budget allocating the financial burdens among the member states.* At present, the principle of sovereignty has not been abrogated even by one iota in the key areas of resource allocation and budget making. According to Pierre Gallois, the West needs a "Strategy of Means" as badly as it needs an operational strategy. The "Strategy of Means" encompasses logistics, but it is more than this, for it embraces the development and manufacture of weapons, their disposition, their emplacement and their readiness as well as their maintenance.[46]

In the thermonuclear age, Gallois wrote,

the problem is to prevent war rather than to wage it, and only a sound and powerful strategy of means can accomplish that purpose. The planning of campaigns that may degenerate into general chaos in a few hours is far less important than the production and distribution of weapons capable of discouraging the resort to force. This can be accomplished only by a pooling of effort and resources.

Unfortunately, the defense community within NATO is not properly organized for the pooling of effort that Gallois suggests. There has been considerable military staff integration, particularly at the higher levels of command. But the officers who compose the international staffs of the various NATO commands have limited freedom to find objective answers to such questions as the most equitable way to raise forces, or the provision of joint training facilities needed to insure the most effective cooperation between the various national contingents.

Terms of conscription, land utilization, weapon choices and related matters are decided by the defense ministers of the various NATO countries. Presently, there is insufficient day-to-day communication between the defense ministries regarding how to solve these fundamental questions equitably. The exchange of technological information and the better coordination of research and development programs should be handled more systematically. In the future, weapons choices might well result from joint decisions rather than unilateral U.S. determination to begin or to abandon a particular weapons project such as Skybolt. More equitable arrangements for joint financing of the NATO research and development program as well as the NATO procurement effort should be established. The choice and location of production facilities should be referred to an appropriate defense coordination committee within NATO. Likewise the matter of international versus national logistics systems requires more intensive study than it has thus far been given. Little progress can be made in this connection unless the parliaments of the various NATO countries frame more unified legislation for the respective member states. Eventually, there might emerge a NATO-wide military budget which would make possible the realistic projection of expenditures and forces for several years ahead. It should be evident that these very difficult and complex problems can only be solved by planning and consultation agencies which treat the military problems confronting the Alliance as a whole.

Nuclear Arms for Western European Union

The contest for supremacy in nuclear weapons is the decisive technological struggle that may one day determine the outcome of the East-West conflict. Since nuclear weapons have become the strongest force in war, a deterrent strategy which does not wholeheartedly incorporate them would be a mere hoax. On the positive side, a comprehensive nuclear strategy for NATO, implemented with adequate technological, industrial and manpower resources, may place that area forever beyond Soviet grasp. Paul-Henri Spaak, prior to his departure from his NATO office, propounded arduously this general view.

Recognizing the obstacles to, and deficiencies in, various schemes for nuclear sharing, the time has come for the United States to assist the Western European Union (WEU) to become a nuclear power within the NATO framework.* On the assumption that wise U.S. policies will induce Britain and France to offer their nuclear capa-

---

* The political rationale for making WEU a nuclear power is developed in Chapter 5, "A Political Framework for Nuclear Partnership."

bilities to WEU control, the practical arguments for United States support of this solution to the nuclear sharing problem are impressive.

A Western European Union nuclear force rather than congeries of national strike forces has the following advantages: First, the individual European nations are not strong enough to develop adequate forces. Second, a European strike force, dispersed geographically, is obviously a superior solution to a coordinated set of small national strike forces. Third, an integrated European strike force removes, or at least lessens, the danger of a strategic attack by an individual nation. Fourth, the creation of a national strike force places, at least initially, considerable strains upon the resources of any single country. Fifth, and perhaps least important militarily but most important politically, a Western European Union strike force will strengthen trends toward the integration of Europe.

Quite naturally, the Soviets, seeking to prevent NATO from being armed effectively with nuclear weapons, want to scotch the idea of U.S. "nuclear sharing."[47] They assert monotonously that nuclear sharing would block any negotiated settlement. In this spoiling operation, the Soviets are assisted by what they themselves have termed those "prudent representatives of the bourgeoisie" who argue that the West should take the lead in unilateral nuclear disarmament and disengagement and a return to a largely conventional strategy.

The Soviets pin their hopes on ultimate victory in their achievement of technological supremacy. The 1962 Soviet feat of simultaneously orbiting two cosmonauts is a foretaste of things to come. Soviet science and disarmament strategy rather than tarnished communist ideology is to be the prime mover of the dialectic of history. Both Marx and Engels understood that the exploitation of the productive forces—which we now call technology—is the true key to political power. And the exploitation of nuclear energy—a force unknown to Marx or Lenin—is the prime mover of the technological thrust. To win the nuclear contest, the Soviets must outpace the United States and the West in all aspects of nuclear technology, nuclear production, and the development, production and deployment of means of delivery and defense. They must obtain better weapons, more of them, and deploy them more effectively.

For years the Soviets have been trying to roll back the American overseas base system. They will continue to try. Nevertheless, unless the West succumbs to the Soviet siren song for disengagement, powerful American nuclear weapons will continue to be deployed overseas, particularly in the NATO area. The Soviets fear the ubiquitous presence of American nuclear power and the prospect that the main European NATO nations might individually or collectively become nuclear powers in their own right.

Were the problem only one of deployment, it would not matter whether nuclear production remained concentrated in the United States. Yet a pooling of NATO technological resources would boost space and nuclear technology, increase the quantity of nuclear weapons, add new weapons types and enhance the strategic and tactical versatility and deployment of the Free World arsenal. This the Soviets know. Effective NATO-wide deployment of strategic, tactical and defensive nuclear weapons would deprive the Soviets of the ability to launch a winning surprise attack. The emergence of the Western European Union as a nuclear force within the framework of the Atlantic Community would assure, in a dramatic, decisive and enduring manner, a shift in the balance of power to the detriment of the Soviet Union. On this prospect hinge both lasting peace and Atlantic unity.

The Soviets recognize that they must not risk major aggression, let alone provoke nuclear conflict, *before* they are ready to destroy the nuclear strength of the Free World and at the same time ward off residual retaliation. *For quite a number of years to come, the Soviets would be foolhardy to risk all-out nuclear conflict. If WEU, within NATO, becomes a true nuclear power, nuclear conflict in Europe could be postponed indefinitely.* Both desiderata could be attained if the Atlantic powers collectively chose and implemented sound military and technological policies.

Conversely, NATO will not survive unless nuclear weapons are incorporated into its forces just as they are in the defense of the United States. If Western Europe remains virtually unarmed, most or all Soviet bombs would be dropped, in case of war, on the United States. This situation, aside from being strategically unfortunate, illustrates how unrealistic policies—such as removing U.S. missiles from Western Europe—might impose severe handicaps upon the U.S. If the countries of Western Europe escaped unscathed from the initial nuclear exchange, they would subsequently suffer the ravages of occupation, with all the horrors attendant upon the imposition of the police state.

The true convergence of interests which nourishes NATO solidarity contrasts with the fear and suspicion which corrode the relations of the Soviet Union and her satellites. The United States is fortunate—far more fortunate than the Soviet Union—in its dependable allies with whom it can share its atomic weapons. It would be unthinkable for the Soviets to place nuclear-warhead missiles in the hands of Poles, Hungarians or East Germans of dubious loyalty. It is primarily this circumstance which warrants any belief that the Soviets might be genuinely interested in unilateral arms agreements with the West.

The American atomic legislation was designed to delay the Soviet acquisition of nuclear weapons. The Soviets now possess such weapons, and some of their weapons are as effective as, or even better than, ours. At present, obsolete American nuclear legislation simply serves to prevent our allies from acquiring the capabilities which they need for their survival and for our own. Illustrative of this attitude was an October, 1962, statement by Representative Chet Holifield, Chairman of the Congressional Joint Atomic Energy Committee, that "it has long been the policy of the Joint Committee to oppose the proliferation of nuclear weapons and nuclear subs to other nations." Mr. Holifield, without naming France, stated on October 17, 1962, that he opposed the transfer of nuclear weapons and secrets "to nations whose political structure is unstable and whose security capability is questionable." Such a cautious refusal to share atomic technology with a leading ally was justified by the conditions of Europe when the Atomic Energy Act was first passed in 1946. In the context of 1963, however, it serves only to exacerbate the strained relations between the United States and France.

As 1962 drew to a close, British support for a European nuclear deterrent force, in return for an easier entrance into the Common Market, was being discussed in the press. Drew Middleton, reporting to the *New York Times*, wrote as follows:

Prime Minister Macmillan and his defense chiefs would prefer that Europe find its nuclear arms with the help of the United States. But the feeling in official quarters is that even without such help the European powers, including Britain, would have their own nuclear system within five years.[48]

The British are obligated by treaties *not* to share information obtained from the United States. But, prior to Nassau, Whitehall seemed ready to take such a step, because membership in the Common Market had assumed vital importance for Britain and for the Macmillan Government. These and other stirrings, including widespread rumors concerning a German-French nuclear deal, were symptomatic of the fact that the United States no longer possessed the nuclear bargaining power which it once held at the apogee of its nuclear monopoly. We are fooling ourselves—and no one else—if we base our policy on the hope that we can prevent the proliferation of nuclear weapons. According to Herman Kahn, "It is not only impossible to fight technology, it is undesirable."[49]

The French developed nuclear weapons with their own resources, an achievement we considered impossible. The Germans invented a new and cheap production process for which the AEC has shown little enthusiasm, but which, nevertheless, is a shortcut to the acquisition of a nuclear capability. In 1962 the Swiss held a referendum approving the acquisition of nuclear weapons. There have been a number of stories according to which the Israelis have acquired secretly some sort of nuclear capability. The Italians have also displayed an interest in the development of nuclear power.[50]

Many American scientific experts contend that European nuclear developments will divert the best European scientific talent to an unrewarding area. Furthermore, they assert that, because of the commanding lead which the United States now enjoys in nuclear technology, most knowledgeable Europeans lack, at present, any serious interest in acquiring their own nuclear capabilities. At the same time, the scientists concede that European interest in acquiring nuclear capability is growing. Yet they do not see the benefits to be derived from encouraging, let alone supporting, this trend. Consequently, they are opposed to promoting greater nuclear cooperation between the United States and its European allies as an approach toward greater political harmony and wider technological exchanges within the Alliance. This attitude—part skepticism, part suspicion—appears to be shortsighted and contrary to the concept of Atlantic partnership.

For the United States to adopt a nuclear policy which stifles the aspirations of its allies, and which it cannot implement, is almost as futile as Canute commanding the sea to stand still. It would be infinitely wiser to give life to that policy of nuclear sharing to which the United States has committed itself formally. Joseph Kraft conceded this to be the prudent course when he asserted, "In the long run, it may be necessary to create a NATO deterrent—if only to head off drives toward independent national nuclear capabilities."[51] By participating in nuclear arrangements which are already coming into being, we can reduce the various secondary dangers with which we seem to be obsessed. By standing outside them, we lose our ability to influence events.

Surveying the pros and cons of nuclear policies, the *New York Times* concluded editorially as follows:

The original project of making NATO a nuclear power, in which the United States would have a voice, is certainly a more practical proposal than is that of a European nuclear force independent of the United States. We hope that Washington will reconsider its policy on this issue, rethink the possibility of giving nuclear arms to NATO, and prepare for the day when France will have no further reasons to oppose creation in this manner of a truly Atlantic military community.[52]

The American entrance into NATO was a revolutionary act. Taking into account our isolationist past we consider NATO revolutionary because *we* entered into an alliance. But the revolutionary impact on Europe was far greater: The Europeans agreed that the United States make for them what once had been their final sovereign decisions about war and peace. For the decision to fight with nuclear weapons then was ours and ours alone. In other words, they agreed to orbit the American planet as virtual satellites. In addition, NATO stationed, more or less permanently, the troops of member states upon the soil of others and created a number of supranational institutions. These, indeed, are revolutionary departures from the historic norm. The Western publics, by and large, are uninformed about developments within European NATO. As presently constituted, there is no other international partnership that equals NATO. The American people are, to say the least, not as fully apprised of this fact as they might be had the same publicity effort that has been expended on the United Nations been devoted to NATO. Worse, our military policy seems designed to weaken rather than strengthen the Atlantic military partnership.

The creation of a NATO nuclear force under WEU aegis would be a token of partnership that will persuade the Atlantic world to speak with one political voice. It is increasingly evident that the defense of genuine national interests requires a higher level of political confederation.* The WEU nuclear force within NATO would be a genuine multinational command, comparable to the European Defense Community. It would provide nuclear support to all Central Front shield forces as well as operate the land-based missile system. It could respond to the political direction of the NATO Council either directly or—and this, of course, is the most crucial issue facing the Alliance—through some yet-to-be-designed European political agency.

There are many who argue that the idea of a multinational NATO nuclear force cannot be put into practice, particularly with respect to control. The control features required, it is said, are incompatible with the single global direction and control over strategic operations which has become a cornerstone of President Kennedy's policy.

The pressing choice is between a globally controlled general war capability under United States direction within an integrated NATO or national strategic capabilities. The latter alternative would spur the creation of a genuine "third force." The trend toward such a "third force," with all of its divisive implications for NATO, will inevitably grow as time goes on *unless* the United States opts for genuine Atlantic nuclear cooperation. We should go further than reluctant consent.†

Unless we want to live in a tripartite nuclear world, the United States must make the Atlantic Community operative. It is time to come down firmly on the side of a practical scheme for nuclear sharing—and take the consequences. Hazards we must accept. No great historical task has ever been accomplished without taking sides and making irrevocable commitments.

If a genuine WEU nuclear force is established, then the strategic problem confronting the Soviet Union will be altered drastically. The Soviets will face two first-class nuclear deployments under coordinated direction. All their strategic calculations, in all quarters

---

* See Chapter 5, "A Political Framework for Nuclear Partnership" and concluding Chapter 8, "The Atlantic Vision: A Question of Choice."

† See note 5, Chapter 8 (p. 386) for a statement by Under Secretary of State George Ball regarding the nuclear sharing question.

of the globe, will be complicated, frustrated and defeated by that fact.

Nuclear sharing is the best way to resolve the schism in the European soul, alternating between fears that the United States will use its nuclear power and fears that it will not. At the present time, however, the United States cannot be expected to share with Europe the decision to use nuclear weapons in the case of either a transcontinental surprise attack or a war in a region where the United States alone, and not NATO, bears the responsibility. If there were an Allied strategic doctrine, the problem of sharing global nuclear decisions would be resolved. But strategic unity presupposes a much higher degree of political unity than now prevails within the Alliance.

If WEU nuclear forces are to be established, new decision-making processes will have to be devised. If NATO were really a single political community, armed with one nuclear force ready to meet any type of aggression, there would be only the one finger of an integrated military command, fully responsible to, and controllable by, a joint political authority which alone could decide whether the safety lock should be unfastened and the trigger pulled.* To solve this thorny problem Pierre Gallois has suggested an ingenious solution: regional groupings within NATO, each linked to the United States. Such an arrangement, Gallois hopes, might ease the problem of dealing with localized attacks against either the northern and southern regions or the Central Front.

The United States cannot have it both ways forever. If it proposes to exercise global strategic leadership of the Free World, it must form a nuclear partnership or else cope with uncontrolled nuclear diffusion on our side as well as the other side of the Iron Curtain.

The Writing on the Wall

There is urgent military business before NATO. Delay in attending to it could well culminate in disaster. NATO, in the light of Marshal Malinovsky's profoundly revealing digressions on the military requirements of the nuclear age, is a military anachronism. NATO's priority action agenda includes: (1) maintenance of over-all

---

* See Chapter 5, "A Political Framework for Nuclear Partnership."

military superiority over the Soviet Union; (2) revision of United States atomic legislation to assist in the immediate creation within NATO of a WEU nuclear force; (3) reorganization of strengthened NATO ground forces for atomic as well as conventional conflict; (4) development of a NATO intermediate-range missile force; (5) development of a NATO-wide defense against ballistic missiles and manned aircraft; (6) development of a rational doctrine and control mechanisms for movement of friendly aircraft in a missile-defended air space; (7) development of citizen armies for a variety of military function; (8) reorganization of the NATO logistics system to make it capable of functioning in a nuclear environment; (9) establishment of an effective system of political direction and military command and control of NATO forces. (Particular attention must be given to the structure, force posture and distinctive problems of the regional commands.) Political arrangements in NATO must be established so that the choice and timing of a response to Soviet attack can be made rapidly at the highest political level. By taking these steps, NATO would confront the Soviets with a "no-win" situation throughout the entire spectrum of conflict possibilities.

But the Atlantic Community must look beyond a "no-win" situation toward a positive goal—the defense and extension of those values which animate its civilization. In Western Europe the Western value system and the Orwellian world of the new Soviet-conditioned man confront one another. Khrushchev pins his ultimate hopes on the superiority of the communist system of values.

We believe that ultimately that system will be victorious on the globe which will offer the nations greater opportunities for improving their material and spiritual life. It is precisely socialism that creates unprecedentedly great prospects for the inexhaustible creative enthusiasm of the masses, for a genuine flourishing of science and culture, for the realization of man's dream of a happy life, a life without destitute and unemployed people, of a happy childhood and a tranquil old age, of the realization of the most audacious and ambitious human projects, of man's right to create in a truly free manner in the interests of the people.[53]

Premier Khrushchev's statement is enlivened by an imagery which draws its appeal from ideals which are the sum and substance of the Western ethos. The Soviet Union is an errant child of the West. The West, while protecting itself from the totalitarianism which has dominated communism ever since Lenin made it operational, must look forward to the day when communism will pass from the forestage of history, and a free community of nations, governed by the consent of the governed, comes into being.

Globally, the West must raise and widen its sights to encompass this wider vision. Sufficient manpower and resources exist in NATO, on both sides of the Atlantic, with which to build, at acceptable cost, superior defense formations capable of restraining the Soviet Union from aggressive actions in Europe and elsewhere. The creation of such forces would block the last remaining avenue through which the Soviets could realize by military action their global ambitions. The essential condition for ending the Cold War is NATO's psychological and military readiness to deal with Soviet aggression firmly and effectively wherever, whenever and under whatever form it may become manifest.*

NATO stands at the nuclear crossroads. The failure of the United States to share its nuclear assets in time could divide the Alliance. Nuclear sharing could be the key to opening up cross-Atlantic technological cooperation, spurring the economic prosperity and political harmony of the West while frustrating indefinitely Soviet political exploitation of military power. Which road will the United States choose?

President Truman laid the foundations of NATO; upon them, President Eisenhower, both as Supreme Commander, Europe, and as President, erected a sturdy edifice; President Kennedy could become the foremost architect of the *Atlantic Community* if he forged from the unlocked secret of the atom the armor of freedom.

---

* A question posed by Walt Rostow, chairman of the State Department Policy Planning Council, regarding U.S. economic policy vis-à-vis Europe, seems pertinent with regard to U.S. nuclear policy: "Is this to be a Europe powerful but turned inward? Or will it be a Europe linked with the United States even more closely than in the past, intimately engaged with us in the great common enterprises of the free community of nations?" (From a speech delivered before the biennial National Convention of the League of Women Voters, at Minneapolis, Minnesota, May 3, 1962.)

The idea that a cooperative U.S. economic policy vis-à-vis the Common Market countries can succeed in opposition to nationalistic nuclear policies is a misleading myth that bars the way toward Atlantic cooperation.

CHAPTER **4** THE ECONOMIC BASE OF

ATLANTIC POWER

For generations before 1914, most of the world was in many respects one common market. Where tariffs existed, they were generally low. Persons moved among countries without governmental restriction. The gold standard, under the management of the City of London, insured a high degree of economic rationality in international trade.

The North Atlantic peoples are now engaged in a great effort to restore something approaching a Free World common market for themselves and, hopefully, for the so-called underdeveloped peoples. The nineteenth-century form of gold-standard common market was shattered beyond repair by World War I. The impact of the war engendered an urgent demand for rapid restoration of destroyed resources and economies, and new vested interests, especially in the new states created by the peace settlements, demanded protection against automatic economic corrections. Furthermore, technological change, particularly in transportation and communication, made unacceptable to the peoples of the world the slow pace of the diffusion of economic benefits under the automatic controls of the gold standard and free trade. The awareness of remote events that is aroused by popular education and rapid communications rendered obsolete and intolerable the harsh correctives of cyclic adjustment under the gold standard and the perpetuation of wide differentials in living standards among peoples.

The nineteenth century was blessed with a semblance of world order, maintained by a pragmatic system for the enforcement of peace. The British balance-of-power policy and navy, together

136

with the Concert of Europe, depended the sanctity of international commitments. After World War I, the British balance-of-power policy in Europe was but a shell of its former self. It was applied for the most part against the wrong party, France. The British failed to understand the meaning of the rise of Hitler, not to speak of the new power of the Soviet Union and of the United States. There was no longer one world, but at least two worlds—the status quo countries and the revolutionary powers, the "have-nots," typified by the communist assault against the legitimacy of the existing order. Today, this bipolar division of the world is blurred by the rise of a third order, the uncommitted. Yet the emergence of that miscellany of nations does not restore the economic unity of the globe, cleft by the communist drive for building a separate economic system outside and independent of the residual world market and consistently hostile to it.[1]

The North Atlantic peoples are now confronted with the task, not of returning to the "good old days" of the world as we now recall them, but of evolving new institutions that will create a twentieth-century stable order within which the West can uphold its ideals against the attrition of the communist world and keep the uncommitted nations within the community of open societies. Ways must be found, not to compel poorer peoples "to face economic reality," for the short or long term, but to create an economic reality that is tolerable. Progress in this task, and the things that remain to be done, will be discussed in this chapter.

The Setting

We have seen in the last chapter that major steps must be taken to secure an adequate and credible defense of the Atlantic frontiers. Large allocations of economic resources will be required. There can be no question of the ability of the economies of the Atlantic countries to provide them. The remarkable economic surge of Western Europe in postwar years, combined with the economic strength of the United States, insures that what must be done can be done—if the Atlantic nations agree on their strategy and find the will to work together to carry it out.

The postwar economic achievements have been realized in large part through newly developed and developing institutions for economic cooperation and integration. (See the chart on p. 139 for a list of political, military and economic organizations that now bridge the Atlantic Community.) In the simplest terms, the ability of the Atlantic Community to defend itself as well as insure the general welfare, will depend on how effectively can be maintained the psychological momentum which has been the true motive force propelling the various vehicles, political, military and economic, of European and Atlantic integration.

Recently, public attention has been focused on the six-nation European Common Market and, to a lesser extent, on the twenty-nation transatlantic Organization for Economic Cooperation and Development (OECD). These institutions of integration and cooperation represent a stage in the continuing postwar trend away from the divisive nationalistic tendencies of the earlier decades of this century. It is worth pausing to consider the factors that generated the new functional arrangements.

The underlying causes of the European and Atlantic movement toward interdependence are both economic and political. On the economic side, common needs and desires reflected kindred technological and sociological developments; external pressures and purposeful leadership supplied the political leaven. Economic interdependence is, of course, far from complete; the institutions are not yet fully adequate, and the trend is still beset by uncertainties. We shall examine some of the political currents, as well as some of the changes in economic policy, that bid fair to remove remaining institutional obstacles to that smooth and matter-of-course cooperation which would exploit to the fullest the economic potential of the Community.

What were the political pressures that brought about the West European drive toward political cooperation? There is no single answer. But the most immediate causative force was war, both hot and cold. When hot war burned itself out in 1945, Europe (as did East Asia) found herself economically prostrate. In spite of great physical destruction, however, Europe was not without resources. Western Europe, in particular, still possessed a trained labor force, entrepreneurial skills, technical knowledge and a not inconsiderable industrial plant. Her most grievous lack was the means with which to procure the raw materials to restart the factory wheels, as well as adequate food to sustain her people. In addition, she needed machinery to restore her damaged industrial plant.

Europe always had been a net importer of many raw materials and foods. Now she had to look to the one prosperous industrial nation in the world, i.e., the United States, for capital goods. Europeans

INSTITUTIONS OF THE ATLANTIC COMMUNITY

	United States	Canada	United Kingdom	France	West Germany	Italy	Belgium	Netherlands	Luxembourg	Greece	Turkey	Iceland	Denmark	Norway	Portugal	Austria	Sweden	Switzerland	Ireland	Spain	Finland	(Yugoslavia)	(Japan)
NATO (1949)	■	■	■	■	■	■	■	■	■	■	■	■	■	■	■								
CEEC (1947)	▨	▨	■	■	■	■	■	■	■	■	■	■	■	■	■	■	■	■	■		▨		
OEEC (1948-61)	▨	▨	■	■	■	■	■	■	■	■	■	■	■	■	■	■	■	■	■	■	▨	▨	
OECD (1961)	■	■	■	■	■	■	■	■	■	■	■	■	■	■	■	■	■	■	■	■			▨
DAC (1961)	■	■	■	■	■	■	■	■						■									■
ECSC (1952) EEC (1958)				■	■	■	■	■	■	▨													
EFTA (1961)			■										■	■	■	■	■	■			▨		
IMF (1947)	■	■	■	■	■	■	■	■	■	■	■	■	■	■	■	■	■		■	■	■		■
WEU (1948)			■	■	■	■	■	■	■														

■ Full memberships   ▨ Associate or partial memberships

GLOSSARY OF ORGANIZATIONAL ABBREVIATIONS

NATO   North Atlantic Treaty Organization
CEEC   Committee for European Economic Cooperation
OEEC   Organization for European Economic Cooperation
OECD   Organization for Economic Cooperation and Development
DAC   Development Assistance Committee
ECSC   European Coal and Steel Community
EEC   European Economic Community
EFTA   European Free Trade Association
IMF   International Monetary Fund
WEU   Western European Union

found themselves confronted by many needs. Their common denominator was the scarcity of foreign exchange, for Europe had to procure the needed supplies from overseas but lacked the liquidity

—that is, the working capital—with which to start again to pay her own way with exports.

As soon as the war ended in Europe, the United States had begun to meet the most urgent needs, primarily in kind. Through the United Nations Relief and Rehabilitation Agency (UNRRA), the United States had been supplying the necessities of food and fuel to its allies. Through a program called Government and Relief in Occupied Areas (GARIOA), the same needs of the defeated nations were also being met. In addition, our allies were still receiving some Lend-Lease supplies. Indeed, the prompt and willing American response to European needs may be traced to the establishment even before our entry into the war of Lend-Lease, which followed the release to Britain of fifty overage U.S. destroyers.

UNRRA and GARIOA engaged in marginal relief activities. They could not restore industrial activity, stability to the currencies nor vigor to European trade so that export earnings would be adequate to support import needs. By 1947, the gold reserves and dollar holdings of Western European countries had declined to $7 billion—equivalent to that year's trade deficit, i.e., excess of European imports over exports.[2] Even these reserves, since they were not well distributed among the individual Western European nations, fell far short of meeting the requirements of European trade.

Early in 1947, the British announced that they could no longer support the burden of assisting Greece in suppressing a communist-supported revolt. The U.S. stepped into the breach. On March 12, 1947, President Truman proposed U.S. military and economic support to Greece and Turkey to prevent them from being drawn behind the Iron Curtain. In May of that year, Congress responded with an appropriation of $400 million.

One may surmise that neither economic necessity nor U.S. responses to Cold War moves made by the Soviet Union would alone have brought about the events that followed. Both the common difficulties and the external pressures of a hostile Soviet Union were driving a hitherto deeply divided Western Europe together. As we shall presently see, these very pressures provided the opportune occasion for the "Europeans" to assert their leadership. The principal "Europeans" were Monnet and Schuman of France, Spaak of Belgium, De Gasperi of Italy and Adenauer of Germany. (Churchill had inspired the European movement in its early days by his wartime proposal of British and French union and his 1945 suggestion of European union; but unlike the "Europeans," he was apparently unwilling to urge his country to the point of modifying her traditional sovereign prerogative, i.e., "freedom of action.")

The aid to Greece and Turkey was recognized for what it was—an interim measure. The creative approach to the long-term problem found dramatic expression in Secretary of State Marshall's historic Harvard address of June, 1947. This speech inaugurated a new dialogue in Atlantic relations, differing not only in the awareness of the challenge which it signified, but also in the sustained response which it suggested. Emergency aid for relieving shortages in individual countries was supplemented by measures enabling Europe to rebuild itself as a regional entity. This new response manifested itself in a succession of varied regional organizations—economic, political and military—which broke Western Europe's traditions of insularity, rivalry and autarchy, and also sealed the U.S. break with the tradition of isolation.

The keynote of Marshall's speech was the proposal that a share of initiative should come from Europe:

> It would be neither fitting nor efficacious for this Government to undertake to draw up unilaterally a program designed to place Europe on its feet economically. This is the business of the Europeans. The initiative, I think, must come from Europe. The role of this country should consist of friendly aid in drafting of a European program and of later support of such a program so far as it may be practical for us to do so. The program should be a joint one, agreed to by a number of, if not all, European nations.[3]

Even in mid-1947, Secretary of State Marshall, speaking for the Truman Administration, was not yet ready to freeze the U.S. position in the framework of a bipolar Cold War world. The offer of assistance to a cooperating Europe did not stop at the Iron Curtain, but was open to all European nations. The Soviet Union declined. Poland was coerced into following suit. Czechoslovakia accepted but, in the course of the events leading up to the communist coup, yielded to force and reversed itself. But Secretary Marshall's proposal met with the instant and fervent approval of Western Europe. Within five weeks, sixteen Western European countries set up the Committee for European Economic Cooperation to prepare a draft of a recovery program.

Following the communist *coup d'état* in Czechoslovakia the Western European Union was formed—the first military response to communist aggression in Western Europe. The Czech coup also accelerated economic cooperation. Formation of the Committee for European Economic Cooperation was followed with startling rapidity by a chain of far-reaching decisions: the Committee submitted its report on requirements and cooperative economic arrangements; the U.S. Congress appropriated funds; the Economic Cooperation Administration (ECA) and the Organization for European Economic Cooperation (OEEC) were established; and the four-year European Recovery Program was launched in the spring of 1948.

Thus opened an era of increasing economic interdependence among North Atlantic countries. The Marshall Plan signaled the awareness of the United States that its national interest had become interdependent with that of the free European countries in the cold as well as a hot war. The formation of the OEEC marked the start of the European countries along the path of cooperative economic effort and showed them willing to submit their respective economic policies to the close scrutiny and criticism of their neighbors.

The first efforts of the OEEC were directed to the objective of achieving liquidity for the procurement of resources, that is, of closing the "dollar gap." At first, this endeavor centered upon determining the distribution of the Marshall Plan funds among the member countries. But the OEEC soon concerned itself with measures that would enable Europe to earn her own way once Marshall aid came to an end in 1952. It was clear that production could expand adequately only in markets opened to increased intra-European trade. The Intra-European Payments Agreements for 1948 and 1949 were followed by the establishment of the European Payments Union (EPU) in September, 1950. The EPU set up a clearinghouse arrangement for intra-European payments that increased the efficiency of the use of funds and thus in effect increased the liquidity of the members. In addition, the Payments Union provided for the granting of credits to cover specified portions of any country's debt to the Union, thus further increasing liquidity and providing assistance to any member in economic difficulty. The price of this aid was the agreement by each nation to submit to a full review of its economic policies and to undertake corrective actions. Consequently, the OEEC attacked the rigid system of import quotas that had grown up to strangle European trade. A Code of Liberalization was adopted in August, 1950, providing for gradual reduction of the quotas.[4]

How much of the economic progress made was the result of the newly acquired habit of cooperation, and how much it owed to the leadership of the "Europeans," no one can now tell. But the cut-off of most U.S. economic aid (though partially replaced by military aid) at the end of 1952 did not mark the end of cooperation. On the contrary, the OEEC went to work on longer-range aspects of economic cooperation. In 1953, for example, the European Productivity Agency was established as an arm of the OEEC to study the problems of productivity and to make recommendations for raising it.

The world-wide boom generated by the Korean War undoubtedly accelerated the recovery of Western Europe and provided a salutary environment for the early years of the OEEC. During these years the dollar gap was closed, intra-European trade was increasingly liberalized and recovery was completed. Currencies had been revalued and were, by August of 1955, sufficiently stable to permit the signing of the European Monetary Agreement and the return to full convertibility of the currencies of several member countries. The objective of convertibility for all currencies was achieved by the end of 1958, at which time the Payments Union terminated its operations.[5]

During the first decade of regional cooperation under the OEEC, Western Europe achieved economic growth beyond all expectations.[6] Western Europe had a favorable balance of trade, foreign exchange reserves had doubled, and GNP had grown at a breathtaking average of almost 5 percent per year.

Dramatic as was this decade of cooperation in the economic sphere—Europe being enticed by the carrot of U.S. aid and driven by the two whips of common needs and shared fears—and spectacular as were the accomplishments, the new approach represented only a limited break with history. True, never before had the Western democracies made explicit the need for economic coordination and the objective of economic growth. Never before had the mechanism for economic cooperation been structured so formally. During the century between Waterloo and Sarajevo the fabric of economic cooperation had been woven from the countless strands of individual, rather than national, decisions. The rules of the game were those of *laissez-faire*, free trade, gold shipments and control by a force that remained largely latent and insured the functioning of the system. The balance-of-power kept the world at peace.

Today, the political aspirations of the Europeans seek more explicit expression. The success of the early functional arrangements in the economic sphere and the demonstrated feasibility of joint effort have encouraged the pursuit of closer political unity. The preferred approach to political unity has been the circuitous detour via economic institutions. It has led to the formation of supranational organizations, a step beyond intergovernmental cooperation. Perhaps the decisive moment came in May of 1950, when a bold plan was put forward just at that psychological moment when strong personal leadership could crystallize popular, business and governmental support. Jean Monnet of France wrote, and Robert Schuman proposed, a plan, which thereafter was to be known by Schuman's name, for the unification of the most basic economic sector of Western Europe, the coal and steel industries. For the first time, a European statesman in office proposed that international economic reform go beyond the elimination of international trade barriers. The plan called for the integration of the industries of the steel-producing nations in the interest of long-term common objectives, even at the cost of short-term unequal sacrifices. The OEEC had successfully established economic growth, rather than protection of national wealth, as the economic philosophy of European governments. Internal barriers not just to trade—the movement of goods— but also to the movement of persons and capital were to be broken down. This could be expected to entail serious costs and painful adjustments for less efficient nations, though, by the very processes of these adjustments, eventual gain for all the participants. Great Britain, restrained by domestic political factors as well as by Commonwealth considerations, was not yet ready for such measures,[7] but France, Italy, West Germany and the three Benelux countries (Belgium, Luxembourg and the Netherlands) took less than one year to reach agreement, signing the European Coal and Steel Community Treaty in April, 1951, to be effective July, 1952. By early 1958, in less than six transitional years, the Coal and Steel Community succeeded in creating a single six-nation market for coal, steel, iron ore and scrap. A High Authority was granted certain real supranational powers over the common market created by the Community. The old dream had come true—sufficient political accord and economic opportunity to exploit modern technology in markets commensurate with efficient production organization.

This demonstration of what could be accomplished jointly by former rivals or enemies contrasted with the breakdown of the efforts to foster integration in another functional field—defense— when, in 1954, the European Defense Community was rejected by the French National Assembly. European leadership was encouraged to pursue its goals through the channel of further economic integration. Negotiations, started in 1955, led to the signing in 1957 of the Treaty of Rome, which established the European Economic Community. Again, Great Britain, haunted by the fear of Franco-German domination, preoccupied with maintaining her "special relationship" with the United States and concerned with her historic ties with the Commonwealth, backed away.[8] The Economic Community was formed by the same "Six" that composed the Coal and Steel Community.

Europe had long dreamed of achieving a customs union, and many attempts toward this objective had been made over more than a century, the most notable being the *Zollvereine* formed in 1834 and 1867 among German states. Negotiations begun among wartime governments in exile had culminated in Benelux, the customs union of Belgium, Luxembourg and the Netherlands, which entered fully into operation on January 1, 1948. But a common market is far more than a customs union. A common market provides for free movement between countries of labor and capital as well as of goods. The Treaty of Rome also provided for restraints on national discriminatory and restrictive measures which might interfere with free trade and competition; for harmonization of the wage, social insurance and related policies of member countries; and for the establishment of common operating agencies, including an investment bank for underdeveloped portions of the community. Most importantly, in the long run, the European Economic Community showed a clear intent to encourage political as well as economic integration. Speaking at the Eighth Annual Session of the NATO Parliamentarians, Dr. Walter Hallstein, President of the Commission of the Community, said:

What is emerging from all this [the progress of the EEC] is not just an economic union. Rather, it is a political union, so far limited to the economic and social fields. *It is because this union is political,* indeed, that the commission recently put forward a comprehensive action program intended to fill out with flesh and blood the bare bones of the treaty: the completion of our "European Constitution" with "European laws" is too great a matter to be left to chance.[9]

Thus the Common Market approach represented a political attack on some of the causes of the national differences in economic welfare and opportunity that tariffs had been designed in part to protect and enhance.

Having stood on the sidelines, and fearing discrimination by the "Six" that would limit her participation in Continental markets, Great Britain established, along with the Scandinavian countries, Portugal, Switzerland and Austria, the European Free Trade Association (EFTA)—promptly dubbed the "Outer Seven" in opposition to the "Inner Six." EFTA planned a schedule for the removal of trade restrictions on nonagricultural products among its members, thus seeking to put pressure on the Common Market through Germany, the heaviest exporter to the Seven, as a first step toward what was envisioned as a nonagricultural free trade area throughout Western Europe. In effect, this represented an attempt to achieve the trade liberalization objectives of the Common Market for all of Western Europe together, while delaying the political integration of the Six. The exclusion of agricultural products reflected, in part, Britain's concern with her Commonwealth ties. European free trade in agricultural commodities would be inconsistent with the system of "preferences," or preferential tariffs, which Great Britain has for many years extended to nations of the Commonwealth to provide them with protected agricultural markets in return both for the advantage which British manufacturers generally hold in the Commonwealth, and for relatively cheap agricultural imports to the United Kingdom.

The spectacular success of the Economic Community, both economically and in terms of political cooperation, eliminated whatever hopes the British had of forestalling the European integration movement. Trade among the Six multiplied more rapidly than any of the members had dared hope. The general prosperity was such that the earlier fears of depression among disadvantaged national industrial sectors subsided. To counter EFTA's tariff reduction schedule and its effects on Germany, the Six were able in May of 1960 greatly to accelerate the planned twelve-year schedule for gradual tariff reduction and creation of the ultimate Common Market.[10] In less than two years—by the summer of 1961—Britain, in a historic reversal of position, applied for membership in the Common Market.

Clearly, Great Britain failed to seize the historic moment in delaying her decision until 1961. Her political as well as economic position vis-à-vis the Continent has declined. As the vicissitudes of the negotiation during 1962 showed, the terms for Britain had worsened, while the price of admission had increased. She was caught between her Commonwealth ties, both economic and psychological, and her dependence on the Continent, politically, militarily and economically. De Gaulle made no secret of his determination that any concession of French independence be minimal and that it was Great Britain, not France, that had the most to gain by the former's admission to the "club." Press stories notwithstanding, the gap between the British position and that of the Common Market countries was not so narrow as to suggest a speedy agreement on Britain's entry. It has been alleged that de Gaulle instructed his representatives at Brussels to break off negotiations because, such an agreement having come within sight, he wanted to torpedo the negotiations for political reasons. It is not proposed here to assess the inwardness of de Gaulle's intentions. It is a fact, however, that M. Couve de Murville, the French Foreign Minister, in a speech to the French National Assembly on January 24, 1963, made it quite clear that some of the most important issues of the fifteen-month negotiations, especially that of the reconciliation of differences on agricultural policy, remained unsettled.[11]

The partial success of the integration movement did not end the course of purely cooperative economic arrangements. On the contrary, by 1959 the emergence of regional blocs within the Atlantic Alliance, as well as the success of the cooperative institutions, suggested to many in this country and in Europe that transatlantic economic cooperation must be strengthened. In 1960, an OEEC committee of "four wise men" drafted the "Dillon Plan," named for the then U.S. Under Secretary of State, a proposal for the creation of a new organization in which the United States and Canada[12] would participate as full members along with the eighteen members of the OEEC. In 1961, the twenty-member Organization for Economic Cooperation and Development (OECD) came into being. Its aims were "to achieve the highest sustainable economic growth and employment and rising standard of living in member countries, while maintaining financial stability . . . to contribute to sound economic expansion in member as well as non-member countries . . . and to contribute to the expansion of world trade on a multilateral, non-discriminatory basis."[13]

Like the OEEC, then, the OECD should enhance the economic element of NATO power by encouraging growth of the resource base. In two important programs, however, the new organization will go beyond the objectives of its predecessor. First, its Economic Policy Committee will provide a mechanism for coordinating actions of financial and monetary authorities to head off episodes such as the sudden flight of U.S. dollars attracted by higher interest rates in Germany and England during the second half of 1960.[14] Secondly, the organization's Development Assistance Committee will provide a means of coordinating aid programs to the less developed countries. (This committee is a successor to the Development Assistance Group established in 1959 by seven capital-exporting countries within OEEC plus the United States, Canada, and Japan.)

The United States, quite apart from its concern with stable international monetary arrangements, well-directed aid programs in critical areas of the Free World and a sensible sharing in the support of such programs, found it desirable to participate in an organization broader in membership than NATO. It is useful, for political and practical reasons, to associate neutral nations directly and closely with the United States in an international economic organization. Countries such as Switzerland and Sweden bring not only the inclination but also considerable resources to this common enterprise, and aid to the uncommitted nations is made more acceptable by the participation of neutral donors. NATO, because it is a military organization, is an unsuitable instrument for administering aid programs.

As one of its first acts, the OECD announced in November, 1961, that its twenty member countries planned to increase their total economic output by 50 percent in ten years. The announcement may have been a shrewd propaganda claim rather than a blueprint for growth, calculated more for its political than its economic effects. The very announcement, however, may generate pressure to attain the goal.[15] Certainly, the statement served at least three political purposes: (1) It furnished a Western response (and a relatively credible one) to the boastful twenty-year economic program announced in 1961 by Premier Khrushchev before the Twenty-second Congress of the Communist Party of the Soviet Union. (2) It created that climate of confidence in Europe's future which the Kennedy Administration hoped would make it easier to win domestic support for trade agreements between the United States and the European Economic Community. (3) The projection of the Western growth rate, although more modest than the communist bloc program, rested upon the assumption of a much larger productive base to start with, and thus carried the hint that, during the next decade, the underdeveloped nations must look to the West rather than to the Soviet bloc for substantial growth through trade and aid.

Whether or not the OECD, as a purely intergovernmental body, will prove capable of coordinating Western growth, trade and development policies in an effective manner remains to be seen. Certainly the presence within OECD of the neutrals—Austria, Ireland, Sweden and Switzerland—may make it a little easier than it would be otherwise for the West as a whole to accomplish certain political-economic objectives in the underdeveloped regions. But their presence also has an undoubted limiting effect. The neutral European states do not wish to become embroiled in any NATO efforts to wage economic warfare against the Sino-Soviet bloc. Thus it is not surprising that the OECD Convention says nothing at all about the coordination of Western policies in such areas as East-West trade. Despite the strategic implications of such trade in the protracted conflict, the coordination of NATO governmental policies in this area has not yet been given an efficient institutional base. The most critical *ad hoc* problems are dealt with as they arise, usually through a process of haphazard cajoling and haggling, while the task of long-range planning to meet the communist economic thrust is ignored.

We have dwelt thus far on the story of the economic, or "functional," development of a European Community, not an Atlantic Community. What is the relation of the European regional developments to the ultimate goal of an Atlantic Community? The signal success of the Common Market marks the transition of the North Atlantic Alliance from one dominated by the United States, economically, militarily and politically, to a partnership of substantial equals—at least in terms of economic strength. In earlier chapters, we have told the story of the strategic shift from a world dominated by the nuclear power of the United States to the bipolar balance of terror, in which the Alliance no longer holds a single strategic view. Perhaps next in importance to this strategic revolution has been the unanticipated degree of success of U.S. policy in restoring the economic strength of Europe. Certainly, over the short range, the competition of a resurgent Europe is fraught with ambiguous implications for the American economy. The division of the Atlantic Community into two economic blocs would seem to be commercially more disadvantageous to the United States than a three-way division among the Continent, the British Commonwealth and the United States. American national policy, however, cleaves firmly to the long-range view that our ultimate interest lies in the maximum economic strength as well as the unity of purpose of the Alliance. During the fifties, economic and political development appeared to move together, at least on the Continent and, up to a point, even in Great Britain. Yet the shift in the distribution of economic power within the Alliance raises crucial questions for the sixties. To date, the responses to these problems of U.S. economic policy have been only partial and tentative.

In October, 1961, the Administration's view—or, rather, what one must presume this view to be—was set forth in a brief report to the Joint Economic Committee of Congress by former Secretary of State Christian A. Herter, appointed chief trade negotiator by President Kennedy in November, 1962, and businessman and statesman William L. Clayton, entitled *A New Look at Foreign Economic Policy, in Light of the Cold War and the Extension of the Common Market in Europe.*[16] The Clayton-Herter Report launched the Administration's program to obtain a new instrument for trade policy —the Trade Expansion Act.[17] Herter and Clayton observed, "The time has come for the United States to take a giant step." This giant step they envisaged as the opening of U.S. negotiations "for a trade partnership with the European Common Market, at the same time stressing the absolute necessity of enlarging the area." While the report also used the phrase "associating itself with the Common

Market," the Administration apparently interpreted both phrases to mean the lowering or elimination of tariffs between the two areas. Instead of the renewal of the Trade Agreements Act, the Administration proposed the Trade Expansion Act, authorizing the "across the board" reduction of duties on large categories of goods by as much as 50 percent, and the elimination of tariffs on all commodities or categories in which the Common Market and the United States together account for 80 percent or more of all world trade. (The effect of the latter provision depended crucially on the question of the admission of Great Britain to the Common Market. The French opposition to Britain's bid for entry early in 1963 cast a shadow upon the rationale of the Kennedy Administration's trade policy. Without inclusion of Great Britain, very few items qualify under the 80-percent-of-world-trade clause, which therefore becomes almost meaningless.) Subsequent to a considerable Congressional and national debate, the Trade Expansion Act was passed in October, 1962, by a handsome majority. It also included the kind of "industrial adjustment" provisions of which the Herter-Clayton Report had this to say:

It is frequently suggested that there be a Federal program to aid industries and workers, and even whole communities, injured by competing imports, to help them adjust to new ways of economic activity. We believe that the dislocations of labor or capital as a result of increased imports can be adjusted better by the affected parties than by the Government, but we would support a public program for extreme cases.

Although the Act, as passed, did not include the provision recommended by Herter and Clayton for elimination of tariffs for the underdeveloped countries, much of the intended purpose may be accomplished by the workings of the most-favored-nation clause, provided negotiations with the Common Market result in extensive tariff reductions.[18]

Two important limitations of the Act must be noted. First, the legislation is permissive only. It authorizes the executive to negotiate tariff reductions but does not guarantee success in tariff negotiations with a prosperous Common Market in the flush of rapid expansion and sheltered by a common protective tariff. Moreover, the common agricultural policy of the Six seems likely to curtail American access to the large and growing European market for agricultural products.

Second, negotiated tariff reductions seem to fall considerably short of "association" with the Common Market, an organization that is far more than a customs union. The achievement of real association would be difficult indeed, not simply because of economic differences to be ironed out, but also because of the political implications. While, in recent years, the United States has fully recognized, and on the whole accepted, the increasing interdependence of nations, matters impinging directly on national sovereignty remain a very delicate subject of political discourse. Certainly, even a modest curb on sovereign prerogatives would raise, in the United States, constitutional issues of great import.

Can the United States remain indifferent to a deterioration in its relative commercial position, while Western Europe—the second most advanced industrial region in the world, with a larger population than ours and a standard of living approaching ours—grows more rapidly? European growth reflects a more rapid rate of increase in worker productivity than that in the United States. Thus there is the danger that this country may lose the productivity advantage that for so long has made possible the high wages and standard of living of the American worker.[19] Another incentive, political rather than pecuniary, for joining in European economic growth is the logic of the Cold War. A North Atlantic Common Market, embracing all the Western European countries as well as the United States and Canada, would be by far the world's largest marketing area and industrial base. Its existence would postpone for many years, if not forever, the threat that the communist bloc economy may overtake that of the West. An Atlantic Common Market could marshal the superior resources of the Western world far more effectively, for the total economic power of the Alliance would be far greater than the sum of its parts.

The economic necessities of the postwar world, combined with the security threat posed by the communist bloc in the Cold War, impelled the West European drive toward political unity. The West Europeans chose functional, economic integration as a means toward such unity. As World War II recedes into the past, however, and people grow accustomed to living with the protracted threat from the East, longer-term factors have tended to become more important. For example, many Europeans have long recognized the tremendous advantages of mass production that have rendered mass markets indispensable. Unlike Balkanized Europe, the United States had long enjoyed a vast internal market. Great Britain derived similar benefits in the last century from a policy of free trade and from the vast empire guarded by her navy and linked politically and economically to the fiscal and political capital of London.

Since World War II, the advantages of mass markets have increased. New technological developments have triggered revolutions in transportation and communication that have helped to standardize tastes, ways of living and socioeconomic aspirations throughout Western Europe. The Common Market is providing a response to this uniformity of demand. The Common Market's success vindicates theories which stress the advantages of mass markets.[20] The Market's success and the trends it enhances are helping in turn to diminish ideological differences within and among European countries.

The basically individualistic nature of Western culture is mirrored in the politico-economic sphere by individual-oriented societies and consumer-oriented economies. West European countries have turned their recovery and burgeoning economic strength to satisfying the individual wants of their peoples. Even more than in the United States, the gross national product (GNP) of Western Europe has been allocated to consumption (including investment to support future consumption). Less than 5 percent of the gross national product is devoted to national security purposes—only half the proportion so allocated during the past decade by the United States and the Soviet Union.[21]

The United States, although its economy remains consumer-oriented, has demonstrated since 1950 a surprising degree of realization of the importance to the consumer of security in the Cold War. The United States has carried the major share of the defense of the Free World. Her annual military outlays are three times those of the rest of NATO put together.[22] Because of differing conceptions of strategy, discussed in preceding chapters, the military efforts of individual NATO partners do not complement one another and an even larger proportion of the actual effective defense is undoubtedly carried by the United States. Nevertheless, our NATO allies have become, collectively, almost an equal partner with the United States in terms of economic strength. The total of the GNP's of our NATO allies was, in 1962, approximately $330 billion, or 60 percent of that of the United States.[23] Because the official exchange rates on which this dollar comparison was based do not fully reflect the higher purchasing power of other currencies in their own countries, the relative size of the non-U.S. portion of the NATO economy was probably larger by as much as 20 to 30 percent than the dollar comparison suggests. In other words, the combined annual product of our allies may be 75 or 80 percent of ours, or more. Moreover, it is increasing faster than ours.

For psychological as well as economic reasons, it is important that the share of our NATO allies in the burden of Free World defense be more nearly proportional to their share in the total of Free World strength. It has already been pointed out that the total military efforts for the preservation of security need to be increased. Investment must be maintained and increased to insure future provision for both the security and the welfare of the peoples of the NATO countries. An increasing effort must be made to improve conditions in the underdeveloped countries of the world. It is therefore clear that the full resources of all the members of the Alliance should be brought to bear jointly on these common purposes. It is not less important psychologically that (1) the U.S. effort be sustained in part by a belief that the sharing of burdens is equitable and (2) our allies be drawn toward agreement on strategy by a sense of commitment engendered by participation in more egalitarian sacrifice. We do not intend here to raise doubts as to NATO's economic capacity to do whatever needs to be done. We have argued in an earlier volume that the U.S. could, if necessary, double its military efforts without even introducing direct economic controls and without curtailing the growth of the standard of living.[24] There is less slack in the economies of many of the other NATO countries than there is in the United States. Nonetheless, given the political will, much greater security efforts by the rest of NATO would be feasible without imposing direct controls or significant curtailment of consumption. Clearly, the issue is not one of economic, but of political, feasibility. Belief in the concept of equity—however difficult it may be to define—is an important element of political practicality. Such a belief, too, provides the necessary lubricant for NATO's military effort, for the requirements of an effective strategy confront many of the member nations with both obligation and incentive to take costly measures within their own borders.

Differences in the attitudes of the Allies on the two sides of the

Atlantic, as expressed in their respective economic strategies, suggest that their national objectives are not the same. But we took as our point of departure for this volume the cultural heritage of the West and the common need for constructing an institutional and political framework for the expression and pursuit of common future goals. It is these common goals that are of overriding importance, and the differences we have noted are differences of emphasis rather than of basic objectives. The consumer orientation of the Western economies remains a valid expression of the value placed on the individual in free societies. National policies within the Atlantic Community must be directed toward the preservation of an open society in all spheres—military, political and economic.

In the light of this requirement, what should U.S. economic policy be in the years ahead? We shall consider the relevant economic policies for the Community in six categories:

1. *Resources:* Economic policy must always seek to broaden the resource base and to increase the ability of member nations of the Alliance to allocate available resources to strategic purposes. (In the present case, Cold War strategy includes not only military preparedness, but also the strategy of aiding and training underdeveloped and uncommitted nations.)

2. *Institutions:* Military and political strategy, as we have seen, is anything but a matter of common agreement among the NATO members. Economic policy should support institutional arrangements that exploit political agreement on cooperative and integrative economic steps, the success of which can feed back to reinforce political accord. (This has actually happened within the Communities of the Six.) Such political accord is in turn vital to the reaching of agreement on military strategy.

3. *International payments:* Although public opinion tends to focus on the U.S balance-of-payments deficit, this issue can be dealt with only by an economic policy that addresses a broader range of questions, namely, those of international liquidity and the commercial and monetary policies of the members of the Alliance.

4. *Burden sharing:* The problem of sharing common burdens among the members of the Alliance has become of immediate concern to this country because of the balance-of-payments problem; but, in point of fact, it is of more fundamental importance with respect to the problem of achieving a concerted strategy. However,

increased shouldering of the burdens by the European members of NATO probably depends first and foremost on reaching a consensus on a credible and mutually acceptable strategy.

5. *Relations with the uncommitted nations:* The preceding four points dealt with U.S. relations with allies. The United States and Western Europe maintain an elaborate set of relations with the uncommitted nations of the world. It was noted in category 1 that the resource base and its allocation must include aid to the underdeveloped nations. Economic policy must consider as well the problems of trade with these nations, and the effect of all national and Western European Community policies and actions on the economies of the underdeveloped countries.

6. *Relations with the communist bloc:* The Atlantic Community must not become so concerned with its internal economic problems and its military relationships to the communist world that it overlooks the problems of developing effective economic policies toward the communist bloc. Such policies would presuppose a determination of both the means and the extent of economic warfare to be waged, in conjunction with a consideration of the effects on the bloc of all other Community policies and actions.

The remainder of this chapter will explore each of these six categories of Atlantic Community economic policy.

Expanding the Resource Base

Let us consider first the problem of the expansion of the resource base. The cooperative and integrative policies of the period of postwar European resurgence have contributed to high rates of growth. Although these rates have tended to slow down in the later stages of the recovery period, they are still impressively higher in Western Europe than in the United States, and compare favorably with the Soviet Union.[25] Further, it seems likely that this general ratio will continue during the coming decade. One of the sustaining forces of the high growth rate in Western Europe is the progressive reduction of institutional constraints on economic activity. Despite the dangers of competition from a unified Western Europe, U.S. policy must support the economic steps that further the breakdown of economic barriers and the strengthening of the economic base.

First on the agenda is to complete the elimination of intra-European trade barriers by the admission of Great Britain to the Common Market. (Others to be admitted eventually to full or associate membership will probably include the Scandinavian countries, Austria, Greece, Ireland, Portugal, Spain,[26] Turkey and Switzerland.) We have already alluded to the great political as well as economic difficulties remaining to be solved before such a widening of the Common Market can become a reality; in any event, the expansion of Common Market membership is not a problem for U.S. decision. More crucial in the long run is the question of U.S. policy if and when the membership of the Common Market is broadened. Will we eventually find ourselves applying for membership in the Common Market? We have already noted that the pressures to do so will be enormous. The passage of the Trade Expansion Act, while not so radical a departure as some suggest from the reciprocal trade agreements policy that has been in force for more than a quarter of a century, is nevertheless regarded as a first step toward some sort of partnership with the European Economic Community.[27]

There is a wide range of developments in the Common Market tending to break down economic barriers other than those of tariffs and similar restrictions on trade between nations. Whenever possible, the United States must be on the side of "liberalization" that restores freedom of trade in its most general sense and reduces limitations on economic growth, not of individual nations but of the Community as a whole.

Already under way in the Common Market are programs aimed at abolishing the very practices that tend to inhibit the free movement of labor. Indeed, the Community cannot realize its maximum potential unless labor mobility is high enough to permit workers to move from less to more prosperous areas. The first step was taken with the passage of regulations insuring that migrant workers in the Common Market would retain their social security rights when transferring to another member country. The United States position on international labor mobility lags far behind those of the European countries. But certainly it would be a most delicate matter in this country to suggest changing the legal limitations of the movement of labor into the U.S. Immigration quotas such as those maintained on the American books are basically incompatible with the concept of integration which has captivated European thinking during the last decade.

Consideration of policy in regard to social insurance automatically raises the question of taxes, since social insurance taxes represent a significant portion of total taxes. While in this country consideration of such matters may seem politically remote, the wide differences between United States and European tax structures, and the implications of these differences with respect to competitive positions, are being vigorously discussed. In particular, the much greater reliance of the United States on direct taxes—income taxes on persons and corporations—is undergoing a reappraisal.[28] During the coming years, trends toward some shift away from direct to indirect taxes on goods and services are likely to gain in strength and public favor.

Many are the legal and historical variations of the climate of enterprise among the members of the Community. Antitrust policy, for example, is one field in which increasing pressure for uniformity, and increasing response to such pressure, may be expected.[29] Perhaps the most important area in which structural variation could take place, however, is agriculture. The story of agriculture differs little from country to country. The demand for agricultural products is highly inelastic; that is, it changes very little in response to changes in price, and it grows only slowly, proportionately with the population, and less than proportionately with an increasing standard of living. The supply of agricultural products, on the other hand, is highly variable because of both the vagaries of weather and rapid technological changes. Prices determined by an inelastic demand and a variable supply tend to fluctuate widely. The farmer's economic status is therefore much more precarious than that of other producers, who can, typically, vary supply in line with demand and thus keep prices stable. Farmers tend, by virtue of their attachment to the land, to be established members of the community, wielding extensive political power. The typical response to this power, the establishment of subsidies to protect the farmer, is only too familiar in this country. The conservative political and social views of the farmer erect ideological barriers against movement into other occupations. Furthermore, disproportionate legislative power is often held by rural constituencies.

National variations on the farmers' power have led to different levels and methods of price support, different price levels for agricultural commodities and different degrees of protection by quantitative and tariff restrictions. Elimination of trade barriers within the EEC is, of course, not compatible with the maintenance of disparate price support levels. In January, 1962, the Common Market started to meet this problem by agreeing on a "Common Agricultural Policy." Uniform prices within the Community will be established above those of the relatively efficient French farmers but below those of the inefficient, high-cost West German farmers.

There will be a common price-support scheme, financed in a transitional period by a complex of "variable levies" on imports designed to equalize prices to the consumer throughout the Common Market.[30] The support prices will be well above those of the very efficient Commonwealth producers—Australia and New Zealand —which have enjoyed protected markets in Great Britain under Imperial Preference. This has been one of the major stumbling blocks to British entry into the Common Market, since the original members were reluctant to grant free entry to products of their efficient overseas competitors, and the British were reluctant to deny to Commonwealth countries the protection afforded by Imperial Preference. Instead, Great Britain sought to postpone the impact of the Market's common external tariff on the Commonwealth, while the Common Market members felt such postponement would jeopardize the position of their agriculture and the hard-won compromise among their own national agricultural groups. In addition, Great Britain stands to lose in the common-price support scheme, because as a heavy importer and a high-cost producer of agricultural goods, she might be paying far more than she would receive.

There seems to be little doubt that these economic difficulties in the negotiations with Britain have been magnified for political reasons. In other words, it is not the economic problems alone which have caused delay, for in themselves most of these economic problems are not insoluble. But issues of pure trade and economic interest have become intertwined with such political considerations as the French fear of British political power in an integrated Europe, and concern with the nature of the European nuclear defense, as well as wariness of the special relationship between the British and the United States, which might keep the British something less than wholly European in outlook.

It is difficult for Americans to give advice on what ought to be done in the agricultural field, in view of the unhappy record of the United States in maintaining the biggest subsidy scheme in all history (although it must be conceded that the subsidies have played a major role in the creation of the most efficient system of agriculture in the world). This country now finds itself, on the one hand, threatened by the Common Agricultural Policy and, on the other, tempted by the growing markets of a prosperous Europe, especially for luxury foods, tobacco and cotton. In time we shall have to "do something" to meet this problem. The prospect is far from hopeless. As the success in passing the Trade Expansion Act showed once again, since World War II it has been much easier to reach a consensus on international than on domestic matters. The first steps to be taken by the United States may be negotiation on tariffs and import quotas to reduce restrictions, especially on imports of French agricultural products, in return for concessions on U.S. exports.

One may suspect that the pattern and pace of more far-reaching changes will be set by the Common Market. More radical surgery has been proposed and, while the patient has demurred, continued discomfort may well lead him to reconsider. For example, Sicco Mansholt of the Netherlands outlined a cartel arrangement designed to accomplish the seemingly impossible, namely, the simultaneous representation of consumer and producer interests. Acting as a "monopsony," or single buyer, the cartel would purchase agricultural commodities at fixed, low prices. The price would be low enough to drive the inefficient farms out of production, and a fund would be established to help in the readjustment of those forced off the land. The cartel would also sell at relatively low prices, and funds would also be provided to help those countries, such as Great Britain, whose consumer prices would be raised. Surpluses would presumably persist, both because marginal farmers would be forced out only gradually and because productivity could be expected to continue to rise on the better farms; these surpluses would be used for aid to underdeveloped countries, much as under U.S. Public Law 480, or the "Food for Peace" program. It seems quite possible that the United States might participate in such a scheme without joining the Common Market. The political road would be difficult, but probably less so than that leading into the Common Market itself. Some rational solution to the problem produced by the program of agricultural subsidies and the consequent snowballing surpluses must be found.

We cannot counsel the Community on its economic growth without taking a look at our own house, which certainly needs putting in order. Since the Korean boom and the subsequent 1955–1957 consumer and capital goods boomlet, economic growth in this country has been painfully slow—less than 3 percent per year, only about 1 percent per capita per year. Unused resources have accumulated. Unemployment fluctuates between 5 percent and 7 percent, and excess capacity persists in many industries. Worst of all, the exploitation of technological progress has lagged, and the resource potential—as measured by actual output plus what could be produced by unemployed people and idle capacity—is much lower than it would be if investment were higher and new discoveries and inventions were put to work more rapidly. The slow growth rate in the United States is still the main drag on the growth of the Atlantic Community and, as noted above, bears vitally on the prospects of realizing the OECD's announced target of 50 percent growth in a decade.

Whatever steps may or may not be taken in concert with Western Europe, many corrective actions can and should be taken here at home. This is not the place to go into U.S. domestic economic policy in detail. Prescriptions for reform are not lacking, as, for example, tax reforms to increase incentives and to decrease deflationary burdens on the economy. While tax reform never comes so rapidly as administrations and economists would like, major reforms of the Federal tax structure, including some reductions, are expected in 1963. The Trade Expansion Act introduced a new approach to that resource-wasting, growth-depressing, escutcheon-blotting sin of our governmental system, the proliferation of subsidies. Subsidies are often necessary to redress inequities, but characteristically they tend to perpetuate the inefficiency thus protected and thus they not only persist but also grow in cost. The adjustment provisions of the Trade Expansion Act are designed to give subsidies to groups disadvantaged by changes in national policy; but these subsidies are to be tied to dynamic reactions, that is they are to be granted only for the transitional period of adjustment to new conditions rather than to perpetuate the status quo.[31] Such use of subsidies is not a new idea, and is not without danger; nevertheless the subsidy plan as advanced in connection with the Trade Expansion Act gives significant promise of increasing the dynamism of the country, of helping to eliminate industrial and geographic pockets of depression and of increasing the growth of the economy. Consideration should be given to extending the adjustment principle independently of the tariff negotiations, so that the shifting of resources out of declining industries may occur in anticipation of tariff reductions rather than simply as a reaction to such reductions. In particular, such a technique may offer promise as a solution to the growth-defeating phenomenon of featherbedding, so widespread in this country and so likely to be a continuing problem as automation works its dramatic effects on one industry after another.

A serious threat is also posed by a possible conflict involved in present monetary policy. This conflict stems primarily from the two somewhat paradoxical motives of present American monetary policy, namely: (1) the quest for economic growth; and (2) the attempt to right our balance-of-payments deficit. A possible solution to this problem may have been found in the change in 1961 of the policy of "bills only" by the Federal Reserve Board. Open market operations in both the long-term U.S. Government bond market and the short-term money market may provide a partial solution to the conflict of these two objectives of domestic monetary policy. If the Federal Reserve is successful in keeping the short-term rate on Treasury bills at a high point while keeping interest rates low in the long-term government bond market, a solution to the dilemma of domestic monetary policy might be in sight. This attempt is now being made by the Federal Reserve. A more far-reaching suggestion has been made by the Bank for International Settlements: as long as the United States has both unused resources and a payments deficit, the Federal Government should simultaneously support high interest rates and budgetary deficits, i.e., a conservative monetary and liberal fiscal policy.[32]

Economic Institutions for the Atlantic Community

We have already indicated the current problems besetting further development of the economic institutions of the Atlantic Community in what has become the main-tent show, the European Common Market. In the center ring, the British entry act is being played out.

The next act may well involve the United States. The United States is beset by a number of problems not too dissimilar to those of the United Kingdom, so that American trials and tribulations might resemble those of Britain:

1. This country, too, confronts a farm problem, although in our case the focus is almost entirely on exports rather than on imports. The difficulties of penetrating the EEC's common external tariff counsel American farmers to enter the tent. However, under the Common Agricultural Policy (or some version of the Mansholt Plan), the United States would be likely to contribute much more than it would receive in financing the agricultural program. This circumstance might create opposition. It may also be noted that no foreseeable reduction of agricultural prices could be substantial enough to reduce significantly marginal farming in this country.

2. The United States' conflict of loyalties would resemble those of Great Britain and the Commonwealth. Our special relationship to Japan and the Latin American countries would make it very difficult for us to become full members of an Atlantic Common Market that left our friends outside its tariff wall. Extreme differences in both levels of economic development and cultural patterns make it unlikely that Latin America and Japan could or would become full members of such a Common Market, although some form of associate membership might be feasible at some time in the future.

3. Finally, the United States will find it even more agonizing than has the United Kingdom to face up to the question of yielding an element of sovereignty to a Common Market organization. One can only hope that national debate will, over a period of years, produce rational solutions, and that the issue will not be shelved, as it was in Great Britain, until a relative decline in national power, wealth and prestige compels action.

However, attention to the main issues should not completely divert us from subsidiary ones. The OECD already includes the United States and Great Britain (and, on a major committee, Japan). As a purely cooperative rather than an integrative body, the OECD has less importance than the Common Market. Nevertheless it may be expected to play a vital role in the coordination of economic policy among the nations and nation groups of its membership, especially in the field of aid to the underdeveloped countries, which will be discussed separately. Suffice it to say here that the United States, which played a leading role in setting up the organization, should press for maximum use of the tools provided by the OECD.

A possible economic organizational alternative to the OECD is NATO. Article II of the North Atlantic Treaty provides that:

the parties will contribute toward the further development of peaceful and friendly international relations by strengthening their free institutions, by bringing about a better understanding of the principles upon which these institutions are founded, and promoting conditions of stability and well being. They will seek to eliminate conflict in their international economic policies, and will encourage economic collaboration between any or all of them.

There has been a long debate within NATO as to the extent to which the organization should broaden its activities under this article. The direct concern of NATO in such matters as production and labor mobility is clear, and there can be little question of its concern with the broader questions of economic growth, trade and promotion of the growth and welfare of underdeveloped countries. The stake of the organization in assisting the less developed countries and areas within its own territories (e.g., southern Italy) has also been pointed out. It has been argued that NATO could gain political support by showing a greater interest and activity in these areas. The North Atlantic Council, meeting at the level of heads of government in December, 1957, issued a communiqué which included the following paragraph:

We have decided that the North Atlantic Council, without duplicating the work of other agencies, shall from time to time, and in the spirit of Article 2 of the treaty, review economic trends and assess economic progress, and make suggestions for improvements either through existing organizations or by the efforts of individual countries, or in special cases by new initiatives.[33]

In order to carry out this decision of the heads of government, the NATO Council in 1958 created the Committee of Economic Advisers.

In general, the debate has been resolved in favor of those who argue that NATO should not deal with broad economic problems, and that neutrals should be encouraged to participate in their solution rather than be driven off by NATO's plainly military connotations. It seems likely that it will continue to be NATO policy to rely on individual members in their respective capacities as members of other organizations to handle economic matters.

Whether developing economic institutions will in the coming years act as a helpful catalyst for, or a hindrance to, political cooperation across the sea remains to be seen. A trend toward regional political unification within the Community is already manifest. Such partial unification exercises potentially divisive effects, as it may substitute two or three strong members of the Alliance for a larger number in which one dominates the others. This phenomenon, of course, has manifested itself in Allied disunity on military and political strategy as well as in the economic sphere. The ultimate role of economic integration is in part a function of policies on strategic and political matters, as has been discussed in other chapters. Timing is also critical. If the United States tarries, as did the United Kingdom, in attempting to come to terms with the Common Market, the making of an Atlantic political unity may be delayed. The gap between the strength of Western Europe and that of the United States at the close of World War II has been almost closed economically and politically, though not militarily. But the United States would be foolish to forfeit the leadership it exercised in bringing about the recovery of Europe. The United States pioneered economic cooperation, but has participated only indirectly in the integration movement that was the lineal descendant of economic cooperation.

The Ebb and Flow of Gold

We have noted earlier that, with or without economic integration, the United States has the resources and economic flexibility to support any foreseeable Cold War strategies, military or nonmilitary. One apparent contradiction to this conclusion appears to have arisen in recent years. We refer, of course, to the balance-of-payments deficit, which became serious in 1958 when it jumped to $3.5 billion from a small surplus in 1957. Although the deficit approached $4 billion in 1959 and 1960, it declined to $2.5 billion in 1961, and less in 1962.

The immediate postwar period was characterized by a balance-of-payments deficit—but at that time a deficit for the Western European countries. Now the shoe is on our foot. Unlike the Europeans, we cannot turn to a wealthier ally for help. (But, also unlike the Europeans in the late 1940's, we have large gold reserves; and, in fact, we have received some help from Western Europe in bringing the deficit down from its peak.)

The deficit is not, in truth, a real constraint on our ability to meet our Cold War commitments and objectives. An occasional small balance-of-payments deficit of, say, $1 to $1.5 billion (the level once more being approached) is not inconsistent with the increasing volume of world trade and the use of the dollar as the principal reserve currency of world markets. The psychological climate has been, however, greatly altered by the larger deficits of the last five years. These deficits have "undermined confidence," as the saying goes, and have weakened the American political position vis-à-vis Europe much more than appears justified by the intrinsic significance of the figures.

The only thing that seems to disturb people more than "burying gold at Fort Knox" appears to be taking gold out of Fort Knox. When the payment deficit began to increase, a portion of it was settled in gold; that is, Europeans demanded gold for some of their dollar balances. The payments deficit and the flow of gold from the United States were further aggravated by European withdrawals of short-term investments in this country—"hot money" moving toward Europe as it had moved toward the U.S. in the forties, when our large gold stocks were being built up. An average of $1.3 billion of gold left the United States from 1958 through 1961, reducing stocks from almost $23 to little over $16 billion (mid-1962).[34] These stocks are still tremendous—nearly 40 percent of the Free World supply and larger in proportion to total annual imports than the gold reserves of any other Free World country except Switzerland. Unfortunately, however, the situation is complicated by our own domestic policy of earmarking some $12 billion of the gold as backing for domestic Federal Reserve obligations, so that only about $4 billion remains as apparent reserve against nearly $20 billion of short-term obligations to foreign countries. The Congress could change this provision overnight by eliminating the domestic reserve requirement; but all concerned hesitate, quite rightly, to recommend this action in the midst of a crisis in confidence, for fear of aggravating the crisis. However, such action should be taken at an opportune moment.

Before considering the measures that have already reduced the deficit and measures that might prevent such a crisis in the future, let us examine the factors that have given rise to it. The common view, which may reflect intentional statistical distortions, tends to exaggerate surpluses created by the favorable balance of the private sector, that is, the excess of exports over imports of goods and services. The exports of U.S. goods and services on strictly private commercial account are not traditionally separated from those financed by U.S. Government expenditures in the official data published by the Department of Commerce. Instead, aggregate exports and imports are shown in a single figure, implying that they are wholly commercial, while U.S. Government payments for military programs and for economic assistance are shown separately. Thus it has appeared that the favorable balance of trade and services has been in the neighborhood of $6 billion in most recent years. This has been more than offset by capital investments abroad of some $3 billion and U.S. military and economic expenditures abroad of some $5 to $6 billion, which, with some miscellaneous transactions and short-term capital movements, have accounted for deficits of $3 billion or so. It can be demonstrated, however, that a large part of government loans, grants and direct expenditures abroad go to finance almost immediate expenditures in this country. Taking account of this factor, net government expenditures abroad can be seen to have been only about $3 billion in recent years, and the commercial balance on goods and services to be, in effect, only about $3 to $4 billion instead of $6 to $7 billion here.[35]

Nevertheless, the adverse balance of payments has tended to be blamed exclusively on our overseas programs, and pressure has been generated for reducing our commitments. One of the last actions of the Eisenhower Administration was, in fact, to inaugurate a program of actions to reduce our commitments without cutting our effective military establishment abroad, by such steps as halting the sending abroad of additional dependents of military personnel. The new Administration rescinded these cuts, persuaded that the military personnel were being made to assume unfairly the burden of national financial problems and that "bringing the wives and children home" tended to affect adversely the credibility of our defense commitment. An extensive program was launched, however, to reduce the deficit by a wide range of actions, big and little, from reducing customs exemptions for tourists and appealing to overseas military personnel to "buy American," through drives to increase tourism in America and exports by American industry, to bilateral arrangements for accelerated repayment of U.S. loans and for purchases of arms in the United States by our allies, notably West Germany and France. In the purely monetary sphere, the U.S. took unilateral action by establishing appropriate interest rates. In addition, eight European countries and Japan participated with the United States in setting up a reserve fund of $6 billion of hard currency (no longer confined to the dollar) to be used to prevent runs on the dollar, that is, hot money withdrawals and other demands for conversion of dollar balances into gold. As the figures show, this program has borne spectacular results.

Thus far, corrective measures have all been essentially short-range in nature. American policy should take a longer view. One country's deficit is always another country's surplus, but the positions are not always the same. The Continent's deficit of a decade ago has shifted to the United States, with Britain continuing in a debtor position. The positions five or ten years hence are not predictable. It is clear, however, that greater stability would strengthen the economies of the Atlantic Community.

In the language of the economist, the long-run problem is one of maintaining the liquidity of the member nations. According to one theory, widely held in Europe, a basic liquidity problem exists because the production of gold has not kept pace with the growth of international trade.[36] This diagnosis seems to suggest that the price of gold should be increased so that existing supplies can take care of current needs. However, increasing the price of gold means devaluing currencies. In the present context, this would mean devaluing the dollar. While this solution is often suggested, it is firmly and rightly rejected by the U.S. Government.[37] The refusal to devalue the dollar is dictated, not simply by distaste for the deflationary internal effects, the "belt-tightening," that it is intended to bring about, but also by the conviction that devaluation would not be an effective remedy to the liquidity crisis. In the first place, such action would aggravate the crisis by further weakening confidence in what is still the world's largest economy. In the second place, it is probable that devaluation of the dollar would be more or less immediately offset by the devaluation of other Western currencies. If all Western currencies were devaluated and relative positions left unchanged, existing deficits would presumably continue or perhaps be aggravated by the side effects, namely, the loss of confidence. A temporary gain would probably be realized by the Soviet Union, which would find its gold stocks increased in value in terms of Western currencies and might be able to make bargain purchases.

But, if we cannot take the simple course of devaluation, there are things which can be done with the mechanisms of international exchange. In the Free World, the institutional arrangements for international payments are centered in and coordinated by the International Monetary Fund (IMF). The Bank for International Settlements, established in 1930, continues to be a focal point for consultation between central banks of the main North Atlantic countries.

This institutional framework was erected for the most part in the early postwar period. The IMF was established as a lender of last resort to countries having balance-of-payments difficulties.[38] Its financial resources, consisting of gold and holdings in the currencies of its sixty-nine members, were increased substantially in 1959 and now stand at $14.5 billion. Still, the IMF does not participate directly and immediately in day-to-day operations relating to payments problems, and many countries hesitate to resort to IMF resources. Moreover, in the period since the IMF was established in 1947, world trade has more than doubled in financial volume. With this increase and the achievement of greater freedom in international transactions has come a natural tendency for wider fluctuations in payments balances. In combination with the slower rate at which new gold is produced and placed in official reserves (only about 3 percent a year), these factors have caused an increasing need for a supplement to gold for international reserves and for international settlements. Since World War II, this need has been filled almost entirely by the use of U.S. dollars as the world's major international currency.

The use of particular currencies to supplement gold as the main medium of international settlement, however, must at some time create problems for the currencies so honored. As the holdings of foreigners in these currencies are built up to meet the rising need abroad for reserves to cope with seasonal or cyclical fluctuations in trade and payments and the secular rise in world trade, the resulting rise in the short-term liabilities of the countries whose currencies are used must soon exceed their own available international reserves. The major international currencies—in particular the dollar—may become increasingly vulnerable to speculative or other uncertainties, with the result that the entire international financial structure may be subjected to heavy strains.

Perhaps the most widely known proposal for relieving these pressures has been advanced by Professor Triffin, who suggests that both internationalization of reserves and a sharp increase in international liquidity are urgently required for the period ahead. The essence of his plan is that countries should agree to transfer to the IMF, in exchange for a claim on the Fund, a portion of their short-term assets in other currencies.[39] As the scheme came into full operation, a progressively greater internationalization of this type would occur. In this manner, the IMF would become not so much a lender of last resort as an International Central Bank. Triffin's proposals also envisage enlarged borrowing and drawing rights on the IMF for member countries. One result of these steps, it is hoped, would be a greater "efficiency" in the utilization of international reserves, with a consequent reduction in the total amount of such reserves needed. Another result would be to place a "buffer" (the IMF) between the users of reserves and the countries whose currencies are used as reserves, thus reducing financial pressures on them.

Considerable controversy has arisen over the basic premise on which Triffin's ideas rest, i.e., whether the more pressing problem is the adequacy of total world liquidity or the maldistribution of existing reserves among specific countries. The IMF itself, in the person of its managing director, Per Jacobsson, has indicated an inclination to support the latter view. Moreover, both Jacobsson and Edward M. Bernstein (formerly a senior official of the IMF) have proposed alternatives to the Triffin plan; their proposals do not envisage extensive international reserves or provide for the degree of expansion in reserves inherent in the Triffin scheme. Jacobsson and Bernstein suggest, in effect, that the existing borrowing powers of the IMF be used to borrow from surplus countries (e.g., Germany), thus creating additional resources for lending to deficit countries (e.g., the United States or Great Britain).[40] One primary virtue of this approach is a purely tactical one: It would not involve so radical a departure from existing arrangements as the Triffin plan, and, apparently, it would not require any new legislative or other enabling acts.

Sir Oliver Franks and Lord Radcliffe, in tacit agreement with Professor Triffin, have proposed that the IMF be authorized to accept from its members deposits which it would treat as reserves. Under this plan, deposits would also be created by the Fund's lending operations. This plan, while aimed at solving the short-run problem of the stability of the key currencies, also seeks to change the nature of the monetary structure of the Atlantic Community through a change in the nature of the liquid reserves held by each member.[41]

A plan for a Community-wide payments union has been suggested, envisaging the creation of a new form of reserve. Under this plan, the members of OECD (plus Japan and possibly Australia and New Zealand) would form a clearing, or payments, union similar to the successful European Payments Union. Deficits and surpluses of the members in ordinary accounts would be settled at an agreed ratio (e.g., one-half or two-thirds) in gold or foreign exchange acceptable to the payee (surplus nation). The remainder would be settled in the form of debits and/or credits on the books of the clearing union. Destabilizing short-term capital movements, however, would be settled entirely in debits or credits in the union. Credit balances in the union would serve as a form of reserves. The scheme would provide an automatic, though only partial, credit offset for any deficit, thus reducing the amount of reserves needed.[42]

This proposal for an OECD Payments Union would serve to strengthen the OECD as an organization of the Atlantic Community. Moreover, management of the Payments Union would be considerably strengthened by virtue of being placed in, or associated with, the Community organization that is responsible for the coordination of development problems within the North Atlantic area. The OECD has a marked advantage over the IMF as a locus for such a union, for the OECD is composed of nations experienced in cooperation and almost all highly developed, whereas the IMF includes practically the full range of noncommunist countries—large and small, developed and less developed, ably governed and badly governed.

An additional source of easing the balance-of-payments problem should be noted, although it in no way lessens the desirability of a long-term solution of the sort we have been discussing. In 1961, both the United States and the United Kingdom held, in addition to each other's currencies, German marks, French francs, Dutch guilders and Italian lire as foreign reserves. This is a start toward diffusion of the pressures on currencies held as international reserves. In the event of the creation of a common European currency a major new world currency would come into being. This step is already being widely discussed. After the entry of Britain and others into the Common Market a common currency and a common tax structure might eventually have to be introduced. A common currency would unquestionably simplify life within the Common Market. It would effectively prevent any tendency to backslide in the unification of many other policies and it would greatly enhance the feelings of integration and economic as well as political solidarity. A common currency would have an impact on international payments arrangements and on the payments position of the United States. One of the functions of such a currency would be to provide a strong store of international reserves. It would be stronger than most of the individual currencies it would absorb, and it would thus take pressure off the dollar.

This solution is consistent with current thinking within the U.S. Government. Under Secretary of the Treasury Robert Roosa, commenting on the initial steps which must be taken to strengthen the Community financial system, said:

At the same time it is conceivable that work can go forward through this and other organs of the OECD toward preparing the way for the next stage of practicable and foreseeable innovations in the area of international financial arrangements—the fusing of the United Kingdom into the Common Market; the evolution of a unified financial mechanism to serve the expanded Common Market; and the forging of appropriate operating and policy links between that organization, once it emerges, and our own financial institutions.[43]

In the history of economic integration, the bold vision of yesterday has brought forth the well-tested institution of today. Thus the quest for currency stability might well lead, first to improved payments mechanisms, then to a common currency for the Common

Market, and finally to the merger of the Common Market currency with the dollar and an Atlantic currency.

One other major possibility for relief of the U.S. situation remains to be considered. We have seen that the balance-of-payments problem is soluble in both the short and the long run and should not be regarded as a real constraint on our present obligations to the Free World. Nevertheless the very existence of the U.S. balance-of-payments problem attests to the success of our policies of the last decade and a half in making possible the re-establishment of strong Western European economies. This outcome means that there are now others well able to share in these obligations. The pressure in this country to establish a fuller measure of "burden sharing" stems in large part from the balance-of-payments problem. Measures such as those proposed by monetary experts could go a long way toward solving the liquidity problem. Yet other considerations argue much more forcibly for a larger measure of burden sharing as an immediate remedy to the problems created by the adverse U.S. payments balance.

Sharing the Burdens

NATO was founded on the conviction that the price of liberty must always be vigilance. This means vigilance to provide for the needs and the security of all members of the open society. The Atlantic Community, being more secure in its own freedom than the underdeveloped nations of the Free World, by virtue of its wealth, political institutions and military power, bears the burden of leadership. The Community must carry not only the burdens of caring for its own people, but also those of improving the lot of its less developed fellow nations. Thus it must defend the indivisible security of all against totalitarian aggression.

The degree of acceptance of the obligations of freedom is not uniform within the Community. We have seen that the military defense of the Free World rests largely on American shoulders. Less disproportionately, the obligation to assist the underdeveloped areas has also been borne largely by the United States.[44]

The unequal distribution of the load has always been offensive to the strong, if vaguely formulated, sense of equity of the American people. This resentment has deepened under the prod of the balance-of-payments deficit. But there are more important reasons for working out better ways of sharing the burden. Successful defense of freedom depends on the soundness of the defense strategy and on the competence and energy expended in its prosecution. Since the burden of risk is shared by all, each has some role in the Community strategy, whether voluntary or not. The success of the strategy depends on the degree to which each participant accepts and plays its respective role. Only to the extent that the members of a group feel themselves contributing to the common effort do they participate in that moral consensus which is the prerequisite of great undertakings.

The acceptance of burdens to be borne in common issues from the formulation of an acceptable strategy, one that the participants view as credible—that is, feasible in performance and promising in effect. We have offered the outline of such a strategy in Chapter 3; we can now consider the economic aspects of recent changes in burden sharing, and the role of economic and military institutions in bringing about such changes.

The determination of equity is not simple. The present measure of equity in the sharing of military burdens within NATO, though not fully explicit, is based on two concepts: (1) the share of total resources devoted to defense, that is, military expenditures as a percent of gross national product; and (2) relative affluence, that is, standard of living, or GNP per capita, on the assumption that the rich can afford to pay higher proportions of their income than the poor. In application, we have seen that these criteria are acknowledged more in the breach than in the observance. The United States spends almost 10 percent of its GNP on national security and the rest of NATO, on the average, less than 5 percent—a ratio inconsistent with the fact that the standard of living and the per capita GNP of other members of NATO are approaching our own. This is particularly true of the richer nations of Europe, including the first three of the "Big Four"—England, Germany, France and Italy.

Reliance on a kind of progressive-taxation concept was perhaps relevant in the early days of NATO, when U.S. ability to pay was overwhelmingly greater than that of its allies. Today, this concept is outmoded. Not only is it inapplicable, but it fails to take account of significant variables. One of these is what may be called economic slack. In some of the countries of the Alliance, there are unused resources which could be put to work at no "opportunity cost," that is, no sacrifice of real alternative uses. In particular, there is unused manpower—unemployed labor in Italy, Canada, Belgium, Portugal, Turkey and even Denmark, as well as in the United States. The employment of the unemployed and of other unused resources would stimulate the economies of these countries and thus both directly and indirectly increase the total resources of the Alliance. Obviously, the total military force of the Alliance cannot be recruited entirely from the surplus manpower countries, but unemployment, and perhaps total available manpower of military ages, certainly might be taken into account in NATO negotiations as one element in determining how burdens should be shared. Other countries have still other available resources such as industrial capacity and gold and foreign exchange reserve. This suggests that the classical economic law of comparative advantage[45] might have very useful application in burden-sharing formulas, giving one country credit for greater than proportional manpower contributions, another for extra contributions to those military supplies which must be procured externally with foreign exchange, and still another perhaps for the making available of land for training or development purposes. (The last is not without precedent in various bases-for-aid arrangements.)

These principles can and should also be employed in negotiating the distribution of the burden of foreign aid. National contributions to a foreign aid pool should reflect many factors in addition to wealth and the availability of foreign exchange. Certainly, agricultural surpluses should be taken into account, as they presently are by the United States. Technical manpower is an important asset and an avenue by which some of the small but highly developed nations may make their maximum contribution. Israel is setting an example which should inspire emulation by Switzerland, the Scandinavian countries and Austria. Even the underdeveloped countries that are recipients of aid have contributions to make by providing land, men, transportation and maintenance services. Both general and particular resource requirements and availabilities may be affected by the interactions among military assistance, economic aid and indigenous military and investment expenditures. Allowance for such effects should be made.

Burden-sharing formulas will always be arrived at by political negotiation, but greater attention to the appropriate economic factors can strongly influence the course of political negotiation. The United

States can make a contribution to the military efficiency, the economic development and the political progress of the Atlantic Community if it does its homework in analyzing the economic criteria and arming its representatives in NATO and the OECD with carefully prepared negotiating positions.

Efforts to optimize burden sharing need not rely wholly on moral suasion in formal negotiation sessions. Tangible incentives need not be regarded as immoral incentives. On the contrary, we should seek to expand participation by a variety of means. For example, there has been insufficient exploration of the potential benefits of possible financial arrangements for the pooling of resources in NATO research, development and procurement programs. There is general recognition among NATO countries of the advantages of standardization and joint logistics in military programs, but there is great reluctance to be guided by criteria other than the attainable share of contracts for one's own industrial plants and the share of military assistance obtainable from the United States. It seems entirely possible, however, to work out a financial pooling scheme for a portion of the cost of research, development and production of agreed-upon NATO defense weapons systems. Such a scheme would offer premiums or subsidies to successful bidders on specific items, with each country contributing to the premiums paid for procurements, even if these are procured from other countries. Such a scheme could maximize contributions by dividing effort along the lines dictated by comparative advantage. To the extent that it induced joint planning and participation in common programs, the scheme would maximize the ability of NATO collectively to direct national activities to conform with NATO objectives rather than with independent national strategies.[46]

Much remains to be done in this area. A successful approach to burden sharing holds promise, not just for the limited objective of alleviating the United States payments deficit, but also for the much greater and longer-term goal of helping the nations of the Community to reach agreement on matters of military and economic strategy, and to expand the scope and effectiveness of their respective efforts.

Success in burden sharing can be an important step in the making of a real Community. A fully developed Common Market, coextensive with a political and military Atlantic Community, would obviate the need for burden sharing or, rather, would make burden sharing automatic within the Community, as it is today in the United States.

The Community and the Rest of the Free World

The external economic relationships of the Atlantic Community involve various kinds of contact with both the Western-oriented and the uncommitted nations outside of the communist bloc. With the primary exceptions of Japan, Australia and New Zealand—who in many nongeographic respects are logically members of the Atlantic Community—these nations are relatively undeveloped. Community economic relations with these countries must for two reasons always be oriented toward improving the level of their development. This orientation is imperative, as we have seen, because of the obligation of a free society to insure and enhance the economic and cultural security of all its members. Such an orientation is made more urgent within the framework of coexistence, peaceful or otherwise, with the communist world.

Direct development assistance is the most obvious and clear-cut channel of economic contact between the Community and the other free countries. For a long time to come, it will be a one-way channel for the transfer of large amounts of capital, both physical and educational (technological, administrative and cultural), from the highly developed, i.e., highly capitalized, to the less developed nations. This transfer may be accomplished by many means, ranging from aid grants through loans for business investment to technical assistance. Because of this variety in the means of transfer, we cannot measure the precise rate of flow of capital through this channel. At this time, it amounts to more than $5 billion a year, but there is general agreement that, in terms of their needs and ability to absorb and utilize the capital, the underdeveloped countries could well receive considerably more, perhaps double the current rates. According to Barbara Ward, the irreducible requirements approximate one percent of the gross national products of the developed nations of the Free World. This figure is close to $10 billion, an impressive amount, yet one that may soon prove inadequate. If all forms of subsidy and commercial investment, in addition to grants and loans, are taken into account, the flow of capital may soon be approaching the figure of $10 billion. Far more will be needed to sustain per capita economic growth rates high enough to demonstrate progress in wiping out the now widening, provocative, destabilizing, threatening discrepancy in the welfare of the rich nations and the poor nations.

We have already discussed the need for a wider sharing of the burden of aid requirements. Wider acceptance of the obligation would, or will, reinforce the need for multilateral planning and administration of aid. The advantages of cooperative effort in this field are manifold:

1. Recipient nations are likely to feel less political pressure from group assistance than from unilateral programs. By the same token, multilateral programs are less vulnerable to communist attack on the ground of selfish interest, imperialism, deprivation of national independence, corruption and so on. More important still, group assistance can establish more rational economic criteria for the giving and monitoring of aid than can a single donor.

2. Multilateral programs can be coordinated to avoid the risks of waste or outright harm by duplication, irrational priorities of projects, incompatibility of independent projects and competition among Allied donors.

3. Cooperative efforts can make available to the recipient nations a broader array of physical and technological resources and planning guidance.

Within the Atlantic Community, collective efforts in sharing the burden of foreign aid have thus far been of limited scope, but the need has been recognized. Two institutions have evolved to date. The Development Fund for Associated Overseas Territories was set up by the European Economic Community in 1958. We have referred earlier to the Development Assistance Committee (DAC) of the OECD (which succeeded DAG, the Development Assistance Group associated with the OEEC).

The ten-nation DAC is the broadest of these organizations, and appears at this time to be the logical organization for the long-range planning of Community aid. Though still largely a paper organization, DAC's potential is great. Barbara Ward has proposed that there be attached to the OECD a number of *ad hoc* organizations—banks, development funds, trade groups, common markets, statistical services and, above all, policymaking committees. In this institutional framework, DAC can appraise the needs of the underdeveloped world as a whole and country by country; weigh the abilities of each member nation to contribute aid quantitatively and qualitatively; evolve workable burden-sharing formulas; plan development programs; and set operating policies for the administration of assistance.

More limited in scope than that envisioned for the OECD, the EEC has nevertheless proceeded farther along the road from cooperation to integration of development assistance programs. In the first place, the EEC Development Fund is specifically intended for the development of the Associated Overseas Territories.[47] Within the EEC, the capitalization and voting arrangements governing the Development Fund (from 1958 to 1963) reflect interesting political compromises among the members:

Contribution to EEC
Development Fund[48]

Country	(In Millions)	Number of Votes
Germany	$200	33
France	200	33
Belgium	70	11
Netherlands	70	11
Italy	40	11
Luxembourg	1.25	1
	$581.25	100

The voting is directly but not proportionately related to contributions, except for the small advantage given Italy. The heaviest contributions are from France, which had until recently the most extensive colonial obligations, and Germany, which had none. This is in line with the concession that Germany made in the basic arrangements for the association of former dependencies of the members of the EEC. On the other hand, Italy's contribution is significantly smaller, a concession by the Community in recognition of Italy's own domestic problems of regional underdevelopment.

From the EEC Fund, the former dependencies of France are granted $511 million; of Belgium, $30 million; of the Netherlands, $35 million; and of Italy, $5 million.[49] This is a statutory allocation, out of which most of the first 50 percent of the grants actually released has gone to the former French dependencies.[50] Since the contributions to the Fund covered a period of over five years, the total amount is relatively small. Nevertheless this is a good illustration of the effectiveness of an integrated institution in reaching an agreement that supersedes the dictates of purely national interest.

Far more difficult problems lie ahead in the planning and administration of intangible aid—that is, aid in the form of technical assistance and educational development rather than of physical resources. Because the monetary amounts involved are likely to be much smaller, however, the political problems of reaching international agreements may be less difficult. The United States, which pioneered "Point Four" technical assistance fifteen years ago, should take leadership in pushing assistance programs within DAC. The smaller advanced nations, who are often closer to the problems of the developing nations, may have much to contribute to DAC programs. Hence membership in the DAC forum should be broadened, since, unfortunately, the largest capital-exporting nations are not always those that inspire the developing nations with the greatest confidence in the donor's motivations.

The big missing element in present plans for Community aid to the underdeveloped nations is an effective plan to stimulate the *recipient's* cooperation that made the Marshall Plan such a resounding success and such an effective progenitor of further successes. In large measure this reflects the vastly less adequate political and administrative preparation of the underdeveloped nations, as compared with those of Western Europe, for the tasks and responsibilities of cooperation. But the Community—starting in DAC—can offer persistent leadership in furthering preparation for and successive steps in economic cooperation by the recipient nations. Effective Community political and strategic policies can go far to induce underdeveloped nations to participate in cooperative organizations.

It is also important to note that both the United States and other Atlantic nations unilaterally and the Community collectively, as it develops its organs of economic policy, can do much to minimize aid needs by encouraging private investment in underdeveloped areas. Such steps as guarantees of convertibility and against expropriation, and expansion of economic information services, can be important in increasing the propensity to invest in Free World lands outside the Community.

The Atlantic Community's economic obligations to the rest of the Free World are not confined to those of a donor or a lender (of technology and culture as well as money and physical resources). The Community also incurs all the normal obligations of a partner in trade. Indeed, the effectiveness of development aid is in considerable measure dependent on the nature and effectiveness of existing and potential trade relations with the underdeveloped countries.

Trade is and has been the principal and traditional source of capital for underdeveloped countries. It can be a means of converting savings into investment. Exportable surpluses from the extractive industries or agriculture—raw materials and tropical foods—can be exchanged for imports of capital as well as consumer goods. There is also a feedback effect: development stimulated by trade or aid creates additional productive capacity (usually in light manufactures) that requires outlets in the markets of the more developed countries. If these outlets are closed, development may be interrupted or seriously inhibited. To keep them open may require far-reaching changes in the economic structure of the developed nations.

The principal means by which countries may close or narrow outlets for other countries is, of course, the imposition of tariffs, sometimes supplemented by import quotas. With respect to agricultural and extractive products, present policies in the Atlantic Community are far from uniform. The Common Market admits primary products duty-free from its associated states, i.e., chiefly the former French colonies in Africa, but levies tariffs on imports from all other areas. Similarly, the United Kingdom grants free entry to the products of the Commonwealth nations but levies tariffs on imports from all others.[51] The United States, to insure nondiscriminatory treatment, applies the most-favored-nation principle (according to which a tariff concession granted to any country is granted to all).

For light manufactures (toys, textiles, etc.), the situation is somewhat more unfavorable to the less developed nations. The Common Market, again, allows free entry of these products from the associated territories, while erecting high barriers against imports from other sources. Commonwealth preference has dictated British policy. For the United States, because many of its indigenous light manufacturing industries find it difficult to compete with those of the underdeveloped nations, the importation of these products has caused knotty problems. The conflict between the pressures of domestic producers and the exigencies of international relations has given rise to ambivalent attitudes in American policy and, in general, has been resolved to the disadvantage of foreign producers.

Perhaps the most serious problem in the category of light manufactures is that of textiles, in which the Western industries have been suffering greatly under the competition of the very cheap producers in Japan, Hong Kong and India. Threatened increases in tariffs (particularly by the United States, which was feeling the effect of imports from Italy and some other parts of Europe, as well as Asia) were averted last year by the signing at Geneva of two International Textile Agreements by a majority of the Atlantic Community nations. This agreement substituted import quotas for tariffs and provided for gradual increases in these quotas—generally 5 percent per year—to soften the impact. In short, the importing nations agreed to share the burden of providing markets for developing countries.

The textile agreements provide a good model for cooperative arrangements in a field in which the problems are bound to increase. Such agreements must be recognized, however, for what they are: interim, compromise solutions. For both primary and secondary products, the United States should continue to press unremittingly for the elimination of discrimination, the application of the most-favored-nation principle and the maximum practicable reduction of trade barriers.

But the conditions of entry into Atlantic markets are only a part of the trade problem of the underdeveloped areas. More crucial is the problem of the demand for, and prices of, their primary products. The wide cyclical variations in both prices and quantities of primary commodities sold make the economies of the underdeveloped countries very unstable. Instability inhibits progress and increases vulnerability to both internal and external pressures. The impact of fluctuating prices on the primary-product-dependent underdeveloped nations is so great that it may, as some experts hold, have cost these nations more in recent years than the value of economic aid they have received.

The causes of this cyclical fluctuation are well known. First, in the short run, both the supply and demand of primary products are highly inelastic. The most important destabilizing influence upon the price structure is the business cycle in the industrial countries. It is a characteristic of this cycle that the demand for raw materials varies even more widely than the over-all business index. While there are other causes of price variation, such as the weather in the supplying countries, the primary importance of variation in demand has been shown by studies indicating that prices and quantities demanded generally move in the same direction.

Some attempts have been made to handle this problem for specific commodities by means of international stabilization agreements. Under the International Wheat Agreement, for example, the consuming nations agree each year to accept given quotas at a fixed minimum price, with an option to accept additional quantities at a lower price; the producing nations agree to provide equivalent quotas at a fixed maximum price, with the option of providing more at a lower maximum. A more direct approach to the heart of the problem is provided in the International Tin Agreement, which provides for the accumulation of "buffer" stocks when demand is weak, and for their resale when demand is strong. Various stabilization agreements, not all of which are consistent with one another, have been reached both separately and collectively by members of the Atlantic Community. Hence the Community still needs to develop a coherent policy and concerted action. The OECD is the logical forum, at least for as long as the Common Market remains a regional organization within the Community. The expansion of the Common Market, since it creates a near "monopsony" or purchase monopoly of primary products, will tend to increase the urgency of the problem. This concentration of demand, and the great disparity in economic strength between buyers and sellers, make it impossible to expect success in the development efforts of the Western world by maintaining a free market in these commodities. A free market in such circumstances would not provide the necessary conditions for economic growth of the underdeveloped countries, but would leave them highly vulnerable to Soviet exploitation.

The dilemma of the primary-products producers does not end with the cyclical problem. There is a long-term, secular trend operating to their disadvantage. The march of technology is continuously toward more extensive processing and refinement of raw materials. An ever larger proportion of total economic effort goes into processing and service activities, leaving a diminishing proportion in the production of raw materials. Put another way, raw materials are used more and more efficiently. Often the process takes place in discrete steps, with sudden and devastating impact on the primary producers. A simple example is provided by the recent development of a greatly improved technique for making powdered "instant" coffee that caught the public fancy and rapidly took over a substantial portion of the coffee market. The impact of this technological change was not primarily in the greater convenience for the housewife but most vitally in the fact that a technique significantly improving the yield of the beverage from a given quantity of coffee beans brought about a shift of demand from Latin American to African types. The net effect is a substantial cut in the total market for coffee, which can be restored only very gradually by population growth and possible changes in consumption habits, particularly in Europe. These factors would operate in any event, and the loss of demand is in a true sense permanent and irrecoverable.

The reduction over time of total demand in the industrial countries causes a gradual deterioration in the terms of trade for the primary-products producers, as the prices of manufactured goods rise more rapidly than those of primary products. It can be argued that the statistical evidence for this proposition is partially illusory, for existing price indices in the industrial countries tend to overstate inflation in the prices of manufactured goods because they do not fully reflect quality improvements. But this is not an adequate or complete explanation, nor is it one that carries any comfort for the injured producer nations.[52]

A vital consideration in the planning of aid to underdeveloped nations, therefore, is the extent to which aid can offset the effect of trade fluctuations and losses. One of the most urgent problems for the Atlantic Community is the development of coordinated plans for an integrated program of trade and aid, designed to help the underdeveloped nations to progress and take their full places in the Free World.

The Community and the Bloc

We have considered the economic problems of the Atlantic Community within its own borders and in its relations with the rest of the Free World. There are also important economic interactions between the Community and the communist bloc. While some may find it pleasant to dream of eliminating these, it is not possible to do so. Nor should all aspects of these relations be regarded as bad—like sin, which is always with us though we may be against it. The communist world has chosen to make economic competition a key phase of the global confrontation. The Western industrial nations have, consciously or unconsciously, accepted the challenge. And well they should, for it is in the economic sphere that the Free World has the greatest tangible advantages.

Conceding these advantages for the present, the communists have emphasized the rate of economic growth rather than the level of economic achievement as the criterion of success. They claim correctly that in recent years they have been growing more rapidly than the West as a whole. The mainland Chinese crisis since 1959 has weakened this claim, but clearly the communist economic accomplishments of the postwar period, however we in the Atlantic Community may evaluate them, have represented a tempting model for the underdeveloped nations.

All that has been said thus far suggests that the Free World under Atlantic Community leadership can do better in the economic competition than it has, provided that it can find the resolve to put Community objectives above parochial interests. The West as a whole has a great deal of slack in its use of resources and in its institutional arrangements. We have already discussed ways and means of taking up that slack. That such slack is available, and in markedly greater degree than in the communist bloc, has been demonstrated anew by recent events. In 1961 and 1962, the United States, in response to the Berlin crisis and other Cold War pressures, increased its arms expenditures by about one-fifth. In an economic sense, this was done without significant cost, for the increase did not absorb all unused resources and thus did not entail giving up any alternative uses of these resources. (There were plenty of alternative uses, but there is no evidence that resources would have been used for them if armaments had not been increased.)

The Soviet Union also has increased its military expenditures, probably by a similar fraction and possibly in direct response to the United States action. But the Soviet Union was not able to do this with otherwise unused resources. At existing levels of technological and organizational efficiency, its resources were fully committed. When military allocations were increased, investments had to be decreased. Planned programs were deferred. The military expenditures also impinged on consumption, as the investment cuts were taken out of the low-priority agricultural sector and were almost immediately reflected in increased scarcity of some foods (primarily meat and dairy products, which had been scheduled to rise considerably). The regime promptly adjusted consumption to the changed supply situation by increasing meat, butter and milk prices (up to 35 percent). It was also forced to renege on the promised elimination of all income taxes. Thus the lack of elbow room in the economy impelled the Soviet Union to give up some of its major objectives in order to meet others. It is likely that one long-lasting effect will be a somewhat lower than expected growth rate in the next few years.

There are more direct ways in which the West can inhibit communist bloc growth rates, at least marginally. The everyday economic life of the Atlantic Community involves a large volume of trade carried on with the Soviet Union by the nations of Western Europe and the United Kingdom. In this trade, the Sino-Soviet bloc seeks advanced machinery and equipment (chemical machinery, for which bloc technology is still much inferior, now has a high priority), as well as many manufactured goods such as iron and steel products (especially pipe with which to develop oil exports and the internal energy economy) and such raw materials as copper. In return, the bloc exports chiefly industrial raw materials, fuels and food.

Within the Atlantic Community, the least interest in trade with the bloc is found in the United States. Basically, this situation reflects the fact that, although sophisticated American goods are valuable to the communist countries, for both economic and military reasons the output of the bloc has only limited interest to the United States. Thus, the United States has favored a restrictive policy to minimize the Sino-Soviet bloc military build-up. Specifically, the United States has denied most-favored-nation tariff treatment to the U.S.S.R., stringently applied United States export controls and, under the Battle and Johnson Acts, prohibited governmental or private credit to the Soviet Union. Though many goods are free of restrictions, Soviet buyers seem to find little attraction in United States goods except those which are banned—and even then they want to buy on credit terms.

United States policy is also influenced by the instability and unpredictability of trade with the bloc and by the imbalance between

Eastern state trading organizations and individualistic Western exporting arrangements. Bloc exports are subject to sudden termination on the basis of political-military considerations; complex products are often imitated at home rather than reordered. Undue dependence on such trade thus could make for weakness in the Western position.

The basic premise of the United States export control policy is that we should do nothing to help a country whose purposes are inimical to our interests. This premise is unassailable, but in practice the program has two weaknesses. First, it is impossible to draw a line between those things which support military potential and those which do not. As we have just seen, increases in one sector of the Soviet economy require cuts in another. (This would be even more true of Communist China in its present crisis.) If a machine tool for making missile components contributes to Soviet military power, does a machine tool for making agricultural tractor parts or even textile machinery components, thereby releasing a Soviet machine tool for missiles, contribute any less? Does an efficient Western textile mill that releases industrial manpower for the armament industry in Russia contribute any less than would a tank plant or even perhaps the tanks themselves? In a tight economy almost any import is helpful. If trade is balanced, as it must roughly be, there is a net gain from any import of an item which must be paid for by exports. Here, again, we find the principle of comparative advantage at work.

Secondly, we have never been able to enforce export controls. While American businessmen have, on the whole, complied faithfully with these controls, our allies, who generally depend more heavily on trade than we do, have never cooperated fully in the program. The West Germans sell steel products, selected machinery and equipment, insecticides and fungicides, and they buy manganese ore, coal, wood, soybeans, platinum and antimony; the British sell nonferrous metals, machinery, steel products, chemicals and rubber (such trade has special appeal to Britain in view of the need to improve its balance of payments); the Danes sell ships and agricultural goods; the Norwegians feel that their fishery industry would be disrupted if sales to the bloc were curtailed; and the Greeks and Turks sell a good deal of mineral as well as agricultural products behind the Iron Curtain. Thus the communist bloc has found ready access in European markets to many items on the United States prohibited list. At least some of the impact of export control has thus been on United States manufacturers who lost out to European competition rather than on the communist bloc, which was not actually deprived of the prohibited goods.

There is also a defensive side to these trade problems. The Soviet Union attempts at times to disrupt prices in Atlantic markets through dumping surplus supplies. One Atlantic country—Italy—is actually the world's biggest importer of Soviet oil, which is being paid for largely by the shipment to the U.S.S.R. of large-diameter steel pipe. The oil is priced at one dollar per barrel F.O.B. Black Sea, which is the equivalent of about seventy-five cents per barrel F.O.B. Persian Gulf —a price so low that it does not quite cover the sums which American and British oil companies must pay as taxes and royalties to Middle East producing countries. Partly because of the low price of Soviet oil, Italy has been able to reduce the price of gasoline at the retail pump, to the satisfaction of the Italian motoring public.

There is economic advantage for the West in receiving these bloc goods at low prices. The danger in accepting them lies in the disruptive effects on Western industries and markets, and possible overdependence on Soviet supplies which can be withdrawn at any strategic moment. Community action to limit such imports and thwart the disruptive trend must be based on strategic considerations and long-run objectives.

Obviously, these are areas in which mechanisms must be designed for increased cooperation within the Atlantic Community. We should not embarrass neutral countries by involving them in economic warfare. To do so would lessen their prospective cooperation on other economic measures, such as trade liberalization and aid to underdeveloped countries, in which the neutrals are both ready and needed partners. NATO is therefore the logical agency within which to coordinate economic warfare techniques. It is a broad enough group which includes all the major countries concerned. The need for coordination of economic warfare measures with other economic acts can be handled through the national delegations to NATO and the OECD. In the past, these delegations have in many cases had overlapping membership, and where this has been the case, coordination between the delegations to the two organizations has been generally close and effective. Coordination of economic warfare plans with other economic activities will lead to the discovery and development of additional weapons for this phase of the Cold War. For example, to refer back to the problem of international payments arrangements, any improvement in the international financial structure, so long as it provides for somewhat greater liquidity, as it must, will tend to reduce the importance of gold. To the extent that the international payments mechanism furnishes the Western countries greater "elbow room" for handling balance-of-payments problems, the relative attractiveness of Soviet bloc markets and Soviet gold should diminish.

The suggestion has been made that a revised international financial structure for the Free World should seek specifically to deny its benefits to nonmembers.[53] This would be accomplished by stipulating that all deficits and surpluses in transactions between a member of the system and a nonmember should be settled fully in gold. In this manner, the contrast between the flexible, multilateral, semiautomatic credit provisions of the Free World system and the rigid bilateral arrangements for trade with the Soviet bloc would be readily apparent, to the prejudice of the latter. There might be some difficulty in enforcing, or providing incentives for, the requirement of gold settlements, but the NATO members as a group might well explore the practical possibilities. More important, however, is the fact that the revised structure would, and should in part be designed to, eliminate some of the existing financial restraints that make trade and other economic relations with the Soviet bloc either attractive to, or necessary for, the uncommitted nations.

In every area of the Atlantic Community's economic policy it appears that one basic problem is the same: There is an urgent need for Community cooperation in the establishment of group instead of national goals and of integrated policies and programs for reaching these goals. There is no easy way to achieve acceptance of the unified goals of a larger group over the diverse goals of smaller groups, whether in a local community, state, nation of states or community of nations. There must be a willingness to try and a will to succeed.

It is clear that the new economic institutions discussed in this chapter have supported the movement toward political unity in the postwar period, and that they can do so in the future. But it is not a foregone conclusion that economic cooperation and integration will bring Community agreement, accelerate economic growth or win the support of the uncommitted nations. Functional integration becomes divisive rather than cohesive if, while it is less than complete, one nation envies the success of others. The United States has had little experience with envying, only with being envied. It has rejoiced in the self-confidence born of pioneering a new world, of building a new nation, of achieving a century and a half of unprecedented success, of reaching unequaled wealth and power, of enjoying an invulnerable homeland. In the last few years, this self-confidence has been shaken by faltering economic progress, by the new experience of being in debt to other nations, by living under the shadow of a new technology that is widely viewed as rendering superior military power useless and self-defeating, and by the fear that the homeland has become totally vulnerable. With feelings of insecurity has come envy of the success of the Common Market, which would not exist without America's help to Europe after the war and America's enduring role in the defense of Europe. This envy colors the American public's view of the economic realities of and the clear advantages of partnership in the Common Market. There is grave danger that the United States will repeat Britain's error, namely, waiting too long. To sulk and to hang back will increase rather than diminish barriers to economic intercourse and to political understanding.

The United States took the lead in postwar economic recovery and the establishment of an environment of cooperation and integration in Europe. It must offer leadership once more. It must find the political resolve to complete the economic institutions of the Community, to secure the recovery it sponsored, and to close the ranks of the West before the divisions become too wide for closing.

CHAPTER **5** A POLITICAL FRAMEWORK FOR

NUCLEAR PARTNERSHIP

The year 1963 finds NATO confronted with new challenges, new problems and new opportunities in a changing international environment. The profound changes which have occurred
within the world as a whole and within the Atlantic Community
during the last half-decade calls for a searching reappraisal of the
concept of the Atlantic Alliance. Nearly everyone pays lip service
to the idea of Atlantic partnership as an imperative demand of the
times. Deep difference exists, however, over the precise form which
the American-European partnership ought to assume. It is no easy
task to convert Western Europe from a latter-day "protectorate" into
a full-fledged partner of the United States. The Europeans achieved
economic independence years ago; but to acquire, at least in some
degree, the mastery of their own political and strategic affairs is,
in the nuclear-missile age, infinitely more difficult a proposition. Yet
acquire it the Europeans appear determined to do.

On the European side of the Atlantic, the three great power centers of the modern nation-state system—Britain, France and Germany
—are once again principal actors in the drama. All three have their
structural weaknesses, to be sure, but today they seem more stable,
politically, economically and psychologically, than they were in the
interwar period. The British are now reassessing their historic attitudes toward the Continent and the Commonwealth. The French,
now that the war in Algeria has been brought to an end, are beginning to experience a new sense of political destiny. The Germans,
who, unlike the British and the French, entertain no well-defined
political ambitions beyond the European continent, face their most

painful dilemma in the apparent contradiction between an ardent desire to achieve national unity and their decision to align themselves actively with the West: the more fully they commit themselves to West European or Atlantic Community economic, political and military integration, the less realistic become their hopes for national reunification in the proximate future. Notwithstanding this dilemma, West German leadership has exhibited a high degree of responsibility in avoiding extremist positions. All three of these elder powers have been casting about in quest of their own creative role in the formulation of Western policy.

Since the days of the Marshall Plan, the United States has consistently supported the trend toward West European integration. Until quite recently, American policymakers have seldom worried about the issues that European unity would raise for NATO. Four years ago, the Foreign Policy Research Institute in its report to the United States Senate Foreign Relations Committee took the position that the trend toward West European integration would be inconsistent neither with United States interests nor NATO objectives provided that: (a) exclusivist groupings be avoided; (b) the pursuit of discriminatory economic policies by the European Economic Community be shunned; and (c) Atlantic-wide Community ties be strengthened commensurately as the movement toward European unity progressed.[1] Under these conditions, the trend toward unity among the West European states was deemed worthy of continued American support. It was long taken for granted that any temptation on the part of Western Europe to veer toward a "third force" position would be held in check by Europe's awareness that her defense will depend increasingly upon the strategic striking capabilities of the United States. Indeed, few doubted that, a NATO strategic nuclear deterrent, if it should be created, would have to be contributed almost exclusively by the United States. The Europeans, therefore, seemed destined to remain completely dependent upon the United States for nuclear deterrence for an indefinitely long period of time.

Fresh political breezes have blown across Europe during the last five years, and the Europeans have been stirred to reassess their role in world affairs. Some of the most important new developments on the far side of the Atlantic—which are often attributed with inaccuracy merely to the appearance of President de Gaulle upon the scene—must be traced back to the period 1956–1957, when two events, a year apart, marked off a watershed in the history of NATO. The first was the policy pursued by the United States in the Suez crisis, which demonstrated to the Europeans how abjectly dependent they were upon their premier ally for the defense of their interests *outside* Europe. Americans are too prone to think that all intelligent Europeans have long since repented the folly of their imperialist misadventures of 1956, that they have come to see the wisdom of American policy in that crisis, and have forgiven and forgotten their humiliation at the hands of their great ally.

The second event occurred in October, 1957, when the successful launching of the sputnik made it clear that the Soviet Union was on the way to acquiring an intercontinental missiles capability which might eventually neutralize American intentions to defend European interests *inside* Europe. Although Soviet achievements in space technology produced no immediate revolution in the world balance of military power, Soviet propagandists, by adroitly projecting the eventual strategic implications of those feats, weakened the confidence of many Europeans in the determination of the United States to defend them against attack, now that American cities were becoming exposed for the first time to the threat of swift missile retaliation. There was a widespread fear that, if the Soviets should come to look upon the U.S. nuclear commitment to its allies as purely declaratory, Western Europe might become a safe area for conventional aggression. Today, in retrospect, such a fear appears to have been premature. But it was real, nevertheless.

It is of the utmost importance that Americans should understand the twofold nature of Europe's misgivings over the possible failure of American support—*outside* Europe and *inside* Europe. Until now, most American analysts have concentrated almost exclusively upon the possible breakdown of deterrence inside Europe. This undoubtedly has been a cause of concern. But it has not been the only cause of concern, and the effort to remove it by reiterating the American pledge and by making the pledge more credible, however welcome such an effort may be, is not likely to prove entirely satisfactory to the Europeans, who are far from indifferent to political-strategic developments outside Europe. Let us first examine the inside problem, and how the United States has sought to deal with it.

In order to assuage the fears of its European allies, the United

States began in 1958 to station Thor and Jupiter medium-range missiles in Britain and on the Continent. The nuclear warheads for these missiles, however, remained exclusively under American control through the operation of the so-called "two key system." The 1958 amendments to the Atomic Energy Act have facilitated the flow of nuclear information, training assistance and equipment to permit the incorporation of atomic weapons delivery systems into European NATO forces, but the United States has always been careful to withhold information on weapons design from all the Allies except Britain.[2] When Washington sought to make sure that Euratom would build reactors suitable only for peaceful and not for military purposes,[3] the Europeans realized that the United States was not merely reluctant to aid in the acquisition of independent European control over nuclear weapons, but actively opposed such a development. The preoccupation with safeguards against nuclear proliferation appeared to dominate American policy, and an increasing number of European leaders resented it.

One of the reasons cited by the British for deciding to manufacture their own thermonuclear weapons was the need for an independent deterrent on the European side of the Atlantic.[4] The British, because of their special wartime relationship with the United States atomic energy program, received American assistance. The French were not able to reconcile themselves to the American view that it was perfectly safe for nuclear weapons to cross the Atlantic to England, but most dangerous for them to cross the Channel to France. At any rate, the British acquisition of thermonuclear capabilities and the assurance thereby gained that Britain would continue to play a special advisory role in the formulation of U.S. policy spurred the French to embark upon their own nuclear weapons program. Even prior to the advent of de Gaulle, the French Government doubted that the United States could be counted upon to uphold French interests in Africa or that it could be fully expected to respond to a Soviet conventional attack upon Western Europe with a nuclear strike on the U.S.S.R. Significantly, it was the government of Guy Mollet, not that of de Gaulle, which initiated the French nuclear armament program.[5] De Gaulle merely pressed forward with increased vigor toward the achievement of an independent *force de frappe*, developed a more eloquent rationale for it and employed France's strategic position as a more effective political lever within the

Alliance.[6] Christian A. Herter gave cogent though unwitting support to de Gaulle's position. In the course of the hearings on his nomination for Secretary of State in April, 1959, he said: "I cannot conceive of any President involving us in all-out nuclear war unless the facts showed clearly that we are in danger of all-out devastation ourselves or that actual moves have been made toward devastating ourselves."[7] De Gaulle's insistence that in the nuclear age no nation could depend upon another for its defense did not entirely lack plausibility.

The negative reasons for trying to develop a national nuclear deterrent outweighed the positive. De Gaulle had cause to wonder in 1960 whether the United States would risk national suicide to defend France—or Europe. American critics of the Eisenhower Administration were then speaking ominously of a "missile gap." The United States, in an effort to correct its international payments imbalance, ordered the withdrawal of American military dependents from Europe—dependents whose presence had helped to inspire confidence in the American pledge to live up to the NATO obligation. The growing U.S. interest in arms control, disarmament and summit negotiations over Berlin stirred up worries that the two superpowers might someday attempt to strike a bargain at Europe's expense. Britain's acquisition of thermonuclear power did little to allay French suspicions. As the campaign for unilateral nuclear disarmament gained momentum and wide publicity across the Channel, the French had little reason to believe that the British would wield an active deterrent—i.e., one that would deter a Soviet attack in Western Europe or a communist takeover of positions in Africa.

Many of the same considerations which originally had led the British to develop their own nuclear force later motivated the French, and these considerations have been essentially negative. In each case, their origins could be traced to a preoccupation with the potentially dire consequences of *not* possessing a national deterrent. In neither case was it clear just what positive purposes the deterrent could be made to serve once it had come into existence. The eastward tug upon nuclear technology continued because none of NATO's major powers on the European side fully trusted its partners to the west to make good its commitment to the defense of the Alliance. Britain did not entirely trust the United States to assign target priority to installations deemed important to Britain, and hence she constructed her own deterrent, later called her "independent contribution to the deterrent." France felt that she could not rely upon British strategy, and so she, too, sought her own national deterrent. Thus the proliferation of national nuclear forces, or efforts to establish them, bespoke a chronic crisis of confidence within NATO itself.

The logical climax of such a process, if not eventually modified, would be an insistence by West Germany upon the right to attain nuclear parity with her West European allies, treaty agreements to the contrary notwithstanding.[8] Such a climax seems logical because, of all the countries of Western Europe, the Federal Republic could make out the best case on the basis of need and, perhaps, technological competence. But the development of an independent national deterrent by West Germany would involve the gravest strategic complications: the issues of active and passive deterrence would be joined.

I

The specter of national nuclear proliferation has compelled the United States, since 1959, to think more seriously about establishing some kind of NATO deterrent. The policies pursued especially by the French Government have made it obvious that the United States must act, even if only symbolically, to placate the European allies and to quiet their misgivings. The present Administration, like its predecessor, seems to recognize that the desire for national deterrents cannot be dampened by strategic arguments alone. The question is whether the proposals thus far advanced by the United States will prove satisfactory to the Europeans, or whether the latter will increasingly resent their continued dependence upon the United States for the defense of what they regard as their vital interests (whether the Americans do or not), and strike out on their own. So far as NATO's political future is concerned, this question goes to the heart of the matter.

Various plans for NATO nuclear sharing have been put forth during the last five years.[9] The problem of devising adequate political controls and decision-making machinery for a genuine NATO deterrent is widely recognized as the crucial stumbling block to its creation. Would the decision to invoke the NATO deterrent be taken by unanimous consent of all fifteen members of the North Atlantic Council, by a special majority, by a simple majority or by a special minority composed of the leading powers? Practically every proposal put forth prior to the Nassau Pact of December, 1962, described a deterrent more cumbersome and less credible than the current United States guarantee. But under the pre-Nassau forms of "NATO deterrent" advanced by the United States, the Europeans would still feel essentially dependent for nuclear defense upon American acquiescence. Under these conditions, it was not likely that a "NATO deterrent" would long satisfy the European allies. Such a deterrent could not meet the political demands of the European situation, for it was not based upon an assessment of all the factors which, in recent years, have prompted the Europeans to aspire to a deterrent of their own.

Perhaps American strategists, as a whole, have been excessively preoccupied with the possibility that the United States might someday fail to respond decisively to a Soviet attack upon Europe. NATO's major ills on the other side of the Atlantic have often been traced to a feeling of insecurity which some American strategic analysts have helped to acerbate by their own speculations about what the United States may deem "thinkable" under this or that awful contingency. The various proposals for a NATO deterrent have usually been advanced as panaceas to soothe the frayed nerves of Europe. But if the diagnosis has not been entirely correct, the prescribed remedy may not prove effective.

The Europeans, no doubt, worry occasionally about the possibility of a premeditated Soviet attack. More often, they are concerned that Soviet probes and pressures in a sensitive area such as Berlin might send tensions spiraling until a slight misstep unleashed violence. In an environment in which excessive reliance has been placed on nuclear strategy, the "pause" which General Norstad has thought desirable to enforce might, if it lasts long enough, give the Americans rather than the Soviets food for thought: the former might be more anxious than the latter to return to the bargaining table.

It is doubtful, however, that the growing European interest in indigenous nuclear capabilities can be traced exclusively or even primarily to fears of a direct Soviet attack. The European peoples as a whole are not given to constant brooding over the issue of survival. Outside of Britain, the campaign for unilateral nuclear disarmament has not gained a great deal of ground. None of the governments which agreed to accept American missiles on its national soil subsequently backed away under the pressure of Premier Khrushchev's blackmail by diplomatic note and press conference. Most informed Europeans seem to regard a Soviet attack as less real a threat today than in years past. They are somewhat more at ease now that the United States has closed up the lead in space technology which the U.S.S.R. enjoyed from 1957 to 1960.[10] As they look eastward, they see a communist bloc beset by economic difficulties and political stresses and strains. By no means has the majority of Europeans been beguiled into thinking that the long-range menace of communism as an international conflict movement has waned. But, in the dominant view, the current *détente* bespeaks the need for a period of strategic consolidation within the communist empire, during which the Soviets can attempt to regain full managerial control of the system and formulate a workable strategy for the next "flow period."

The Europeans, therefore, are breathing a little more freely for the time being. Since the Cuban missile crisis they appear to be paying even less attention to the communist danger. Even if the Soviets should, as is to be expected, shift back to a hard policy line, European statesmen seem to be of the opinion that an outright Soviet attack on Western Europe is most unlikely. The Europeans have had enough experience to realize that the strategy of protracted conflict enjoins adventuristic moves, the full consequences of which can be neither calculated nor controlled. Next to an all-out attack upon the United States, aggression against a nuclear-armed Western Europe constitutes the greatest strategic gamble which the Soviets could take. Both the Soviets and the Europeans (at least the Continental Europeans) understand this rather well.

As Western Europe's economic prowess develops, an American determination to defend that region to the hilt becomes increasingly important. The United States, making a rational calculation of its own vital interests, cannot possibly permit a Soviet takeover of Western Europe with all its productive potential, for it would pose the issue of survival to American society as a distinctive cultural-economic system. Subtle discussions of the conventional-nuclear dilemma notwithstanding, this possibility must still be admitted: If war should come in Western Europe, the United States may very well decide that it has no choice but to commit itself fully to the defense of the area defined in the North Atlantic Treaty, regardless of cost. The concept of irreducible national interest has not been rendered completely obsolete in the age of the nuclear missile. When President Kennedy, in the spring of 1962, announced that the United States reserved the right to initiate the use of nuclear weapons against a deep Soviet penetration into Western Europe, his words had the ring of credibility.

Europeans on the whole seem satisfied that the United States is a responsible keeper of the peace. Nevertheless, it is not at all surprising that many European statesmen, and not de Gaulle alone, should like to have a voice in the making of nuclear decisions. Alastair Buchan, in an important statement of recent political trends within NATO, writes:

What is beyond dispute, in my view, is that the restored pride and dynamism of Europe makes it likely that these countries will tend to play a critical or even obstructive role in the formulation of allied policy, unless a means can be found which gives them full responsibility of playing a constructive role. Moreover there can be no reason to assume that this is not a permanent development or is likely to be less marked when certain grand old men of a passing generation have quit the European scene, for the new Europe is not the creation merely of de Gaulle, Adenauer and Macmillan.[11]

In an effort to dispel confusion in the contemporary debate over the NATO deterrent and European aspirations, Buchan draws an interesting distinction between the English word "control," which in this context connotes actual physical possession of the buttons and levers whereby nuclear warheads are armed and fired, and the French term *contrôle*, which implies access to planning and policy decisions.

If one analyzes European fears, or examines the reasons why first Britain, then France, embarked on an independent nuclear capability, it becomes clear that the basic European desire is not so much for operational control of bombers or missiles as *pour contrôler* American strategic policy, to gain some measure of control over the context of peace and war. . . . If the United States could present a clear and continuous picture of its strategic policy . . . and accept informed criticism of its plans, then not only would European governments at last have a clear picture of the considerations which must govern their own defense policies and diplomacy, but their main motive for wishing to acquire operational control of nuclear weapons would disappear.[12]

Buchan was quite right to call attention to the need for much closer cooperation among the Allies in the constant process of formulating strategic policies which might someday lead to the taking of hard decisions—decisions that would vitally affect the security not only of the United States but of the European countries as well. What is required is regular, intimate and frank discussion of such things as R & D (research and development), nuclear weapons deployment, the conventional-nuclear relationship and the "rules of engagement," leading toward an agreed definition of situations and thresholds appropriate for the use of certain types of nuclear weapons. In no other way can an atmosphere of mutual confidence be sustained among the Allies; in no other way can a community of strategic thought be created. It may be impossible to devise contingency plans for the entire range of conceivable challenges which might arise. It should be possible, however, to fashion a consensus among the overwhelming majority of Allied policymakers so that they will size up a Soviet challenge within the same frame of reference and move quickly toward similar conclusions as regards the response to be made. Indeed, it seems that NATO has already made definite moves in the direction indicated by Buchan. There was a more intensive exchange of views among the NATO foreign and defense ministers and the NATO military planners at the Athens meeting in May, 1962, than ever before. The pertinent passages from the Ministerial Council communiqué bear quoting in full:

The Council noted the progress which has been made in the direction of closer cooperation between member countries in the development of the alliance's defense policy. In this respect ministers welcomed the confirmation by the United States that it will continue to make available for the alliance nuclear weapons necessary for NATO defense, concerting with its allies on basic plans and arrangements in regard to these weapons. In addition, both the United Kingdom and the United States Government have given firm assurances that their strategic forces will continue to provide defense against threats to the alliance beyond the capability of NATO-committed forces to deal with.

So that all member states may play their full part in consultation on nuclear defense policy, it has been decided to set up special procedures which will enable all members of the alliance to exchange information concerning the role of nuclear weapons in NATO defense.

The purpose of NATO is defense, and it must be clear that in case of attack it will defend its members by all necessary means. The Council has reviewed the action that would be necessary on the part of member countries, collectively and individually, in the various circumstances in which the alliance might be compelled to have recourse to its nuclear defenses.[13]

Prior to the Nassau Agreement for a joint NATO Polaris force, intensified consultation represented the U.S. answer to the demands of Europe. The United States has made it clear that it will not assist France in her effort to acquire an independent national strike force. American officials have been unmoved by the argument that if the French are stubbornly determined to build such a force, the United States may as well earn their goodwill and reduce their costs instead of depriving them of technical data already known to the Soviets. Under no circumstances does the United States wish to see the Western deterrent undergo any further mitosis. According to the present policy of the United States, independent national deterrents are dangerous, since they invite attack, may provoke war and are likely to lead to further proliferation; are expensive and prone to obsolescence in an age of fast-changing military technology; and lack credibility. The Kennedy Administration, in insisting upon the continued indivisibility of the Alliance's nuclear defenses, has marshaled some compelling strategic arguments for unity of planning, concentration of executive authority and centralized direction of NATO. Secretary of Defense Robert McNamara, in a commencement address at the University of Michigan on June 16, 1962, delivered a sharp warning against the development of "competing and conflicting strategies to meet the contingency of nuclear war." He said:

We are convinced that a general nuclear war target system is indivisible, and if, despite all our efforts, nuclear war should occur, our best hope lies in conducting a centrally controlled campaign against all of the enemy's vital nuclear capabilities, while retaining reserve forces, all centrally controlled.

We know that the same forces which are targeted on ourselves are also targeted on our allies. Our own strategic retaliatory forces are prepared to respond against these forces, wherever they are and whatever their targets. This mission is assigned not only in fulfillment of our treaty commitments but also because the character of nuclear war compels it.

More specifically, the U.S. is as much concerned with that portion of Soviet nuclear striking power that can reach Western Europe as with that portion that also can reach the United States. In short, we have undertaken the nuclear defense of NATO on a global basis. This will continue to be our objective. In the execution of this mission, the weapons in the European theater are only one resource among many.[14]

In pure strategic reason, the Defense Secretary's position cannot be easily controverted. The question remains, however, whether a centralized deterrent, adumbrated by intensified transatlantic consultation, will satisfy the statesmen of Western Europe. This is the best solution for the NATO area itself until a better, a politically more comprehensive one has been found. But no one outside the top levels of the Administration can say for certain whether the present arrangement will prove satisfactory politically if and when a military crisis should arise in a non-NATO region. Let us suppose, for example, that the Communist Chinese attempt to embark upon a "final solution" of the Formosa question and that, in the midst of the build-up of military preparations and international tensions, Peking announces that it has acquired nuclear weapons.[15] Will the Europeans be content to defer to the judgment of American decision-makers on the grounds that the latter have almost exclusive strategic responsibility for the security of Far Eastern positions, or will the Europeans insist that they should be allowed to exercise a veto over the prospect of a nuclear engagement, with all its attendant dangers, in a part of the world where European vital interests are not directly at stake? To what extent is the United States prepared to admit its European allies to participation in the development of strategies in Asia—or, for that matter, in the Western Hemisphere—which might, at some future time, entail the use of nuclear weapons? De Gaulle, who has long desired a veto power in such instances, has never received satisfactory assurances on this score—a fact which helps to explain his uncooperative attitude.

More important still, the Europeans want to place themselves in a position where they can, with greater freedom, pursue their own international initiatives. This they cannot do unless they reduce their military dependence upon the United States. Particularly keen is the interest of West Europeans in the future of Africa, now that the process of decolonization has entered its final phase. The economic interdependence of Europe and the Dark Continent is expected to grow with the Common Market. The West European states have virtually liquidated all their strategic responsibilities in the Far East, Southeast Asia and the Middle East (except for Kuwait). But for years President de Gaulle has been lecturing them on the importance of retaining their strategic responsibilities for the defense of an independent Africa, and the lessons have begun to sink in. U.S. policy in the Congo crisis has given rise to dissatisfaction with the American approach to decolonization and its aftermath, not only in France and Belgium, where it was to be expected, but even in Britain, where it was not. Washington's handling of the Congo tangle has reinforced the suspicions of U.S. policy which many Europeans have entertained ever since Suez. European statesmen and officials, who are somewhat resentful of the fact that the United States does not attach greater importance to their longer experience and broader knowledge in African affairs, are not quite willing to forfeit the future security and political evolution of Africa to the neutralist bloc in the General Assembly.

Africa is every bit as vital to Europe as Europe is to the United States. Although the African situation seemed relatively settled as of mid-1962, the Europeans doubt that the Soviets have written it off as a bad investment; they fully expect trouble to brew again. In some future crisis, the government of an African state may very well call for effective Western assistance to quell a communist or procommunist guerrilla insurrection in which the insurgents are supported by the Soviets (under the doctrine of the "just war of national liberation"). At that time, the Europeans may not wish to follow the United States in relying on a United Nations solution. But, given their present power position, if the Europeans attempted to apply pressure by supplying conventional arms and military advice, they would almost certainly run the risk of Soviet nuclear blackmail. The Soviets would order the Europeans to cease and desist or else face direct embroilment with Soviet military forces either in Africa or in Europe, or both. The next move would then be up to the United States, and there is no guarantee that Washington would be any readier to underwrite Europe's African interests than it was at Suez. United States policymakers might once again join the Soviets in applying leverage against European "boat-rocking" policies, thereby undercutting much of the popular support that activist European statesmen might otherwise enjoy. (It is European statesmen, more than European publics, who feel the need for enhanced flexibility.)

Up to now, most Europeans have seemed fairly satisfied that the United States can be counted upon to defend essential American interests in Europe. For all practical purposes, that means defending Europe. But European leaders have no impelling reason to believe that the United States will take a strong stand against the Soviet Union for the sake of European interests outside Europe—interests which impinge more directly upon European prosperity than upon American security. Hence thoughtful Europeans discern a powerful motive for acquiring an independent nuclear deterrent, so that they may guarantee their extracontinental interests just as effectively as Americans ensure their own. To a considerable degree, this motive stems from policy differences over Africa, deep-rooted as they are in divergent historical experiences and attitudes on the relations which should prevail between the industrialized nations and the politically and economically less advanced peoples of the world.

The year 1962 witnessed the rise into fashion of what some writers have called the "dumbbell theory" of Atlantic politics. This theory postulates a strongly armed United States on the one side and another strongly armed grouping in Europe.[16] The metaphor conveys the notion of weight evenly distributed at both ends, which is exactly what the Europeans want.

II

One of the most noteworthy diplomatic revolutions of this century was the British decision in the summer of 1961 to seek entry into the European Economic Community. This decision signaled a shift of British policy orientation from the Commonwealth and the European Free Trade Association (EFTA) toward closer ties with the Six. The Macmillan Government accepted the fact that, having been unable to bring significant influence to bear upon the Common Market from the outside, it had little choice but to apply for membership, regardless of how difficult the adjustment might be. The decision undoubtedly disturbed many Englishmen, just as it did the statesmen and publics of the Commonwealth countries. Nevertheless it seemed to reflect the logic of historical change.

The U.K. market by itself can no longer be expected to furnish the growing outlet that Commonwealth exporters need, nor can Britain alone meet the capital requirements of the developing Commonwealth countries. The plain fact is that within recent years British trade with the Commonwealth countries as a whole has actually begun to decline, while Commonwealth buying from other regions of the world, including Western Europe, has been on the rise.[17] At the same time, the Common Market has been increasingly important to British industry, both as buyer and as international competitor.

In other ways, too, the Commonwealth has changed. Canada, Australia and New Zealand have remained loyal in their political sentiments, but the newer members in Asia and Africa have been very critical of Whitehall's policies in respect to decolonization and the struggle between the Soviet bloc and the Western Alliance. The Indians have complained of the scarcity of British economic aid and of Britain's unwillingness to support them in Goa and on Kashmir. Commonwealth neutralists in Africa have loosened the frail bonds that, at least formally, tied them to London. In England itself, many a Conservative who believes stoutly in justice between the races has watched with regret the departure of the Union of South Africa, wondering whether it was to be the harbinger of the end of an era. The Parliamentary enactment of the Immigration Bill in late 1961 signaled an ominous change of attitude in Britain. The world's oldest and most unique political community of states appears to be on the verge of final dissolution. The British Government has said more than once that if the choice had to be made between the Commonwealth and Europe it would unquestionably choose the former, but that no such stark choice need arise. After the first year of negotiations, however, it seemed clear that Britain had already chosen Europe and was now determined to obtain the best possible arrangements on behalf of those Commonwealth countries which depend most heavily upon her market. The Commonwealth heads of government, meeting at London in September, 1962, after airing their resentments, finally resigned themselves to the fact that the British were bent upon pursuing the negotiations through to a finish —one way or the other.

If it were only a matter of economics, British diplomatists might be able to persuade the EEC to sew together an intricate patch quilt of protocols, escape clauses and gentlemen's agreements which would ameliorate most of the serious transition problems. But the problem of admitting Britain to the EEC is much more than an economic one. It is fraught with political implications of a most far-reaching character.

Britain's approach to the EEC has given rise to two sets of political problems. The first, which is complex enough in itself but rather simple when compared with the second set, arises within Britain as she contemplates the ultimate aim of political unification to which the Rome Treaty makes guarded reference.[18] The precise form of the projected union never has been made clear, but the original architects of the EEC, following the same line of thought which runs through the Schuman Plan for the Coal and Steel Community, hoped that the Common Market would serve as a forerunner to some kind of federalism. The British, for constitutional reasons, have always been wary of subscribing to the Community's objective of eventual political unification. The Conservatives shy away from the notion of federal practice codified in a written constitution—a device unpopular in England ever since Cromwell's time. Labour, too, has been cool to the idea of a supranational authority, not because of any Burkean attachment to the customs and conventions of the realm, but because of its apprehensions as to the maneuverability of a future Labour Cabinet. It might be difficult to pursue socialist welfare policies so long as a majority of Community decision-makers are unsympathetic to the Fabian concept of planning.[19] Conservatives and Labourites alike prefer intergovernmental cooperation to supranational decision-taking. The English are at root an insular people. They wonder whether, having subordinated their sovereignty to European institutions, they might not often be outvoted by the Franco-German partnership and such support as it can muster among the Continental members. Italy and the Benelux countries welcome the prospect of Britain's presence as a counterweight to France and Germany. On many issues, Britain could probably expect to find Germany on her side. Furthermore, as the British advocates of entry have often pointed out, joining the EEC would not involve a one-sided surrender of national sovereignty. Her Majesty's Government would be doing no more than the Six have already done, and by becoming a member it would acquire a significant policy voice in the economic affairs of the entire Community.[20] But there is always the possibility that when important issues arise, whether economic or political, the British might balk at the course of action desired by the majority of the EEC, and it is this unknown and unpredictable contingency which gives pause to many Englishmen who cherish the nation's traditional freedom of action.[21]

The very ambiguity of the British attitude—wishing to get in and yet being afraid of the consequences of getting in—has thrown the European federalist movement into confusion. The federalists at first could not make up their minds whether to welcome or dread the overtures of the Macmillan Government. They realize that the British application has the full backing of Washington, and, since Washington has heretofore given enthusiastic support to the European unity trend, they assume that Britain's adherence to the EEC cannot but represent a gain. Presumably, Britain's adherence would help to put Europe on the high road to that federal structure which Winston Churchill, speaking at the University of Zurich in 1946, acclaimed as the "United States of Europe." Moreover, since most European federalists are numbered among the staunchest advocates of a stronger Atlantic Community, they are hopeful also that Britain's entry would provide the essential bridge between a united Europe and the two North American allies. The United States, for its part, favors British admission for a number of reasons. As one British review put it:

The provisions of the new Trade Expansion Act, which allow for the reduction or elimination of all tariffs on products in which the EEC and the United States together account for 80 percent or more of world trade, would lose practically all their meaning if Britain were to stay out of Europe. The main attraction of British accession to the Community, however, is the added guarantee of European political stability which it brings with it. . . . British membership of the EEC would in the first place mean the end of the EFTA with its "unhealthy" tinge of neutrality. It would also presumably counteract any European pretensions to "third force" status and help to weld Europe more firmly into the Atlantic partnership.[22]

The "Europeanists" are uncertain as to what the net effect of British entry would be. They are undoubtedly aware that Prime Minister Macmillan's decision to seek entry into the EEC has been facilitated by President de Gaulle's appeal for a "Europe of the Fatherlands" (*Europe des patries*)—i.e., a confederation of sovereign states rather than a federal structure—as the goal of the movement toward closer political unity. So long as de Gaulle remains at the helm, France will not abdicate national sovereignty and Britain will not be obliged to do so. De Gaulle may never have intended to ease the Conservative Cabinet's decision of July, 1961, but paradoxically enough, that is just what he did.

Both Gaullist officials and some staunch European federalists have at times suspected the British application for membership in the EEC as a move aimed at diluting the political objective of the Continental states. Although the interpretations of the European federalists and the French Government happen to coincide, the motives that prompt their misgivings differ. Not a few "Europeanists," who have been keenly disappointed at de Gaulle's proposal for a confederation, fear that British adherence to the Common Market will further buttress opposition to the growth of truly supranational institutions. The noticeable lack of enthusiasm of the de Gaulle Government, on the other hand, reflects a concern lest the admittance of Britain, accompanied by a "massive escort" of Commonwealth and EFTA countries, thwart the potential development of the emerging European Community as a vehicle of French hegemony in Europe. Despite the fact that Edward Heath, Lord Privy Seal, who has conducted the negotiations for Britain, has declared that his country stands ready to join in planning the political future of Europe, and to play a "full part" in that future,[23] President de Gaulle apparently has long felt that the British would like to gain all the economic advantages of EEC membership while withholding the political entrance fee.

When President de Gaulle first came to power, he spoke of the EEC—if he spoke of it at all—with a perfunctoriness that, at times, seemed to give way to annoyance. But gradually he discerned in the economic integration of the Six an opportunity to realize his dream of a European confederation, led by France, which would eventually be able to defend itself militarily, to match the economic-technological prowess of either the United States or the Soviet Union, and to play an economic, political and strategic role in the underdeveloped areas of the world (especially Africa) comparable to that of the two superpowers. De Gaulle's project, in American and

British political literature, has often been described as the effort to create a "third force," and has usually been dismissed rather cursorily as the vain and unrealistic ambition of a mystic nationalist, a latter-day Jeanne d'Arc, still smarting under the memory of the humiliating treatment which, so he fancied, was meted out to himself and to France by Roosevelt and Churchill during World War II. As a statesman, de Gaulle is, to be sure, a unique type within the Western Alliance. But it is not wise to ignore his aspirations, however odd their formulation might seem to an Anglo-American audience. Much less prudent is it to regard him with a certain amount of levity (as many American political observers have been wont to do ever since he retired in 1946 to await the "call of destiny"), or to assume that he will conveniently be removed from the political scene once he has completed his function of liquidating the Algerian problem.

There can be little doubt that de Gaulle has his heart set on a Europe capable of acting independently of both the United States and the Soviet Union. The term "third force" fails to convey an appropriate description of what he envisages. In contemporary discourse, "third force," rightly or not, is taken as a sort of neutral posture in the global conflict between the Soviet Union and the United States. Indeed, it has often been suggested that de Gaulle hopes to preside over a confederated Europe which would be strong enough to arbitrate between Moscow and Washington. This interpretation of his intentions may be misleading. The French President, after all, is an ardent proponent of Western values precisely because he is a Frenchman *à outrance*. As a matter of fact, the burden of much of his criticism of U.S. foreign policy has been that it is excessively oriented toward a United Nations universalism and is not sufficiently pro-Western in its concrete actions. His contempt for the United Nations, the rigidity of his stand on Berlin negotiations and his refusal to attend the Geneva disarmament talks in the spring of 1962 struck some Britons and Americans as little short of scandalous. Would his quest for a single Europe stretching "from the Atlantic to the Urals" lead him into temptation—the temptation to make a deal with that *chère et brave Russie*—or would he favor a more vigorous policy to reverse the status quo in Eastern Europe? With de Gaulle, no one can say for sure whither he is trending. But it is at least conceivable that what he seeks for Europe is not so much the role of umpire between East and West as the role of a Western player more active than the United States has been. If anyone turns out to be the umpire or moderator, it may well be the United States, not Europe, for the latter would in a sense replace the former, at least in some areas of the world, as the strategic antagonist of the communist bloc.

These are indeed no more than speculative glimpses of the future. But to dream great dreams is not the least of the requisites of statesmanship. De Gaulle is a long-range strategic thinker—perhaps the only one among the leading Western statesmen, most of whom are pragmatist at heart. De Gaulle must realize that the translation of his dream into political reality will require many years. He may not be certain that the task he has set for himself can be accomplished in his own lifetime, but he seems determined to make a start. His formidable schedule called for the following accomplishments: (1) to resolve the Algerian problem; (2) to build a lasting French community with the new African states; (3) to make France a nuclear power; (4) to gain acceptance for French political leadership in Western Europe; (5) to cement the Franco-German *rapprochement;* and (6) to demonstrate his superior statesmanship by forging an appropriate link between Great Britain and Europe at the propitious time and under the right conditions—meaning, of course, under terms that he himself will lay down. Each of these objectives has at one time or another appeared downright fantastic. No other Western statesman has defined for himself political tasks of such magnitude.

Some of de Gaulle's aspirations are, without doubt, immoderate or quixotic. But for all that, his policy objectives cannot be discounted. The French President has already exerted a significant impact upon European thinking, both as a catalyst of new ideas and as a mirror of new trends of thought. He speaks not only for himself, nor only for France. In a sense, he speaks for Europe, or at least he is a spokesman for a point of view which many Europeans, including even some federalists who ridicule his confederal ideas, are convinced needs to be expressed. His message to his fellow Europeans is fairly simple, and might be paraphrased as follows:

We are Europe, greatest of all extant civilizations, origin of most of the dynamic forces sweeping through the world. We have made some colossal blunders in modern times, culminating in two world wars, and as a result we have gone into decline. Think where we would be today had we not suffered such gross internal failures! Our international position would be unchallenged. We would now be the leaders and teachers of mankind in every sphere—political, economic, scientific, social and cultural. Let us, then, strive to undo our mistakes and restore our greatness. Why should we quail before one outside power or depend entirely upon another for our defense? We can, through the application of our native intellectual genius, become again the masters of our own destiny. We have the knowledge, the skills, the resources and the productive base required for power; all we need is to inspire ourselves. Remember, we are Europe.

Such ardent European federalists as Jean Monnet and Paul-Henri Spaak have been trying for years to convince their fellow Europeans that they could accomplish great things together if only they would unite. But since the demise of the proposal for a European Defense Community, the federalists for the most part have concentrated too much upon economic integration, assuming that it would lead gradually and inexorably to some form of political unification along federal lines. In recent years, however, it has become apparent that economic integration, even when it proves eminently successful, does not necessarily ensure the growth of closer political unity. Indeed, if economic difficulties sometimes spur the movement toward political unity, the removal of these difficulties as a result of sector integration may very well modify the strength of the forces which originally furnished the propulsion toward unity. At any rate, political unity is achieved not merely by raising the standard of living; it demands a decision of the political will. De Gaulle understands this very well. He is also convinced, rightly or wrongly, that Europe's destiny lies not in a "United States of Europe," but in a family of the historic nations, with all their old nationalistic illnesses cured, working out cooperative policies under the leadership of the nation with the most universal intellectual outlook, namely, France.

Neither the Germans, nor the British, nor the Italians nor any other European nation can be expected to embrace a plan which embodies the dream of French leadership of Europe. Perhaps de Gaulle himself never expected them to do so; he may be playing the role of the pedagogue, trying to demonstrate a point which, in his view, the "utopian federalists" have overlooked, namely, that at the present time all European governments are bound to entertain reservations about political supranationalism. In the long run, his analysis may turn out to be no less out of tune with the facts of Europe's political sociology than will that of his critics. Chiding those supranationalists who want to postpone defining the political form of Europe until after Britain has become an EEC member, de Gaulle has issued a public reminder that Great Britain, "in its capacity as a great state and a nation loyal to itself, would never agree to lose its identity in some utopian structure."

I have never personally, in any of my statements, spoken of a "Europe of nations," although it is always being claimed that I have done so. It is not, of course, that I am repudiating my own; quite on the contrary, I am more attached to France than ever, and I do not believe that Europe can have any living reality if it does not include France and her Frenchmen, Germany and its Germans, Italy and its Italians, and so forth. Dante, Goethe, Chateaubriand belong to all Europe to the very extent that they were respectively and eminently Italian, German and French. They would not have served Europe very well if they had been stateless, or if they had thought and written in some kind of integrated Esperanto or Volapuk.

But it is true that the nation is a human and sentimental element, whereas Europe can only be built on the basis of active, authoritative and responsible elements. What elements? The states, of course, for, in this respect, it is only the states that are valid, legitimate and capable of achievement. I have already said, and I repeat, that at the present time there cannot be any other Europe than a Europe of states, apart, of course, from myths, stories and parades.[24]

De Gaulle believes that the EEC is a creature of the states which furnish it with funds, provide it with staff members and define the political limits within which the EEC can make economic policy. When it is decided to bring agriculture under the Common Market, or to allow the association of Greece, or to admit Britain or to negotiate tariffs with the United States, says de Gaulle, all these are political questions which require political action on the part of the states. He agrees that the economic development of Europe cannot be assured without its political union, but he is skeptical about the possibility of accomplishing union through a European parliament.

These are ideas that may, perhaps, beguile certain minds, but I certainly do not see how they could be carried out in practice, even if there were six signatures on the dotted line. . . . Would the French people, the German people, the Italian people, the Dutch people, the Belgian people, the Luxembourg people dream of submitting to laws voted by foreign

deputies if these laws were to run contrary to their own deep-seated will?
    This is not so; there is no way, at the present time, for a foreign majority
to be able to restrain recalcitrant nations. It is true that, in this "integrated"
Europe, as they say, there would perhaps be no policy at all. This would
simplify things a great deal. . . . But then, perhaps, this world would
follow the lead of some outsider who did have a policy. There would perhaps be a federator, but the federator would not be European.[25]

De Gaulle's fear that Europe might have its policy imposed upon
it by an outside "federator" is directed more toward Washington
than Moscow. Indeed, the fact that the United States has been such
an enthusiastic advocate of European integration since the days of
the Marshall Plan makes the integrationists doubly suspect in his
eyes.[26] He does not relish a movement toward unity which often
seems to draw both inspiration and support from the U.S. Department of State. This helps to explain why de Gaulle has sought to
gain acceptance among the other members of the EEC for *his* idea
of European union before Britain should be admitted. The British,
in discussing their reorientation toward the Continent, might concede confidentially that their "special relationship" with the United
States seems to be on the wane and that, since the Americans are
taking such a keen interest in the Common Market, Britain had
better prepare to go in or else face isolation. But de Gaulle seems at
times to suspect that Whitehall's application masks an Anglo-American plot to upset his schemes. Moreover, he seems to regard the
"European federalists'" support for British entry more as a peeved
reaction to his own policies than as a coherent move toward European unity.

De Gaulle has sought to devise a formula for political unity which
the British would be required to ratify at the time of their admission. The negotiations, in a sense, have turned into a contest between
France, anxious to shape the political character of Western Europe
before the British enter, and the British, who would like to see the
settlement of the major political questions postponed until after they
have acquired a full voice in the deliberations of the EEC. In
November, 1961, the EEC's Committee on Political Organization
produced a draft plan of union which was attributed in large measure to the Committee chairman, Christian Fouchet. The Fouchet
Plan called for an indissoluble European Union in which all decisions would be taken unanimously. No decision would bind a gov-

ernment that had abstained in the voting. The Union would be headed by a council consisting of the heads of government of the member states meeting three times a year. Between meetings, a permanent political committee meeting in Paris would serve as the executive. A parliament was provided for, vested only with consultative powers, and consisting of the members already serving in the assemblies of the three integral European organizations—the EEC, Euratom and the Coal and Steel Community. The Fouchet draft, which was generally identified with the position of President de Gaulle, placed emphasis upon the executive rather than upon the legislative as the distinctive institution of European integration.[27] The call for treaty revision at the end of three years was designed ostensibly to win approval among at least some federalists who demand a stronger union eventually, but who might be persuaded that de Gaulle's plan was the best that could be hoped for at the time.

De Gaulle, to be sure, holds out for national sovereign prerogatives in the decision-making procedures of the proposed European Union. Nevertheless, he seems to envision common functions of a sweeping character, especially in the fields of coordinated foreign policy and defense activities.[28] De Gaulle looks toward a more independent European approach to Africa, where in recent years the anticolonialist orientation of U.S. policy has displeased European statesmen; toward the creation of a political-economic association that would exert, for several underdeveloped countries, a more magnetic attraction than either the United States or the Soviet Union; and toward distinctly European solutions to problems which are primarily European, such as the status of Berlin and the reunification of Germany. Finally, he desires the establishment of military capabilities and the formulation of strategies which would enable Europe to achieve a greater degree of autonomy and flexibility in the pursuit of its shared interests.

A year and a half after the date of their application, the British still found themselves looking in from the outside. Although they had offered to discuss European political union, they were not admitted to detailed discussions of the subject. British participation, in the eyes of the French, was still premature, and de Gaulle's views seemed to have prevailed with Chancellor Adenauer, over the strenuous objections of the Italians and the Benelux countries.[29] De

Gaulle, no doubt, played his German cards to force the British to come to terms, and also to keep the Germans tied to French policy, lest they succumb to the temptation to strike out on their own. He managed in the spring of 1962 to induce the Bonn Government to line up with France in opposition to the Anglo-American position on Berlin negotiations. Adenauer, who always attached paramount importance to Germany's ties with the United States, nonetheless was increasingly attracted to the Gaullist thesis, namely, that London and Washington would have reached an accommodation with Moscow over Berlin had it not been for the intransigence of France. The German Chancellor, who worked assiduously for a decade to restore the political respectability of his nation, had another good reason to lean toward de Gaulle: The latter was the first European statesman to show himself ready to accept the Federal Republic as a full-fledged partner in the new Europe. The summer of 1962 marked progress toward erasing the unpleasant memories of 1870, 1914 and 1940 when *le grand Charles* and *der Alte* attended High Mass together at the Rheims Cathedral and afterward reviewed a binational military parade at Mourmelon. Some weeks later, the French President was warmly received on his reciprocal visit to the Federal Republic. The exchange of visits paved the way for the signing, in January, 1963, of the Franco-German Treaty of Cooperation, by which the two nations declared their historic enmity to be past, and seemed to be tightening their political solidarity without waiting for their other European partners.

The British, not for the first time in the twentieth century, were suffering a spell of diplomatic jitters at the sight of political developments on the Continent. They realized that a new Europe was in the making, and they did not wish to be left out (even though they have some qualms about going in). They were aware, too, that de Gaulle was in a strong bargaining position, and that this position had improved now that the Algerian settlement had freed him for more active politicking among the statesmen of Western Europe. The longer he delayed approving the terms for British entry, the higher the membership fee Britain might have to pay. De Gaulle's ideas on the emerging shape of Europe and on international affairs in general appeared less unpalatable to the British than they did a year earlier. Indeed, in the summer of 1962, the British hinted openly that they were willing to discuss a delicate matter which undoubtedly had been in the back of de Gaulle's mind for a long time—an offer to grant nuclear assistance to the French in return for favorable concessions on Commonwealth trade exigencies.

The British had grown sensitive to allegations from the Continent that their entry into Europe would seem halfhearted if they left their nuclear capability outside. One suggested solution, made with a nod toward the Labour Left and the other unilateralists, was for Britain to renounce her nuclear weapons and thereby reduce (hopefully) the incentive for proliferation in favor of greater reliance upon the United States deterrent. But this proposal failed to generate a ground swell. A more interesting straw in the wind was a question posed in April, 1962, by the *Economist:* "Will some kind of gesture to France, in nuclear matters, be required to get this country into the Common Market?"[30] A week later the same periodical asked whether Britain and France could "be persuaded to merge their efforts in a single force that could adequately guard Europe without adding another name to the list of nuclear powers."[31] (Just how many names were then on that list was left vague; no one could say whether the point was to head off a French or a German national deterrent.) Later still, the *Economist,* in commenting upon the Prime Minister's forthcoming visit to Paris, counseled him as follows:

> While Mr. Macmillan should not go to Paris with the idea of buying Britain in, he should make it quite clear that—once in—Britain will regard itself, atomic bombs and all, as wholly committed to Europe, and not just a part-time representative from another Anglo-Saxon world.
>
> In particular, Mr. Macmillan should try to come to a preliminary understanding with General de Gaulle about how Britain might dispose of its nuclear armoury if and when it joins the Common Market. . . . [If nuclear renunciation proves impossible, the next best aim] should be an *entente nucleaire:* a bilateral Anglo-French arrangement to replace the bad example the two countries are currently setting with their separate, national, atomic forces.
>
> General de Gaulle might still not be interested. . . . Yet there would be powerful advantages for him in such a pooling of effort. His defence planners, if not the General himself, must be aware that the new generation of weapons that will come to birth in the second half of the 1960's will be beyond the pocket of all but the richest powers—or combinations of powers. A joint Anglo-French nuclear arm might provide a credible deterrent for the whole of Western Europe; its bases would lie away from

the politically sensitive middle of the continent; it would need no third recruit.[32]

It is doubtful that de Gaulle, even if he should see his way to accepting the concept of a joint deterrent, could subscribe to an arrangement so patently directed against Germany. But the very fact that a leading English journal could unblushingly disclose its views on so delicate a matter provides telling evidence that profound changes are afoot on the other side of the Atlantic. The three leading European states, the powers of old, are engaged in a kind of cat-and-mouse diplomacy that has not been seen for several decades. The historic political rivalry of France and England for prestige and leadership has once again been joined. Of imperial grandeur, little is left. But there is still a Commonwealth and a French Community; the new states of sub-Saharan Africa are categorized as English-speaking or French-speaking. The question is whether the rivalry of old can be smothered in a merger—whether Paris and London will adopt a policy of mutual support in Africa against Soviet penetration and against the proneutralist policies of the United States. The resurgence of German economic power on the Continent adds impetus to the movement toward such a merger. Both England and France are anxious to enlist Germany's economic power in the cause of preserving Europe's overseas position while at the same time keeping Germany's military potential under careful control. Britain would accomplish this latter objective by freezing Germany out of the nuclear club, France by admitting the Germans to a joint nuclear effort. The logic of the situation points unmistakably toward a European Community deterrent, jointly built and jointly controlled. There is reason to believe that nothing less than agreement on a plan for a European nuclear force can break the impasse which has been reached in the historic effort to marry Britain to the Continent.

III

The problem of European deterrence represents the most complex and delicate political challenge yet to arise within the Alliance. The manner in which it is handled is a matter of crucial import for the future of the Atlantic Community. The issue brings into play all the political interrelationships of the United States, Great Britain,

France and Germany, and it is doubtful that a satisfactory solution can be worked out by any three of them over the strong objections of the fourth. The challenge calls for a return, within the Alliance, to the congress diplomacy of an earlier age in which the leading dramatis personae are present as full participants, the spirit of compromise and concert predominates over national egoism, and all the parties are equally satisfied (or equally dissatisfied) as the result of a sometimes painful process of mutual accommodation. Quite obviously, the first step to be taken is to heal the breach between the older Anglo-American and the younger Franco-German axes within the coalition. The key to the solution of this problem is most likely to be found in the concept of an independent European group deterrent—a concept that the United States for a long time has been reluctant to discuss, much less embrace.

It is not at all clear that the British Government has yet fully made up its mind on the direction in which it wishes to move. The ambiguity of her policy during the last year and a half suggests that Britain is undergoing a profound reassessment of her international position. The British have often professed reluctance to link themselves too closely with Europe because this might impair the Anglo-American friendship, based upon similar constitutional, legal and political traditions, linguistic unity and wartime cooperation.[33] But strangely enough, the British did not originally support the proposal for a NATO deterrent, which would seem calculated to perpetuate the special Anglo-American prerogatives in nuclear decision-making. One of the favorite British arguments against a NATO deterrent was that it could be created "only at the expense of something much more important—the establishment and maintenance of strong conventional forces."[34] This argument did not ring true, since Britain, of the four leading NATO powers, had shown herself least interested in increasing her conventional contribution to Continental defense. Another argument frequently advanced by British spokesmen sounded more plausible, namely, that a deterrent with fifteen fingers on the trigger lacks credibility. The real source of British disaffection, however, was that a NATO deterrent, as envisaged prior to the Nassau Pact, would not really give Britain the kind of entree to American nuclear decision-making which she wished to have.

Alastair Buchan, in a brilliant summary of British points of view, outlined the role which Britain would wish to play in the development of American nuclear strategy.[35] In Buchan's view, the United States is cast in the part of bodyguard for Europe, since it possesses all the economic and technological resources to maintain the "fastest gun in the West." In his eyes, the Europeans need not duplicate the costly American deterrent provided that the United States agree to serve as a model bodyguard—impressive-looking and trained well enough to know that he should not draw to fire unless directly attacked or given the sign by those he is retained to protect. The NATO deterrent offered by the United States since 1960, in which the American near-monopoly of nuclear weapons is preserved intact so long as *all* the members of NATO cannot arrive at agreement on joint control, does not exactly fulfill the requirements of Buchan's "bodyguard theory." The promise of Secretaries Rusk and McNamara, given at Athens to keep the Allies apprised of the number, location and capacity of nuclear warheads stationed in Western Europe, as well as the hypothetical conditions in which they might be used, was probably less than the British had in mind on the subject of *contrôle* —to use the term which Buchan had stressed.

Just how far the United States is willing to go to bring its European allies into nuclear strategic planning no one can say. If Americans themselves cannot be sure, a fortiori the British cannot. This is probably one reason why the Macmillan Government in 1962 seemed attracted to the idea of a European deterrent. Could the Americans but be awakened to the fact that the Europeans are thinking seriously about acquiring their own deterrent, the former might be persuaded to convert their entire deterrent, and not just a fraction of it, into a genuine NATO deterrent under the joint control of the leading NATO powers. This still seems to be the hope of some Englishmen; others appear to be coming round to the conclusion that the Anglo-American partnership has reached the point of diminishing returns, and that henceforth Britain, while remaining loyal to NATO, should shift the emphasis of her Alliance policy from across the Atlantic to across the Channel.

Prime Minister Macmillan, speaking to the House of Commons in June, 1962, hinted broadly at the possibility of a joint European deterrent, leaving the impression that this might be the goal of his Cabinet's policy. The Prime Minister, to a certain extent, was reacting to criticisms directed at his government after Defense Secretary

McNamara had deprecated national deterrent forces.[36] In a statement celebrated for its vagueness, Macmillan noted that "the ultimate future of what might be a European defense system must be adapted to the changing situation."[37]

Just about the same time, West German Foreign Minister Gerhard Schroeder, following talks with Secretary of State Dean Rusk, announced that the two countries had agreed on the desirability of a "multilateral European nuclear force."[38] As indicated previously, the British were, at least for a time, inclined toward an Anglo-French nuclear force. The Germans, however, who do not like having to make a political choice between France on the one hand and the United States on the other, have wanted a European deterrent in which they would be able to play an active part, but one meshed with NATO. It seems likely that France, for economic, technological and political reasons, would resist a British proposal for a joint deterrent which excluded the Bonn Republic. Adenauer sided with de Gaulle in the policy of delaying action on the British application, despite the fact that Britain had the support of the United States. Not a few American military leaders would like to make nuclear weapons available to the Bonn Government if adequate political controls satisfactory to the other Europeans could be assured.

The British Government was reported, early in November, 1962, to be interested in the establishment of a multilateral European nuclear deterrent.[39] The time seemed propitious for an American diplomatic initiative which would have a fair chance of breaking the current stalemate: an offer to make the Western European Union (WEU) an independent nuclear power, provided that Britain and France will subject their nuclear capabilities to joint control within the WEU framework.

The concept of a WEU deterrent has received relatively little attention from Western strategic analysts.[40] Yet it commends itself for a number of reasons:

1. The WEU furnishes a vehicle for the transfer by Great Britain and France of their national nuclear forces to joint control. If the United States, by encouraging the creation of a WEU deterrent, could induce its two European allies to make such a transfer, it could not be charged with promoting nuclear proliferation; actually, it would be moving to reduce the number of nuclear powers from four to three.

2. Through the WEU, the United States can assist in advancing the process of European unification to a higher stage. Since the defeat of the European Defense Community, the prospect of achieving European military integration has not appeared very bright. In 1954, the attempt to integrate traditionally organized national armed forces failed. But the fact that nuclear capabilities represent a new military component in Europe, combined with the factor of the geographic homogeneity of the region (which makes it inconceivable that one West European state could wage nuclear war without involving its neighbors), militates in favor of nuclear integration. Furthermore, if Britain should undertake a full commitment to Europe (beyond the partial commitment which she has already undertaken through the WEU),[41] one of the main reasons for the French defeat of EDC—the fear that France without Britain could not be assured of control over a rearming Germany—would be removed.

3. The West Europeans, de Gaulle included, appear determined to establish a European Political Community capable of pursuing common defense and foreign policies. No European political union, however, can rely merely upon the economic prowess of the EEC for its ability to wield power as a major actor on the world scene; it must have a nuclear deterrent at its command.

4. A WEU deterrent would pose less complex political problems of achieving multilateral control of nuclear weapons and strategy than would a genuine NATO deterrent under circumstances now prevailing. It will be a difficult enough task for Britain, France, Germany, Italy and the Benelux countries to work out satisfactory control arrangements through the WEU. But then at least the problem of devising a solution satisfactory not only to the seven countries mentioned but also to the Canadians, the Norwegians, the Portuguese, the Danes, the Turks and the Greeks (leaving the Americans aside for the moment, and passing over Iceland, which has no interest in nuclear sharing) would be reduced to more manageable proportions. For purposes of strategic planning, the WEU countries form a relatively compact geographic unity, and they have a longer experience in intimate political-military conversations than do the members of NATO as a whole.

5. The political control of a WEU deterrent could be expected to be more responsible and more restrained than the control of any purely national deterrent. Furthermore, a WEU deterrent could

provide a framework in which West Germany would be able to make a contribution toward the construction and maintenance of the European nuclear capability and participate in the strategic planning process while remaining under the surveillance and control of her neighbors so far as her own nuclear activities were concerned.[42] Since German scientists and technicians are already cooperating with the French on military nuclear projects, it would be wise for the United States to propose formally a type of multilateral deterrent for Europe which will help to allay the misgivings of the British, the Italians and the Benelux countries over the possibility of a Franco-German atomic partnership.

6. If Britain enters the EEC and Euratom, as well as the projected European Political Community, there would then be a confluence of membership as between the organs of European integration and the WEU. The latter could become the military arm of the new Seven and gradually be converted into a European Defense Community. The WEU exists; the wording of the agreement has already been negotiated. If the United States wishes to encourage the further unification of Europe, with the British participating fully, there is no more appropriate instrument at hand for the purpose than the WEU. A timely announcement by the United States that it is willing to help the Europeans build their defense community on the WEU base might resolve the nuclear-sharing problem and resolve the deadlock between Britain and the Six. But whether or not Britain successfully negotiates entry into the EEC, the problem of the European deterrent would remain, and it might be solved through a revitalized WEU.

7. The WEU, moreover, can furnish a meeting ground for both supranationalists and intergovernmentalists. At first glance, the WEU looks very much like an intergovernmental organization such as NATO, but it contains several additional noteworthy features. The WEU Treaty runs for fifty years, and the wording of its mutual defense guarantee is somewhat stronger than that of NATO. One of its stated objectives in addition to defense is to encourage the progressive integration of Europe. The WEU Council, which normally consists of the Foreign Ministers, may be convoked at the request of any member "to consult with regard to any situation which may constitute a threat to peace, in whatever area this threat should arise."[43] The last phrase takes on particular significance in the light

of what has been said above concerning the desire of many European leaders to formulate common foreign policies for non-European areas. Furthermore, within the WEU Council Britain and the Six have accepted a modest form of taking decisions by less than unanimous agreement.[44] It is in this respect that WEU comes closer to being a political community than does NATO. The WEU Assembly, which is composed of the signatory powers' representatives to the Consultative Assembly of the Council of Europe, is the only intergovernmental parliamentary body in Europe empowered to debate defense questions. It has, as a matter of fact, debated such issues as the need for revising Western strategy in view of "nuclear equipoise," the importance of meeting the prescribed goals for conventional forces, and the problems of establishing joint political control over nuclear weapons. Hence, from the standpoint of existing structure, WEU seems to be the most suitable of all *available* instruments through which the United States could carry out a nuclear-sharing decision. It provides an opportunity for working out appropriate political controls for a European nuclear deterrent which could circumvent some of the problems implied in the overworked metaphor of "fifteen fingers on the trigger and fifteen fingers on the safety lock."

8. In terms of geostrategic space, a West European deterrent utilizing mobile land-based missiles makes a great deal more sense than either the British or the French national deterrent. Measured in square miles, the land target area of Western Europe is two and a half times greater than that of France, and nearly six times larger than that of the United Kingdom. Admittedly, an area of 542,000 square miles is not large in the calculation of thermonuclear exchanges with the U.S.S.R., but it substantially complicates the Soviets' problem of working out a first-strike strategy against Europe alone sufficiently powerful to ensure destruction of Europe's retaliatory capabilities (with the United States standing in the background as *tertius gaudens*). If the eventual ability of Europe to develop a sea-based, mobile deterrent be taken into account, the strategic computations are altered further toward the comparative advantage of Europe over any single European state. There can be no disputing the fact that it would be substantially more difficult for the U.S.S.R. to contemplate a strike against the entire WEU than against France alone.[45] To this extent, the credibility and effectiveness of the de-

terrent would be enhanced, even though a great deal would still hinge upon command and control arrangements.

9. As for economic-technological factors, Western Europe holds a similar comparative advantage over any single European state. The WEU countries, taken as a whole, can boast a total population more than four times greater than either Britain or France, as well as a GNP superiority almost as great. There is no reason to suppose that, with U.S. assistance, Europe could not develop a significant nuclear capability, both tactical and strategic, within a period of from five to ten years. (Without U.S. cooperation, but with political determination, a united Europe, including Britain, can probably achieve a similar capability in from ten to fifteen years.) What is more, the abandonment of national deterrents in favor of a multilateral force would put an end to wasteful duplication of spent resources, and perhaps leave more room in military budgets for the support of "conventional" or "multicapability" forces. The seven European states, working through Euratom and an expanded European Launcher Development Organization, would in time be able to make specialized contributions toward the establishment and maintenance of an up-to-date Western deterrent capability.[46] The Europeans, no doubt, are several years behind to start. But they would be able to take advantage of technological failures and unwise strategic choices in both the United States and the Soviet Union. With an economic growth rate surpassing that of the U.S.S.R. and nearly double that of the United States, Europe will probably be able to sustain increasingly costly programs of military technology nearly as well as will the two superpowers. As a matter of fact, the Europeans are likely to conclude that in order to become one of the world's leading scientific-technological complexes and to retain a position among the leaders over an extended period they have no other choice but to pursue nuclear and missile programs. Governmental expenditures in the areas of advanced military technology generate national overhead capital in the development of several key industries: fuels, metals, plastics, engines, ceramics, electronics, chemicals and others. In the absence of a significant effort to build a deterrent force, Europe's economic growth may lead to an excessively "soft" productive system in which investment capital will be attracted increasingly toward consumer-satisfaction industries and away from the producer durables on which continued growth depends, and also away from

new industries on the technological frontier on which strategic power must be based.

10. A WEU deterrent will enable Europe to achieve its political objective of bringing to an end the nuclear monopoly of the United States within the Alliance, without undermining the Alliance itself by setting the stage for the withdrawal of U.S. military power from Europe. For purposes of military planning the WEU has always been a subsidiary of NATO. The WEU has delegated to NATO certain responsibilities, e.g., in the field of weapons standardization. One of the reasons why the WEU Council has been reluctant in the past to take its own initiatives in the realm of defense was the fear of creating an unpopular consortium within NATO.[47] It is not difficult, however, to postulate a WEU nuclear consortium which would continue to be tied in closely with NATO at the heads of government, foreign ministers and defense ministers levels. There is no reason why the acquisition of nuclear power by the WEU states must necessarily spell an end to U.S. involvement in Europe. At times many European analysts have feared that a stubborn French policy of "going it alone" would create dangers which might induce the United States to disengage itself militarily from the Continent. But a European deterrent, meshed into NATO as a responsible partner of the U.S. deterrent, would provide conditions for continued American participation in the defense of Europe.

There are three very cogent strategic reasons why NATO must endure and why the United States must maintain its military presence in Europe beyond the establishment of a West European deterrent: (1) The United States will remain largely responsible for extending the deterrent to the defense of the five European members of NATO who are outside of WEU—Turkey, Greece, Portugal, Norway and Denmark. The United States would probably keep nuclear weapons on the soil of some of these countries under bilateral agreements, as well as on the soil of the WEU countries under bilateral agreements, or under a joint U.S.-WEU protocol, or both. (2) Although two foci of Western deterrent strength will be in existence, centralized planning and coordinated targeting will be indispensable, and these can be accomplished only through NATO. There will, in short, be two fingers on the trigger of the Western deterrent within the framework of NATO. One will be an American finger, the other a WEU finger. To paraphrase Prime Minister Macmillan, each of the two parties may for a time be "constitutionally free" to invoke the deterrent, but both will, "as a matter of practice," closely coordinate their strategic plans. If American-European partnership means anything, it must mean at least this.[48] (3) It would be most unwise for the United States ever to disengage itself completely from the European region, leaving the Soviets to surmise—foolish as this might be—that they could, at a time of crisis, drive a political wedge through the Atlantic Community by threatening to deal with one part while leaving the other untouched. Under the WEU plan, the Soviets could never be quite sure whether there were one or two deterrents in the West. This circumstance alone could prove highly embarrassing for the Soviets were it not for the possibility that they themselves cannot decide whether they would prefer to face one deterrent or two.

Far from contemplating military disengagement from Europe, the United States should begin thinking of inviting a nuclearized Europe to engage itself in the defense of the continental United States. This would be partnership carried to its logical conclusion. If the United States is committed to the hilt in the defense of Europe and helps Western Europe to acquire an independent nuclear capability, then it is essential that Western Europe tender a credible pledge of its reciprocal commitment to the defense of the United States. Implicit in such a suggestion is the ultimate homogenization of the defense of the Atlantic Community. Given the indivisibility of nuclear defense and the fundamental identity of interests of all Atlantic countries, nothing less than a perfect *quid pro quo* will satisfy Europeans and Americans.

The task ahead, so far as NATO is concerned, is more delicate diplomatically than difficult technically. Technologically and economically speaking, a European deterrent is feasible. The most important pitfalls along the way are political and strategic. Undoubtedly the first question to arise is whether President de Gaulle will agree to place the French national nuclear force under any joint control. This is a question which can be answered only by President de Gaulle, or later by his successors. But it should not be forgotten that even if the European federalists at some future date regain the leadership of the unity movement, the desire for a European deterrent is not likely to diminish.[49] As for de Gaulle himself, it is possible that he will gradually submit to the logic of the economic, technolog-

ical and geostrategic facts which can be marshaled against the national deterrent as well as the arguments in favor of a West European
deterrent. The French President has talked as much as any supranationalist about the need for common European defense and foreign policies. In no area is the need for a common policy more urgent
than in nuclear weaponry and strategy. If Britain agrees to place her
national deterrent under the WEU, one of France's motives for
creating a nuclear force of her own would be removed. Furthermore,
a WEU deterrent is likely to be the very least that Germany would
accept, and the most that the British would be willing to concede.
Therefore, if de Gaulle is in earnest when he speaks of common
policies for Europe, he must realize that they cannot possibly be
created without a joint European atomic policy.

The second set of questions raised by a WEU deterrent concerns
its organization. This, President Kennedy suggested at his press
conference on July 5, 1962, will be primarily a matter upon which
the Europeans must agree among themselves before the United
States can act.[50] The United States cannot draft detailed blueprints
and then try to impose them upon the Europeans. It is up to the
governments of Europe to demonstrate that they have devised a
formula for joint political control and a credible plan of development, production, deployment and military strategy before the
United States can begin to schedule its assistance program. But this
does not mean that American policymakers can afford to sit back and
do nothing but wait. The pattern established by this country when
it promised Europe help in achieving economic recovery and independence through the Marshall Plan after the Europeans had composed their differences through the OEEC may yet prove useful in
stimulating the Europeans to strive toward nuclear unity. Whereas
the United States clearly discerned the need for an economic recovery program and assumed the initiative in announcing the Marshall
Plan, up to now it has not shown a similar enthusiasm for a European
deterrent program. American policymakers keep on saying that they
will cooperate if and when the Europeans agree—only to add quickly
that they do not see a need for a European deterrent. Indeed, the
Nassau Pact can be interpreted as a veering away by the U.S. from
the idea of a genuine multilateral European force.

It seems logical to assume that a WEU deterrent under joint control, especially one that was expected to evolve into a full-fledged

European nuclear defense community, would eventually entail all or most of the following components: (1) a single atomic energy authority, such as Euratom, to supervise the production of all fissionable materials within the member countries; (2) a single international military staff, responsible to the WEU Council for all nuclear strategic and tactical planning, training programs, deployment of weapons under prescribed safeguards and conduct of military operations; (3) the creation of "mixed" (rather than homogeneous) international military teams to staff, guard and operate stockpiles of nuclear weapons and deployed weapons; (4) a WEU system of adequate arms control safeguards to prevent diversion of nuclear materials from production plants, unauthorized sequestration of weapons and accidental occurrences or strategic miscalculation; and (5) the establishment of mutually acceptable political controls governing both the deployment of weapons and the rules of nuclear engagement.

It is most unlikely that a simple formula for the control of a WEU deterrent could be found. There might have to be one set of controls for strategic weapons, another for tactical weapons and still another for whatever conventional forces would be placed under WEU command. "Mixed" military teams might control nuclear weapons deployed in any one member country. Thus, for example, nuclear weapons deployed in Germany might be under the joint control of Anglo-French-German units. If WEU nuclear weapons were deployed in Italy, they would be manned by Anglo-French-Italian units, and in Belgium by Anglo-French-Belgian units. Perhaps the nuclear weapons in Britain and France would be simply under the control of Anglo-French teams, or perhaps nationals of other WEU countries would be allowed to participate in the control of the original two national deterrents which had been pooled to form the basis of WEU.

A similar type of "crazy-quilt" pattern might also turn out to be the only feasible approach to political controls, however disorderly it may seem to those strategists who prefer mathematically precise rules. In the making of certain WEU decisions, unanimity might be required (with Britain, France, Germany, Italy and Benelux each casting one vote). For other decisions, a "qualified" majority may prove practical (e.g., three votes, provided that two of the three are cast by France and Great Britain, or four votes if France and Britain are divided on the issue). In addition to this, each nation might reserve the right to veto the deployment or the use of nuclear weapons or certain types of nuclear weapons on its own soil. Finally, special arrangements might have to be made governing the decision to use nuclear weapons against a Soviet attack upon West Germany. In the early phase of the conflict, or up to a prescribed geographic line of Soviet penetration, tripartite agreement (i.e., British, French and German) may be required to initiate the use of nuclears. Beyond that point, a Franco-German decision might be sufficient. The Europeans, in the various institutions which they have already constructed, have shown themselves quite adept at working out decision-making procedures which seem very complex to the outside observer but which have the merit of taking into account the unique political problems involved in every international decision.[51]

The United States would be wise to announce that it will look favorably upon the concept of a Western Europe deterrent; that it will construe the 1958 amendments to the McMahon Act to authorize the sharing of nuclear weapons information once it is clear that irreversible progress is being made toward merging the two European nuclear forces into a single deterrent under joint WEU control; and that it will insist upon the centralization of nuclear strategic planning between this country and the Western European Union within the framework of NATO. The United States should also declare that during the period of transition, i.e., from five to ten years, it will continue to provide the principal deterrent for the defense of Europe in NATO, and that it will during that time reserve its freedom to employ nuclear weapons if necessary to meet its solemn treaty obligations or to preserve its own national interest. Moreover, the United States ought to acknowledge that during the transitional period the political control of the developing WEU deterrent would, as a matter of course, rest entirely with the WEU members themselves, to be exercised according to agreed procedures. (The authority of Defense Secretary McNamara and Prime Minister Macmillan can be cited to support the thesis that independence of political control is not incompatible with centralization of technical command and control. If Britain can do it, why cannot the WEU?) Finally, there should be an understanding that, at the end of the transitional period (to be defined in a mutually satisfactory manner), when Western Europe possesses its own credible deterrent, the United States and the

Western European Union will come together and bargain as equals. for the purpose of creating a single, joint NATO deterrent.

At that time, there will be two fingers on the trigger, one American and one European. The two transatlantic nuclear partners will naturally turn their thoughts to the notion of two fingers on the safety lock. What is suggested here is not necessarily the deadlock of reciprocal veto powers, but rather the merging of two "constitutional freedoms of action" into a single constitutional freedom of action, vested in the appropriate institutions of a like-minded Atlantic Community.

CHAPTER **6** THE GRAND DESIGN AND ITS

OPPONENTS: A WESTERN RESPONSE

Many are the opponents of greater unity in the North Atlantic area. The communists, because of ideology and strategic objectives, are irreconcilably committed to the destruction of the Western Alliance, their chief competitor for the prize of molding tomorrow's world. Communist ideology postulates the disintegration of capitalism, and the Soviets seek, first and foremost, to hasten the West's decline and fall. In Africa and Asia many newly independent peoples look with suspicion, if not with hostility, upon the efforts of their erstwhile rulers to achieve greater unity. Although they retain, in some cases, a residual respect for the legacy bequeathed by the West, the new states often seek to exploit their position in the struggle between the prime contenders. Last but not least, in Europe and the United States there exist forces in many guises, from unilateralism to neo-isolationism, which oppose Atlantic unity.

According to Lenin, wars among the Western powers were the logical and natural consequence of "capitalist" expansion. But Lenin also predicted that the countries of the West, in order to forestall their "predictable" extinction, would lash out against the communist world. Thus, according to Lenin (and Stalin), war between communism and the capitalist powers was inevitable.

Khrushchev reaffirmed his adherence to Lenin's precept when he declared, in his celebrated speech of January 6, 1961:

Even the window of the so-called Atlantic solidarity hides an ugly picture of internal discords and conflicts; the opposition to U.S. leadership and diktat is increasing. The revival of German militarism and revanchism

231

in the center of Europe restores a most complicated range of Anglo-German, Franco-German, and other imperialist contradictions. If we compare the present position of capitalism with its position after World War II, it becomes clear that a great deepening in the general crisis of capitalism has taken place.[1]

Nevertheless, Khrushchev holds, the West represents the primary obstacle to the establishment of peace, communist style, even though the Soviets believe that they have taken great strides toward the "socialist encirclement" of the Atlantic Community. The communists foresee a period in which the Sino-Soviet bloc will outstrip the West in military, technological and economic growth, and thus become predominant in world politics. According to the communists, a primary way to achieve this objective is to nurture the disunity of the West.

Peaceful Coexistence

Nikita Khrushchev, in his speech of January 6, 1961, far from sounding a clarion call to genuine peaceful coexistence, declared war anew upon the noncommunist world.[2] He did not introduce a new variant into communist strategy. He merely returned to the historic alternative of *peredyshka,* the soft line, or the intermission which has been part and parcel of Soviet diplomacy as far back as Brest-Litovsk. Although it is not *new,* this strategy of the "ebb," of the "popular front," of "cooperation with progressive forces among the bourgeoisie," is an intrinsic, ever-present element of communist dialectic. The term "peaceful coexistence" is not imbued with the benign meaning which it connotes in *our* parlance, just as the Japanese "co-prosperity sphere" was meant to couch a most uncivilized aggression in the language of civilized international behavior.

In fact, Khrushchev's pronouncement provided guidelines for communist expansionist strategy for this decade and perhaps beyond 1970. It called for the intensification of all forms of political warfare, supported by growing Soviet military might. This directive will remain in force as long as, according to Soviet calculations, the U.S. retains an over-all military edge. In 1957, Shepilov, for a brief time Soviet Foreign Minister, described the character of "peaceful coexistence": "As long as different social-political systems continue to exist, the antagonisms between them are unavoidable. Peaceful co-existence is a struggle, political, economic and ideological."

The carrot-and-stick technique of "peaceful coexistence" has reaped rich harvests for the communists in the past. It is ideally tailored to the mentality in the West, which fancies each Kremlin easing of Cold War tensions as the dawn of a *rapprochement*. In the West, hopeful forecasts on the impending transformation of Soviet society and the confusion of communist bargaining technique with a change in purpose provide a fertile ground for communist political warfare.

NATO, an alliance created to forestall armed aggression, finds itself engaged in an unconventional conflict demanding joint political positions and actions. The absence of a shooting war tends to obscure the unorthodox threat against which joint efforts are required. Yet the real inroads of Soviet political warfare behind the screen of "coexistence" make demands for joint action that greatly exceed those usually confronting an alliance in peacetime.

Whereas the Soviet objective is plainly the neutralization of the Western Alliance, that very Western Alliance cannot bring itself to engage in the extensive and integral use of political warfare techniques which offer the defense against its neutralization. In World War II, the West regarded political warfare operations as insignificant appendages of policy. The fact that, when the shooting started, the Nazi threat was no longer primarily a psychopolitical one militated against the expansion of the West's political-psychological capabilities. The pursuit of war by other means did not appeal to the Western leaders. It is enough to recall General Bradley's comment that the U.S. was concerned not with political problems, but simply with defeating the enemy.

Communist psychological warfare has been effective—in any case effective enough to deter the West from waging the Cold War more extensively in nonviolent forms. Instead, the West has lavished its attention on hopeful speculation over the Sino-Soviet rift, deciphering the meaning of de-Stalinization, exploring the constructive possibilities of so-called national communism, gloating over the corruption of communist ideology or the mistakes of communist leadership, and the "mellowing" of Soviet society as standards of living improve.[3]

The West has been deflected from the pursuit of realistic policies by the illusion that it could foster by conciliatory policies the emergence in the Soviet Union of new leaders and groups who stand for moderation, and thus achieve a general *détente* with the communists.

Much attention has been given by Western spokesmen to the concept of overlapping interest, particularly in the field of arms control, between Khrushchev who speaks about "burying us" and ourselves, his opponents, who presumably wish to stay alive. As Dean Rusk put it:

There is another matter in which, objectively examined, all the great powers have a genuine common interest. I refer to the halting of the upward spiral of the arms race. Let us be clear about what this means and what it does not mean. We have a security interest in turning the arms race downward; otherwise the path ahead means increasingly vast diversions of resources away from the unfinished business of mankind as well as increasing dangers for all concerned as weapons systems tax or exceed the capacities of the mind of man. But disarmament measures cannot be unilateral; surely the free world learned that lesson from the demobilization after World War II.

After discussing both the technical and political difficulties involved, Secretary Rusk concluded:

We hope that self-interest and the yearning of the Soviet peoples for a better life will cause the Soviet Government to reconsider and sit down with the rest of us to work out practical steps which will begin to reduce the burdens and dangers.[4]

These hopes, which we share, advanced before the Cuban missile crisis, are at variance, however, with Khrushchev's assertion that "the struggle for disarmament is an active struggle against imperialism, for restricting its military potentials."[5]

Khrushchev's revealing words unmask the deep strategic significance behind the Soviet disarmament campaign. In a report prepared for the U.S. Senate Committee on the Judiciary, the Foreign Policy Research Institute concluded:

Acceptance of any precipitate program of disarmament by the West would mean in a basic strategic sense that the West no longer felt capable of insuring its own survival. This acknowledgement alone would constitute for the West a strategic defeat of enormous magnitude, leaving an irresolute Western World only the recourse of seeking accommodation with an aggressive movement which is dedicated to achieving mastery of the globe.[6]

Communist strategy for emasculating Western power is abetted by that political pseudo sophistication which has become so fashionable in certain Western intellectual circles impatient with the stark realities of the power conflict. Thus, for example, it is argued that the West should "fraternize" with the communists in order to promote ideological dissension among them.[7]

Armed with insights such as these, the West, ignoring the consistency of communist aggression conducted under the banners of "peaceful coexistence," treats each conflict confrontation tactically rather than as a part of a vast strategic campaign. Each concrete dispute is to be settled once and for all on its merits. To this end, the West seeks to persuade the Soviets of its good intentions. The score card of this diplomatic contest makes melancholy reading: The West offers concessions; these concessions, when the Soviets deign to accept them, enable the Soviets to continue the conflict from a more advantageous position.

Until recently, the Soviets' latitude for maneuver in Western Europe had been comparatively narrow. But the Soviets' growing military power, achievements in space and adroit political strategy, abetted by a widespread feeling that there are gaps in the Western military posture, open up new opportunities for communist initiatives. Until the Cuban missile showdown, nuclear blackmail tactics were beginning to pay off. The growing Soviet nuclear capability tended to diminish the effectiveness of the United States' strategic deterrent as the principal restraint on Soviet moves in Central Europe. Until the Soviet missile deployment in Cuba, communist attempts at atomic blackmail had been pure bluff. Having learned from this setback the communists are likely to speed their arms drive so that future "adventuristic" actions will be backed by a force which makes the threat of nuclear devastation seem much more plausible.

Communist psychological operations have become more opportunistic. They have shifted from the proletarian class to a multiple-class basis, exploiting the economic, political and social shortcomings within a target country. Internationally, the communists pose as champions of national liberation movements, anticolonialism, peace and ban-the-bomb movements. In the remaining colonial areas, communist propaganda ascribes all ills to imperialism; everyone will gain wealth and happiness through liberation from colonial rule. Further-more, the communists have almost immobilized Western counter-moves. They have conditioned the West to accept their own ground rule for the waging of the Cold War, namely, that the communist empire is the "peace zone" and the Free World the "war zone."[8] The general euphoria which has pervaded Washington since the President first cut off and then reversed the flow of Soviet missiles to Cuba (in itself an admirable use of power with restraint) ought not to be allowed to becloud our judgment. The oft-repeated as-sertion that "the tide is running in the West's favor" has yet to be backed up by solid and sustained empirical evidence.

Communist psychological warfare operations, directed at exploit-ing the internal vulnerabilities within target countries, are geared to the "objective" situation. Their propaganda is pinpointed toward sympathetic and discontented groups. Their ultimate goal is the cor-ruption of non-Marxist ideological symbols such as liberty, liberalism, democracy, religion and justice. This propaganda of demoralization seeks to destroy anticommunist leadership and to discredit indige-nous social systems and institutions, and to plunge noncommunist societies into a welter of frustration, confusion, pessimism, guilt, hopelessness, fear and defeatism. The communists generally manage to sustain the psychological initiative and, particularly in the inter-national sphere, they are still largely responsible for the items that go on the agenda of the East-West conflict.

Communist propaganda peddles a variety of merchandise labeled "peace." Its "peace" drive is particularly directed at Asia and Africa and, with suitable adjustments, at a growing neutralist movement in Europe which equates peace with disengagement. The communists foster the neutralist spirit in Europe by fears of the re-emergence of a strong Germany. The growth of neutralist sentiment in Western lands impedes the development of true nuclear power in Europe and strengthens those factions that agitate for the withdrawal of the United States from Western Europe. As part of their "peace" strategy, the communists seek to infiltrate legitimate peace move-ments and organizations. These "fronts" invite public support by sponsoring popular causes. Any group advocating unilateral dis-armament for the West can be sure to gain strong communist sup-port. The radical left wing of the British Labour Party, for example, has become a channel for communist unilateral disarmament propaganda. The leaders of the two main unilateralist groups in Britain, Lord Bertrand Russell of the Committee of 100 and Canon Collins of the Campaign for Nuclear Disarmament, were invited to the World Peace Congress in Moscow in the summer of 1962.

Until recently, Moscow did not entertain exaggerated notions about the true strength of NATO and the potential threat of its arms to the Soviet position in Europe. The Soviets were all too aware of the numerous weaknesses of the Western Alliance. The real deterrent to Soviet aggression in Europe was America's strategic nuclear force. Of late, a noticeable change has occurred in the Soviets' attitude. They are now genuinely apprehensive about developments in Western Europe. *The intensity of the political warfare campaign against NATO remains one of the constants of Soviet policy.* Now, Soviet propaganda, while waxing lyrical over the blessings of neutralism and unilateralism, calls for the elimination of all American bases as the only alternative to the nuclear annihilation of the host country.

Communists rarely originate issues on which to pin their political warfare strategy. It is far easier and more profitable to exploit the numerous frictions and conflicts that thrive within the Atlantic world. Most useful to the Kremlin are the disagreements that divide the nations of Western Europe and North America on such matters as, for example, nuclear weapons, their proper individual and collective responses to communist challenges, and the proper policies, individual and collective, toward a host of issues arising in Asia, Africa and Latin America.

NATO: The Permanent Threat

A careful study of communist propaganda reveals the objectives of Soviet strategy. For example, communist propaganda has always portrayed NATO as an "aggressive" military bloc bent upon the destruction of the Soviet Union. In his speech of January 6, 1961, Premier Khrushchev reiterated this theme: "We set ourselves the task of exposing the aggressive essence of military-political alignments of the imperialists like NATO, SEATO, and CENTO, of seeking their isolation and ultimate liquidation."[9] The communist propaganda campaign is directed toward five specific objectives: to prevent the spread of nuclear weapons within NATO, to forestall the creation of a NATO nuclear force, to impede West German rearmament, to slow the increase of national military budgets and to force the withdrawal of United States troops from Europe.

Should the communists once succeed in separating one or more countries from NATO, they would not only have gained a tactical advantage by depriving the West of territory for its defense, but they would also have scored a psychological victory by reducing the prestige of NATO throughout the world. Therefore the communists have sought, by persistent efforts, to frighten NATO members, from Norway to Turkey, by warning them of the liabilities inherent in membership in an "aggressive" Western Alliance. The Soviets periodically warn selected NATO countries that their cities and populations are vulnerable to the nuclear capabilities of the Soviet Union, and that, should they accept NATO missile installations, they will become prime targets in the event of nuclear war. Such propaganda, though it may not achieve the demise of NATO, provides the principal stimulant for the growth of unilateralist and pacifist sentiment.

In the propaganda campaign against NATO, the communists combine the strategy of peaceful coexistence with increasingly blunt military threats. By the adroit alternation of "peace" appeals and threats of nuclear blackmail, the communists seek to weaken the credibility which the Europeans attach to the United States nuclear deterrent. Communist propaganda portrays the United States as seeking its own security behind a European shield. The United States, it is claimed, seeks to pursue "aggressive" policies and to engage Europe in a war which will result "inevitably" in Europe's own destruction. Thus the communists seek to condition the peoples of Western Europe to believe that opposition to communist expansion is not worth the risk of all-out war and that the West does not possess the means by which to respond appropriately to graduated Soviet challenges. Missiles, bombs, space exploits and nuclear testing have replaced the wonders of the workers' paradise as the favorite themes of communist propaganda.

At the heart and center of the communist effort is the perennial attempt to detach West Germany from NATO. The Soviets know that without West Germany the prospects for European integration would be considerably less promising. The communists are also aware of the significance of West Germany's contribution to NATO in terms of men and territory vital for the defense of Western Europe. The communists realize, furthermore, that the reduction of the German Federal Republic to a secondary NATO power would deprive the United States of a most important ally on the European Continent and give rise to neutralist forces in the Federal Republic.

The communist strategists recognize that the future of the Atlantic Alliance and of European integration is related closely to the future of West Germany. Soviet propaganda, therefore, decries the "German peril." West Germany is to be separated first psychologically and then physically from the West. The communists maintain that West Germany, through its influence on NATO policy in Europe and its alleged domination of the Common Market, is about to accomplish by intrigue what Hitler failed to achieve by conquest: the control of Europe. The Germans are said to be bent upon the building of a military machine with which to threaten the Soviet Union and the communist states of Eastern Europe. According to Khrushchev, "The struggle against the revival of German militarism is of particular importance for the consolidation of peace in Europe, and not only in Europe."

On November 27, 1958, in a formal note, the Soviet Union demanded that the Western powers leave Berlin and proposed the creation of a "demilitarized free city" in West Berlin. Because Berlin is a Western outpost in the so-called "peace-zone" of communism, it is "a bone in [Khrushchev's] throat." But Berlin also represents for the communists a means of prying loose West Germany from NATO and European integration. In short, Khrushchev's objective in Berlin extends far beyond the former German capital to the future of NATO. Berlin is a pressure point to be taken one day, if possible, by the communists, but to be used in the meantime to sow dissension within the Atlantic Alliance.

Shortly after he revived the Berlin issue, Khrushchev reaped rewards in the form of Western division over the response most appropriate to the new Soviet threat. The Western Allies, in identical notes, on December 31, 1958, rejected the Soviet Union's note of November 27 on the status of West Berlin. However, on February 21, 1959, Prime Minister Macmillan began a series of talks in Moscow with Khrushchev. The joint communiqué issued at the conclusion of the talks stated that "further study could usefully be made of the possibility of increasing security by some method of limitation of forces and weapons, both conventional and nuclear, in an agreed area of Europe coupled with an appropriate system of inspection." The communiqué did little to allay French and German apprehensions that the British might be prepared to make concessions to the Soviets at Germany's expense. The West German Government has always feared that the day might come when the United States, having agreed to "disengagement," might leave West Germany exposed to Soviet encroachments. The communists at various intervals have put forth proposals for "disengagement" in Europe which would have left the Soviet forces within easy striking distance of Western Europe while removing American forces across the Atlantic. These proposals found favor among influential circles in many NATO countries. Nowhere did they receive a more respectful hearing than in Britain.[10] Thus it was not surprising that not a few NATO partners came to doubt British firmness on Berlin—if not on most crucial West-East issues.

Differences among the Western Allies centered upon the means most appropriate for safeguarding the freedom of the inhabitants of West Berlin. Officially, agreement existed on the necessity to preserve in West Berlin a Western outpost behind the Iron Curtain. However, General de Gaulle, bent upon solidifying his *entente* with the Federal Republic, took the position that the West need not respond with concessions to a crisis manufactured by Khrushchev. Chancellor Adenauer, moreover, asserted that so long as the Soviets threatened West Berlin, the West should not negotiate under duress.

The communists, in the course of the Berlin crisis, have proposed, as the *quid pro quo* for the reduction of tension in and around Berlin, the removal of nuclear forces from West Germany, the restriction of nuclear weapons to those Western Allies now possessing them and the prohibition of exchanges of nuclear information among NATO countries. The Soviets know that the West has largely staked its defense of Berlin and of Europe upon the use of nuclear weapons. NATO strategy, despite efforts to create a more flexible posture, is in large measure nuclear strategy. Should the Soviets succeed in achieving a *modus vivendi* on Berlin at the expense of Western strategy and security, they would not only have achieved the objective of casting a shadow over the effectiveness of the West's defenses;

they would also have removed the major obstacle to the conquest of West Berlin.

The Western Allies have announced that a Soviet attack against Berlin would be a *casus belli*. Khrushchev knows that he cannot seize Berlin without the risk of nuclear war. Nor can the communists be certain of what else the Western Allies might do, should they decide not to wage a nuclear war on behalf of Berlin. To be sure, there exists the possibility that, were the Soviets to succeed in demonstrating the inability of Western countries to defend what, on so many occasions, they have termed a vital interest, NATO might not survive the calamitous loss of its prestige and might fall apart. Yet, the communists cannot be certain that the loss of Berlin might not arouse the United States and its European allies to vastly increased defense expenditures and new steps toward integration.

If the Soviets ever have their way in Berlin, they will have removed a "crisis faucet" with which to raise or lower tensions with the West. For this purpose the Berlin issue has served Khrushchev well since 1958. In sum, the communists, should they effect a quick grab of West Berlin, might risk Western nuclear retaliation. They would confront the prospect of a vastly increased United States armaments effort, and possibly even steps to strengthen the Western Alliance. The Soviets would have scored an impressive victory, but they would also have lost an important pressure point in their strategy of protracted conflict against NATO.

In Cuba, the communists have acquired a territorial foothold in the very heartland of the North Atlantic Community. Throughout the year 1962, up to the time of the missile crisis in October, many of the European allies of the United States—and indeed many observers in this country—were inclined to deprecate the magnitude of the threat to the Western Hemisphere and to NATO posed by the presence of communism on the island. President Kennedy's policy of naval blockade turned back the missiles but not communism from Cuba. In fact, it did not turn back Soviet military power from the Caribbean. Even after the Administration's triumph in October, the U.S.S.R. continued to consolidate its newest political satellite and its only overseas military base. By February, 1963, the Administration was admitting that the shipment of conventional military equipment to the island had been proceeding apace. American equanimity in the face of this situation was justified by the interpretation that the arms were "purely defensive." Such an interpretation was almost tantamount to recognizing the right of the communists to remain in permanent occupation. It was especially remarkable in view of the fact that, at the time of the missile crisis, the Administration claimed to be able to control the situation because it possessed not only superior strategic nuclear capabilities but also superior conventional capabilities in the Caribbean, meaning that it could have ordered the invasion of the island if necessary without provoking general war. But after October, the Soviets were allowed to modify the balance of conventional forces in the area to the disadvantage of the United States. Three months after the withdrawal of the missiles, communism was more firmly entrenched than ever upon the island. Some observers took comfort in the thought that the image of Castro had been tarnished in Latin America. But throughout history, communism has displayed a remarkable ability to survive recurring blots on its escutcheon and to regain respectability. Tarnished image or no, in the early part of 1963 it appeared as though one of the tasks assigned to the several thousand "weapons instructors" who the Soviets admitted were in Cuba was to train revolutionaries for future activities in Latin America. Even though communism in Cuba posed no immediate threat to the security of the United States, it nevertheless presented a threat of the first magnitude to the other Latin republics. Despite the periodic emanation of confident statements from U.S. policy-making officials, it was not yet clear that the United States possessed a coherent strategic plan for countering the danger.

The Cuba crisis left many disconcerting bits of debris. At the height of the crisis, quite a few persons had uncritically compared the emplacement of Soviet missiles in a country where the communists had seized power by deception and force with the positioning of American bases in Europe at the invitation of free countries. Those who drew such comparisons apparently did not realize that they were casting doubt upon the morally superior rights of a free, defensive alliance over an aggressive totalitarian movement. It is discomfiting to imagine toward what uncharted ground this line of analogous reasoning will lead the West—a line which propounds as a guiding standard for policy a simple, disarming rule: "Let's be fair to the communists."

Communism and the Specter of Europe

The communists, in 1962, showed their apprehension over trends toward unity in Western Europe by directing their psychological warfare against European integration. The communists could not gainsay the fact that the prosperity of the European Economic Community stood in sharp contrast to the failures of communism in East Germany and other communist satellites. Moreover, the application of Britain and of other European countries for membership in, or association under protocol with, the Common Market raised the prospect of yet a more formidable obstacle to communist expansion. Accordingly, the communists asserted that "The Common Market is a component of the imperialist policy of organizing reactionary political and military and economic blocs to fight the world socialist system, the young sovereign states, the national-liberation movements in the countries still fettered by colonial chains and the progressive forces at home." As in their earlier propaganda against NATO, the communists portrayed the European Economic Community as a last-ditch effort by the capitalists to stem the advance of communism. The communists thus revealed once again their irreconcilable hostility toward Western unity.

On May 30, 1962, Premier Khrushchev opened the communist campaign against the Common Market when, speaking officially at a rally in Moscow during the state visit of the President of the Mali Republic, he denounced the European Economic Community. The Soviet Premier declared that the Common Market represents "a state-monopoly agreement of the West German financial oligarchy which threatens the vital interests of all peoples, the cause of universal peace, because the imperialist aggressive circles are using it to strengthen NATO and to speed up the arms race." Although Khrushchev suggested that the Common Market was "directed against the Soviet Union and other socialist countries," his most detailed criticism concerned the alleged aim of the European Economic Community "to tie a number of liberated countries to the economy of the imperialist states, to keep them in servitude." Thus Khrushchev added yet another dimension to the communist propaganda campaign to undermine Western unity and to exacerbate tensions between Europe and the states of Africa and Asia.

Khrushchev probably realizes that the creation of the European Economic Community has dealt a grievous blow to communist dogma as well as to Soviet policy in Europe. The increasing wealth and rising living standards in Europe have refuted the dogmas of Marx and Lenin, for European prosperity, contrary to communist doctrine, has come at a time when European colonial systems have been in the process of dissolution. Moreover, the political stability and growing military strength of Western Europe hinder the communists' expansion westward through subversion and limited military probes. Western Europe's glittering prosperity stands in sharp contrast to the shabbiness of life in Eastern Europe and the Soviet Union. Economic growth rates in West European countries as of 1962 approximated or exceeded those of the Sino-Soviet bloc. In short, contrary to Marx's opening passage in the *Communist Manifesto,* the specter of capitalist Europe haunts communism.

Communist tactics against the Common Market are not confined to propaganda. The Soviets have attempted to weaken the Common Market in trade talks with West European countries. It was probably the ominous prospect of "competitive coexistence," EEC style, which led the Soviet Union, on June 13, 1962, to suspend trade negotiations with France. The Soviets thus brought into operation another of their techniques of political warfare. They offered to resume talks if the French granted to the Soviets a most-favored-nation agreement on a par with concessions given to members of the European Economic Community. To have agreed to the Soviet demand would have been tantamount to the refusal of France to live up to her commitments in the Common Market. Moreover, such an agreement with the Soviet Union would have endangered not only negotiations between Great Britain and the European Economic Community, but also those concerning the admission of Denmark, Norway and Ireland. The Soviet proposal to France undoubtedly had as one of its objectives the disruption of the Franco-German *entente* which has formed a mainstay of European integration and, within the Western Alliance, a barrier to accommodation with the communists in Berlin.[11]

The Soviets sought to exploit British resentments and misgivings after the Brussels negotiations on entry into the Common Market were suspended. *Pravda,* on February 7, 1963, deplored what it termed the "humiliation" of Britain by her NATO partners. The communist newspaper also shed crocodile tears over the U.S. decision to cancel Skybolt on the grounds that it deprived Britain of her independent nuclear deterrent. At the same time the Soviet Union, in notes to the governments at Paris and Bonn, vehemently denounced the Franco-German Pact. These various propaganda ploys, undoubtedly calculated to appeal to British nationalist sentiment and to arouse British suspicion of the Franco-German coalition, happened to come on the eve of a visit to Moscow by 170 prominent U.K. businessmen, arranged by a leading British newspaper publisher to explore the prospects of increased Anglo-Soviet trade. The communists held out the alluring prospect of orders to Britain's depressed shipbuilding industry, together with purchases of factories and other capital goods, in exchange for British imports of Soviet goods, including petroleum. The Soviets in effect offered Britain increased trade with the communist bloc as an alternative to closer economic links with Western Europe.

European Neutrals and Outsiders

The opposition to Atlantic and European integration expressed by neutralist leaders in Africa and Asia has no counterpart in the official statements of those noncommunist European countries who are not members of NATO. European neutrals do not oppose in principle the Atlantic Alliance or the European Common Market. Where their neutrality permits, the European neutrals actively seek ways of participating in those schemes which promote the integration of the West. But the participation of the European neutrals, Finland, Sweden, Switzerland and Austria, is limited, by and large, to cultural and economic cooperation with the other nations of the Atlantic Community, while precluding formal ties with them.

Finland's proximity to the Soviet Union dictates a foreign policy of neutrality. The Soviets have always voiced their hostility to Finnish membership in European or Atlantic organizations. For example, when the Finnish Prime Minister, in 1948, declared that he favored expanded cultural relations with other Scandinavian countries, but was not contemplating military cooperation, the Soviet press accused him of trying to lead Finland into a northern bloc protected by the United States. In 1961, after Finland had signed an agreement giving her associate membership in EFTA, the

Soviet Government expressed its dissatisfaction. But Finland, despite Soviet pressures, conducts more trade with Free World countries than with the Soviet Union. Her contacts are primarily with the West rather than with the Soviet Union. Her neutrality is dictated more by geographical and strategic considerations than by affinities of ideology or culture.

Swedish neutrality is conditioned by such factors as geography and a history of 150 years of noninvolvement in the political struggles of Europe. Common among Swedes is the belief that membership in NATO would provoke the Soviet Union into applying greater pressure against Finland. Swedes sometimes suggest that the fact that they would join NATO in the event of a Soviet seizure of Finland acts as a deterrent against the communists and thus preserves Finnish independence. Some defend Swedish neutrality by asserting that for Sweden to join NATO would increase the risk of a war in which Sweden could neither affect the outcome nor be assured of adequate protection by the Alliance. Nevertheless, in addition to her membership in the OEEC and the OECD, some Swedes have suggested the possibility of Sweden's joining the European Economic Community. Her neutrality, moreover, does not prevent Sweden from allocating for defense a larger share of GNP than most NATO countries.

Certain groups, including the publishers of *Dagens Nyheterm* and a minority of the Swedish Conservative and Liberal parties, have urged Sweden's membership in NATO. Through much of its history, NATO has enjoyed considerable popular support in Sweden. Those Swedes who support NATO agree that in a conflict between the Soviet bloc and the West, Swedish territory might easily become a battleground irrespective of Sweden's professed neutrality. Thus, it is suggested, the only way to minimize the likelihood of war is for Sweden to join NATO, for the Swedes could then make more effective defense preparations in collaboration with other NATO countries, and in case of attack could be certain of allies.[12]

Swiss neutrality, guaranteed by the Instrument of Vienna, evolved from a delicate domestic compromise, and sheltered by the protective umbrella of the European power balance, prevents Switzerland from seeking membership in NATO and other programs designed to increase the military and political cohesion of the Atlantic Community. Nevertheless there is recognition in Switzerland of the need for military collaboration with NATO in the event of armed conflict in Europe. The Swiss Federal Council, in 1960, received legislative approval for the creation of three new mobile divisions which could be used in conjunction with NATO military units in case of a communist attack against Switzerland.[13] The Swiss joined the OEEC, and later EFTA, in order to preserve their trading position in Europe. But the Swiss are not prepared to participate fully in European integration. According to Willy Bretscher, editor of the *Neue Zürcher Zeitung:* "Joining a structure designed to evolve into a European super-state, would in the case of Switzerland, a neutral, small nation, imply abandoning essential parts of its national sovereignty, with the result of a real danger to its political independence, its neutrality, its federative structure, and its democratic way of life."[14] For the same reasons, the Swiss are unwilling to associate themselves formally with the Atlantic Alliance, even though their sympathies, history, trade and defense link them firmly to the West.

After World War II, Austria participated in several West European organizations of economic cooperation. Austria, for example, was a founding member of the OEEC. As the price for regaining her independence and effecting the removal of foreign troops from her soil, Austria agreed, in 1955, to become a militarily neutral country. As a result of this status Austria is bound not to join military alliances and not to allow the establishment of foreign bases on her soil. Nevertheless Austria's neutrality did not prevent her from rendering assistance to Hungarian refugees during the Budapest uprising of 1956. Austria, like other European neutrals, joined EFTA. Many Austrians, moreover, favor Austria's membership in the European Economic Community, for Austria does 60 percent of her foreign trade with the Common Market. Austria remains firmly in the Atlantic Community and is willing to consider participation in the nonmilitary forms of Western integration.

Spain, though for different reasons from the European neutrals, is excluded from NATO. Franco's regime, however, is unique in Europe in having expressed unremitting hostility toward communism before, during and since World War II.[15] The Spanish Government, moreover, permitted the United States, by the Pact of Madrid, signed in 1953, to construct a complex of naval and air bases, thus providing the West added deterrent strength in the Iberian Peninsula against a Soviet attack upon NATO in Europe.

In 1957, the United States Government evinced its interest in possible NATO membership for Spain. In April, 1959, the French Government suggested that it was prepared to support Spain's admission to NATO, and President de Gaulle, in June of the same year, proposed the creation of a Western Mediterranean Alliance with Spain as a member. There was evidence, moreover, in 1960, that West Germany, lacking suitable space at home, was negotiating for the use of territory in Spain for the training of German military forces. This revelation brought sharp protests in Europe.

The idea of Spain joining NATO also arouses considerable opposition in some North Atlantic countries, particularly in Britain, Norway and Denmark, because of the nature of Franco's authoritarian regime, even though similar objections might be raised about Portugal and Turkey. Nevertheless, on July 20, 1959, Spain was granted full membership in OEEC after her government pledged itself to the adoption of an economic stabilization plan. Spain, like the neutrals of Europe, faces the task of reconciling herself to European economic integration as represented by the Common Market. There were signs, early in 1963, that the Spanish Government was not unfriendly to suggestions that it might enter into closer economic and political cooperation with France and Germany just when the question of U.S. bases in Spain was about to be re-opened.

The Developing Areas

The communists, in recent years, have focused their attention upon the reduction of European and American influence in the underdeveloped areas. Both Lenin and Stalin regarded the communist movement's objective to be the removal of all vestiges of Western power from Latin America, Africa, and Asia. As we have seen, Lenin held that the West, because of its control of the underdeveloped areas, was able for a time to postpone its own demise. According to Khrushchev, "With the collapse of the colonial system, imperialism has become considerably weaker. Vast territories, tremendous masses of people, have already ceased or are ceasing to serve as its reserve, a source of cheap raw material and cannon fodder."[16] Therefore, the reduction of Western influence in the underdeveloped areas, according to communist reasoning, leads inexorably to the weakening of Europe and the United States, and contributes to the expansion

of communism. The communist effort to penetrate the underdeveloped areas provides a wedge for splitting the Western Alliance,
for many extra-NATO problems, from the Congo to Cuba—not to
mention Suez and Taiwan—have opened breaches among the North
Atlantic countries.

Although Western Europe is relatively secure, the underdeveloped
areas are vulnerable to communist penetration through subversion
and "wars of national liberation." From South Vietnam to Cuba, the
middle and southern reaches of the globe furnish the communists
with numerous opportunities for exploiting the anti-Western sentiments of former colonial peoples and of those countries in transition
from old to new social, political and economic orders.

The problems of the underdeveloped areas have aroused intense
and compassionate interest in the United States, and American
policymakers have sometimes provoked European resentment by sid-
ing with African or Asian countries against their former rulers. Some
Americans have found in neutralism a stance to be encouraged as a
means of lessening tensions in the Cold War. Others have suggested
that the United States, if it fosters Atlantic unity, runs the risk of
alienating the neutrals and of incurring their displeasure for joining
a "rich man's club."

It is the goal of Soviet foreign policy to strengthen all those forces
alive in the underdeveloped areas which are hostile to the West and
to greater Atlantic unity. No doubt, former colonial peoples will
harbor resentments against their erstwhile rulers even without communist encouragement. The neutralism or nonalignment which char-
acterizes the foreign policy of most new states exists as a function
of bipolarity. Former colonial peoples exploit the prevailing global
strategic equation to assert their independence from the West and
to enhance their national stature. In short, neutralism, because it
reflects African and Asian conceptions of national interest, does not
yield easily to American persuasion—even persuasion laced with
concrete tokens of goodwill.

Strategically, the underdeveloped areas are of greater importance
to the West than to the Soviet Union. The communists undoubtedly
realize that the United States, in order to provide for its own security
and that of its allies, requires the deployment of military forces far
from North America. Therefore, the reduction of the Western presence in Africa and Asia represents a deterioration of the West's de-

fense position vis-à-vis the communist bloc. Similar consequences would attend the withdrawal of NATO installations from such forward positions as Turkey. Hence the communist efforts to convert the West's friends to neutralists and neutralists to communists. Because of its geographic expanse, the Soviet Union controls, to a far greater degree than the United States, territory from which its military forces can safeguard its strategic heartland. The geographical asymmetry of the Soviet Union and the United States creates for the former both a useful propaganda device with which to harass the West and a potential counter for bargaining the Soviet presence in, say, Cuba for that of the West in some European or Asian country.

Neutralism has many faces, ranging from the benevolence displayed by some of France's former colonies in Africa to the truculence toward the West which marks the foreign policy of Ghana and the Mali Republic. The attitudes of the neutralist countries are conditioned in part by an anti-Western bias which is a legacy of European rule. The logic of anti-imperialism leads some neutralist leaders to pursue their campaign against all remnants of Western domination or neo-colonialism. The popularity of such a cause permits neutralist leaders to oppose it only at great risk to their domestic political position. Therefore, the "compleat neutralist" keeps on waging the struggle against the West, even after independence has been gained and Western imperialism has shrunk to a semantic abstraction. In the reduction and elimination of Western influence, his objective coincides with those of the communists. For this reason, if for no other, on *some* issues he is likely to make common cause with the Soviets.

But neutralism is more than just the product of unpleasant experience under European rule. Neutralism corresponds also to the internal needs of many underdeveloped countries and compensates them for their relatively weak position in world politics. Underdeveloped countries have neither the resources nor the national cohesiveness to enable them to play an impressive part in world politics. A policy of neutralism, however, permits them to encourage both the Soviets and the West to compete with largesse for their allegiance. Neutralism also enables them to adopt a posture in international relations above and beyond that justified by their stature. They may pose as peacemakers between the two prime contenders while being courted and feted by both. The neutralists appear to favor stalemate in the Cold War, not primarily because they are indifferent to the consequences of communist domination, but because the prevailing bipolarity permits neutralists to maximize their own meager power potential and, in some cases, simply to exist. It is in their interest to promote actively a stand-off between the United States and the Soviet Union. Undoubtedly, they know that the power which they may individually contribute to one side or the other is miniscule and therefore unlikely to affect appreciably the outcome of the protracted conflict. One by one, underdeveloped countries can afford the luxury of moving toward or away from the communist position without greatly endangering the East-West equation.

Some neutralists, by their actions and by their words, equate the defense needs of the Soviets and the West. Hence their opposition to Western military bases on foreign soil. The United States is no more entitled, in neutralist eyes, to bases in Africa, Asia and Latin America than is the Soviet Union. (In fact, since, until recently, the Soviets have never had bases outside the Iron Curtain, the symmetry which neutralists perceive between Soviet and Western defense needs leads logically to the acceptance of Soviet military fortification of Cuba and to requests by neutralists for the withdrawal of the United States from its naval installation at Guantánamo.) Neutralists such as Nehru have condemned indiscriminately *all* military alliances, including NATO and SEATO, as well as the Warsaw Pact and the alliance between the Soviet Union and Communist China. Alliances, according to Nehru, may "lead to final catastrophe," for they increase international tension and fear.[17] Similarly, according to Nasser, a "policy of military blocs and pacts inevitably results in an arms race, causes misunderstanding . . . and tensions."[18] In Nkrumah's estimation, defense pacts between African and non-African states "bring the Cold War to Africa."[19]

Many Africans and Asians look upon the Atlantic Alliance as an organization which the Western powers have created in order to perpetuate colonialism. Some maintain, for example, that Portugal retains her overseas territories because she has the support of other NATO members, together with weapons supplied by the Alliance. Much of the Indian press condemned the Atlantic Alliance when Portuguese arms bearing NATO labels were found in Goa following India's seizure of that small enclave in 1961. In short, the Africans and Asians evaluate NATO, like other questions of foreign policy, in terms of its relationship to what they deem to be the most pressing issues confronting them.

Because of their conceptions of national interest, African and Asian leaders, even if they understood the origin and purpose of NATO, could probably not be expected to abandon their neutralism. The Chinese communist military incursions into India and the successes of communist guerrillas in Southeast Asia did not precipitate an Asian or African repudiation of neutralism and a consequent rush to join an alliance with the West or even to assist a beleaguered India. Nehru, whose armies were no match for those of the Chinese communists, was prepared to uphold his policy of nonalignment and hoped to obtain arms from the Soviets as well as from the West.[20] Although Nehru's doctrine of "positive neutralism" made no allowance for this contingency, the West responded with offers of military aid, while the Soviets, after much hesitation, finally delivered in January, 1963, a token shipment of MIG aircraft promised long ago to India.

Neutralist thought on international relations appears sometimes to postulate little or no difference in ethical quality between the West and the Sino-Soviet bloc. If there is a difference, it seems to reside in the relative vulnerability of Western governments to neutralist pressures, compared to the relative inability of African and Asian countries to influence Soviet or Chinese communist foreign policy. But both contenders stand equally guilty before some neutralist tribunes. The West is portrayed as adopting a stance of inflexibility when it refuses to accede to communist proposals for general and complete disarmament, an unpoliced test ban and the elimination of overseas bases, despite the fact that such arrangements might tip the balance of power toward the Soviet Union. Such judgments by neutralists are likely to have a greater effect upon the "open societies" of the West than controlled public opinion behind the Iron Curtain.[21]

Much of the antipathy of neutralist leaders toward the West is focused upon the growing unity of Western Europe. Understandably, some Afro-Asian countries face problems of readjustment as a result of the European Economic Community and, especially, of the gradual ending of Imperial Preference should Britain gain membership. The European Economic Community, however, has offered to many underdeveloped countries generous arrangements providing for preferential treatment of their products in the Common Market. Underdeveloped countries associated with the European Economic Community would retain the freedom to impose their own tariffs upon European exports, while gaining access to a fund for economic development. It is difficult to conceive of such a relationship in terms of "neo-colonialism."

Nevertheless, the Common Market has evoked the opposition of such neutralists as President Nkrumah. Addressing Ghana's Parliament on July 4, 1961, Dr. Nkrumah declared that "Recently a new threat has loomed up to the cause of African unity which is no less ominous for being unobtrusive. It is the creation of the European Common Market." On this and subsequent occasions Nkrumah expressed his fear of the Common Market as a threat not only to Ghana but to the whole of Africa. Nkrumah described the Common Market as a "cloak for perpetuating colonial privileges in Africa," exerting economic pressure upon newly independent states. Other African and Asian leaders have voiced similar apprehensions about the European Economic Community.

Africans do not oppose in principle *all* programs of economic integration. While condemning unity in Europe, African leaders espouse in Africa the idea of a common market and various forms of political collaboration. They allege that their opposition to the European Economic Community is motivated by fears of its adverse repercussions upon African unity. The Common Market is said to discriminate against independent African states economically by retarding industrial development and diversification and by perpetuating the artificial barriers which are a legacy of European rule. To be sure, much of the trade of African states is with Europe rather than with other countries in Africa. To increase economic exchanges within Africa is a desirable goal. However, so long as African economies are competitive rather than complementary with each other, trade will continue to move to Europe. Yet the West, in such schemes as the Common Market's Development Fund, has offered to assist in bringing about the economic diversification and specialization necessary to increase trade among African states—without, however, diminishing markedly African opposition to European economic unity.

Nevertheless, Africans are bent upon advancing their own unity. Economic experts of the Casablanca Group met in Conakry in July, 1961. Their closing communiqué indicated their intention to eliminate trade barriers among their countries over a five-year transitional period and to establish a clearing mechanism to facilitate currency exchange. Other conclaves of Africans have issued declarations of support for political and economic unity in Africa. Nkrumah gave additional impetus to African unity when, at the Belgrade Conference of neutralist leaders in September, 1961, he suggested that "the political unification of Africa has assumed even greater importance in view of the new danger facing the continent in the form of the European Common Market."

Africans are not alone in their opposition to West European economic integration. Asians have voiced their apprehension that the European Economic Community represents a danger to their exports and economic development. One appropriate remedy is greater regional trade in Asia. According to an Indian commentator, "Under the shadow of the European Common Market, Asian countries are growing more interested in intra-regional trade."[22] Prime Minister Nehru has expressed agreement with such a remedy, but he stressed in September, 1962, at the Commonwealth Prime Ministers' Conference in London, yet another fear held by neutralists: that integration in Western Europe might lead to heightened tensions in the Cold War. Again, neutralist criticisms paralleled communist propaganda against the European Common Market.

Like the policy of neutralism itself, Afro-Asian opposition to military pacts and to economic integration in the West flows from several motivations. But basic to Afro-Asian attitudes is the likely impact of the Western Alliance and European economic integration upon their conception of national interest. Because they do not understand the differing defense needs of East and West, they do not comprehend the significance of alliance systems in the Free World. Nor do neutralists, at least in public statements, acknowledge their utter dependence upon the West's strength for their own independence and the freedom to opt for a policy of neutralism—a choice denied to those states which have fallen into the communist orbit.

The nationalist leaders of Africa and Asia have their own plans for unity, some of which, as in the case of the Pan-African Movement, antedate NATO and the European Economic Community. Undoubtedly, the drive toward unity in Europe and in the North Atlantic area may give additional impetus to similar efforts in Africa, Asia and Latin America. African and Asian leaders, while condemning the

West's efforts to unite, will seek to take the steps which they deem essential for their own welfare and development. Afro-Asian leaders decry the West's quest for the very objectives which they strive to attain for themselves.

The West should, where possible, take into account the interests of Afro-Asian countries. But a foreign policy which has as its primary objective to "identify" the United States with the newly independent states at the expense of the Atlantic Community courts disaster for the entire Free World. Underdeveloped countries, as India's anguished leaders have begun to learn, will be permitted the luxury of neutralism only so long as the West maintains its strength vis-à-vis the Sino-Soviet bloc. If the United States and its European Allies forgo necessary efforts toward military, political and economic unity because of the adverse reaction of neutralists, they run the risk of endangering themselves as well as the neutralists. Indeed, Khrushchev, disdainful of neutralism, has declared that liberation from European rule is not the sole objective of communist strategy in the underdeveloped areas.

The correct application of Marxist-Leninist theory in countries which have freed themselves consists indeed in seeking forms for uniting the whole [nation] while taking account of the special features of the economic, political, and cultural life of the peoples, in insuring the leading role of the working class in the national front, and in the struggle for resolute extermination of the roots of imperialism and the remnants of feudalism . . . *for clearing the way for an eventual movement toward socialism.*[23]

In contrast to many other Asian countries, there is considerable understanding in Japan of the defense needs of the Free World. Japan has allied herself in a defense pact with the United States, and its government has acknowledged that cooperation with the West forms the primary basis for Japanese prosperity and economic development. To be sure, there exists in Japan, as in other noncommunist countries, a vociferous minority which advocates Japanese neutrality in the Cold War (i.e., the withdrawal of United States forces from Japan and the termination of the Mutual Security Defense Treaty). But proponents of such policies—socialists, communists and pacifist groups—have not won over the majority of Japanese public opinion. Most Japanese still stand opposed to cooperation with the Sino-Soviet bloc at the expense of Japan's ties with the West. Japan, because of her highly skilled population, her great industrial capabilities and her strategic position near the coasts of China and the Soviet Union, provides an important increment to Western security. Japan is the one non-Western country in Asia which, by virtue of its industrial power, can make a significant contribution to the economic growth of other Asian countries. In short, Japan resembles in many ways the most advanced of the North Atlantic countries. Therefore Japan should be included, wherever possible, in the plans for achieving greater unity in the West—as the West's major partner in Asia and, indeed, by virtue of her political aspirations and her economic and social achievements, a "Western" country.

European Reservations

Forces within the North Atlantic area which weaken the drive toward Atlantic unification spring from many roots. In part, they stem from the residual elements of the historical geographic isolation of some parts of the North Atlantic area, from differing conceptions of national interest and, in part, from the anxieties about human survival in the nuclear age. In Britain, for example, a formidable alignment of Right and Left opposes closer links with Europe, as well as United States military installations on British soil. Some Englishmen seem to share the fears of Africans and Asians, namely, that a united Europe, not to mention a united West, might heighten tensions in the Cold War. Because a goodly portion of British thinking in foreign affairs focuses upon the danger of nuclear war and the need for reducing tension, the British Government has taken the lead in proposing summit conferences or, as in February, 1959, has actually undertaken unilateral talks at the highest level with the Soviets.

Groups such as the Campaign for Nuclear Disarmament in Britain suggest that the United States and the Soviet Union share in equal measure the guilt for international tensions. According to Bertrand Russell, "There is in the West much more regimentation and much more misleading propaganda by the Establishment than is generally known. Nor is it admitted that all such restrictions diminish the difference between East and West and make the claim of the West to be called 'The Free World' derisory."[24] The implication is that man must be saved even at the expense of his freedom. Unilateralists are led therefore to call for the nuclear disarmament of NATO and the withdrawal of American power across the Atlantic. The unilateralist movement depicts Britain as the hostage to American "militarism." The logic of unilateralism does not argue for the strengthening of the West to meet a ubiquitous Soviet challenge, but for surrender, either on the installment plan or all at once, in order to escape nuclear annihilation. The communists have given their blessing to the unilateralist movement, for its objectives are in consonance with those of the Soviet Union: to create disillusionment with the prevailing social and political order and to disarm NATO.

On the Continent there are those who fear that British membership in such European institutions as the Common Market may impede progress toward political unity. They point to the many interests and obligations of Britain outside Europe and to the "massive entourage" of Commonwealth countries whose interests British diplomacy attempted to safeguard in negotiations with the European Economic Community. In short, some Europeans tend to view the unification of the Six as a goal more important than the creation of a broader European and Atlantic unity. Not a few Europeans, moreover, because they resent the pivotal position of Britain in NATO and the privileged place assigned to the British by the United States in the formulation of Cold War strategy, see European unity as a means to regain for Continental countries a status commensurate with their new economic power.

Some European countries have shown a renewed emphasis on national issues. This trend gained impetus after 1953 for four main reasons: (1) the restoration of economic strength and a resulting feeling of new confidence on the part of some European nations; (2) the apparent lessening of the Soviet military threat after the death of Stalin; (3) the increasing preoccupation by some European nations (particularly France) with extra-European affairs; and (4) the advent of a new nuclear weapons technology and attendant disagreements over the decision-making processes of the Atlantic Alliance.

In Great Britain, the Labour Party's rejection, in September, 1962, of the terms negotiated by the Conservative Government for Britain's entry into the Common Market suggested that British insularity had by no means been relegated to history. Nevertheless, according to public opinion surveys, the government's decision increasingly appeared to be gaining support among the majority of the electorate.[25]

Other manifestations of nationalism—the Austro-Italian conflict over South Tyrol, the British-Icelandic fisheries dispute and Irredentist strivings in West Germany—frequently have been characterized as a resurgence of nineteenth-century European chauvinism. There is little doubt that old *mystiques* and mutual distrusts continue to color European attitudes. The current frictions between France and Great Britain over the military and economic organization of Europe, for example, are sparked by a rivalry which has spanned many centuries of European history. French leaders are doubtful of Britain's determination to stand by Europe in the event of a Soviet thrust to the Channel. These sentiments have their counterparts in London, where many Englishmen consider France the great barrier to closer cooperation in Europe and in the Atlantic world.

These rivalries, however, no longer conform to the mold of the exclusive nationalism of the late nineteenth century. The stakes are no longer Continental hegemony, or even national power per se, but equality within the councils of an alliance. President de Gaulle, for example, despite his devotion to French grandeur, has reiterated his loyalty to the partnership of the West. He has rejected the idea of French neutrality with the observation that this would destroy the Alliance and leave no alternatives but a nuclear holocaust or Soviet domination of Europe. Despite his public opposition to European supranationalist schemes, he has led France into the European Economic Community. His bid for Franco-German *rapprochement* is undoubtedly an effort to establish a bloc which would strengthen the hand of France in dealings with the other members of the Alliance. Whatever the motives, the settlement of differences between these traditional rivals represents an important milestone in the postwar evolution of European unity.

It is imperative, therefore, that in evaluating the phenomenon of European neo-nationalism, the distinction be drawn between its *mystique* and practical demands. General de Gaulle, for one, combines an evangelical striving for French greatness with a hardheaded evaluation of the facts of the twentieth century. He maintains that the inescapable unity of world-wide commitments by the Allies demands unity of world-wide strategic planning. He objects to American policy which prevents the sharing of atomic secrets with its major allies in Europe. His principal objectives are: participation with Great Britain and the United States in global-strategic planning and acquiescence in the French effort to develop a *force de frappe*.

The fact that nationalism does not constitute an immediate threat to European unity as such, however, does not detract from its debilitating effects upon the Atlantic Alliance as a whole. Nationalist resentments are mainly directed against the leadership of the United States. The demand for equality is essentially a rejection of aspects of this leadership. Equally significant for the continued viability of the Alliance, nationalism could engender a new regionalism within the Alliance. President de Gaulle's proposal for a Mediterranean pact composed of France, Spain, Italy, Morocco and Tunisia bespeaks this trend as does the Franco-German Pact of January, 1963, and de Gaulle's subsequent overtures to Spain for closer political-military links.[26]

Some European socialist parties tend to embrace national objectives at the expense of European integration. At the same time, certain socialist factions advocate a settlement of the East-West conflict that cannot be reconciled easily with Atlantic unity. The Italian Socialist Party, for example, under the leadership of Pietro Nenni, entered a coalition with the Christian Democrats in 1961 in what was termed the *apertura alla sinistra*. Yet the Italian Socialists are avowedly neutralist in foreign policy, and oppose in principle "military blocs" such as NATO.[27] Moreover, there are those in the British Labour Party who advocate disengagement in Europe while opposing Britain's entry into the European Economic Community because it would, allegedly, heighten tensions in the Cold War.

Nevertheless, there is, in Western Europe, a broad consensus which recognizes the necessity for unity. Yet opinion divides on the question of precisely what shape West European unity should assume. In the Benelux countries, as well as in West Germany, there is considerable official support for the erection in Western Europe of federal institutions. The Gaullist idea of European unity, however, postulates a *Europe des patries*, in which nation-states, rather than supranational institutions, provide the basis for confederal arrangements. Such appears also to be the British vision of European integration. Yet the federal approach has numerous advocates in most West European countries. There was, moreover, throughout Western

Europe considerable sympathy and support for Britain after the breakdown of the Brussels negotiations in January, 1963. Persons of the federalist persuasion as well as those who have shared the Gaullist conception of European unity found themselves in agreement on the issue of Britain's entry, though unable, because of France's veto, to alter events.

There exist, too, differences of opinion about the purpose of European integration. There are those Europeans who see Europe as a "third force" between the United States and the Soviet Union. After the Suez crisis of 1956, a good many disenchanted Europeans advocated European integration as a means of reducing Europe's dependence upon the United States and as a way of bolstering her power position in world politics. Yet, fortunately for the Atlantic Community, European integration is not motivated primarily by the idea of a "third force" as a counterweight to American influence. At this juncture, however, no one can foretell with certainty the exact shape of European unity or the extent to which Western Europe may grow within or outside an Atlantic framework.

American Critics

Some of the arguments against greater unity in the North Atlantic area are common to Americans as well as Europeans. Like their European counterparts, some American critics of closer ties between the United States and Europe see, albeit erroneously, a strengthened NATO as contributing to the intensification of the Cold War. In the interest of peace they would seek an accommodation with the Soviets at the price of reducing American forces in Europe and, if necessary, the dismantling of NATO. According to one such suggestion, NATO should be pared down to an Anglo-Saxon alliance:

If the United States should advance a serious proposal for disengagement, it would immediately relax tensions aroused by the Berlin issue. . . . A disengaged West Germany would cease to be a member [of NATO]. At a subsequent date Italy and Scandinavia might also prefer neutrality. Similarly France might be left to follow its own nationalist course. . . . Indeed, the logic of such a position might lead to an eventual neutralization of the whole six-nation area. This would leave NATO a truly Atlantic Alliance based on the United States, Canada, and Great Britain.[28]

Implicit in such proposals is the underlying assumption, shared by the British unilateralists, that security through alliances and deterrents is illusory in the nuclear age, or, as the advocates of "disengagement" argue, that demilitarized neutrals are preferable to armed, committed allies. In short, according to these dismaying views, the United States must be willing to whittle away its own security and that of its allies in the name of a peace which never quite comes within reach.

There exists, however, in the United States a form of isolationism which has no counterpart in Europe. Not a few self-styled American patriots view efforts to achieve greater unity in the North Atlantic area as tantamount to the repeal of the Declaration of Independence. Western Europe is alleged to consist of "socialist" countries. Therefore, the United States, were it to opt for closer ties with Europe, would be led down the road to socialism and, by implication, to communism. The best hope, therefore, for American victory in the Cold War, it is suggested, lies in United States withdrawal from its alliances and in its reliance solely upon its own power for its security.

Although both extremes of American political thought have as their points of departure radically differing assumptions about the nature of the threat posed by communism, the remedies which they propose are in some respects similar. Both appear to advocate dissolution of our alliance systems and suggest that American power should be confined to North America. *Yet this is precisely the objective of communist strategy.* Clarion calls for a withdrawal to "Fortress America" serve, therefore, to frighten those allies who wish to safeguard their freedom; they do not frighten the communists. Both extremes, moreover, favor greater concentration by the United States upon domestic problems as a panacea for the Cold War. According to the "left," a solution lies in internal economic and humanitarian reforms. For the "right," communism is to a large extent an internal conspiracy upon which attention must be focused rather than upon pressing international issues. The United States, to be sure, must seek wherever possible to promote the well-being of all Americans and to guard against communist subversion from within. The communists, however, have made gains not primarily because of inequalities in American life or because of the alleged disloyalties of key Americans, but *because the United States and its allies have not taken together the steps necessary to counter the multidimensional communist strategy of protracted conflict.*

Canadian Reservations

Canada represents a synthesis of many of the features of the European and American traditions, modified and adapted to the Canadian environment. There exist, nevertheless, in Canada opponents of the Atlantic Alliance, who propose instead a Canadian policy of neutralism. Canada, it is suggested, then might be able, unencumbered by military ties to her giant neighbor to the south, to mediate between the communists and the United States.[29] Undoubtedly, such ideas can be traced to a hostility against the United States engendered by the pervasive influence of this country upon Canadian life. Election campaigns in Canada, at least since 1958, have provided the occasion for outbursts of anti-U.S. sentiments. The long-standing U.S.-Canadian dispute about Canada's role in the nuclear defense of North America precipitated angry condemnations in February, 1963, of the "colossus to the south" for its alleged unwarranted interference in Canada's internal affairs. Furthermore, the Diefenbaker Government had as one of its objectives to reduce United States influence upon Canada by increasing, where possible, trade and other contacts with Britain. Yet Canada is dependent upon the flow of foreign capital, especially from the United States, for her economic growth. This dependence is likely to grow as British attentions focus more upon Western Europe than upon the Commonwealth.

The Other American Republics

Latin Americans, in the early postwar period, looked with envy at the massive injections of United States capital into the European economies by the Marshall Plan. Not a few Latin Americans contrasted the impressive program to rebuild Europe with the more modest aid granted by the United States to her sister republics of the Western Hemisphere. However, Latin Americans, by and large, did not view with apprehension the participation of the United States in NATO. In fact, many leaders in Latin America recognized the need, in the interest of the Western Hemisphere, for the United States' military links with its West European allies.

The emergence of the European Economic Community, however, raised in Latin America apprehension about possible unfavorable consequences for the primary producers of the Western Hemisphere. Some Latin Americans were fearful of European discrimination against their exports in favor of the products of African states holding associate membership in the Common Market. But Latin American fears of economic discrimination have stimulated efforts to develop closer ties with the European Economic Community. In July, 1962, Dr. José A. Mora, Secretary General of the Organization of American States, journeyed to Europe for consultations on Latin America's relationship with the European Economic Community. He received from several European governments promises to increase their technical assistance to Latin America and to channel training fellowships through the OAS.[30] Moreover, in September, 1962, as a result of Dr. Mora's consultations in Europe, the OAS established a European office in Brussels to maintain liaison with the European Economic Community, and to increase Latin-American collaboration with the Organization for Economic Cooperation and Development. According to José Figueres, former President of Costa Rica, "Western Europe should share in the responsibility for Latin-American development. Historic ties, culture and trade link our republics with Europe as much as with the United States. Although we have direct relations with the mother countries, the good offices of the United States are essential, especially in coordinating the efforts of what is really a triangular economy."[31] Thus European and North Atlantic unification has spurred the Latin Americans to new efforts to find for themselves a place in the grand design.

Growing Western unity has given impetus to regional trade agreements in Latin America. As the European Economic Community took shape, Latin Americans, fearing the loss of markets in Europe to African producers of coffee, cocoa and bananas, saw in regional organization a device for dealing effectively with possible discrimination. The result was a series of meetings, culminating in proposals for regional associations. In 1960, Argentina, Brazil, Chile, Mexico, Paraguay, Peru and Uruguay signed the Treaty of Montevideo establishing a free trade zone.[32] Central American republics took renewed interest in their regional economic problems. Consolidating earlier efforts, El Salvador, Guatemala, Honduras and Nicaragua signed in 1960 the General Treaty on Central American Integration and established the Central American Bank for Economic Integration.[33] But Latin Americans have only just begun to give thought to the broader problems of their relationship to the North Atlantic Community.

An Appraisal

The many groups which oppose the unification of the North Atlantic area do so for diverse reasons. The hostility of the communists to NATO is implacable; little that the West can do will alter their attitude. Within the Atlantic area itself, historic national antagonisms have been, for the most part, muted, but it would be unwise to overlook the fact that they have left a residue which still bars the road to that trust required by partnership. The canny detachment of the uncommitted peoples is a different matter again. Although they retain in many cases a residual respect for the Western legacy (as reflected, for example, in the willingness of a Panikkar to acknowledge India's debt to Britain for the legal, political and administrative structure of the nation's unity), most of the uncommitted peoples seem permanently unable to embrace the West's cause with the slightest bit of enthusiasm. Their virtual indifference to the outcome of the clash between the two social-state systems seems, at the present time, almost beyond change. Exhortatory appeals to Western political concepts of human freedom have little effect upon them. Only the convincing image of economic-technological success, as well as of the total strength—military, intellectual and otherwise—needed to shape the course of international events, not elevated rhetoric, will induce them to identify their fortunes with one side or the other.

The Soviets realize this only too well. Aware that the control of organized masses of people constitutes the decisive element of power in the contemporary global contest, they ardently woo the masses or the men who can manipulate the masses. The possession of advanced nuclear weaponry, queen of the global game of chess, would profit the Soviets little were they to lose the pawns, the many captive millions who must sustain the brunt of their power play. In the present situation, in which the communist bloc still finds itself inferior to the West in the realm of strategic military implements, the communists seek to woo the masses from their historical allegiance through the mediation of the elites shaping the "thought environment" of modern society. For nearly five decades now, the communists have tried to cast themselves upon the world scene in the role of the vigorous young challenger. They have sought to present their doctrine as a new post-Christian doctrine of salvation —a new youthful springtime in the life of mankind and a promise of better things to come. It is precisely the emotional appeal that communism is capable of making to the disenchanted and the naïve which renders dangerous any readiness in the West to rest on the laurels of temporary military superiority, measured in the number of deliverable megatons. The insight expressed by Jules Monnerot a decade ago has lost none of its relevance for today:

The historical innovation of contemporary communism is the virtual unification of the forces of an external and an internal enemy, a combination of subversion with invasion—so that as it expands the system can absorb simultaneously both societies and individuals, and can make not only territorial and economic but also political and spiritual conquests. The innovation also consists in raising an issue and persuading a certain number of people, by various methods of intimidation and psychological pressure, to accept it as predestined. . . .[34]

Those who have devoted the greater part of their intellectual lifetime to the study of Soviet strategy have developed a healthy respect for the adversary. Over the years, they have grown wary of recurring reports from supposedly well-informed analysts that the Soviet communist leadership is tottering on the brink of a more mellow world outlook; that the communist demesne is ready to crack from within; or that communism has lost its *élan vital* and its image as the inexorable wave of the future. Undoubtedly, all these things are devoutly to be wished. But the wish should not be allowed to become father to the thought. In the present situation it is premature, to say the least, to be seeking ways of strengthening the "soft" communists against the "hard" communists when the execution of these ways involves any policy concessions which risk weakening the security position of the Atlantic Alliance. From the experience of the postwar period, it can be fairly inferred that the

United States stands to lose little by viewing the current twists and turns in Soviet policy with traditional Yankee skepticism, if not bemusement.

NATO, unfortunately, has not paid sufficient attention to the task of parrying the communists' psychopolitical thrust. Much of the communists' success in this field must be attributed to the kind of systematic analytical effort to which the Atlantic nations have simply not seen fit to allocate their resources and their concerted labors. The Americans have often demonstrated their consummate mastery of the techniques of mass persuasion for domestic commercial and political campaign purposes. Time and again, Americans have shown that they know *how* to approach people, even though they have not always been sure about the proper substantive basis on which to approach them. The Europeans, for their part, possess a vaster fund of experience in trying to understand the values that motivate people—the Russians, the East Europeans, the Asians and the Africans. By harnessing the knowledge and the skills available on both sides of the Atlantic, NATO could probably do a great deal to improve the West's political-psychological performance in the international arena. This is not to suggest, of course, that the formation of another committee, or a dozen committees, is likely to bring about startling Western successes or revolutionary transformations in the world political climate. But up to now, the West has not done as much or as well as it might have done in this realm, despite the urgings of such groups as the NATO Parliamentarians, the Atlantic Convention of NATO Citizens, the Atlantic Institute and various committees of the North Atlantic Council and NATO Secretariat.

No one need be under any illusion that it is an easy thing to mount a global psychopolitical offensive against communism and on behalf of the Western pluralist ideals. The meaning of freedom, for individuals and groups, cannot be sold, as the utopian ideas of communism can. Genuine human liberty can be understood only by being lived, or by being sought after at the price of life, as those who tried to conquer the Berlin Wall sought it. Dostoevsky has assured us that freedom is not something that the masses seek. To the extent that they have it, they will enjoy its pleasurable benefits and shun its dreadful responsibilities. As Polybius long ago observed, only the noble soul carries on the struggle to preserve human liberty, irrespective of cost to himself. In the nuclear age

more so than in any other, the crass soul will buy physical safety at the expense of virtually all values that fall short of physical survival itself. If even in the West there are widespread doubts about the prudence of defending human freedom at the risk of war, it should hardly come as a surprise that the Atlantic nations encounter some difficulty in propagating the cheap, sloganized editions of their most cherished values in the non-Western regions of the world.

The main reason why the West has often fared badly in the Cold War is so basic and uncomplicated as to be almost ludicrous: The West has no firm, popularly comprehensible policy for winning the Cold War. The arguments against seeking to win it range all the way from the assertion that the effort to do so would lead the West to adopt totalitarian institutions of its own—the "garrison state"—to such subtle propositions as, for example, that on humanitarian grounds there can be and should be no victory over the communist menace. We are told that it is sophomoric to speak of winning, and that life and liberty are, at least in the nuclear age, mutually exclusive. These kindred arguments, which stand Western humanism on its head, are not unconnected with the formulations of the communist dialectics of war and peace. The efficacy of communist brain-washing is not confined to victims who are physically captive. By remote control it cleanses those who will not learn, or have no one to teach them, psychopolitical warfare.

Secretary of State Dulles, on January 10, 1958, told a press conference of the failure of one of President Eisenhower's efforts to win the support of world opinion for a sincere and reasonable disarmament proposal. Secretary Dulles confessed that "the Soviet Union has smothered our proposals with words . . . they have developed their propaganda to a much higher degree than we have . . . [they are] winning the propaganda war, and there is very little the United States can do about it."[35] This admission of defeatism in the area of propaganda was made ten years after the establishment of the U.S. Information Agency. It led James Reston to write:

Is the West so lacking in originality, imagination and persistence that it cannot articulate good policies as well as the communists can articulate bad policies? Washington cannot leave the field of public excitement and propaganda to Moscow, without continuing to lose the psychological initiative.[36]

The task of the West is not eased by those of its spokesmen who would have the West win its case by publicizing its defects. "Telling the whole truth no matter how much it may hurt us" is their motto. In James Warburg's words, "Honest self-criticism is better propaganda than criticism of an adversary."[37] Montesquieu wrote: *"On peut être menteur, mais on ne peut pas être faux."* It is not necessary to present a litany of failure to win credibility. Furthermore, to conduct a propaganda campaign *for* democracy by being *impartial toward it* comes close to promoting the rival product.

The propaganda efforts of the West suffer from a confusion of terms. Thus far, the communists have been permitted not only to select the issues of the controversy, but also to couch them in their own vocabulary. Khrushchev, for example, insists on identifying the contending systems as communism and capitalism—a potently simplistic disjunctive which is false. The confrontation is not one between two systems seeking peace and plenty, divided only by economic differences. The struggle is essentially a political one, and what is at stake is the shape of human society and the quality of man's life on this planet for centuries to come.

The Magna Carta, the Declaration of Independence, the call of the French Revolution for Liberty, Equality and Fraternity and our own Bill of Rights do not mention capitalism. But communism is the dominant theme of the *Communist Manifesto* and in all things Soviet, from law to science to sport to education to culture—an ideology that grates on every ear like a perpetually revolving broken record.

Democracy is nonideological. Democracy does not enjoin us to seek divine guidance or to trust in human reason, to invest funds for profit or to reject the profit motive, to educate our children as we see fit or to send them to public schools. Democracy is a method for sharing power on the basis of legal equality, and for holding the rulers accountable by periodic political scrutiny. This definition leaves out much of what is claimed by various schools of thought as being the complete or desirable features of democracy. It describes, however, the characteristics which have distinguished working democracies from other known types of government in history. These characteristics are methodological. Many social goals, per se, are not democratic—or, for that matter, undemocratic. Many goals can be reached by some other route. Economic equality, for example, can

be attained under despotic rule; in the Leninist phase, the economic status of the Soviet Union's rulers was not appreciably above that of the working masses.[38]

The communists deliberately obscure the philosophical differences between democracy and communism. They offer their system to the unwitting as being nothing more than an economic system that is better than "capitalism." The communists will continue to gain ground by misrepresenting the nature of the two systems. They will never debate the real differences between them. For us to confine the argument to the relative merits of two kinds of economic organizations is to fall into a semantic trap.

"Capitalism" only partly describes one aspect of the economic structure of society. "Capital" is but one of the factors necessary for the production of goods. If this term does not give a complete picture of our economic system, it is even worse to use the word "capitalism" to describe our entire way of life and all the various institutions of our society. The communists, true to their "broken record" mentality, still speak of "capitalism" in very much the same terms as did Marx more than a hundred years ago. Actually, the Western nations are almost as far away from the capitalism of the 1840's as the communists are from pure communism!

The word "democracy" applies to the entire functioning of our society—to the interplay of all the individual separate structures taken together as a whole. The conflict then is one between two complete social systems, and the economic structures, while they are important, are still only parts of, and not all of, each social system.

Consequently, wherever the reference is communism, the West's counter must be representative institutions; where the reference is peace, the West's should be freedom and justice; where it is "relaxation of tensions," the West's should be self-determination. The combinations may be changed. What matters is to cut loose from the glossary of communism.

The Western position is also being undercut by that curious and studied "objectivity" which tends to equate the evil doings of the West with those of the communists. On the issue of military bases, the imposed presence of the Red Army in Soviet satellites is made one with the deployment of U.S. forces in America's "satellites" in Europe and Asia. The character of an alliance of free peoples is studiously ignored. There is a *qualitative* difference between arm-

ing the police and arming the gangsters, between aggressive communist imperialism and the defense of freedom. The passion of many Westerners for drawing analogies demeaning for the West and bending truth to their purpose is not exactly conducive to hardening the Western peoples' will to join the issue and fight for their survival.

It is the primary responsibility of those who make policy and its attendant propaganda to address themselves specifically to political issues as they are, not as they might be, and least of all as mere momentary phenomena in history which will pass. Each moment links the chain of historical continuity. What men do and suffer here and now will determine the future of the race. Yet an increasing number of those concerned with Western policy have acquired such a detached view of responsibility that they can declare that: (a) most problems would be with us still in aggravated form even if communism disappeared tomorrow; (b) national sovereignty and rivalries were problems before communism appeared; (c) the expectations of underdeveloped countries would haunt us even if communism were gone; and (d) popular demand for better health, education and culture would be with us whether communism stayed or went. These things may all be true, yet have nothing to do with the threats posed by communism. One cannot help having second thoughts as to why they are even raised. It is as if the Allied High Command, as the Battle of the Bulge began, should have said, "Ah, this too shall pass," and retired to Paris for the weekend.

Closely related to a failure to discriminate between persistent world problems and the communist ability to aggravate them is the assiduous courting of neutralism as preferable to any commitment to face the reality of communist global ambitions. Detachment from the global struggle is increasingly advocated within the United States. David Riesman and Michael Maccoby made the point quite candidly: "As the cold war continues, it becomes increasingly difficult for decent Americans, humane enough to prefer peace to an egocentric national honor, to be outspoken and genuinely anticommunist."[39]

Perhaps the ink of this sticky humanism has rubbed off on some documents of state. Our global view has so "mellowed" that it has become hard for the detached observer to see how the United States distinguishes between friends, genuine neutrals and the "nonaligned

neutrals" who manage to side with the communist world on nearly every international test. Indeed, McGeorge Bundy, the President's Special Assistant for Security Affairs, admonishes his readers as follows: "It would be an erring logic which would set our unaligned friends always behind our allies."[40] The European NATO countries who have experienced the abrasive logic of this position may reasonably ask if they are ever to be set ahead of nations who cover hostility toward them with the cloak of neutralism.

In the last few years Belgium, Portugal, France, Great Britain and the Netherlands have found the United States indifferent, if not down-right hostile, to what they regarded to be their national interests. Dutch animosity toward the United States for the latter's role in turning over West New Guinea to Indonesia provided a fair sample of sentiments engendered by American statecraft. Marquis Childs reported from The Hague in September, 1962, as follows:

> Scornful words are poured on Robert Kennedy's five-day visit to Djakarta and his assumption that he understood the problem. The visiting reporter is told that the Russians were keeping hands off as late as last March and only when they saw that Washington meant to force a so-called compromise did they come through with extensive military support for Sukarno.
>
> At the height of the outcry Joseph Luns, who has been Netherlands' Foreign Minister for 10 years, said that while his country would continue to be allies of the United States they could no longer be friends.[41]

The exaggerated attention which the United States pays to neutralist opinion reinforces communist propaganda. The principal United States problem is how to commit those nations who wish to maintain their freedom to the defense of freedom everywhere. The indiscriminate treatment of neutrals and allies is scarcely the way to rally other nations to our cause.

Shortly after the summary settlement of the Dutch-Indonesian conflict, Thailand voiced its distress at the United States decisions to create a neutral Laos and to increase military aid to neutralist Cambodia. Thailand, so it seems, took new bearings and initiated trade relations with the Soviet Union. A press report tells of the Thais' "agonizing reappraisal":

> Interior Minister Praphas Charusathien, a leading exponent of "thaiism" and the most outspoken critic of the United States on the Cambodian

issue, said that the announcement that trade relations with the Soviet Union will be made formal was "not in any way" a retaliatory measure against the United States for stepping up aid to Cambodia.[42]

By itself this incident would be of relatively little importance. But as part of the pattern of change in inter-Allied relationships, resulting from a trend toward United States political and potential military isolation, it is symptomatic.

The Political Front

Victory in the conflict with the communists lies within the West's grasp once it raises its sights beyond purely military defense and enters resolutely the political and psychological arena. But first the peoples of the West must scotch the idea that in the thermonuclear age it is impossible for one social system to triumph over another except at the unacceptable risk of war. The communists believe that the road toward victory can be pursued safely without risking thermonuclear war on the one hand or compromising with "capitalism" on the other. There is no reason why the West should not be allowed to face the future with hopes every bit as high. Greater emphasis by NATO upon political goals would remove the sting from the criticism of those—not only communists by any means—who charge that the West scarcely thinks of meeting the communist challenge on any but military grounds. It is incumbent upon the statesmen of the Atlantic world to express openly their resolve to compel the global political retreat of communism and to terminate its control over peoples who have never freely accepted it. Once this goal has been clearly defined and expressly stated, but not before, the West can determine upon the appropriate policies, prudent yet efficacious, for mounting a sustained political and economic offensive against the system that Lenin built. A prerequisite for carrying out this task is a wider and deeper understanding among Western publics as to what NATO is, for what it really stands and why it must not merely endure but grow stronger and more united in the future.

The images of NATO and other institutions of Western unity stand in need of greater popularization. If these institutions could attain within the nations of the Atlantic Community a status and prestige commensurate with that of the United Nations, the path would be greatly smoothed toward solving the many perplexing problems which currently beset the Western Alliance. Furthermore, increased cultural exchanges between Western Europe and the United States offer the greatest promise for smothering residual anti-Americanism in Europe and anti-Europeanism in the United States. The attitudes of many European intellectuals toward the United States are shaped by half-knowledge or abysmal ignorance, both of them dangerous. An intimate familiarity with American values and institutions would contribute toward stilling harsh and unwarranted criticism, and leave European intellectuals less vulnerable to Soviet divisive tactics. For example, exchanges of civil service workers among the nations of the Atlantic Community would encourage a more sympathetic understanding of the nature of each nation's problems. Private organizations such as the Atlantic Institute, fostering a continuing dialogue among the elites of the Atlantic partners, can remove many of the intellectual and psychological hurdles on the road toward increased cooperation. (North Atlantic countries sometimes appear more interested in expanding cultural exchange with the Soviet Union than with other Western nations.) The spread of the "third force" idea in Europe and the growth of neutralism and nationalism might be checked through increased cultural contacts among the nations of the Atlantic Community. Such a program could be implemented through the establishment of an Atlantic Organization for Cultural, Scientific and Educational Affairs.

Perhaps the most immediate need is for a better information program to publicize the military, economic and political problems of the North Atlantic area. Publicity about NATO has all too often stressed its weaknesses, unfilled quotas and unmet goals. Much less publicity has been given the Atlantic Alliance's achievements—its substructure of political agreement and military cooperation. Above all, the North Atlantic Community itself—member governments and nongovernmental organizations—should develop information programs designed to create a greater public awareness of the nature and importance of the North Atlantic area and to meet on the battleground of the intellect those who are hostile to NATO.

The important task of explaining and reporting the activities of the North Atlantic Community (especially NATO) rests primarily on national information services. They cannot discharge this task if member governments fail to make adequate provision for this purpose in their national programs. But, at the same time, the promotion of information about the North Atlantic Community should be conceived as a joint endeavor of the North Atlantic nations. Therefore NATO countries should forge links between their national information programs in order better to publicize the merits of North Atlantic unity.

National information services of the North Atlantic Community should submit to the NATO Council for mutual discussion and co-ordination relevant information programs which they plan to initiate. Provision should be made for the translation and widest dissemination of Atlantic publications and films and the conduct of NATO tours for educators, journalists, civic, business and labor leaders and private citizens.

National information services should be encouraged, as a matter of course, to make imaginative and extensive use of radio, television and publication. They might report on legislative activities and present debates among political figures—a "Meet the Press" approach on a large intra-European and intra-Atlantic scale. For the first time, the nations of the North Atlantic area have within their means the capabilities to develop a communications system embracing the 300 million people of Western Europe, as well as the 200 million inhabitants of North America. The experimental broadcasts of Telstar in 1962 illustrated the possibilities which exist for increasing through communications the cohesiveness of the North Atlantic area.

In view of the proper sensitivity that all governments display toward propaganda conducted within their boundaries, a centralized psychological warfare agency for NATO is not desirable. Yet NATO nations might agree, for example, upon beaming broadcasts into the U.S.S.R., though they might not wish to entrust this task to NATO. The impact of broadcasting to the Sino-Soviet bloc could be improved by increasing the cooperation among governments in devising common policies and objectives. The collective task is to blunt communist propaganda within the West and the uncommitted world, to strengthen cooperation within the Atlantic Community, and to chop away at the pretense of communism to be "the wave of the future."

The United States is the NATO nation most actively engaged in the propaganda battle for the minds of men. Yet, in measurable propaganda output, the United States runs fourth behind the Soviet Union, Communist China and the United Arab Republic. The Kremlin outspends the United States ten to one on overt propaganda and by more than twenty to one on covert propaganda outlets, including indirect support of supposedly independent publishers. The Soviet Union manages to distribute over fifty million copies of books throughout the Free World compared to about four million which are subsidized by the United States Information Agency. The "market surveys" conducted by the communists for their propaganda campaigns—the fetching ideas, issues, promises and semantics—cover far wider ground and probe more deeply than those undertaken by the United States.

What actions should the Atlantic nations in their information programs seek to inspire? First and foremost, they should press for a much more closely knit alliance. Secondly, they should urge the new nations to adopt constructive future-oriented policies in lieu of emotion-ridden anticolonialism. Finally, they should foster the desire for national independence and representative government behind the Iron Curtain. Most importantly, the Atlantic peoples must be better prepared psychologically to cope with the realities of conflict with communism.

Just as the communists sincerely and ardently embrace the Marxist-Leninist prescriptions, so the West must back up its political warfare operations with a philosophy of freedom. The universal appeal of Western values, institutions, technology and economic achievements is a formidable weapon in the West's arsenal. The answer of communism to the world's economic, social, and political ills has been proven for a long time to be woefully inadequate. Communism, or rather, the communist version of state capitalism, is an obsolete system. Yet the articulate spokesmen of Western ideology who are capable of exploiting communist failures are few. The democratic West has not presented forcefully enough either to non-Westerners or even to influential intellectual milieus within its own ranks the social failures of communism and the immense improvement throughout the last century of the average citizen's lot in the North Atlantic area. To be sure, in developing political counterweapons we must beware of presumptuousness, of posing as the Children of Light battling the Devil Incarnate. Clearly, too, some of the methods employed in Soviet political warfare, such as lies, fraud and slander, are incompatible with Western values. Fire is not the best means of fighting fire.

The communist system is guilty of most of the sins of which its propaganda accuses the West. Through a greatly expanded information program, the West can alert the world to the dulling and warping of human life which communism brings. This theme should be hammered home persistently by the West in its diplomatic communications, in the United Nations and especially in those circles where it is possible to discuss frankly the political fate of man.

Communist political warfare is designed to expose and magnify the flaws of Western society, even though incurable political, social and economic diseases are endemic in the communist system. The communists preach abundance, yet live in the grip of enforced privation; they preach beauty, but produce ugliness; they preach liberation, while retaining the world's largest colonial empire.

The West should ask, and keep on asking, the Soviet Union why it does not grant independence to its colonies, and demand that a date be set for their independence. By substituting the word "colony" for "satellite," the Western "voice" can deprive the Soviets of a semantic fig leaf which hides the truth and thus deceives many, particularly in the so-called nonaligned regions of the globe. This, it may be argued, is a mere matter of words. But, so the Chinese sage tells us, the rectification of terms is the principal business of philosophy.

The Soviet system has many of the characteristics of fascism. This point should be made frequently and with force. The Soviets came to power on the strength of the claim that they would improve the social and economic conditions of the masses; but, instead, they have exploited the masses to enhance the military power of the U.S.S.R. The West refutes communism with a weak and muffled voice; in most instances, it refrains from doing so altogether. Thus, for example, the West permits the Soviets to lay claim to space while ignoring their responsibilities to operate a humane and tolerant society on earth. U.S. Attorney General Robert Kennedy put it this way:

Throughout most of the world no one is prepared to counter the communists' arguments with facts and figures. No one raises questions or stresses opposite opinions or positions. . . . We are victims of a smart, articulate, well-organized minority which has kept us continuously on the defensive. We have permitted it to happen, we have allowed it to continue. If we do not meet the problem head on, if we are not ourselves imaginative, tough, dedicated, willing and self-sacrificing, the struggle with the enemy will not be won by them, but lost by us.[44]

The Economic Front*

According to Marxist ideology, economics are the determinant of politics. Yet communist leaders have usually managed to subordinate economic policy decisions as well as the doctrine of economic determinism to political objectives. The communists regard economic productivity as an instrument of global power accumulation, not as a mere means of satisfying human wants. The purpose of the Soviet productive effort is to expand the communist power base for the successful waging of conflict. Economics, as a significant underpinning of communist strategic power, now increasingly supports policies designed to promote disturbances in the free economic system and to carry on the political penetration and reorientation of the "in-between" regions, thus diminishing the zone of Western political influence.

The communist bloc's transactions with the Free World comprise less than 5 percent of total international trade. A real menace arises, however, from the mischief a flexible state trading monopoly, backed by immense resources, can wreak on individual firms and unwary governments in free countries. Concentrating their resources on promising targets, the Soviets can wage economic warfare in selected commodities and in selected markets. Divisive effects of Soviet trade with Europe have already assumed serious proportions, notably in oil. Within five years the U.S.S.R. will control, at its present rate of progress, a quarter of the Free World's export trade in oil.

In Italy, the ENI, the state-owned oil agency which obtains a large part of its crude oil imports from the Soviet Union, is probably the most powerful interest group. Its influence reaches far beyond oil exploitation. The ENI, a state-within-the-state, conducts its foreign relations with sovereign nonchalance. Its aspirations seem to be at variance with postwar Italian policy and to point away from Italy's commitment to NATO.[45] ENI and the coalition of Fanfani's

---

* Chapter 4 contains a recommendation that NATO should be the primary Western instrumentality for waging economic warfare. This section examines some of the issues involved and policies which might be pursued.

Christian Democrats with Nenni's wing of the Italian Socialist Party give the Communist Party a powerful lever in Italian politics.

The Soviets can undersell Western producers whenever they wish to practice dumping. "The state trading apparatus can intensify its offensive against a specific target country simply by manipulating the proper line of goods. It can purchase a free country's export surpluses and dump them in another market (e.g., Egypt's cotton, Burma's rice, Indonesia's rubber and tin), either to acquire foreign currencies or disrupt local market economies. Barter can become a weapon to reduce the earnings of Western countries. For instance, Soviet oil bartered for Brazilian coffee cuts Brazilian purchases of oil in hard-currency areas. . . . When Western businessmen succumb to the lure of communist bloc trade, they help to open the state planners' bottlenecks, thereby alleviating popular dissatisfaction with the performance of communist regimes. At the same time, they aid the communists in laying the foundations for future export capacities which will someday be harnessed to the conduct of further economic warfare against the West."[46]

Aeroflot, the aviation arm of Soviet political-economic warfare, has thrust deep into North and West Africa and, across the Atlantic, to Cuba. In the East, Soviet transport planes now span the Red Sea, the Indian Ocean and fly over the South Pacific. Strategically, the east-west air thrust represents a vast pincer operation converging on the Western Hemisphere. In North Africa, Soviet penetration has been vastly facilitated by the twice-weekly Aeroflot flights from Moscow by way of Belgrade to Libya, Mali, Guinea, Ghana and Morocco. Soviet influence via air transport is most perceptible in Mali and Morocco, but it is already well entrenched in Guinea and Ghana. Soviet air services, unlike even the nationally owned Western lines, are political instruments of the communist state. Upon acquisition, additional routes are immediately used to shuttle agents, arms, propaganda and money into target areas.

This complex of problems should be made a topic of discussion in the NATO Council, where it might be possible to suggest common policies and to agree upon a strategy which would force the Soviets to come across with real value as a *quid pro quo* for Western imports.

Against the backdrop of Soviet economic penetration of the Free World a U.S. Senate report written by Samuel Pisar warns:

The key to an effective strategy is the coordination of allied economic policies toward the Communist bloc. The present patchwork of individual and contradictory national policies cannot possibly yield the necessary response. In the first place a new and imaginative U.S. approach to the alliance is indicated, reflecting a more genuine concern with the requirements of military and economic security on the one hand and the legitimate needs and interests of our allies on the other. Fundamentally, the strategy must be broadly based on a foundation of vigorous economic momentum and collaboration within the Atlantic Community, and a liberal foreign trade climate within the free world with ample alternatives to the more hazardous varieties of trade entanglement with the block.[47]

The NATO Allies might agree to the following ground rules, namely: to take measures to insulate NATO currencies from speculative manipulation; to refrain from extending any credit to communist countries; to minimize the sale to communist countries of capital goods in any form and to concentrate on consumer goods sales; to prevent communist bloc penetration of European markets through dumping and other devices and to screen purchases from the communist bloc as to comparative economic and political desirability. The potentialities of Western economic warfare can be illustrated by the case of an economically vulnerable area, namely, East Germany. Notwithstanding all its gritty political problems, East Germany ranks first among the Soviet satellites for it makes the largest contribution to Soviet economic growth. Communist economic planning in East Germany depends for the fulfillment of quotas upon machinery replacement parts, chemical products, transportation and electro-technical equipment from West Germany. By holding the threat of an economic boycott over East Germany, the West would have a powerful lever to put the Soviets on their best behavior in Berlin and elsewhere. Furthermore, markets for these West German goods are available elsewhere. This would be an extremely powerful weapon which could throw into disarray communist plans for economic expansion and cut East Germany's share in communist aid to the underdeveloped areas. One need only recall the demonstrated effectiveness of the West German cancellation, in reprisal against restrictions on West German travel to Berlin, of the interzonal trade agreement in the fall of 1960.

The immense resources of the Atlantic Community should be

marshaled to bottle up Soviet political and economic pressures until the *only* alternatives open to the Soviets will be naked aggression against the NATO Alliance or a negotiated withdrawal. Although, from time to time, thoughtful Western observers have proposed such a policy, the leaders of the Western Alliance, while professing their agreement in principle, have not yet managed to concert their national policies for the purpose of bringing the West's overwhelming economic power to bear against the communist bloc. In this direction lies one of the best hopes for a peaceful and beneficent transformation of the international environment.

The Promise of Victory

For all its weaknesses, NATO stands as the one rock against which Soviet power has beaten in vain. Thus far, NATO has checked Soviet ambitions and, it is hoped, will continue to do so for an indefinitely long time—as long as may be necessary.

Although the West Europeans still view with mixed emotions the United States' role in the Alliance, there is good reason to assume that they would welcome resolute and dynamic United States leadership. At the very least, the United States has the obligation of presenting them with an alternative to confusion, cynicism and defeatism. The resumption of Soviet atomic testing shocked Europe; yet the European NATO members did not step up their contributions to common defense. If Pavlovian conditioning is not to sap the Europeans' will to defend themselves, a tougher and more forward-looking United States must rally, by the force of its own resolve, its faltering Allies. The United States handling of the Cuban crisis in October, 1962, provides an instructive example. The diplomatic and military means are at hand. For example, the sight of a nuclear-armed Europe can insure Premier Khrushchev's return to a more civil comportment, if not to sobriety. The actual possession of nuclear weapons by our European Allies would lessen Europe's vulnerability to Soviet psychological warfare as well as military aggression. It would greatly complicate any Soviet plans for military adventures in Central Europe, for even limited probes would court the danger of an all-out nuclear war. Moreover, the nuclear arming of Western Europe confronts the Soviets with the difficult task of explaining *their* nuclear sharing policies to *their* allies.

During the next decade, the one overriding objective of American foreign policy must be the strengthening of the NATO Alliance so that it can bar communist expansion and keep open the approaches to the uncommitted world. In the last analysis, NATO will be as strong as the United States cares to make it, for the state of the Alliance reflects truly the sureness of American leadership. Of course, the average American believes that, in the moment of truth, his country will stand firm and thus takes umbrage at European doubts about America's good faith. But widely publicized ruminations on the imminent transformation ("liberalization") of Soviet society and the blessings that are about to flow from the Sino-Soviet split are not apt to strengthen Europe's confidence in American judgment, especially when these musings are echoed by high American officials as they intensify negotiations with the Soviets.

The principles which should infuse Allied Cold War diplomacy and the dangers of failing to adhere to them were succinctly set forth by McGeorge Bundy when he reflected upon the pitfalls into which the democracies fell in coping with Hitler:

> The greatest of our failures, of course, was in the failure to develop common policies and purposes of sufficient coherence to prevent—and later to deal with—the rise of Adolf Hitler. In this failure there is blame enough for all of us. . . . In the first place, one must put the dangers of neutrality or appeasement as means of dealing with a determinedly expansionist power. . . . Second, and more subtly, we can, I think, discern in the history of the years from 1925 to 1939 an astonishing tendency to miss the real issues. . . . A third lesson from the 1930's is that governments without courage can be expected at critical moments to take wrong decisions which they will defend on grounds of domestic political necessity. . . . Finally, in this set of gloomy flashbacks, let me recall what we may call the error of the empty commitment.[48]

NATO is founded on the premise that the Western democratic nations shall not a second time lapse into the errors of appeasement which led to what Winston Churchill called the "unnecessary war."

In sum, the key to Western unity lies in the attainment within the Atlantic Community of a consensus on the nature of the communist threat. Salvation lies in what the West *does*. It does not reside in a never-ending debate over the basic intent of every Soviet move abroad and the meaning of every shift in the tortuous course of internal communist politics.

Fundamental changes within the communist bloc cannot be wrought by wishful thinking. It is not likely that the communists, as their relative power grows, will be so reckless or so stupid as to abandon capriciously their avowed beliefs and objectives. If fundamental changes are to occur in the communist world, they will be brought about by the pressures of a purposeful and unified Western counterstrategy immune to communist blandishments. It is Western disunity that sustains the ideological fervor and self-confidence of the communists. The communist flame will flicker when the West ceases to fuel it.

It is the task of statesmen in the West to plan for all kinds of likely and even some unlikely contingencies. Hardened by many battles, communist operational doctrine has developed a tough pragmatism which reconciles what, on the face of it, seems irreconcilable. The communists who read our press are fully aware of our difficulties in evaluating their real intentions, platform controversies and secret palace intrigues. It is not their purpose to make it easier for us to fathom their minds. Nor has a certain tendency toward over-sophistication, which sometimes flaws our intellectual output, escaped their attention.

No doubt, our intelligence community keeps track conscientiously of events in the Soviet Union, of the ideological tug-of-war between Moscow and Peking and of a good many wrinkles of intraparty strife in the satellite regions and elsewhere. Yet the margin of the unknown remains wide. We should not consider troubles within the communist camp as a source of comfort, particularly in the unlikely case that these troubles should reach crisis proportions. Despotic regimes in the throes of crisis are most dangerous, especially when they are heavily armed. If the Atlantic world is to take advantage of opportunities presented by communism's many internal dilemmas, it must keep its powder dry and thus frustrate Soviet diversions abroad as an easy escape from failures at home.

The nations of the North Atlantic area do not lack the means to influence those on both sides of the Iron Curtain who are either the supporters or the opponents of the West. But the test of the effectiveness of the policies which the North Atlantic countries adopt depends not upon the degree to which the West attempts, in an "other-directed" fashion, to curry favor with its opponents, but rather upon the extent to which Western programs provide progress and security for the Atlantic Community and the rest of the Free World.

For some years now, Europe has been engaged, as it were, in a great constitutional debate over what might aptly be called the "interstate commerce clause." More recently, the Atlantic Community as a whole has launched itself upon a constitutional debate over the meaning of "the common defense." At the beginning of 1963, it seemed as though these two constitutional debates were about to be merged into one—a most historic one—the outcome of which would determine whether the Atlantic peoples would succeed in their efforts to form a "more perfect union." The debate, to be sure, might require a long time to run its full course. To the extent that it is conducted in a serious vein, and not merely at the level of abstract political rhetoric, it will deal increasingly with the reform of NATO's institutional structure. It is this aspect of the NATO problem to which we now must turn.

CHAPTER **7** INSTITUTIONS FOR THE FUTURE
ATLANTIC COMMUNITY

Many factors have combined, during the last fifteen years, to exert a unifying impact upon Europe and the Atlantic world as a whole. Now that the worst chauvinist excrescences lie buried beneath the rubble of World War II, the common spiritual and cultural values of Western civilization have reasserted themselves. The political squabbles which, in recent years, have divided the Atlantic Community have occurred within a common cultural framework. This framework defines the limits of intra-Alliance political and strategic jockeying. Whereas the Soviet bloc is bound together by a single intolerant ideology (despite occasional heretical protests) and is menaced by the divisive force of national cultural differences, the Atlantic Community can afford to indulge in a high degree of ideological pluralism precisely because it is united in basic cultural values. The Atlantic Community, fortunately, is not beset by a cultural cleavage so profound as that which separates the Soviet Union from China.

New technological developments within the West have set in motion revolutions in transport and communications which, along with mass production techniques, are helping to standardize not only consumer tastes and socioeconomic aspirations, but even political ideas throughout the Atlantic countries. Within the countries of the West the alignments and programs of political parties are evolving along remarkably similar lines. There are, no doubt, healthy disagreements between Democrats and Republicans, Labourites and Conservatives, Socialists and Christian Democrats. Most hearteningly, in the postwar period the major European parties have begun to

develop—as the English and American parties did long ago—the notion of a basic political consensus underlying partisan and even, to
a certain extent, ideological differences. Although "ideologized"
politics seems to be in the ascendancy in the United States, its sharp-
ness has been noticeably attenuated within the European states
since 1945.

Generally speaking, the peoples of most Western democratic
countries are beginning to see the internal and external problems of
their societies within a relatively homogeneous framework. Internally, they aim at a rational political and economic order. They aspire
to representative government and the rule of law, government which
is responsive to the will of the voting majority and subject to the
criticism of an intelligent opposition. They seek a sensible balance
between maximum liberty for individuals and groups and the essential requirements of public unity, order, progress and security.
In the economic sphere, they seek to strike an equitable balance between voluntary activity and the public interest, i.e., a system of
mixed enterprise keyed to widely shared prosperity and sustained
growth. Externally, the peoples of the Atlantic democracies are willing to support defense policies calculated to halt the international
march of communism. They are gradually coming to see the need
for intelligent political and economic approaches to the underdeveloped areas of the world. In sum, although it would be premature to
say that a political and social consensus exists within the Atlantic
region, the foundations for such a consensus are present, waiting for
the day when the leaders of Western society proceed toward the
erection of the edifice.

This is not the place to attempt a detailed assessment of the loyalty
of individual citizens of the NATO Alliance states either to the "idea
of Europe" or to the concept of Atlantic Community. It would be
very difficult to measure the degree to which the peoples of the
Western countries are now widening the focus of their political
consciousness from the traditional nation-state to a broader type of
"nationalism" founded upon a regional cultural unity. Perhaps popular attitudes are not entirely relevant to the question under review.
History shows that federative and confederative movements have
usually issued from the efforts of prominent leaders and elites
rather than from mass sentiments. More revealing than the views
of the average European or American in the street is the actual

record of: (a) official actions, commitments and proposals on the part of the governments concerned; (b) the programs of major political parties; (c) the declared attitudes of organized interest groups which play a significant political role in the life of their national societies; and (d) the published preferences of intellectuals and journalists, who do much to mold public opinion in their countries. Despite numerous differences, divergent interpretations and fluctuations in enthusiasm, one of the major themes articulated during the last decade by the majority of Western statesmen, governmental officials, party leaders, interest group spokesmen, and "opinion makers" has been the desirability of closer association within Europe and the Atlantic regions.

Both Western Europe and the Atlantic Community as a whole are closer to accepting the notion of political unity than they have been for centuries. At no time since the modern nation-state period began have Western governments felt so keenly as they do today the urge to unite for a dual purpose: the defensive one of thwarting a threat to their security and the constructive one of coordinating their policies for the benefit of the entire international community.

Nevertheless, in spite of these pleasing portents, neither political leadership nor public opinion in the Atlantic democracies is yet prepared to come to grips with the making of a permanent Atlantic federal union. Significant strides have been made in the exchange of ideas in both official and unofficial international conferences, but the movement for closer political integration has not yet been geared into the domestic political processes of the Atlantic societies. The constitutional questions raised in the Senate Foreign Relations Committee during the debate over "unanimous decision-taking" procedures in the OECD Treaty indicate that the United States, among other NATO allies, is far from ready to sign over any of its national prerogatives to an Atlantic political organization. The Secretary General of NATO, Dr. Dirk Stikker, speaking to the NATO Parliamentarians in Paris in late 1961, went to some lengths to point out the conception of NATO which the member governments were willing to accept:

We must not forget, after all, that NATO is not and was not intended to be a supranational institution; NATO is an alliance of sovereign and independent states who reserve to themselves ultimate responsibility for all their decisions in domestic and foreign affairs.[1]

Before examining such practical steps as may be taken to expand existing Atlantic institutions and to improve their performance, it will be useful to review the recent history of the Atlantic unity movement. The Third NATO Parliamentarians' Conference, in a resolution unanimously adopted on November 16, 1957, issued a call for two important meetings.[2] First, it proposed that arrangements be made for the Atlantic Congress which met in London in June, 1959. The Atlantic Congress, consisting of 650 prominent citizens of the NATO countries, launched several important new initiatives, including the concept of the OECD and plans for the creation of an Atlantic Institute. Second, the NATO Parliamentarians' resolution recommended that the governments

bring about, in accordance with the constitutional and governmental processes of their countries, a conference of leading representative citizens selected on a non-partisan basis and directed to convene as often as necessary in order to examine exhaustively and to recommend how greater cooperation and unity of purpose, as envisaged by the North Atlantic Treaty, within the Atlantic Community may best be developed.[3]

The resolution further urged that the delegates to this conference be officially appointed but should be expected to act in accordance with their individual convictions. In subsequent annual conferences, the NATO Parliamentarians reiterated their appeals for a formal Atlantic Conference. In September, 1960, acting upon the recommendation, the United States Congress passed Public Law 86–719, which created a U.S. Citizens Commission on NATO of twenty persons appointed by the President of the Senate and the Speaker of the House of Representatives, thereby making it an official though uninstructed body. The United States Commission, under the co-chairmanship of former Under Secretary of State William L. Clayton and former Secretary of State Christian A. Herter, assumed the lead in organizing the Atlantic Convention, which met in Paris in January, 1962.

Some of the planners and delegates looked upon the Convention as an historic event, which they likened to the Constitutional Convention in Philadelphia in 1787. But the meeting was not designed to draft an Atlantic Constitution to be submitted to the peoples of the fifteen states for ratification. Indeed, the subject of political unification was treated with great circumspection. At the plenary session of January 19, Adolph W. Schmidt, one of the delegates from the

United States, raised a question about a statement in the Preamble of the final Declaration of the Convention: "A true Atlantic Community must extend to the political, military, economic, moral and cultural fields." Mr. Schmidt proposed that this be amended to read as follows: "In organizing a true Atlantic Community, the eventual goal must be government extending to the political, military, economic, moral and cultural fields." The crucial addition, of course, was the term "government." The amendment was defeated by a vote of 36 to 19.[4]

The Declaration of Paris, which attracted a good deal of attention in the Western press, proposed several measures for strengthening the Atlantic Community,[5] Among the more important political recommendations were these: (1) the creation of a permanent High Council to concert and plan, and, in certain agreed cases, to decide policy on matters of concern to the Community as a whole; (2) to develop the NATO Parliamentarians' Conference into a consultative Assembly which would review the work of the various Atlantic institutions and make recommendations to them; (3) to establish an Atlantic High Court of Justice to decide specified legal controversies arising under the treaties linking the members of the Community; (4) to harmonize political, military and economic policy on matters affecting the Community as a whole; (5) to treat the formulation of an agreed NATO policy with respect to nuclear weapons as a matter of urgent business for the North Atlantic Council; (6) to establish within the earliest practicable period a Special Governmental Commission, appointed by the NATO governments, "to draw up plans within two years for the creation of a true Atlantic Community."[6]

It is noteworthy that the Atlantic Convention was a product of initiatives taken by national parliaments. National executive branches, except for a few permissive and sometimes grudging gestures, kept aloof. Indeed, the fact that the meeting had its origins in a series of legislative resolutions furnished one of the bases for comparing it with the Philadelphia Convention. It should not be forgotten, however, that in 1787 the Articles of Confederation did not provide for a powerful executive branch. Today, the conduct of NATO relations comes under the rubric of foreign policy for all Allied governments, and in every case the executive branch is more important than the legislative in the execution of foreign affairs. Interestingly enough, while executive personnel have often justified

their skepticism of schemes for closer NATO unity on the grounds
that national legislatures are extremely jealous of sovereign prerogatives, one could argue that in recent years the NATO Parliamentarians have pressed somewhat harder toward unification than have the
NATO Ambassadors or Foreign Ministers. A similar condition obtained in the case of the European unity movement. Among the
Six, the members of the various consultative assemblies have usually
displayed a more daringly experimental attitude than the national
ministers, whose job it is to reconcile joint decision-making with
national policy requirements.[7] Since parliamentary representatives are not, in the strict sense of the term, "responsible" governmental agents, they can feel free to adopt *avant-garde* positions
which may provoke frowns or smiles from executive personnel in the
intergovernmental bodies, and also from many of their own colleagues in the legislative chambers back home. (In the case of the
Atlantic Convention, although it issued from legislative action, the
delegates were private citizens, not members of the national parliaments.)

Normally, the NATO Parliamentarians themselves are very careful
not to appear to be advocating any diminution of domestic legislative
prerogatives. But, at the same time, most of them are anxious to
make sure that if the North Atlantic Council, or its equivalent, is
vested with an enhanced executive power for the Atlantic Community, some method will be devised to hold it accountable to a
regional representative body. It would seem that, as the Atlantic
Community is slowly being built, the historic struggle between
executive and legislative power which characterized the evolution
of Western democratic government will be re-enacted, almost unconsciously, on a regional scale. This is by no means a symptom of
the West's political ill health. Although the Parliamentarians do not
enjoy a legal status under the North Atlantic Treaty comparable to
that of the Council, nevertheless they can play an extremely important political role in educating their fellow legislators on the
issues of the Community, helping to build support for the pro-
Atlantic programs which, it is hoped, the executive branch will pursue, and preparing popular sentiment for the day when far-reaching
commitments will have to be undertaken and ratified.

The effort to achieve closer political unity among the NATO countries should not be conceived of, as it often is, in terms of "giving up

national sovereignty." It is misleading, irrelevant and self-defeating to pose the problem in a manner which focuses attention unnecessarily upon an outmoded legalistic abstraction of dubious validity. Instead of being asked to delegate sovereignty, the members of NATO should be asked simply to work together more closely and more intensively for the attainment of their common purposes, to increase their mutual interdependence and to devise more practical and more efficient mechanisms for getting things done. It will be wiser for the statesmen of the Atlantic Community to let the idea of absolute national sovereignty die quietly of inanition rather than to insist upon a formal execution before a firing squad.

Nor is it necessary to assume that the only kind of progress toward closer political unification within the Atlantic Community that is worth pursuing is the kind that can be embodied in formal, written instruments. The NATO governments, no doubt, should be thinking seriously of treaty revision before 1969, when NATO reaches its twentieth anniversary. But treaty amendment is not the only way, or necessarily the most important way, in which the institutions of the Atlantic Community can be developed. Treaty-making, after all, is an essentially *international* process; it implies accommodation to *foreign* interests. Besides, a treaty is a formal contract in which traditional diplomatic language often masks an egoistic regard for national prerogatives, a reluctance to make a genuine commitment and underlying distrust of how the other party will behave when the *casus foederis* arises. Treaties, moreover, reflect mutually acceptable arrangements at a given point of time. Often, before their expiration, they are outmoded, at least partially, by rapidly changing historical circumstances. Finally, the practice of writing treaties and, for that matter, constitutions, too, connotes a bias toward the Roman law method of describing the evolution of political institutions and legal rules.

There is in the Western tradition, and not only in the Anglo-American branch of it, another important path to political evolution, namely, the customs, conventions and precedents of political life, which serve as guidelines to the kind of political action that is expected as a matter of course. The British, of course, are famous for the customs and conventions of their unwritten constitution. But most American and West European politicians also understand quite well the notion of informal ground rules. These emerge from the inner life of a community. Their very existence testifies to the reality of that practical consensus without which no community can endure. Customary developments, therefore, ought to play their part in the growth of Atlantic institutions, and a certain amount of "elbow room" should be left for this purpose.

No one would suggest that the treaty method lacks utility in the process of regional integration; it is an indispensable part of regional constitution-making among modern, sovereign, bureaucratic states. One of the most useful purposes to be served by the treaty method is to clarify the developing consensus among all the members of the community. Certainly, the OECD Convention served to codify common economic purposes which could scarcely have been formulated by the member governments five years earlier. Hence if the NATO Treaty should be revised, the new document will represent a "lowest common denominator" of the factors binding the Allies. It will not, and cannot, be expected to define the total political content of the Atlantic Community, any more than the present Treaty did, say eight or ten years ago. If a NATO Parliament should come into being by formal consent of the governments, its political functions and prestige will depend just as much upon the skill with which it continues to refine its informal, routine operations as upon any treaty clauses which purport to define its formal role. The NATO Parliamentarians first earned their political spurs without any benefit of treaty status. Their annual conference is already a political reality of NATO—one which has had profound effects upon the direction of the Atlantic Community.

Within the last three years, the process of integration has been carried forward at a more rapid rate in Western Europe than in the transatlantic community as a whole. This is particularly true at the economic level, as the most cursory comparison of the EEC and the OECD will show. The point of dangerous asymmetry has not been reached, at least not at the political level. Within a very few years, however, the gap in the evolution of the respective systems might widen irremediably unless steps are taken soon to insure that the consolidation of NATO will henceforth take place at a speed commensurate with the progress of Western European integration.[3] NATO must keep abreast of the European Community in the pace toward unification; this strategic imperative is addressed to both the United States and Western Europe, i.e., to every part of the Atlantic Community.

There are at least five institutional dimensions in which efforts should be made to improve the collective political performance of the Atlantic Community: (1) the North Atlantic Council; (2) NATO's political-military relationships; (3) the Secretariat; (4) an Atlantic parliamentary body; and (5) an Atlantic Community Court. A brief comment on each is in order.

The North Atlantic Council. The Council, which is the meeting ground of the various national executives and the "permanent-session workshop" of their legates, is undoubtedly the most important of all NATO institutions and will remain so for the foreseeable future. Since it is the only organ mentioned by name in the Treaty, and creates all other "subsidiary bodies as may be necessary," it presumably wields whatever executive, legislative and judicial powers inhere in the intergovernmental organization. Because of this importance, it would be desirable, as Alastair Buchan suggests, to enhance its prestige by choosing the permanent ambassadors from the ranks not of professional diplomats but of those who enjoy high political standing in their own countries.[9] (It must be admitted, however, that in countries such as the United States, where public stature often depends upon command of local party organizations, politicians who accept this assignment might quickly lose the political standing on which their selection was based.) The task, as Alexander Hamilton might have advised us, is to invest the Council with such an aura of honor and power of influence as will attract the finest, albeit not the most ambitious, political figures.

Even more important, perhaps, than the role of the permanent ambassadors is the performance of the Council at the ministerial levels and at the heads of government level. Although the ambassadors have a vital part to play in the continuous exchange and sifting of views and in furnishing week-to-week guidance to the various planning and operational groups within NATO, their function is necessarily circumscribed by the fact that they are legates and not executives in their own right. No matter how extraordinary the insights which they acquire into the problems of NATO, they lack the prestige which goes with command of foreign offices, defense ministries and treasury departments. Therefore the trend of recent years toward intensifying the participation of foreign ministers, defense ministers (with their chiefs of staff) and finance ministers should be reinforced. For optimum results, this requires constant efforts to increase competence and efficiency in the work of the ambassadors, the committees of the Council, and the divisions of the Secretariat.

The NATO Council should meet at the heads of government level at regular intervals (e.g., once every two years) instead of only at times critical to the fortunes of the Alliance. The heads of government meeting should serve mainly a symbolic purpose; it should be arranged as a solemn display of coalition unity and trust. Questions which can be decided at the ambassadorial or ministerial level should not be held in abeyance so that they can be passed up to the heads of government, nor should the NATO "summit conference" become an occasion for the public airing of intra-NATO differences. Such regularly scheduled conferences would enable Western leaders to exchange their views frankly within an Alliance atmosphere, free of those suspicions which bilateral meetings may breed among absent allies. In this way, too, the heads of government could be brought completely up to date on the great issues of the Alliance. They could identify the major political and strategic issues looming on the horizon, and lay down broad directives to the ministers and ambassadors for the coordination of national policies before critical disputes arise. Finally, these gatherings would enable the heads of government to breathe the air of the Atlantic Community and to engage in healthy rivalry for intellectual leadership of the Alliance. If substantial portions of their discussions were televised and broadcast throughout Europe and America, nothing could do more to bring home to the millions the vital role NATO plays in their lives and thus help to mold a new Atlantic consciousness.

One important step which can be taken immediately within the Council is to intensify further the process of consultation, with a specific view to improving the Alliance's contingency planning. George W. Ball, U.S. Under Secretary of State, addressing the NATO Parliamentarians in November, 1962, spoke as follows:

There are those who suppose that the requirements of speed and secrecy necessarily preclude all possibility of consultation. They are wrong. Time factors may render it difficult to consult on every step in a swiftly developing situation; they may telescope the exchange of views at moments of crisis, but they should not impair the continuum of the consultative process.

The Cuban crisis, in our view, makes manifest the need for a deeper, franker and more continuous exchange of views. For, by such exchanges, we can block out in advance large areas of agreement so that when the moment of crisis comes we will all instinctively move along similar lines.

The fact is that if the nations of the Alliance are to be able to respond with the necessary decisiveness to the challenges ahead, we must be able to act on the basis of solid planning directed at a great variety of contingencies. We are engaged in this planning in the case of Berlin—working through the North Atlantic Council, and the Quadripartite Ambassadorial Group in Washington. But I believe we can make more progress. I think we can and should develop further the techniques of contingency planning, applying it across the board to situations of danger confronting the Alliance.[10]

To take a longer-range view, the permanent ambassadors should begin immediately to explore the possibilities of modifying the decision-taking procedures within the Council. The argument can be made, on traditional constitutional grounds, that since "foreign affairs" are in all countries primarily the responsibility of the executive, the latter, in dealing with his peers from other sovereign states, may agree to abide by a set of rules for taking certain coalition decisions which do not impinge upon the constitutional prerogatives of the national legislature. In brief, there is nothing in the Atlantic Treaty which requires the Council to reach every decision via the unanimity rule. The present rule should eventually be replaced, through carefully contrived transitional stages, by provisions for reaching some decisions by a system of weighted majority vote.

For certain classes of questions, such as those involving fundamental nuclear strategy and centralized command and control, it may eventually be necessary (within a period of five to ten years) to structure the voting in such a way that the veto power will be reserved to either the United States or the WEU. The WEU nations are entitled to a preponderant voice in crucial decisions (concerning, e.g., the rules of nuclear engagement) which affect the defense of Europe. For other classes of questions, either the United States or the WEU might be allowed to adopt the initiative in developing policies which, when concurred in by both the United States and the WEU, would be considered as binding upon the entire Alliance. For example, it might be logical to have the WEU assume the leadership in working out an Atlantic policy toward Eastern Europe while the United States does the same toward China. Still other classes of questions could be handled in such a way as to safeguard the essential national interests of the smaller powers. On all important matters, it would be desirable, of course, to adhere as much as possible to the concept of the "concurrent majority," which implies mutual respect for the basic interests of all.

But the requirement of unanimity is unnecessarily inflexible. It fails to give due weight to a normal fact of international relations: that on some questions the interests of certain Allies are more important to the common good of the whole Alliance than the interests of others. In sum, the Allies should begin to think of treating with each other not necessarily on a basis of strict legal equality, but rather on a basis of equity, arrived at through frank communication and mutual agreement. The Allies themselves, in the Council, should decide in what respects they ought to be treated equally and in what respects they accept the logic of unequal treatment as embodied in various procedures for arriving at policy conclusions by weighted vote.

NATO's Political-Military Relationships. The concept of civilian supremacy over the military reflects much more than a purely Anglo-American tradition; it springs from deep-rooted convictions in Western culture which are traceable as far back as Plato. If it is true, as Alastair Buchan charges, that the Council "has little authority over military planning in the Standing Group or Supreme Headquarters Europe, and therefore . . . little control over the military environment in which it may be asked to reach political judgments,"[11] the situation demands early correction. The remedy lies in strengthening the Council, in improving the process of long-range planning in all policy sectors, in devising more effective liaison mechanisms, and in harmonizing the interrelationships of the Council, the Secretariat, the Standing Group, the whole Military Committee (i.e., the chiefs of staff of all members) and the Supreme Allied Commander.

There is a growing feeling that the Standing Group cannot properly carry out its assigned mission in Washington. What has happened in effect is that the burden of operational planning for Western Europe has been shifted from the Standing Group to SACEUR, whose headquarters is located on the defense front and enjoys ready access to the NATO Council. SACLANT, with headquarters in Norfolk, Virginia, is responsible for the security of the Atlantic Ocean linking North America and Europe. Neither SACEUR nor SACLANT, the two principal NATO commanders, plans for the military security of the Alliance as a whole. Presumably, the Standing Group has this responsibility, but its representatives have less authority and prestige than the Supreme Allied Commanders. Consequently, the focus of NATO planning is not in the military body directly responsible to the NATO Council. In view of the fact that military planning should be conducted within an established political framework, this situation obviously calls for some remedy. We do not intend to suggest a solution. We call attention, however, to an interesting proposal made by Alastair Buchan. Buchan suggests that the Standing Group (representing the chiefs of staff of the United States, Britain, France and—this would be an addition—West Germany) be transformed into the NATO military staff, under a NATO Chief of Staff who, with three deputy chiefs, would be the highest military authority in the Alliance. Buchan suggests placing the NATO Chief of Staff wholly within a civilian secretariat, four steps down in the hierarchy, namely, under the Chairman of the Council. The Secretary General (who would be separated from the Council chairmanship, as he was before 1957) and a civilian deputy secretary general would be responsible both for military planning and arms control policy. But this would seem, Sir John Slessor observed, "to be carrying the perfectly sound principle of civilian control to an extravagant extreme." Slessor is of the opinion that the NATO Chief of Staff, as the officer who will be responsible for the execution of military plans, should also be responsible for advice in their formulation, and that he should not be insulated against direct access to the chairman and individual members of the Council by two layers of civilian officials.[12]

Buchan's plan poses another difficulty, insofar as it subordinates the NATO Chief of Staff to a civilian deputy who is responsible for both military planning *and* arms control. While there is much to be said for combining the two functions, there is a danger that a civilian deputy, partial to a certain approach to arms control, might be tempted to convert military planning into a political instrument for the reduction of international tensions to the detriment of the defense posture of the Alliance. Defense planning should always be carried out with a view to current defense needs, and not primarily with the hope of creating at some future date an atmosphere congenial to disarmament. The balance between the two exigencies should be struck by the Council after availing itself of the arguments on both sides.

The Secretariat. Buchan's suggestion concerning the separation of the Secretary General from the Chairman of the Council is a good one, and deserves to be supported by the member governments. The chairman, he urges, should be a distinguished European political figure who would serve as the Council's principal public spokesman. (If the WEU joins the United States as the second power nucleus within NATO, there will be no need for the courteous gesture of always having a European chairman, presumably to counterbalance the American Chief of Staff. All key positions in NATO should eventually be alternated between Americans and Europeans. In the case of the Council, it might be advisable to have co-chairmen, one European and one American. Then, when an American was appointed Chief of Staff, the Secretary General would be a European, and vice versa.) In Buchan's view, the Secretary General would not be a policymaking official, but one who would draw together the threads of planning so that the Council might be presented with priorities and choices—"a powerful but not a public position."[13]

The Secretariat itself is in need of reorganization. The Secretary General might well be provided with five deputies: (1) one for European questions; (2) one for extra-European affairs, including liaison with such other Free World alliances as ANZUS, OAS, CENTO and SEATO; (3) one for arms control; (4) one for coordinating NATO economic affairs; and (5) one for Atlantic Community informational, scientific and cultural affairs.[14]

An Atlantic Parliamentary Body. Efforts should be made forthwith to facilitate the deliberations of the NATO Parliamentarians and to strengthen the informal links between them and the Council. The Council should furnish the Parliamentarians with as much official information as possible (even in executive session if necessary), encourage them to deliberate upon certain matters which the Council deems appropriate and take into due consideration their committee reports and resolutions. Granted that, at present, the NATO Parliamentarians have no official status (and it is doubtful that the United States Senate and some of the European parliaments would wish to accord them such status), nevertheless they are, because of their standing as individual members of the national legislative bodies, a significant and, potentially, highly influential group. Secretary General Stikker recognized this when he said:

Nothing we are doing, or trying to do, can be accomplished without the support of the legislative institutions of our member countries and that implies without your help; you are in that sense the living link between the public opinions of our fifteen countries and those who are responsible in an official capacity for the execution of policy. . . .

I have noticed in several publications that there is a feeling that the NATO parliamentarians' conference has not sufficient standing because your conference is not formally an integral part of NATO institutions. I doubt whether such an attitude is justified. On the contrary, I believe that your strength lies in the very fact that your institution has grown up spontaneously and unofficially. In custom, if not in law, you have become an essential institution of NATO.[15]

Eventually, a NATO Parliamentary Assembly must be created. The time, no doubt, is still not ripe for the establishment of a true Atlantic Parliament, elected by direct suffrage according to the principle of proportionate representation. Any premature effort in this direction would probably encounter the vigorous opposition of national legislatures, fearful as they are of supranational lawmaking institutions. But it is not too soon to be thinking seriously about such an institution, to be studying its implications carefully and to be debating intelligently how an Atlantic Assembly might work, what its proper powers might be, and how it might be related to other institutions of the Community. The Europeans have thought much more than the Americans have about these problems. They have, for example, learned from experience in the European assemblies—the assemblies of the Council of Europe and the Western European Union, and the Common Assembly of the Coal and Steel Community, the EEC and Euratom—that the main parliamentary groups have formed themselves according to ideological-party affinities instead of national allegiances.[16] The Europeans, therefore, are beginning to understand how party government might operate in a region-wide parliament. American legislators could benefit from discussions in the NATO Parliamentarians' Conference of these European experiences.

If, in the near future, a NATO Assembly should be formally

established under a revised Atlantic Treaty, or by a protocol to the present Treaty, it will be mainly an advisory and consultative body. During the early stages of its life, such an Assembly should not be endowed with policy-formulating or policy-directing powers of a binding character (binding, i.e., upon other NATO bodies) except in very modestly circumscribed areas. Such an Assembly would naturally be able to address questions to the Chairman of the Council and to receive answers; to adopt reports; to render opinions; and to pass resolutions of censure, admonition, praise or exhortation. But the Council, beyond owing it a respectful hearing, would not be deemed politically responsible to it, nor would the Assembly wield the power of the purse. Its principal function would be to provide a continuous review of NATO public policy through mature, informed and inspirational debate, and by asking penetrating questions of the national executive spokesmen who appear before it from time to time.

The Assembly would be expected to concentrate upon the common problems and great challenges confronting the Allies, such as: (a) the political defense of freedom; (b) methods of parrying communist bloc offensives along the economic warfare front; (c) methods of marshaling the West's technological, scientific and productive resources for purposes of military defense and social improvement throughout the Free World; (d) the vigor and seriousness with which the national governments comply with the policy recommendations of such existing bodies as the NATO Council and the OECD, as well as the manner in which NATO Assembly recommendations are followed through within the Alliance; (e) the means of maximizing the Atlantic Community's political and psychological impact upon the satellite nations of Eastern Europe and the neutralist nations; (f) the stimulation among Western publics of a sense of allegiance to the political and social ideals of the Atlantic Community, and to NATO as the instrument for preserving them. It may not be advisable to assign to the Assembly the function of debating publicly defense matters, but it should be allowed to subject broad military policies to critical review in closed session. Furthermore, the Assembly might be given substantive responsibilities for monitoring progress in information and educational programs, and cultural, intellectual and scientific-technological cooperation.

An Atlantic Community Court. The Atlantic Convention recom-

mended the "creation of a High Court of Justice, reserved to the
Atlantic Community, in order to settle legal differences between
members and between members and the organizations arising from
the interpretation and application of treaties."[17] The purpose of this
proposal would not be to replace the International Court of Justice,
so far as the Atlantic nations are concerned, by an Atlantic regional
court of all-encompassing legal jurisdiction. The function of an Atlantic Court would be more modest and more restricted. It would not
be created specifically for the purpose of applying those basic and
universal rules of international law which the World Court normally
applies. Actually, the Atlantic Court would be supplementary to the
International Court. From time to time, NATO members become
involved in disagreements or disputes over the interpretation of
countless international instruments which have been executed in
pursuance of the Atlantic Treaty and the OECD Convention. At
present, these issues are not suitable for submission to the adjudica-
tion of a universal membership court. Many of the agreements are
of a confidential nature; often the issue involves matters which bear
upon the security or the political interest of the Alliance. It would
be unthinkable for any member of NATO to request that such a
case be carried before the World Court, whose membership includes
judges from the communist bloc countries. Frequently, the Atlantic
parties would be willing to have these issues settled according to a
body of Atlantic legal principles if an appropriate judicial mechanism existed. As things now stand, these matters must be settled by
diplomatic negotiation. In the future, the number of treaties, conventions, protocols and executive agreements among the Atlantic nations is likely to increase. It is inevitable that the codes of NATO
administrative law will grow. The concept of the rule of law to
which all NATO nations subscribe suggests that there should be some
agency to which recourse can be had against the Atlantic Community administrators. This Court will become increasingly necessary to relieve the political bodies of time-consuming negotiations
over problems which could be settled by an impartial agency. The
justices of the Court, who would be drawn from several Atlantic
countries on a rotational basis, would be expected to develop an
Atlantic "constitutional law," based upon the written treaties and
the common principles of the Anglo-American and the Continental
Roman law traditions. Drafting a statute for an Atlantic Court, with

equitable provisions for the selection of judges and careful definitions of the jurisdiction and procedures of the Court, is one of the
most likely ways of fostering the growth of a Community spirit.

The foregoing recommendations, to be sure, may strike the un-
compromising advocate of Atlantic federation as falling disappoint-
ingly short of the ideal of a larger union. But they trace the lines of
an evolution which seems to lie within the range of political practicality. Indeed, it is by no means certain that even these relatively
modest suggestions for the future political development of NATO's
institutions will immediately prove acceptable to all the members
of the Alliance. It is tempting to envisage political evolution as a
spontaneous and inexorable movement upward and onward, conforming to an immanent law of progress. In fact, however, everything depends on the strength or frailty of political purpose. In the
final analysis, NATO will be able to advance toward a higher stage
only if the member governments will it so and deliberately execute
the grand design. The initiative, as always, must come from the most
important and the most influential members—in this case, the United
States, Great Britain, France and West Germany.

The establishment of a basic political consensus among these four
nations is the linchpin of a more closely united Atlantic Community,
for it is these states that are most directly concerned with the
making of crucial policy decisions on such matters as defense
strategy, burden sharing and negotiations with the Soviets. In brief,
what would seem to be required is a dusting off of the French proposal for a tripartite directorate and an appropriate alteration of the
concept, namely extending it to include West Germany and thus
acknowledging the changed circumstances of the international situation. It may not be advisable from the standpoint of the United
States, Britain and France, not to speak of the Federal Republic itself, to have the latter assume a share of strategic responsibility for
the defense of areas outside the NATO theater. But it is absurd to
presume that the Big Three, without Germany's concurrence, could
coordinate their policies on questions that bear vitally upon the future of Central Europe. At the present time, the divisions of opinion
among the leading members of NATO seldom find Germany in a
three-to-one minority; more frequently of late differences among the
Allies have congealed into an Anglo-American position and a
Franco-German position. President de Gaulle, since his European

policy pivots on a firm political friendship between Paris and Bonn, could hardly cavil at the suggestion that an informal quadripartite "directory" (conforming to the membership of the Quadripartite Ambassadorial Group which already exists in Washington) should determine at least certain categories of Alliance policy issues. The United States might find that this proposal holds the promise of closing the political fissures within the Alliance and of satisfying the Continental power on whose economic and military cooperation the United States has depended increasingly in recent years. Perhaps the most vocal objections to such a scheme will come from Britain. It is likely, however, that the British can be persuaded to acquiesce in a four-power directorate in which the voice of the United States will always be heard and in which West Germany's policy would be subject to the critical review of her three partners. As for the other NATO powers, it is unlikely that they will oppose an arrangement that so closely fits the realities of power and relieves them from responsibilities which extend beyond their strategic horizon and the limits of their economic resources.

CHAPTER **8** THE ATLANTIC VISION: A QUESTION
OF CHOICE

Santayana said, "He who does not learn from history
is condemned to repeat it." The immense complexity of international relations and the pressure of events tend to divert the attention of the statesman from underlying issues. More often than not,
his energies are consumed by warding off the crisis of the day and
coping with that unforeseen and, more often than not, unforeseeable
emergency which is the commonplace of contemporary international
politics.

Since World War II the United States has pursued a number of
strategies designed to halt the disintegration of what we call, for
want of a better term, the Free World and block communist expansion. Some of these strategies have paid off; others have failed.
Drawing upon our historical tradition, our principles of government
and humanitarian ideals, we have fashioned an image of the kind
of world we want to live in. Yet our endeavors have not been informed by an understanding of history that could accommodate our
principles and aspirations to the realities of our times.

The overarching reality of our times is the transformation of the
nation-state system. International law, formal diplomacy and the
Charter of the United Nations pay homage to the concept of
inviolate national sovereignty. The public declarations of our government abound in eulogies of national self-determination and national independence. Yet the most powerful trends of our age are
working against both. The progress of military-industrial technology
and the increase of international economic interdependence have
reduced the sovereignty of most states, old and new, to a polite

fiction. The sovereignty of most nation-states is now at the mercy of forces that they cannot control.

Mankind stands at the threshold of a new era—of the Age of Global History, as Hans Kohn has called it. The passing of the nation-state system constitutes the true revolution of our times. If there is a lesson to be learned from the history of similar historical transactions—the passing of the Greek city-state, of the Roman Empire and of the feudal order—it is that the new order, however radical its innovations, conserves much of the old. To some, this fact signifies the deplorable inertia of the human race; to others, this fact bespeaks the reassuring continuity of historic evolution. Be this as it may, the desuetude of the nation-state system should not blind posterity to its immense achievements. For a long time, many of its problems will keep intruding upon the new order. The conservation of the nation-state's rich bequest to human progress calls for as great an exertion of imaginative statesmanship as does the liberation of the new life-giving forces. Vulgar notions about evolution to the contrary, history has never been a one-way street. The nation-state has been an essential step along the path of mankind's political development. Under specific conditions, it still is—notwithstanding its obsolescence within the perspective of global history. For not a few peoples in Africa and Asia, the nation-state represents the necessary stage in the transition from preindustrial to industrial civilization. For the more mature peoples, the nation-state represents the necessary stage in the making of a wider union. In the West, national and supranational loyalties not only need not conflict but should re-enforce one another, for supranational integration furnishes the best guarantee for the preservation of the best in nationhood. National diversity—and diversity is the spice of international life—finds its haven in supranational unity. This is the meaning and purpose of federation.

The real world has been unkind to Marxist-Leninist economic theory. The evolution of capitalism did not conform to Marxist-Leninist analysis and prediction. Yet the Marxist-Leninist dialectic did contribute one important element to communism as a power philosophy: it attuned the initiate to revolutionary change. The communists understood far better than their opponents that the international political system had failed to adjust itself to rapid technological and economic change. They also latched onto the potential of nationalism in the underdeveloped world. Although there is no place for the nation in the communist utopia, the communists allied themselves with the nationalisms of Africa, Asia and Latin America. The enduring objective of communist strategy has been the destruction of Western empires and the isolation of the Western peoples amidst the rising tide of anticolonial revolt. In the communist scheme of things, destruction is the necessary step toward construction. From the wreckage of the nation-state system the communists propose to construct what they now call "the commonwealth of socialist nations"—a euphemism for world-wide communist rule. The communist mind, displeasing as is to us its twisting casuistry, is far more sensitive to the forces making for change in the world than the status quo mentality still so prevalent in most Western chancelleries.

The critics of our foreign policies, although they divide on many issues, contend that our foreign policies have been largely "reactive" and have left the initiative to the communists. So sweeping an indictment appears unjustified in the light of the United States' real achievements throughout the post-World War II epoch. The restoration of Western Europe, the creation of the Atlantic Alliance, the reconstruction of Japan, the defense of the Far East and the making of the European Common Market would have been impossible without American leadership and power. The United States, whenever and wherever it pursued, after World War II, firm policies and stood up to hostile challenges, attained its objectives. If this had not been so, all of Europe and all of Asia would, by now, have disappeared behind the Iron Curtain. Yet memorable as have been these successes, they have been offset by the rapid growth of Soviet power and the penetration of communist influence into regions which, only yesterday, seemed to rest safely within the Free World's fold. More important still, the Western Alliance, though it has grown stronger militarily and has defied successfully Soviet pressures, now seems incapable of reconciling its internal dissensions—and of growing with the times and their necessities. In the eyes of the European peoples, the image of American leadership appears blurred by unaccountable hesitations and ambiguities. Not that the official spokesmen of America have failed to affirm their devotion to the idea of

Atlantic cooperation! But on specifics, the context of American policy has added up to a great deal less than unreserved commitment to Atlantic unity.

It can be argued—and argued cogently on the high level of sophistication—that the United States, the strongest of the Free World peoples and bearer of global responsibilities, cannot but pursue many policies and that these many policies need not necessarily jibe with one another. Yet even the diversity of situations and of policies appropriate to them does not preclude explicit commitment to a clearly defined hierarchy of values and goals. It is the lack of such explicit commitment which has engendered the chronic malaise of the Atlantic Alliance. Increasingly, American efforts have been expended on the intricacies of particular solutions—how to devise a Berlin settlement; how to complement the U.S. deterrent by the right quota of NATO "conventional" forces; how to increase the budgetary contributions of NATO's European members—rather than on the grand design of the Alliance and the definition of its over-all purpose. A great deal of ingenuity has gone into devising a variety of strategic responses to a variety of contingencies as well as keeping these responses safely under the latch of the American nuclear veto; only a fraction of this considerable cerebral and material effort has been expended on creating an Atlantic climate of confidence.

American policy, so thoroughgoing in particulars, has been less than precise in defining a schedule for Atlantic development for the future. Put in its simplest terms, the question is—or should be: "Do we want an Atlantic Community and, if we do, what shall it be like?" The answer to this question cannot be based on the expectation that fortuitous events—the advent of new political personalities and the subsidence of current crisis situations—will ease the burden of American statesmanship. The West is passing through a period of profound readjustment; its perplexities should not be confused with the idiosyncrasies of individual statesmen. Political leadership requires adeptness at improvisation; without an overriding purpose, firmly held, it cannot inspire a people, not to speak of an alliance of many peoples, with the will to do great things together. It is on the latter score that American leadership has been most vulnerable to its critics.

Although the launching of the Marshall Plan and the creation of the Atlantic Alliance stand to the enduring credit of American statesmanship, even these two attempts at a grand design are marred by inconsistency—by failure to follow through and to complete the task that had been so boldly conceived. Instead of concentrating our resources on what should have been our primary task, namely, to organize that part of the world which we were powerful enough to organize, we dissipated our energies on a series of minor and often conflicting objectives. It is as if the sum of America's postwar achievements were smaller than its parts.

The Atlantic Community is still a loose and brittle thing; our immense efforts expended on the United Nations and the many compromises have been rewarded by ambiguities and embarrassments; and our extremely costly efforts and compromises for the sake of the emerging nations have produced results that are, to put it charitably, inconclusive.

Western thought has always held man to be a rational being, notwithstanding his irrational impulses. We can assess rationally the forces arrayed against us and go about rationally developing a suitable counterstrategy. An assessment of communist strategy must start from the prudent assumption that the dynamism of the communist movement is far from broken.

That dynamism now feeds on forces that differ from those upon which communist power drew in the past. No doubt, the socialist myth has lost some of its attraction. Massive "contradictions" have asserted themselves within the communist system itself. But neither internal changes nor increasing tensions between the communist power elites warrant the belief that the communist system is about to break down under its own weight. More likely than not, the communist system will stand up as long as the communists retain the instruments of state power—a vast military arsenal, effective police control and the unbroken monopoly of political indoctrination—and manage to increase and consolidate their gains abroad. It is this law of totalitarian dynamics which is at work in the Moscow-Peking controversy: how to expand in order to exist. No doubt, the Cuban crisis marks a setback for communism—communism qua conflict strategy rather than political ideology. Yet the communists have suffered not a few reverses, and periods of "ebb" have always been succeeded by those of "flow." Out of acrimonious and bloody party controversies have emerged new leaderships and new unanimity in purpose. In Cuba one important round went to the West; the communists yielded to the West's superior force and determination. Cuba taught a lesson, predictable but immensely gratifying. Yet, the very fact that the Soviets could conceive of mounting a deadly military challenge at the very doorstep of the United States reveals alarming gaps in the United States strategic circumspection. The denouement of this particular episode might qualify as a Happy Ending; yet the United States steered clear of a disaster by a slim margin—so slim indeed as to suggest a searching reappraisal of the basic precepts which have guided United States conduct during these last seventeen years.

The communists, like many totalitarian rulers before them, seek to sublimate discontent *within* into success *without*. The contested grounds between the Western Alliance and the communist bloc are the so-called uncommitted peoples—the colonial world at which Lenin directed his strategic analysis. This third part of the globe, with two-thirds of the world's population, possesses only 20 percent of the world's productive wealth, whereas the Western peoples control 60 percent and the Soviet Union and its European satellites 20 percent. In other words, the wealth of 600 million Europeans and Americans is three times that of three times as many Afro-Asians. This great disparity tends to widen rather than diminish, for rates of Afro-Asian population growth outpace rates of economic growth. It provides the most explosive issue on which communist conflict management can fasten its disruptive tactics. It will challenge for generations to come the wisdom of Western statesmanship.

For the West, development aid is not a novel experience. The West has always assisted the underdeveloped toward development. Economic improvement was inherent in the very logic of colonialism, if only because it was in the self-interest of the colonizers. During the last 150 years the West has succeeded far beyond the boldest expectations in raising the standards of living of the peoples of Africa and Asia, who throughout history had lived at subsistence level. The needs of these peoples and their aspirations toward improvement are facts. So are the West's contributions to international economic development. But it does not follow from these facts that the conflict between despotism and freedom, between communism and democracy, will be won in the underdeveloped world.

The antics of neutralists have not been prompted exclusively by past resentments of "colonialism." Nor can the Western peoples win the sympathies of the ex-colonial peoples by displaying their contrition at the past transgressions of "colonialism." The rise of "neutralism"—especially the special brand of anti-Western "neutralism" —has not been solely the consequence of poverty or abiding anti-Western resentment. Its principal cause has been a much simpler one: a good many "neutralists" believe that, one day, the communists will gain the lead in the race for world power.

We have insisted on telling ourselves that we can win over the uncommitted peoples, who, for the best of power political reasons, wish to remain uncommitted, by economic largesse and deference to their opinions—"world opinion"—on such matters as nuclear testing, the recognition of Red China, disarmament and the defense of Southeast Asia. On none of these issues is "world opinion" particularly helpful to our cause. Our manifest eagerness to help and understand will not persuade the "uncommitted" to throw in their lot with us so long as we ourselves appear uncertain of our power and purpose. Since the "uncommitted" will not and cannot help us in our conflict with communism, we and our friends must fight it out according to the dictates of our best interests and best judgment.

It is the task of the leading Western power to shape world opinion by the rightness and efficacy of its actions, rather than take its cue from the changing views of a handful of articulate Asian and African leaders who have managed to impersonate "world opinion." At best, the West can hold the position that it still occupies throughout the underdeveloped world and strengthen its ties with those Asian and African peoples who have not committed themselves irrevocably to the communist camp. Western initiative in these continents is confined to a holding action—until Western policy has made it evident that the balance of power will remain weighted in its favor.

Such a change in the balance of power can occur only by virtue of the consolidation of the Western Alliance. In sum, the Western powers must seek to achieve greater unity among themselves and organize effectively their own vast resources. Once they have succeeded in this task, many of the problems which they still attempt to solve unilaterally will solve themselves.

On the basis of potentials of industrial productivity and skills, there is no reason why a united West cannot win the military-technological race with the Soviets. It was the West's apparent lag in this race which did more than anything else to lower its prestige in Asia and Africa and to strengthen the "neutralist" tendencies of Asian and African leaders.

A Western program for the economic development of the backward peoples, informed by a unitary strategic concept, will not only raise the standard of living of the Asian and African peoples, but also bar the intrusion of communist influence which is now magnified by the divided counsel of the Western peoples on such issues as the devolution of colonialism, trade with the communist bloc and the question as to who should receive the major share of economic aid, the West's proven friends and allies or the sulking "neutralists."

Hence the major task of United States foreign policy is to labor for the unity of the West. The core of that unity is NATO, the principal and most effective international organization in the Free World. Around this core are clustered the several European unions: the European Coal and Steel Community, the Common Market, Euratom, the Council of Europe, the West European Union, and the Organization for Economic Cooperation and Development, which includes the NATO countries as well as Sweden, Finland, Switzerland and Austria. Some of these experiments in integration are still inconclusive; some are overlapping, and some conflict with one another. But what matters is the quest for integration, the creative surge. To sustain this movement and enhance its sense of direction, to reconcile conflicts of national interest within it and to shield it against the divisive strategies of the communists—this should be the overriding purpose of American diplomacy.

Neither the plaudits and catcalls of the "neutralists" nor the menacing gestures of the Soviets should be allowed to divert United States policy from its major task. In the 1930's, a united West could have scotched the Nazi menace and prevented the Second World War. In the 1960's, a united West provides the most powerful deterrent to the communist strategy of conquest and the strongest guarantee of world peace.

A policy that places the making of the Atlantic Community above all other American international objectives conforms to our traditional ideals: an international order under law composed of peoples under representative governments. Furthermore, such a policy derives its historical warrant from the unity of Western culture. The ideal of humanism is a Western ideal. Historically, American leadership at its best has known how to identify the strivings of the

American people with the aspirations of all mankind. The peoples of the world now aspire toward a new order that will supersede the increasingly unworkable international system of national sovereignties, of whom all but two cannot defend themselves unaided against aggression from without.

The United Nations, whose Charter clings to the idea of national sovereignty, may well prove the last and most tragic failure to marry the nation-state system to a world order under law. No one can tell now whether or not the United Nations will be able to resolve the fundamental contradiction that warps its politics and negates its purpose. The United States can now less than ever bank all its hopes for a better world on the United Nations. The making of an Atlantic federation, however, does lie within the scope of American power. The undertaking seems formidable. Yet in the light of past achievements, such as the creation of NATO and the European unions, it is not an impossible undertaking.

The ideals which, after World War II, inspired the American quest for a world order under peace and justice have been so lofty, and the popular hopes pinned on the United Nations so great, that a sober reappraisal of the United Nations still poses considerable psychological difficulties. It is only in the last few years that American public opinion has awakened to the discordance between ideal and reality. Yet, when the United Nations was born, its congenital weakness did not escape the scrutiny of the observant few. Herbert Hoover said:

I urged the ratification of the United Nations Charter by the Senate. But I stated at that time the American people should be under no illusions that this Charter assures lasting peace. But now we must realize that the United Nations has failed to give us even a remote hope of lasting peace. . . . If the free nations are to survive they must have a new and stronger worldwide organization to meet [the communist] menace. For purposes of this discussion I may call it the Council of Free Nations. *It should include only those nations who are willing to stand up and fight for their freedom and independence.* [Italics added.][1]

The controversy on the alternatives of international order cuts across the alignment of the political parties. Senator J. William Fulbright wrote:

The question is how and whether a dynamic "concert of free nations" can be put together. It is clear that the United Nations, although it was designed to form just such a concert, has fallen far short of the hopes which attended its creation; we must look elsewhere for a system that can unify the forces of freedom effectively.[2]

Senator Fulbright's conclusion coincides closely with that which Herbert Hoover drew:

A "concert of free nations" should take its inspiration from the traditions of the nineteenth century Concert of Europe with its common values and accepted "rules of the game" . . . The North Atlantic nations represent an almost-existing community and, because they do, they can press forward in the development of supranational institutions.[3]

Our understanding of the historic task and our commitment to our historic mission should inform all our policies. Thus armed with a unitary view of historic evolution, we will be able to challenge communism on its own ground and confound its universal aspirations. The Atlantic peoples, united in a common undertaking, have the power to change the course of history and to give the lie to the "inevitability" of communist doctrine. Until the Western Allies have settled their own disagreements, developed an appropriate structure for political decision-making, integrated (in fact and not merely on paper) their enormous technological and military resources, and confronted the rest of the globe with a common purpose, all talk of "taking the initiative" vis-à-vis the Soviets is idle talk indeed. Western disunity supplies the openings for communist penetration. The operational code of the communists is but the counterimage of the strategic and tactical opportunities afforded by their divided opponents. The decision alone to proceed with the making of the Atlantic union would deliver a tremendous blow at the façade of communist solidarity. NATO's growing strength and resistance to communist wrecking tactics compelled a revision of Soviet strategy. It is highly improbable that communist leadership would have on its hands the chronic tribulations of dogmatic heresies and intrabloc tensions, had the Western Alliance foundered. The divisive forces within the communist bloc stand in direct ratio to the unitary forces in the West. Once the chinks in the West's armor are closed, the strategy and tactics of the communists will be reduced to that *real* "peaceful competition" which they, not we, need fear. To thwart communist management of conflict is to strike at the roots of communism. The communist system feeds on conflict. It cannot survive peace. A united West would have reason to hope that communist power would succumb to a long truce enforced by the superior power of the Atlantic Alliance. Even so, peace will not be certain, for nothing ever is certain. But, here and now, the brightest prospect of a peaceful world for all peoples—and not the Western peoples alone—opens from an ever stronger and ever closer Atlantic Community.

The task of making the Atlantic Community is beset by many problems some of which—and this is in the nature of politics—either cannot be solved as speedily as mere logic suggests or can be solved only partially. Most of these problems are highly complex, as complex as are the relationships of a score of highly developed nations rooted in their long and proud histories. Yet the basic issues are simple. Every so often, during the last fifteen years, the leaders of the Atlantic Alliance have called for unity lest the Alliance fall apart and its enemies pick up the pieces. Thus, for example, the NATO Council of Ministers, in December of 1956, declared that "it was wise and timely to bring about a closer association of kindred Atlantic and West European nations for other than defense purposes alone; that a partial pooling of sovereignty for mutual protection should also promote progress and cooperation generally." The NATO Ministers agreed unanimously that "there was, in short, a sense of Atlantic Community, alongside the realization of an immediate common danger." Yet, this unanimity on the desirability of "a partial pooling of sovereignty" has not been carried over into the creation of political institutions that could take on those "pooled" sovereign rights and responsibilities—and govern.

The creation of new political institutions has always met with the resistance of entrenched bureaucracies and vested political interests. True enough, the consummation of the Rome Treaties entails a progressive surrender of heretofore cherished sovereign prerogatives. It can be argued that NATO itself represents a stage in the evolution away from national sovereignty toward an organism endowed with the potentiality of growth toward a higher stage, a confederation. In fact, however, both the European Economic Community and NATO are neither more nor less than functional arrangements, the one economic and the other military. Historically, organizations such as NATO, though designed as permanently standing military alliances, have displayed neither durability nor, even during their epoch of greatest vigor, cohesiveness. The historic record of economic unions is even less impressive. The path of history, across the last one hundred years or so, is littered with the wreckage of *Zollvereine* (customs unions).

By themselves, economic ties are frail, and all the implications of a real economic community, i.e., a community in which everyone can plan ahead for at least the life span of a generation, are acceptable only if they are not fraught with the risk of sudden dissolution. That the survival of the economic community depends upon the common interest and the goodwill of incumbent governments, and that the present economic constellation favors the maintenance of the functional arrangement, does not furnish sufficient guarantees for unqualified commitments and the spontaneous growth of supranational loyalties. Governments and their philosophies might change —they usually do; economic trends, too, may alter—they usually do. The "Europeans" themselves admit that, no matter what progress has already been achieved, complete economic integration of Western Europe is only conceivable within the framework of some form of political integration. Conceivably, the path of the European Common Market toward the future might become smoother; Britain might enter and all the goals of the Rome Treaties might be achieved —and achieved sooner than anticipated. Yet even then the ingrained urge toward national self-sufficiency would keep on asserting itself within the Community. Even then only a political community, either superimposed upon the Common Market or created, so to speak, around it, could master the trends toward autarchy and thus toward disintegration. The historic lessons that apply to economic unions apply, of course, even more cogently to economic "partnerships." Strictly speaking, between sovereign states there can be no such thing as "partnership" as this term is understood within the context of personal and business relationships. Treaties, even if they do not contain self-contradictory escape clauses, are not, as is marriage, made in heaven. The right to abrogate treaties is inherent in national sovereignty. Again, the history of mankind can be told as the history of innumerable "perpetual" treaties abrogated or simply broken. In fact, we know little about the forces that keep economic unions together and cause them to fly apart.

The achievements of the European Common Market have been remarkable. Yet European progress has benefited from a number of extraordinary circumstances, none of which need necessarily endure or recur within the context of a future wider economic union such as an Atlantic market or an Atlantic Economic Community. No one now knows what would happen to the proud edifice of Brussels if Western Europe or the Free World were to be seized by a great economic crisis. Nor is it certain that the forces that labored for the cumulative increase of exchange and productivity of West Europe will come to the aid of an "Atlantic partnership," not to speak of an Atlantic Common Market, which, at present, is no more than a gleam in an academic eye.

As a matter of fact, the future of the development of the common economic institutions of Europe is fraught not only with economic uncertainties but also with not inconsiderable psychological dangers. It is unlikely that economic integration constitutes the first step toward political integration and that, as an ever larger school of thought seems to believe, political integration must follow as a matter of course upon the completion of economic integration. Maurice Allais, addressing in January, 1962, the Atlantic Convention of NATO nations, said: "Economic integration . . . would in fact be a certain means of increasing the awareness of the various national interests, with the result that the future of a real Community, and with it our own future, might be fatally endangered. I believe that political union should precede or at least accompany economic union. This is an essential condition."

Indeed, the Western publics derive easy comfort from the idea that an economic community by itself brings forth a true political community. Not so surprisingly, this belief is encouraged by all those, especially government bureaucracies and vested political interests, who propose to do nothing except compose a stream of memoranda showing why political integration, today, tomorrow or next year, is premature, impossible and deleterious to national interests. Paradoxically, the very accomplishments of the great European planners such as M. Monnet have tended to obscure the difference between economic and political integration. They bypassed strongly held political positions; to this dexterous performance the European Common Market owes its existence. Yet the supple pragmatism of M. Monnet and his brilliant helpers, so effective in reconciling the interests of many, mostly private groups, should not be mistaken for an effective substitute for statesmanship. The strong points of national sovereignty still stand. Wisely, perhaps, the problem of their reduction has been shelved; in truth, it has not been solved.

In the hierarchy of national interests the military ranks a close second to the political. Indeed, in the age of protracted conflict no less than in preceding historic ages, foreign policy and defense are the two sides of the same coin. The crisis of Atlantic relationships has arisen from profound disagreements on the military strategy of the Western Alliance. That "sense of Atlantic Community" of which the NATO ministers spoke in December, 1956, will be as strong or as weak as the structure of NATO strategy. There is a reciprocal relationship between the cohesiveness of the Alliance and the agreement of its members upon the meaning of technological-military change and, hence, of modern conflict.

It is the thesis of this book that the meaning of military-technological change and of world conflict argues for the closer political integration of the Atlantic Community and the creation of appropriate political institutions. If this thesis can be shown to be invalid, then, here and now, the case for the Atlantic Community falls to the ground. True enough, the Atlantic Community can lay just claim to the common heritage of Europe and American culture; true enough, it is the peoples of the Atlantic Community that do the bulk of the world's trade. Yet if the common cause of military defense does not spur the Western peoples to make the leap from political separateness to political community, then neither the promise of cultural enrichment nor the prospect of good business can furnish the impulsion. The Western peoples have exchanged their cultural and commercial goods for a long time—in some respects, more freely in the nineteenth century than they do now. If common survival is not a matter important enough to inspire us to seek political unity, then, certainly, our common concern with beauty, truth and profit, deep as it might be, will not move us by one inch beyond the limits of national sovereignty.

The styles of statesmanship vary from generation to generation, from nation to nation, from statesman to statesman. No doubt, there are several conceivable alternatives for the making of the Atlantic unity. Historically, the making of wider unions, especially unions of free peoples, has been a disorderly process. Conceivably, the "dumbbell" approach to Western unity is more promising than might be the attempt to transform NATO into a political confederacy. The idea of a strong and united Western Europe deliberating, on equal terms, with the United States on the future shape of the Atlantic Community has won powerful support on both sides of the Atlantic.[4] Awkward as is the metaphor, the "dumbbell" approach derives its warrant from a tried and trusted principle, namely, that of the balance of power. Its dangers, too, are obvious: a United Western Europe might look inward, a "third force" between East and West. Furthermore, a number of NATO members such as Canada, Norway and Denmark, not to speak of Turkey, would be placed in the embarrassing position of having to opt between clustering around one or the other bulbous weight of the "dumbbell" or drifting into an isolation that would be far from splendid. Yet the consolidation of Western Europe, particularly were it to sublimate the issue of nuclear proliferation into the creation of a multilateral force under the control of the Western European Union, might well be the sole alternative to the collapse of the Western Alliance and the nuclear Balkanization of the West. This solution is far from an ideal one. It is still possible, however, to diminish its attendant risks. To do so requires, however, speedy political action. The one and only vehicle for such action is NATO. The greater the political cohesiveness of NATO, the more effectively can it curb the divisive potentialities that are latent in the development of two power centers within the Atlantic world. In brief, the growth of European unity should not be taken as the first step toward the making of the Atlantic Community. Rather, the political integration of the NATO Allies *and* the integration of the West European economies should proceed simultaneously.

The central issue of NATO integration is how the resources of the Alliance are to be combined in order to achieve technological and, in a broad sense, military superiority. Technically, NATO integration is a matter of efficiency; politically, it is a matter of equity. The future of NATO hinges on the reconciliation of techniques with politics, of strategic requirements with a sense of participation. The task is fraught with a host of problems, military-technological, economic and psychological, most of which can be solved only by considerable exertion and sacrifice. Over time, not a few of them appear soluble; new ones are likely to arise. Here and now, however, the most important military problems before NATO are the control of nuclear weapons and their availability to all and every ally wherever and whenever they are needed. The fundamental question of NATO strategy is simply whether it will provide to all members the degree of security they bargained for when they joined NATO. If NATO strategy does not do exactly that, then the Alliance will fall apart and there will be no need to debate the finer points of "political consultation" and who should or should not have a "finger on the trigger."

The declared policies of the United States are faulted not so much by lapses in military-technical logic as by psychological ambiguities. Perhaps our European Allies are concerned less than they avow with strategic exigencies and perhaps more than they care to admit with the lack of trust which they read between the lines of American policy declarations. It is here that we come to the heart of the matter.

The avowed purpose of U.S. policy is to halt "nuclear proliferation" and thus to diminish the danger of general nuclear war triggered by "accident or inadvertence." U.S. policy is based on the assumption that the limitation of the nuclear club to two members, the United States itself and the Soviet Union, offers the basis for a nuclear disarmament agreement, whereas the accession of other members would make such an agreement more difficult, if not altogether impossible. It is easy to infer that U.S. policy is guided by the idea of a U.S.-Soviet partnership in nuclear matters, a partnership that, so to speak, cuts across all other alignments of the two powers. Though their other interests might diverge, the United States and the Soviet Union have a common stake in nuclear hegemony. If this concept were to govern U.S. conduct, then nothing less than a revolutionary realignment of power would be in the making —the two major nuclear powers against all the lesser and would-be nuclear powers, irrespective of ideological and alliance commitments. If this is indeed the U.S. purpose, then the nuclear policies of the United States vis-à-vis its NATO Allies, especially France, make sense—whatever may be their military technical rationale and however distasteful their ideological implications. Then the question is not whether the United States "trusts" its Western Allies, but whether, in nuclear matters—i.e., the matters of life and death—the United States "trusts" the Soviets more than anybody else, its own best friends included.

Such an orientation—a policy that places a U.S.-Soviet nuclear limitation agreement above all other policy considerations—might be compatible with many worthwhile aspirations; it is contrary to the ideal of an Atlantic Community founded upon common political institutions and shared values. In fact, such a policy, were it indeed the preferred and chosen policy of the United States, would be doomed to failure. A few years ago, the voice of the United States' nuclear paternalism dominated the counsels of the Western Alliance; today, "nuclear proliferation" in Europe is a fact of life, impervious to scholastic arguments. The technologies of nucleonics are now entering the possession of several powers other than those who belong formally to the not-so-exclusive club. This increase of membership is in accord with modern scientific-technological development as well as with the exigencies of state power in the twentieth century. This circumstance confronts the U.S. with the necessity of choice: to arrest the march of science and technology and to freeze, for the sake of an illusionary nuclear status quo, the world into the unnatural mold of a U.S.-Soviet entente—or to take its allies into the bosom of nuclear partnership, if only to insure its safe and orderly management. The United States has offered its European Allies a few samples from its bountiful nuclear arsenal, attaching forthwith the proviso that the offering be surrendered to the control of NATO.[5] Since, under present circumstances, the control of NATO is tantamount to the control of the United States, the U.S. proposal is redundant. It will remain redundant as long as national sovereignty remains the alpha and the omega of the discourse on the making of the Atlantic Community.

The case *against* the development of independent *national* deterrents in Europe is strong on military as well as economic grounds. But it does not answer the case *for* a *collective* European deterrent. It is in the logic of the present historical situation that Europe will, sooner or later, develop an indigenous deterrent. The crucial issue is whether it will be built with the assistance of the United States and in such a way as will reinforce the trend toward a genuine NATO confederation, or whether it will be built despite the United States, in which case it will not augur well for the future of the Alliance. The question as to whether Europe's nuclear forces should be coordinated and deployed under the writ of the Western European Union can be answered only by the Europeans themselves

—although United States diplomacy can do much toward easing such a decision. It can be argued that the United States' reluctance to open its nuclear trove to the Europeans will spur the latter to develop the requisite technologies by their own efforts, and that, anyway, the Europeans would rather take the necessary pains than depend on American bounty, if not tutelage. The United States has every reason to stimulate Europe's technological endeavors—conceivably, the Europeans might come up with discoveries in the field of nucleonics which neither we nor the Soviets have thought about—and to confirm the Europeans in their self-reliance. Yet, sooner or later, both Europe and we will approach the point of decision: to join efforts or go separate ways. Unless the development of a European deterrent is paralleled by an intensive effort toward creation of political institutions that can accommodate a transatlantic nuclear partnership, Americans and Europeans will each go their way not only in nuclear affairs but also in most other matters of strategic and political import.

The United States is still the most powerful country on earth. The powerful can choose between alternatives; the weak cannot. Conceivably, the United States can let its European Allies go their own way and develop an alternative to NATO. More likely than not, so radical a change of course will be attended not only by incalculable psychological consequences but also by a steep increase of national expenditures. The strategic services of our NATO allies—their contributions in real estate, such as ubiquity of bases and forward warning systems, and in military forces—would have to be replaced by alternate devices and American manpower respectively. It is difficult to see how these strategic "substitutions" can be effected lest the United States proceed to a mobilization in peacetime beyond the upper limits of the Korean War effort. At present, the United States is not a "garrison state," the charges of the more eccentric fringes of the disarmament and accommodation lobbies to the contrary. The break-up of NATO, however, would result inevitably in the increasing militarization of America. The defense of an isolated citadel must be insured by a strong, ever-ready garrison. Permanent peacetime mobilization at heavy material and moral costs seems an inordinately high price to pay for the retention of the United States nuclear-strategic monopoly.

Thus far, the failure to solve the problem of nuclear sharing has been attended by not a few unfortunate consequences. The most unfortunate of these has been the rise of what might be called European nuclear chauvinism. Americans may rightly decry the phenomenon; yet, for some of its causes, U.S. official policy cannot waive responsibility. More than any other disagreement between the Allies, the European-American conflict over nuclear strategy endangers the survival of NATO.

No doubt, it is on this issue that NATO may founder. Then the dream of an Atlantic Community might turn into a nightmare. Then the historians who cast their eye upon us from the vantage point of 1987 (assuming that they will still be free to pass an authentic judgment) will be likely to trace the demise of the noble Atlantic coalition less to the grandiose visions of a de Gaulle than to the inability of the Americans to accept the full implications of "Atlantic partnership." If, on the other hand, steps are now taken, while there is still time, to raise Europe to a parity of political-military interdependence with the United States in the framework of NATO, historians a quarter-century hence will have good reason to concur that the United States, having proclaimed the ideal of "interdependence," kept faith with it. Within NATO, the problem of nuclear sharing can be solved only by the creation of a political authority—confederal to start with and, since on this road one cannot turn back, federal in the end.

A flair for compromise solutions is an indispensable ingredient of the art of statesmanship. No less important is the cool courage to take calculated risks. To go shares with our European Allies in strategic decision and arms signifies a cession of American national sovereignty to a yet-to-be determined Atlantic authority. This fact must be clearly understood and put bluntly to the American people. To be sure, the United States would remain the most influential member of the Alliance, and the institutional arrangements could be worked out, according the United States a place at the council table commensurate with its resources and contributions. Although the United States could not settle for less, the danger that the European members would "gang up" on the United States in order to overrule it appears infinitesimally small, for the historical divergencies which separate the European states from one another and divide European society preclude the creation of a monolithic European faction. Relatively simple institutional devices, as for example, the provision for weighted voting, could safeguard American interest:[6] The European members could not "vote" the United States into a nuclear war, or "veto" the use of the United States' nuclear forces in its own defense.

Indeed, the strongest argument against the sharing of strategic decision and arms derives its force from a consideration far weightier than that of all the foolish things our European Allies might do to drag us, against our will, into a nuclear war—or keep us out of it. By and large, our European Allies have not redeemed their pledges to NATO; they have not met the agreed quota of forces, and, even if they now lived up to agreements concluded a long while ago, they would contribute proportionately far less than does the United States. Some of our European Allies may legitimately question the United States' wisdom in asking them to field certain kinds of forces as, for example, conventional ones, and to desist from developing others as, for example, nuclear ones. The United States, however, stands on firm ground when it calls upon its European Allies to contribute more, a great deal more than they have contributed in the past, to the *over-all strength* of the Alliance. In brief, the purpose and justification of a U.S. policy of sharing strategic decision and arms must be the increase, as a *quid pro quo,* of the West's collective power. The price is well worth paying, and the offer to pay it would place the United States in the strongest position for exacting fair value from its Allies. It follows as a matter of course that the United States must see to it that the bargain be kept. It is bad to coddle one's enemies; it is worse to coddle one's friends.

It is not at all certain that the Western peoples, distracted by the trivia of their overabundant civilization and susceptible to the lure of "easy" solutions, will rise to the immensely difficult task of building a new, a vaster edifice upon ground furrowed by national rivalry and distrust. Perhaps, here and now, the most important task is not to agree on exactly how high will be the edifice, but rather to agree that it be built and that the cornerstones be laid. Such agreement will not issue spontaneously from the confabulations of harassed functionaries, panting from crisis to crisis. It will issue only from the exertion of supreme leadership. The United States still holds the leadership of the West. For how long it will be able to do so, no one now knows. The currents will not necessarily run in our way forever. It is prudent to make the most of today's favorable constellation—to lead those who still consent to be led. Time that is not used is never on one's side.

Organization, however efficient, is not a substitute for leadership. A nation may be imbued with the collective will to lead. Yet that will stands for naught if there are not a chosen few who articulate it. Thus, for example, attention has been given to the machinery of NATO rather than to the men who service it. Senator Fulbright wrote:

> The problem of NATO is not one of machinery, of which there is an abundance, but of the will to use it. The NATO Council is available as an executive agency, the Standing Group as a high military authority.[7]

Yet neither the United States nor the major Allied countries have chosen their representatives to these bodies from the small band of the strongest and wisest. Perhaps the task of breathing new life into the existing forms of Atlantic cooperation and of building new ones should begin with the selection of those men of truly national stature who could speak not only for their respective governments but also for their peoples. A former Presidential aspirant, holding Cabinet rank, speaks for the United States in the United Nations. The affairs of the Atlantic Community can lay just claim to as august a representative of American interest, possessed of the highest attributes of statesmanship and public esteem. Once the right policy has been entrusted to the right man, the appropriate organization will develop more or less as a matter of course. The making of the Atlantic Community presents, in the perspective of historical time, a task that will surely be not less exacting than the founding of the United States. It is the good fortune of the American people that the wisest and the strongest turned their hand to the making of the Union. The task of building the Atlantic Community challenges the most competent, imaginative and forceful minds of both the Old World and the New. The transformation of the NATO Parliamentarians' Conference into a NATO Consultative Assembly[8] would provide, not only for a closer link between NATO and the NATO peoples and among the NATO peoples themselves, but also the best school for Atlantic leadership. Here, the great issues could be debated, and the Assembly could serve as the forcing house of Atlantic personalities. Every political edifice must have a room for rhetoric. The making of the Atlantic Community calls for many skills. Among these perhaps the most important is that of pleading the Atlantic cause in a language as clear and as inspiring as that which ennobled the deliberations of the Founders of the United States.

U.S. foreign policy, like the foreign policies of all world powers, must thread its way through the welter of conflicting purposes and commitments. The cares of European and Asian alliances, the quest for security through strength and peace through reconciliation, the facts and the myths of international order, the clamors of the un-committed and underdeveloped—all these concerns converge upon the sanctum of American statesmanship. Now the United States speaks firmly and forthrightly; then it seems to speak with two voices; and then again, it is as if it could not speak at all even on the gravest issue. Thus far, the United States has stood by its Atlantic commitments. Thus far, despite internecine bickerings and cease-less communist pressures, NATO has withstood every major crisis —from Suez to Berlin to Cuba. More important still, the storms of crisis have cleansed the air of phantoms. In the United States, there is no longer a need for pleading the case for American leadership; the American people accept it. In their historical experience lies the blueprint of the new order—the new order that can be built because the American people have it within their power to build it. President Kennedy, speaking on July 4, 1962, in Independence Hall, Philadel-phia, issued the Declaration of Interdependence. He said:

I will say, here and now, on this day of independence, that the United States will be ready for a declaration of interdependence—that we will be prepared to discuss with a United Europe the ways and means of forming a concrete Atlantic partnership—a mutually beneficial partnership between the new union now emerging in Europe and the old American union founded here a century and three quarters ago.

All this will not be completed in a year—but let the world know that this is now our goal.

In urging the adopting of the Constitution, Alexander Hamilton told his fellow New Yorkers "to think continentally." Today Americans must learn to think intercontinentally.[9]

Statesmanship has its own grammar. The President spoke of part-nership; he did not elaborate the terms of "intercontinental" relation-ship. His reticence on Atlantic specifics is redeemed by his allusion to American precedent. Eleven years elapsed between the Declara-tion of Independence and the adoption of the American Constitution. Lest we forget, in Hamilton's day the question was not so much the surrender of the sovereignties of the American states as their peoples themselves delegating to a higher authority some of their inalienable rights. They did not surrender; they transferred. In our case, just as in theirs, the real issue is not national sovereignty for its own sake, but material prosperity and the preservation of fundamental political liberties—the welfare, as the American Constitution has it, of the people. If Atlantic political institutions can do just that, citizens of the Atlantic states have every reason to delegate some of their rights to these Atlantic political institutions.

The great transformations of political systems manifest the popular will. Dwelling on the prospect for the transmutation of Europe's economic union into political union, Paul-Henri Spaak has this to say on the political "take-off" point: "At any rate, we are now at a point where the peoples themselves are directly concerned. It is at their level that the final choice must be made."[10] What is true of Europe today will be true of the entire Atlantic world tomorrow. The most sublime leadership cannot evoke a popular will that is not there in the first place, but it can grasp—or fumble—the precious moment when that popular will needs be made articulate and harnessed to purposeful action. Not all of us may see the consummation of the Grand Design. The making of the sovereign Atlantic Community may well absorb the energies of this generation. What matters is that we and the world know "that this is now our goal."

POSTSCRIPT

The manuscript of this book was submitted to the publisher at the end of December, 1962. Within the ensuing month a series of fast-moving and closely-related events brought on one of the most serious diplomatic crises in the history of NATO. Just before the close of the year, President Kennedy and Prime Minister Macmillan concluded the Nassau Pact, by which the United States offered to supply Britain with Polaris missiles for a NATO sea-based deterrent. Because of certain stipulations, the proposal, when offered to France, did not satisfy President de Gaulle's nuclear aspirations and was rejected. In January, after signing a Franco-German Treaty of Cooperation which seemed to institute a special political relationship between the two leading continental nations, the French President vetoed Britain's application for membership in the Common Market over the official protests of France's five Community partners. In doing so, he pointedly gave offense to the United States, which had long advocated British entry.

The ensuing controversies which threatened the solidarity of NATO as gravely as had the discords at the time of Suez were perhaps inevitable, given the divergence of Anglo-American and French policies during the last five years. Yet, the long-range result of this eruption may prove to be quite salutary—if it clarifies the issues and leads to a reconciliation of views. The authors of this book do not subscribe to the thesis, advanced by Raymond Aron, that the "Grand Designs" of President Kennedy and President de Gaulle, respectively, are necessarily incompatible.

President Kennedy has often spoken with eloquence of the need for a genuine Atlantic partnership; President de Gaulle, of the need for Europe's equality with the United States within the Alliance. In the foregoing pages the argument has been made that these two designs—for a strong, united and self-reliant Europe and for a more closely knit Atlantic Community—are complementary. The issue under dispute lies elsewhere: the policies pursued by the United States and France in respect to the political control of nuclear weapons have been diametrically opposed. It is this conflict over the control of nuclear weapons and strategies which has precipitated the latest crisis of NATO and western unity. Economic issues, especially those involving the discrepancies between the agricultural policies of Britain and France, have played an important part, but not the decisive one. The nuclear question, because it raises the issue of Alliance leadership, is the crucial question.

In preceding pages we adverted to credible information suggesting that the British, from June to November, 1962, were contemplating the establishment of an Anglo-French joint atomic force, or at least an *entente nucléaire* whereby the two countries would render mutual assistance in the effort to maintain national nuclear deterrent forces.[1] It seemed logical to assume that the British, who were several years ahead of the French in nuclear technology, might be able to work out a cooperative arrangement with the French, who expected to have a Mach 2 bomber (the Mirage IV) operational by 1964, superior to any delivery capabilities possessed by the Royal Air Force. Neither British nor French strategists were convinced by American arguments that as larger numbers of ICBM's became available the manned aircraft would become completely obsolete. Indeed, the U.S. decision to invest billions in the yet-to-fly TFX would suggest the contrary.

Since each weapons system possesses its own distinctive advantages and disadvantages, only a judicious mix of systems assures strategic flexibility. In view of these and other considerations, the possibility of an Anglo-French agreement over nuclear cooperation was not farfetched.

In brief, there is some reason to believe that President de Gaulle had assumed a tie-in between Franco-British nuclear cooperation and British admission to the Common Market, and that the British understood this *quid pro quo* very well.

American policymakers frequently expressed themselves willing to assist the Allies in an effort to create a European deterrent once the Allies could agree among themselves as to its political framework. But after scuttling the Skybolt missile, the Administration offered the British Polaris weapons for their national forces. In the Nassau Pact of December, 1962, the United States offered to make Polaris missiles available to the British, French and, presumably, other allies, provided that the allies themselves furnish the submarines and the nuclear warheads which they would then contribute as national components to a NATO Polaris submarine force.[2] A significant aspect of the Nassau Agreement was the provision that each country's nuclear component would revert to the control of its own government at times when the "supreme national interest" required it. President Kennedy, at a year's end press conference at Palm Beach, reflected upon the proposal as follows:

It will be independent in moments of great national peril, which is really the only time you consider using nuclear weapons anyway. It will serve as a basis for a multinational force or multilateral force. . . .

Our whole policy has been against the diversion of resources towards independent national deterrents. We think it doesn't make strategic sense, and we think it really would cost the Europeans a great deal of money. . . .

So we have the problem of whether—on the other hand, there is the desire of Europe for a European deterrent or greater control over the deterrent. The question really would be whether a deterrent composed of a multinational force made up of the British, the Americans and French elements . . . would satisfy the desires of other Europeans to have a greater control over the use of nuclear weapons.[3]

There was, at least on the surface, a contradiction in the American proposal. On the one hand, the United States appeared to be adamantly opposed to the proliferation of independent national deterrents.[4] On the other hand, the Nassau Pact specifically permitted independent national control in precisely those critical situations where individual national interests are at stake. Undoubtedly, the phrase "in the supreme national interest" was calculated to satisfy both the Macmillan Government and President de Gaulle, but it served to placate only the former. The British appeared to be acting the role of "honest broker" between Washington and Paris, but they were not able to bridge the divergent positions. President de Gaulle at first showed polite interest; his response was neither "yes" nor "no" but "tell me more." Apparently, the more he learned about the details of the proposal, the less he liked it.

In the first place, the United States did not offer a submarine, but only information from which a nuclear-powered submarine could be constructed. Secondly, the U.S. offered only the Polaris missile, not the warhead without which the weapons system has no military utility. Thirdly, as it became clear in subsequent Anglo-American conversations, the Europeans would be expected not merely to purchase finished Polarises but also to participate in the financing of their advanced development. Fourth, since the new Polaris-armed submarines would not become available until 1968, the French, in the meantime, if they did accept the offer, would have to integrate their Mirage IV bombers with other Western bombing forces in NATO. De Gaulle, in other words, would have to give up his bargaining leverage in 1964 without knowing what kind of voice he would be accorded in the control of Western nuclear power in 1968. Finally, almost simultaneously with the offer of the Polaris complex to France, the U.S. hopefully reopened test ban negotiations with the Soviets, who were insisting that there could be no treaty unless the United States would somehow secure a French renunciation of further testing. Without nuclear testing, the French would never obtain a warhead for the Polaris missile. Finally, in abandoning the Skybolt the United States revealed its old penchant for making decisions of great strategic importance unilaterally and not within the framework of the NATO Alliance. Under the circumstances prevailing in early 1963, de Gaulle did not find the proposals embodied in the Nassau Pact irresistibly attractive. He saw in the Nassau Pact a last-ditch attempt by the Kennedy Administration to reunify all of the West's nuclear forces, not on the basis of a European-American partnership, but under conditions that would permit the United States to retain its monopoly of leadership within the Western Alliance. Therefore, at his Seventh Press Conference, held at the Elysée Palace on January 14, 1963, President de Gaulle rejected the plan for a NATO Polaris deterrent. He criticized the effort of the U.S. to perpetuate its monopoly in the West's strategic affairs, contradicted the U.S. argument that France's atomic force was useless because it could not become a match for that of the Soviets or the Americans, and called attention to the fact that, while Britain would be expected to turn over all her nuclear weapons to the sea-based force, the bulk of American nuclear weapons would remain outside the integrated NATO deterrent. Then he said:

France has taken note of the Anglo-American Nassau Agreement. As it was conceived, undoubtedly no one will be surprised that we cannot subscribe to it. It truly would not be useful for us to buy Polaris missiles when we have neither the submarines to launch them nor the thermonuclear warheads to arm them. Doubtless the day will come when we will have these submarines and these warheads. But that day will be long in coming. . . . When we will one day have these submarines and these warheads, what will the Polaris missiles be worth? At that time we will probably have missiles of our own invention. In other words, for us, in terms of technology, this affair is not the question of the moment.[5]

Two weeks after making this statement, de Gaulle brought to a halt the negotiations for Britain's entry into EEC. The historic veto, which set off pessimistic speculations about the future of the Alliance in all Western capitals, came just a few days after U.S. Under Secretary of State George W. Ball had chided the French President for harboring "obsolete ideas" that echo a "distant and earlier age," and after President Kennedy had delivered a solemn reminder of the "hard and fast realities of this Nation's relationship with Europe—realities of danger, power and purpose, which are too deeply rooted in history and necessity to be either obscured or altered in the long run by personal or even national differences. . . ." President Kennedy added:

In unity this Alliance has ample strength to hold back the expansion of Communism until such time as it loses its force and momentum. Acting alone, neither the United States nor Europe could be certain of success and survival. The reality of purpose, therefore, is that that which serves to unite us is right, and what tends to divide us is wrong. . . . If we are to be worthy of our historic trust, we must continue on both sides of the Atlantic to work together in trust.[6]

While occasionally overlooking the possibility that U.S. policies might be included among "what tends to divide us," American and British writers heaped most of the blame on de Gaulle for the breakdown in transatlantic cooperation. Western analysts were prone to attribute de Gaulle's performance to many different motivations, some of them objective, most of them uncomplimentary: (1) He was trying to protect the integrity of the Treaty of Rome against assiduous British efforts to dilute its provisions with special economic arrangements that all of the Six had once unanimously judged to be unacceptable.[7] (2) He was disappointed that, under the special arrangements sought by Britain both for her domestic agriculture and for her "massive escort," French farmers would be deprived of their coveted role of "grocers of the Englishman's table." (3) He was motivated by a spirit of vindictiveness—a crass desire to humiliate the land of Churchill. (4) He feared that Britain, once in, would lead an Anglo-Italian-Benelux coalition to bring to naught his Grand Design of a Franco-German partnership as the basis of European political unity. (5) He represented a new menace of Continental authoritarianism to the traditions of parliamentary democratic government—a new Napoleon if not a Hitler. (6) He suffered from an irrational phobia of *les Angle-Saxons,* who were united in a con-spiracy against the restoration of French grandeur. (7) He deemed the English an incorrigibly insular people who could never really become a part of Europe. (8) He resented the fact that at the Bahamas Conference, Prime Minister Macmillan "knuckled under" to the Kennedy Administration and agreed in effect to merge British nuclear weapons into an "indivisible" U.S. deterrent instead of giving them to Europe.

In his press conference of January 14, 1963, President de Gaulle presaged his veto of British membership in the Common Market. De Gaulle stated that the Nassau Agreement showed clearly a con-tinuing Anglo-American special relationship. Once again, in de Gaulle's estimation, Britain had proven that attachments to the transatlantic English-speaking world took precedence over loyalties to her friends in Europe with whom she was negotiating for political as well as economic integration. De Gaulle speciously concluded that the economy of Britain, because she continued to be "insular" and "maritime," was not adapted to the Common Market member-ship. "In short," he suggested, "the nature, structure and economic context of England differ profoundly from those of the other states of the Continent."

Because the British had focused many of their hopes for future leadership—both political and economic—upon Common Market membership, the failure of the Brussels negotiations produced an-guished outbursts. Within Europe itself new fissures in the Alliance also opened. Thus the French encountered in the Common Market the opposition of the "Friendly Five," their EEC partners who favored British entry. Moreover, the United States found not only its leadership in the Alliance in question, but also in jeopardy the whole conception of Atlantic Partnership, upon which rested the success of the Trade Expansion Act as well as much of the Kennedy Administration's design for foreign policy.

Anyone who tries to interpret de Gaulle's motives does so at his own peril. But it should be clear from the contents of this book that the authors do not subscribe to any of the extreme attitudes, either of adulation or condemnation, to which the French President's personality and policies have given rise in recent years. Some of the explanations of his behavior cited above can be dismissed as absurd. He is not a victim of self-delusion, nor is he a dictator. On the contrary, he has proven himself a very shrewd politician, anxious to accomplish certain pondered objectives to the best of his political ability, which is not inconsiderable. If he has had certain reservations about the "Anglo-Saxons," these have been no more serious than the reservations which the "Anglo-Saxons" have expressed toward him before and after his return to power. If his views on executive preponderance have given offense to the advocates of parliamentary government, let the latter determine whether France, plagued with more serious troubles than any other member of the Alliance, could possibly have come through the last five critical years quite so well without his leadership, and whether Algeria's suffering would have been greater or less. Indeed, it should not be forgotten that, in some respects at least, the entire Alliance has been indebted to President de Gaulle for his achievements in Africa.

This is not to suggest that de Gaulle's policies do not pose obstacles to the growth of a genuine Atlantic Community. In the opinion of the authors, the divisions that have opened between de Gaulle and the United States or between de Gaulle and Britain need not portend either the collapse of the Alliance or a halt to the movement toward European unity. In fact, by forcing the basic issues into the light of public controversy, the crisis generated by de Gaulle's actions, if properly diagnosed, might conceivably mark a turning point on the road toward Allied cooperation. American policymakers were surprised by the frankness of the General in explaining his opposition to British admission. One of the deputies who was present at a reception held at the Elysée Palace for members of the National Assembly paraphrased de Gaulle's remarks as follows:

At Rambouillet [French official guest château], Mr. Macmillan came to tell me that we should unite our two forces, putting everything in common. Several days afterward he went to the Bahamas. Naturally, this changed the tone of my news conference of January 14.[8]

To some officials in Washington, this seemed to be an attitude not quite in keeping with a man who professes to be building a new Europe according to his own Grand Design. But if this was the reason for de Gaulle's action (and a plausible case can be made for it), then one may surmise that he has not made an irrevocable decision to exclude Britain from Europe.

The primary differences between the General and the Anglo-American element within NATO are far more political and military than economic. It is grossly unfair to say that the impasse at which the Alliance finds itself must be traced solely to the diplomatic style of the President of the Fifth Republic. From an analysis of his statements and his actions, it would appear that he does not believe that there can be a viable Atlantic partnership unless Europe and America achieve equilibrium. They are not in equilibrium today, especially since the U.S. defense budget is three times as great as that of the rest of NATO combined. Despite this discrepancy, de Gaulle argues that the trend of British and American policy in recent years has not been calculated to bring about a true equilibrium. Rather, Anglo-American policy, as he sees it, has been formulated with a view toward perpetuating the monopoly of Anglo-American leadership within NATO—a monopoly which has virtually reduced the Atlantic Community to a grouping of the English-speaking peoples on both sides of the ocean. In his view, Western Europe cannot be more than the geographical term that it is today, let alone a full partner in a larger Atlantic world unless the nations of the Continent can be brought into a political-economic union whose combined resources and power will approach those of the two super powers. To admit Britain while she still gives priority to her special relationship with the United States (a bias reflected in the Nassau Pact), and does not identify herself wholeheartedly with Europe as such, would be "premature" and would probably serve only to prolong the imbalance from which NATO has always suffered. On more than one occasion de Gaulle has asked for a coalition in which the United States, Great Britain and France would de-

vise common policies for coping both with Soviet ambitions and
with the challenges posed by the emerging non-Atlantic world. His
vision of the future may differ in certain respects from our own. But
it is yet to be demonstrated that this vision is essentially incompatible with the broader objectives of Atlantic interdependence frequently proclaimed by President Kennedy.

Those who question de Gaulle's Atlantic loyalties point ominously
to his statements concerning a future Europe stretching from the
Channel to the Urals, and suggest that de Gaulle seeks to open a
dialogue with the Soviet Union. De Gaulle hopes that one day
Russia will return to the Community of Europe. Even so, he need
not be unfaithful to the Alliance. After all, the Kennedy Administration (like its predecessor) has explored quite actively the possibility
of a Soviet-American *détente* via negotiations carried on outside
the framework of NATO. We, too, must recognize the implications
of such a bilateral approach for the solidarity of the Alliance. Few
observers doubt that when the Soviets speak of *détente* they mean
the liquidation of U.S. overseas bases and the elimination of U.S.
military force from the European Continent. De Gaulle has often
alluded to the possibility of an eventual American withdrawal from
Europe and has defended France's decision to create a nuclear capability on the grounds that Europe must be in a position to protect itself if the American pullback should come to pass. Many Europeans,
scanning the situation in Berlin, the Geneva arms negotiations and
the changes which are being made in the U.S. defense posture, conclude that the United States is striving for a military posture which
will mitigate the threat of nuclear war—even though it might render
Europe more vulnerable to Soviet pressure.

The issue of nuclear proliferation is at the heart of the disputes
concerning defense concepts. Opposition to proliferation has become, in some Washington circles, an *idée fixe* unchallenged and
unchallengeable.

The United States has sought to halt the trend toward proliferation
of nuclear weapons by exerting a variety of political, military and
economic pressures on its allies. The present Administration has been
primarily concerned over the possibility that nations, once they
acquire nuclear weapons, will be unwilling to act in concert with
Alliance strategies and policies. Since 1961, the Administration has

been unsuccessful in slowing the trend toward proliferation of nuclear weapons. But it has overlooked the dangers inherent in the fragmentation of policy and strategy engendered by its obsession with nuclear proliferation. In the real world one must deal with things as they are rather than with things as one would like them to be. The possession of nuclear weapons by certain of our allies would pose little danger provided they were jointly controlled and disposed in accordance with a coherent and well-understood strategy.[9]

Only a coherent Free World strategy made operable by an adequate allied system of command, control and communication will achieve the objectives—desirable ones, indeed—sought by the Kennedy Administration. If the problems of political control and strategic doctrine were resolved, the problem of the physical possession of nuclear wepons would become relatively insignificant.

We have offered Europe a series of disparate strategic edicts. We have not sought to work out a coherent strategy jointly with our NATO allies. In the course of the American debate with de Gaulle, U.S. ideas of the optimum methods of defending the NATO area against attack have been changing rapidly, thus compounding the confusion at the political level. It was pointed out in Chapter 3 of this book that in June, 1962, Secretary of Defense McNamara enunciated a doctrine of "counterforce"—based upon a sufficient nuclear superiority to enable the United States to absorb an enemy first strike and still prevail over him by retaliating selectively against military targets. During the Cuban crisis, the Secretary advanced a modified version of this doctrine: he said that to leave to the enemy the option of launching a nuclear war did not necessarily mean that the U.S. must actually absorb the enemy's entire first strike capability, since we would be able to destroy a substantial portion of it before it could be launched. But in his statement before the House Armed Services Committee on January 30, 1963, the Secretary shifted from the counterforce idea and announced a strategic doctrine based not upon superior U.S. nuclear forces (which permitted the Cuban crisis to be handled successfully) but upon a rather nebulous concept of "stability" which has been long in the making.

U.S. military policy today suffers from certain ambiguities

which, according to Henry Kissinger, "have been obscured by the fact that those most responsible for developing it belong to a single school of thought and after years of association have come to take for granted some assumptions which are not really so self-evident as they have tried to make them appear."[10] Presumably, the Administration espouses the concept of flexibility across the entire spectrum of conflict. Yet in planning the future defense of Europe, it appears to be relying upon a single weapons system, viz., the Polaris missile. Admittedly, the Polaris system is one of the best single weapons systems ever developed by the U.S. Nevertheless, it has its weaknesses and may one day be rendered obsolete by technological developments. De Gaulle is not the only one who has raised his voice in warning. In the British Parliamentary debates of early February, 1963, Labour party spokesmen criticized the Macmillan Government for making Britain unduly dependent upon a single weapons system which, within a few years, may turn out to be inadequate in the face of Europe's defense problems.

The Administration's efforts to persuade the European allies of the "indivisibility" of nuclear defense and the nuclear interdependence of the whole Alliance deserve praise. So does the U.S. attempt to induce the Europeans to increase their manpower commitments to NATO. Certainly the Alliance can use more manpower. But an increase in manpower should not be thought of merely in terms of conventional forces and conventional strategies, backed up primarily by the threat of *strategic* nuclear retaliation. This is a monolithic notion of nuclear weapons which, at a time of crisis, could have disastrous consequences. Increased manpower for NATO makes military sense only if it is also related to the development of a flexible, carefully-controlled nuclear capability—both strategic and tactical.

Many European observers are convinced that the United States is anxious to bring about the early denuclearization of NATO defenses in Europe. The two main obstacles to the achievement of this goal are the existing or emerging national nuclear capabilities and the current reliance on atomic weapons to defeat aggression. This explains, in the eyes of these Europeans, why the U.S. has sought either to eliminate French and British nuclear forces or to "integrate" them into NATO. In the latter case, the United States has emphasized sea-based systems, which remove the nuclear weapons clearly outside a European combat zone. Hence they would be usable only in general war, and they would be more responsive to "permissive links" (a technical device preventing the firing of nuclear weapons except when authorized by the highest authority), multinational manning and other controls.

General Norstad's attempts to modernize his atomic strike forces with medium-range missiles met constant opposition from officials in Washington.[11] Actions to harden delivery aircraft against atomic attack have been deferred on the supposition that their primary role in the 1960's will be to support conventional operations. The manner in which the role of tactical nuclear firepower has been played down, combined with the demands for a conventional build-up, suggests that there is little intention to modernize present land-based atomic systems. The motives underlying the U.S. effort, in the face of strong Allied opposition, to emphasize conventional concepts for the defense of Europe are seen by the Europeans as flowing from three American strategic assumptions:

First is the assumption that a primarily conventional strategy will improve deterrence of limited aggression. According to this line of reasoning, it is not credible to the Soviets that NATO should meet a limited attack with an immediate atomic response. Hence, the lack of an adequate conventional capability to cope with less-than-massive aggression constitutes an invitation to attempt it. Such an argument has considerable validity with respect to the lower spectrum of military operations. But it does not justify a costly effort to develop a capability for waging sustained, large-scale conventional war without the support of tactical nuclear weapons. Hence it does not justify the withdrawal of tactical atomic weapons from the Continent, especially in the face of Soviet forces armed with them. Within recent years, Soviet military planners have exhibited no interest in a return to conventional forces or to conventional strategies.

Second is the assumption that an increase in conventional forces is essential if the United States is to obtain a choice of responses to a specific act of aggression, i.e., to enhance flexibility. President Kennedy has said that he wishes to have options between "defeat and all-out nuclear war." Theoretically, it would appear that this argument looks toward the maintenance of both conventional and local nuclear capabilities so that NATO can face Soviet challenges across the spectrum. But concrete policy measures which are directed toward the reduction of atomic capabilities in the European NATO theater belie the professed goal of providing a greater range of choices, and suggest that the real purpose is to execute a transition to a conventional posture for NATO in Europe, backed by the threat of strategic nuclear retaliation. It is extremely difficult for the majority of experienced military analysts to see just how the downgrading or the virtual elimination of the possibility of a calibrated tactical nuclear response to aggression fits into a policy of "enhanced flexibility."

Third is the assumption that the United States is now in the process of shifting its interest from the defense of the NATO area against Soviet aggression to the conclusion of an arms agreement with a Soviet leader who seeks "peaceful coexistence" and labors under considerable difficulties with his principal ally, China. President Kennedy's frequent affirmations of Atlantic solidarity would seem to be tantamount to a categoric rejection of the idea of nuclear disengagement according to the Rapacki Plan or to any of its Western equivalents. Nevertheless, the Europeans have plausible grounds for wondering whether the United States is heading toward nuclear isolationism. Since Cuba, there have been persistent rumors of an impending arms accommodation between the U.S.S.R. and the U.S., perhaps to be arranged through NATO-Warsaw Pact talks. Furthermore, in January, 1963, the United States hastened to liquidate its land-based missile installations in Turkey and Italy. Although these were replaced by Polaris submarines, the number of operational missiles was reduced. Administration spokesmen were at pains to assert that the phasing out of the Thors and Jupiters was part of a long-planned modernization program, and denied that it represented a unilateral U.S. initiative in reciprocation for the Soviet withdrawal of missiles from Cuba. Nevertheless, many more analytically-minded Europeans could not help wondering at the significance of the measure for which no earlier Presidential statements had prepared public opinion—theirs and ours. Their puzzlement was in no way dispelled by the fact that, in justifying the removal of the missiles from Italy, the United States employed the same arguments which had been advanced by the Italian Communist party three years previously in voicing its opposition to the stationing of missiles on that country's soil.

The rapidity with which the United States has altered both its military doctrine and its military posture has not been conducive to European acceptance of the idea of Atlantic partnership.[12] The Europeans were understandably perplexed in January, 1963, over the policy adopted by the U.S. toward Canada. To them, it appeared that the Canadians were being chastised for embracing the same kind of nuclear policy which the Kennedy Administration was trying to persuade the European allies to accept. The Canadians were berated for refusing to take American nuclear warheads; the French were advised in effect that they should not have nuclear weapons on their territory under any circumstances. To be sure, there were good reasons for insisting that the Canadians should acquire nuclear weapons in order to discharge their responsibilities toward North American Air Defense (NORAD). But the timing of the U.S. criticism of the Diefenbaker Government's distaste for nuclear weapons reinforced European suspicions that Washington policymakers were moving toward a "Nuclear Fortress America" while executing at least a partial nuclear disengagement from the rest of the world.

Suspicions, by a dialectic of their own, cause attitudes to polarize. When the United States takes certain steps—calculated perhaps in the minds of American policymakers to reduce the "hostage mentality" of the Europeans—the latter leap to the conclusion that the U.S. is preparing to "sell Europe down the river." Conversely, when President de Gaulle tries to inspire his fellow Europeans to become more self-reliant with regard to their own defense in the nuclear age, Americans accuse him of seeking to create a "third force" and to take Europe someday out of NATO. This is what the pundits meant when they spoke of a "crisis of confidence" within the Alliance. It is to be fervently hoped that the mutual prophecies of betrayal do not become self-fulfilling by feeding on each other.

There were those in Washington who believed that the difficulty that the United States experienced in gaining acceptance for its nuclear policies in Europe could be overcome by the departure of Adenauer and de Gaulle from the political scene. They overlooked the fact that the issues involved were greater than these two men, neither of whom lacks greatness. They forgot that de Gaulle inherited France's nuclear program from his predecessors. The American detractors of de Gaulle and Adenauer—those aged and archaic Europeans—forgot the remarkable transformation which the two leaders wrought in the historical relations between France and Germany. In the perspective of history, to have put an end to a hostility which erupted into the two most devastating wars in history and was universally accepted as "hereditary" will deserve more than passing notice.

It is tempting, though mistaken, to view the "crisis of confidence" as if it had occurred in a political vacuum. All the speculation, for example, about the possibility of an early understanding between Paris and Moscow fails to take into account the significance of the Franco-German Treaty of Cooperation. It hardly seems likely that the Soviet Union will warm up toward a France that has aligned herself so completely with West Germany. The Soviets have been quick to denounce violently the Franco-German Treaty, branding it as a military pact aimed at the U.S.S.R. No doubt, the Soviets now have a better reason than ever for trying to woo France away from Germany. But it is very unlikely that they can offer France as attractive an arrangement as a close Franco-German relationship.

At the present time, there is no need for the United States to view the Franco-German pact with alarm. Advocates of European integration on both sides of the Atlantic have always taken it for granted that Franco-German amity must form the foundation of European unity. In the current political impasse within the Alliance (which is often interpreted rather narrowly as a triangular personal debate among President Kennedy, Prime Minister Macmillan and President de Gaulle) West Germany stands in a position of crucial importance. It is highly probable that the future of NATO will be decided by the kinds of choices which the Germans make. Chancellor Adenauer has frequently demonstrated his attachment to the idea of Franco-German reconciliation within the larger context of the Atlantic Community. In a statesmanlike way, he has long pursued two fundamental objectives: (1) the closest possible integration of Europe's military defense efforts with those of the United States through NATO; and (2) the establishment of ever closer relations with France through the Communities of the Six and within the NATO framework. Adenauer was one of the first of Europe's statesmen to favor British entry into the Common Market. It was only after Britain decided to establish EFTA as a separate organization that Adenauer's ardor cooled. During the debates which took place in the Bundestag in February, 1963, over the question of the Treaty of Cooperation, the Chancellor, however, reaffirmed his support of

Britain's entry and hewed to a middle course between Paris and Washington. Adenauer was admirable in his efforts to hold the Alliance together. Neither Macmillan, de Gaulle nor Kennedy cast any doubt upon the commitments which *der Alte* had assumed with respect to each of them. But all three of them seemed to overlook the fact that the Federal Republic can meet none of its obligations unless the other three Allies resolve their policy differences. West Germany's difficulties in the quest for balanced relationships with the United States, Britain and France are likely to be compounded after Adenauer's mantle has fallen upon the shoulders of his successor. The diplomatic tug of war among the Three over the allegiance of the young republic could place an unbearable strain upon its nascent parliamentary institutions. The three seasoned democratic Allies are most unwise in allowing the fate of the Western Alliance to hang so vitally upon the choices of the Germans. If the Three fail to arrive at agreement among themselves while a man of Chancellor Adenauer's experience is still on the scene to hold Germany to a responsible pro-NATO course, the situation might conceivably end in tragedy, not only for Germany but for the entire Atlantic Community. The prospect—unfortunately, a real one—of political chaos in Germany could be calamitous to the Western Alliance.

There are those who contend that de Gaulle's Grand Design, if there be one, is incompatible with the continued presence of American forces in Europe. There can be no argument that if de Gaulle aims, as some of his critics insist he does, for the total withdrawal of the *présence Américaine* from Europe, then he is no friend of NATO's. But the possibility still remains that de Gaulle's policy, however tortuous it may seem, however exasperating it may be to us, represents a climactic phase in a development that was always implicit in America's postwar policy of helping Europe to recover economically, of encouraging her to unite politically, and of defending her until she could take her place as a full and equal guardian of the ramparts of Western civilization. It would, therefore, be unwise to pass summary judgment on de Gaulle's political strategy before sufficient and clear evidence has been presented as to its concrete meaning for Europe and its actual implications for future transatlantic relations.

The most detailed and candid acknowledgment of the task facing the United States and "our collaborators in Europe" was made on

February 12, 1963, by J. Robert Schaetzel, Deputy Assistant Secretary of State for Atlantic Affairs. In a speech at Pomona College, Claremont, California, Schaetzel said that what the United States and the Europeans must do is "to look again at our premises for a united Europe and for the Atlantic partnership and to test these premises against the questions that have been recently raised." He added: "If the premises stand up against the challenge, as *I have no doubt they will,* then the problem is not to fall away from our views in the face of these obstacles but to put renewed effort into the construction of the European and Atlantic relationship." Schaetzel went on to say, "we are ready to discuss any subject and to respond to any criticism on political, military or economic policies or action."[13] On this path—the path of open discussion—rather than in the absolute certainty of our premises, lies the chief hope of accord.

In the troubled months between Secretary McNamara's stern admonitions of June 16, 1962, and the moment of this writing, the Administration proceeded toward a re-evaluation of its own position. In the light of realities that do not yield to arguments however well intentioned, American policy has undergone, between then and now, some remarkable modifications. W. W. Rostow, Counselor of the State Department, speaking on March 28, 1963, at Philadelphia, dwelt on the virtues of discussion and partnership on the basis of equality. He said:

> The transition in our relations with Europe from dependence to partnership—a transition taking place in economic, political and military affairs—requires changes in attitude and policy by *all* the nations in the Alliance. It is a complicated and delicate transition. In no field is it more critical than nuclear matters; for on a credible nuclear deterrent the security of the 400,000,000 human beings who live within the Atlantic system depends. The debates and explorations that accompany this transition should not be viewed as petty squabbles or as evidence of disarray. They are part of a living constitutional debate of the first order of magnitude—a debate that must take place if inescapable problems are to be solved and Europe move from dependence to global partnership within the Free World. [Italics added.]

A leading French journalist, M. Servan-Schreiber, summed up the conflict between French and American policies, both of which he deems unrealistic, in the following passage:

General de Gaulle wants France and the other nations to regain their independence in matters of war and peace through their own efforts and at their own expense. This is impossible.

President Kennedy wants the European nations to have complete confidence in the United States in those matters and to rely on Washington for their defense and their destiny. This also is impossible.

Out of the clash of these two policies comes the crisis. The problem of war and the decision of armed defense or attack have always been the most important ones in politics. Indeed, to judge as to the necessity of war is the gravest and the most inalienable mandate entrusted by any people to its government.

The advent of the atomic era did not relieve the political authorities of that responsibility; to the contrary, it has increased it immensely. Then who—which elected political authority—should have the finger on the trigger? That is the whole problem. And everybody knows quite well that nobody will allow it to be a foreign finger—a foreign political authority.

In other words, any American proposal of a purely technical nature which leaves political sovereignty (the finger on the trigger) with the United States is inadequate. A proposition for military integration will not be plausible and serious until the day when it will be accompanied by genuine political co-sovereignty.

If America values Europe, it must then propose to it a political confederation in one form or another. If not, the U.S. will lose Europe, and the sudden burst of General de Gaulle will have been only a premonitory symptom.[14]

The conclusions of this book are in accord with Servan-Schreiber's recommendation: The United States must propose a political confederation in one form or another lest "the United States lose Europe." The gestation period of political federation is long. Organisms in gestation are both fragile and mysterious things. There is a limit to the shocks which they can withstand. The yet-to-be-born Atlantic Community is perilously close to this limit. So great have been the recent strains that the most reasonable prescription is a period of calm during which certain specific treatments can be applied.

What measures seem most appropriate to enable us to achieve, eventually, a genuine Atlantic confederation? The solution must not be so radical as to be rejected by peoples long steeped in the lore of sovereignty, nor so trivial as to be a mere gloss on the status quo. The following measures seem to fall within these bounds: The

United States pledges itself to assist in the creation of a European nuclear force under the aegis of the Western European Union and within the framework of NATO. This pledge must, in turn, be accepted by both France and Great Britain, the only existing nuclear powers in Western Europe. This pledge would signify the widening of the agreement on nuclear cooperation arrived at by President Kennedy and Prime Minister Macmillan at Nassau. For this purpose, U.S. atomic legislation would have to be modified in order to permit the early transfer to France of a limited number of nuclear warheads of a kind appropriate to the French *force de frappe,* once the latter has been integrated into a European deterrent.

On the issue of Britain's bid to enter the Common Market, the next move is logically Britain's. Whatever may be Britain's proposal for the settlement of the questions left open in the course of the Brussels negotiations, it must not dilute beyond recognition the Treaty of Rome. Just as in the matter of nuclear cooperation, France must evince a willingness to achieve an equitable solution. If the *will* to find an answer to questions which are essentially technical animates both London and Paris, this answer can be found.

The issues of nuclear sharing and economic cooperation are inseparable. If both are settled, the stage will have been set for the next and climactic act of political confederation. The United States has constantly urged economic cooperation while dragging its feet, because of its fear of nuclear proliferation, with respect to the creation of a European atomic force. An American pledge to assist in the creation of a European multilateral deterrent should inspire the Europeans to design those arrangements which President Kennedy has called for as the prerequisite for transatlantic nuclear sharing. A historical American pledge and the collective European response were the launching devices of the Marshall Plan, the very plan which made possible the restoration of Europe and the growth of a powerful Atlantic Community. What better example of initiative and response could we follow?

Nothing less than the creation of a confederacy will halt the drift of NATO toward impotence and dissolution. The attempt to keep NATO a military alliance and *no more than a military alliance* is tantamount to seeking its destruction. If there is one feature all military alliances throughout history have held in common it is a far shorter life expectancy than that of any, even the most short-lived, political organism. The best ally of NATO and the champions of Atlantic Union, J. V. Stalin, lies unfortunately in his modest grave; not all Western statesmen are immune to the charms of "peaceful coexistence"; and the Atlantic peoples have become so used to living with the nuclear stalemate that they can no longer envisage that it might be broken. Fear alone will no longer keep together NATO.

The future of the Atlantic Community depends on a feat of political imagination rather than on the ingenious shuffling and reshuffling of NATO weaponry. Rather than argue over how genuine is Premier Khrushchev's dedication to peace or how real are the schisms of the communist bloc, let us assume that communism has disappeared altogether. Such a happy event, unlikely as it is, would not by one wit diminish the need for a strong, truly united Atlantic Community, for the Atlantic Community is not and has never been a mere community of fear, but, in the words of Alexandre Març, a "community of fate": The American and European civilizations, as widely as they may differ, spring from the same sources and live by the same values. Both are confronted with the same global challenge: to build a new, decent and safe world for all men. Justified as has been, in the past, the defensive stance of NATO, and great as are the threats against which it stands guard, communism, far from disappearing, is still the most formidable danger that ever threatened human freedom—the time has come when NATO must grow beyond itself. The chapter: NATO, the military alliance, will soon be closed; the chapter: the Atlantic Community, the Closer Union, must soon begin.

March 30, 1963

NOTES

CHAPTER 1. THE MEANING OF THE ATLANTIC COMMUNITY

1. Hans Kohn, *American Nationalism: An Interpretive Essay*, New York: Macmillan, 1957, pp. 32–33.

2. Hans Kohn, *The Age of Nationalism*, New York: Harper & Brothers, 1962, p. 34.

3. Norman Angell, *The Political Conditions of Allied Success*, New York: G. P. Putnam's Sons, 1918, pp. 4, 9, 11, 13.

4. *New York Times*, May 16, 1962, p. 1.

5. Daniel J. Boorstin, "American Nationalism and the Image of Europe, 1914–1945." Paper read before the Mississippi Valley Historical Association, April 22, 1954.

6. From Secretary of State Dean Rusk's address to the Veterans of Foreign Wars in Minneapolis on August 13, 1962. For the text of this address, see Ernest K. Lindley, editor, *The Winds of Freedom*, Selections from the Speeches and Statements of Secretary of State Dean Rusk, Boston: Beacon Press, 1963, pp. 341–351.

CHAPTER 2. THE POLITICAL HISTORY OF NATO

1. Cf. J. T. Delos, *La Nation*, Montreal: L'Arbre, 1944; and Jacques Maritain, *Man and the State*, Chicago: University of Chicago Press, 1951, p. 3.

2. North Atlantic Treaty, Article IV.

3. When the Senate Foreign Relations Committee was deliberating upon the Treaty, the question was raised whether Article II imposed any obligation to adopt enabling legislation in pursuance of the objective of economic cooperation. Apprehensions were allayed when the Committee concluded that "no such obligations were contemplated by the negotiators." Report of the Senate Committee on Foreign Relations, June 6, 1949.

4. *United States Foreign Policy: Western Europe*, A Study Prepared

at the Request of the Committee on Foreign Relations, U.S. Senate, by the Foreign Policy Research Institute, University of Pennsylvania, October 15, 1959, p. 5.

5. Under the weak Articles of Confederation, e.g., Congress had the power, among other things, to declare war and conclude peace; conduct foreign relations; levy military and monetary assessments; settle disputes between states; and create courts for limited purposes.

6. Under the Articles of Confederation, nine votes were required for major decisions by Congress. Under the Swiss Confederation as restored in 1815, each state had one vote in the Diet; important decisions were taken by a three-quarters majority.

7. The North Atlantic Council, the principal instrument of decision-making in NATO, is composed of representatives of all fifteen member governments. It can meet at three levels: (a) Heads of Government (as it did once, in December, 1957); (b) Foreign Ministers (as it usually does twice yearly); occasionally, the Council at the ministerial level brings together Defense and Finance Ministers; (c) Permanent Ambassadors (once a week or more frequently). Unanimous decisions of the Council, once taken, are deemed binding upon the member governments. Lord Ismay, former Secretary General of NATO, wrote: "When governments hold divergent views, negotiation continues until unanimous agreement has been obtained. It is true that unanimity is not always achieved without considerable patience and a good deal of give and take; but it has always been reached in the end. That is because the interests and objectives of all NATO countries are fundamentally the same, and because the habit of thinking alike and acting alike for the common good is growing daily." *NATO, the First Five Years: 1949–1954*, Paris: North Atlantic Treaty Organization, 1955, p. 60.

8. The most important of these were the Committee of Political Advisers, the Committee of Economic Advisers, the Committee on Information and Cultural Relations, the Annual Review Committee, the Defense Production Committee and the Infrastructure Committee.

9. A. H. Robertson, *European Institutions,* London Institute of World Affairs, New York: Praeger, 1958, p. 89.

10. Carol Edler Bauman, *Political Cooperation in NATO,* National Security Studies Group, University of Wisconsin, Madison, Wisconsin, June, 1960, p. 10.

11. The Egyptians credited the United States with having assisted them in bringing about the accords on both the Sudan and the Suez Canal. Cf. *Department of State Bulletin,* Vol. XXXI, August 16, 1954, p. 234. The British, for their part, have been ready to blame the United States for exerting "pressure to hustle the British out of the Canal Zone."

John Marlowe, *Arab Nationalism and British Imperialism*, New York: Praeger, 1961, p. 90.

12. Cf. Walter Z. Laqueur, *The Soviet Union and the Middle East*, New York: Praeger, 1959, pp. 189–246; Keith Wheelock, *Nasser's New Egypt*, a Foreign Policy Research Institute Book, New York: Praeger, 1960, Chapters VII–IX; and James E. Dougherty, "The Aswan Decision in Perspective," *Political Science Quarterly*, Vol. LXXXIV, March, 1959.

13. Geoffrey Crowther, "Reconstruction of an Alliance," *Foreign Affairs*, Vol. XXXV, January, 1957, pp. 180–181. Cf. also Susan Strange, "Strains on NATO," *The Yearbook of World Affairs 1956*, published under the auspices of the London Institute of World Affairs, New York: Praeger, 1957, pp. 21–41.

14. Foreign Ministers Gaetano Martino of Italy, Halvard Lange of Norway and Lester B. Pearson of Canada.

15. *Report of the Committee of Three on Non-Military Cooperation in NATO*, reprinted from the *Department of State Bulletin*, January 7, 1957, Department of State Publication No. 6449.

16. *Ibid.*

17. *Ibid.*

18. *Ibid.*

19. *NATO: Meeting of Heads of Government, Paris, Text of Statements, December 1957*, Department of State Publication No. 6606.

20. M. Spaak said: "You will, I am sure, realize that this is an innovation, even a revolution, in diplomatic practice. It is really extremely significant that the most powerful nation in the world should accept this form of consultation and adopt the new practice of inviting even the smallest of its allies to discuss with it, on a footing of complete equality, matters of mutual interest and that in the vast majority of cases it should take account of suggestions it receives. This is of cardinal importance if the alliance is to live and develop." Address to the Atlantic Treaty Association, Boston, September 27, 1958, *NATO Letter*, Vol. VI, September–October, 1958, pp. 18–19.

21. President Eisenhower's Letter to Premier Bulganin, January 12, 1958, *Department of State Bulletin*, Vol. XXXVIII, January 27, 1958, pp. 122–127; and the Western Three Power Memorandum, May 28, 1958, *Department of State Bulletin*, Vol. XXXIX, July 7, 1958, pp. 12–16.

22. Trial balloons sent up by individual Western statesmen were often the cause of confusion and premature apprehension. Secretary Dulles, for example, at a press conference on January 13, 1959, suggested the theoretical possibility that there might be some way of unifying Germany besides free elections. Prime Minister Macmillan a few weeks later agreed with Khrushchev that some consideration should be given to

promoting European security through the limitation of forces and weapons, both conventional and nuclear, in an agreed area of Europe. Shortly thereafter, President de Gaulle implied that Germany ought to accept the Oder-Neisse boundary in the East. Chancellor Adenauer regarded these statements as indicating a piecemeal surrender of Allied positions. Cf. Richard P. Stebbins, *The United States in World Affairs, 1959*, for the Council on Foreign Relations, New York: Harper & Brothers, 1960, pp. 146–147.

23. West Berlin is not mentioned specifically in the North Atlantic Treaty as part of the area to be defended against attack. But the wording of Article II of the Protocol of October 22, 1951, signed at the accession of Greece and Turkey, makes it clear that an armed attack on one of the parties includes an attack on the forces of any of the parties in any European territory in which occupation forces of any of the parties were stationed on the date when the Treaty entered into force. The necessity for defending Berlin arises not out of the strategic importance of the territory but from: (a) the rights of 2.2 million West Berliners to remain free; (b) its symbolic meaning as an island of freedom in Communist East Europe; (c) the implications which any seemingly irrevocable change in its status may have for the eventual reunification of Germany; (d) the incalculably adverse psychopolitical effects which the ouster of Western forces from Berlin would have on Germany's willingness to adhere to NATO, and on the solidarity of the entire alliance.

24. De Gaulle apparently believed that any weakening of the West's position with respect to Berlin might lead to a reassessment among the Germans of their pro-Western orientation, and a temptation to come to terms with the Soviet Union. Such a development would, of course, upset de Gaulle's plans for Franco-German partnership. By refusing to negotiate on Berlin, the French President appeared to the West Germans as their staunchest ally.

25. In all fairness it should be admitted that, although there had been wide divergences of opinion on the possibility of reaching an understanding with the Soviet leaders prior to the Paris Summit of May, 1960, when Premier Khrushchev seized upon the U-2 incident as a pretext for wrecking the conference, the Big Three manifested the spirit of "all for one and one for all."

26. Article 6 of Protocol II on the Forces of Western European Union embodied a British promise to maintain four divisions on the Continent and "not to withdraw these forces against the wishes of the majority of the High Contracting Parties." This undertaking was not to be binding in the case of an acute overseas emergency. If it came to constitute too great a financial strain, the U.K. was to invite the North Atlantic Council to review the financial conditions under which U.K. forces were main-

tained. Quoted in M. Margaret Ball, *NATO and the European Unity Movement*, published under the auspices of the London Institute of World Affairs, New York: Praeger, 1959, pp. 392–393.

27. The question of U.S. opposition to nuclear proliferation and the American-British-French tangle over the problems of nuclear sharing are treated at length in Chapters 4 and 5.

28. De Gaulle, at a press conference on March 25, 1959, scored that form of military integration "where the states and peoples and governments see themselves, within the sacred domain of their own defense, deprived more or less of their role and responsibilities." *New York Times*, March 26, 1959. Cf. Stebbins, *op. cit.*, pp. 196–201. The only French military units which have been integrated are those which are stationed in West Germany and along the Franco-German border.

29. The texts of these letters have never been published.

30. René Pleven, "France in the Atlantic Community," *Foreign Affairs*, Vol. XXXVIII, October, 1959, p. 22.

31. *Ibid.*, pp. 22–23. For a thorough account of the French attitude toward Alliance problems, cf. Edgar S. Furniss, Jr., "De Gaulle's France and NATO: An Interpretation," *International Organization*, Vol. XV, Summer, 1961, pp. 349–365.

32. The campaign reached a peak in December, 1961, when the Soviet Government handed to U.S. Ambassador Llewellyn Thompson a note demanding that the United States turn over General Adolf Heusinger, on duty in Washington as chairman of the NATO Military Committee, to stand trial for "crimes against the peace, war crimes and crimes against humanity." *New York Times*, December 13, 1961. The United States quickly branded the Soviet demand "a crude and ludicrous propaganda exercise."

33. Under the WEU Protocol III, the Federal Republic undertakes not to manufacture any atomic, biological or chemical weapons. It can manufacture guided missiles, warships and strategic bombers only with the approval of two-thirds of the WEU Council. Protocol IV establishes the Agency for the Control of Armaments whose task is to ensure compliance with the provisions of Protocol III by carrying out an inspection system on a basis of majority decision.

34. Cf. Lawrence S. Kaplan, "NATO and Adenauer's Germany: Uneasy Partnership," *International Organization*, Vol. XV, Autumn, 1961, pp. 618–629.

35. The West German Government had not cleared its negotiations with Spain through the proper NATO channels.

36. From the time the Soviets evacuated the naval base at Porkkala in 1955 until they hinted in late 1961 that they might invoke the joint

defense provisions of their 1948 pact with the Finns, their policy was designed to encourage neutralist tendencies on the northern flank of NATO. Cf. Lyman B. Burbank, "Scandinavian Integration and Western Defense," *Foreign Affairs*, Vol. XXXV, October, 1956.

37. This seemed particularly to be in the offing at the time of the flare-up over the Holy Loch submarine base and in the immediate post-U-2 period, when many Britons protested against what they deemed to be "provocative" U.S. flights from U.K. bases.

38. After the *Santa Maria* incident and the seizure of Goa by India, Portuguese friendship toward the United States continued to wane. The Portuguese Government began to study the possibility of charging the United States rent for the Azores base on an annual contract basis. One aspect of U.S.-Portuguese relations commonly overlooked was the effect which they might have on the future of the quasi alliance between the United States and Spain. The Spanish Government has strongly supported Portugal's stand on Angola. Many officials in the Franco Government have become so critical of American policy in Africa as to raise doubts about Spain's willingness to renew the quasi alliance, which Spain has hitherto looked upon as a form of protection against liberation movements within her own North African possessions. The authors are indebted to Professor Arthur P. Whitaker of the University of Pennsylvania for calling this point to their attention.

39. It sometimes seems that the French Government would like to see the United States reduce its commitments on the mainland of Southeast Asia and fall back to an allegedly more efficient island chain defense in Asia in order to be in a better position to help Western Europe maintain its primacy of place in Africa. Perhaps the French cannot but resent the fact that the United States did not come to their assistance against the Viet Minh when the latter was supported by Communist China in a campaign which reached its culmination at Dienbienphu, but later replaced French strategic responsibility in Southeast Asia through its mutual security programs. A desire to restore France's political influence in Southeast Asia might explain the French attitude toward the United States presence in that region. Or the French may share U.S. concern for the independence of new pro-Western states but may act stubbornly in Southeast Asia precisely to impress upon the United States the need for joint tripartite strategic planning for the defense of areas not presently covered by the NATO Treaty.

40. The following editorial reaction was not untypical: "No one outside the States sees anything sacrosanct in the Monroe Doctrine—any more than most Americans saw anything sacrosanct in Britain's claims for a special status in the Middle East. . . . At the time of Suez, the United States rightly put her obligation to maintain world peace and interna-

tional law above the immediate interests of her allies. If Britain has the courage to act now as the United States did then, she will do as great a service to the real interests of the alliance." Manchester *Guardian Weekly*, April 20, 1961.

41. *New York Times*, February 21, 1962.

42. Sydney Gruson, "Our Policies Bother Allies," *New York Times*, February 25, 1962.

43. Karl E. Meyer, "Back from the Abyss," *New Leader*, November 12, 1962.

44. George Liska, *Nations in Alliance: The Limits of Interdependence*, Baltimore: Johns Hopkins Press, 1962, p. 74.

45. *Ibid.*, p. 78.

46. The steps which the Western nations have taken through the Organization for Economic Cooperation and Development to ensure a high growth rate among themselves, to contribute toward sound economic development within the less privileged countries of the world, and to facilitate the expansion of international trade are described in Chapter 4, "The Economic Base of Atlantic Power."

47. "Building the Frontiers of Freedom," a Statement before the Foreign Relations Committee, U.S. Senate, May 31, 1961. Text in the *Department of State Bulletin*, Vol. XLIV, No. 1147, June 19, 1961.

48. Indians, e.g., have been much less exercised over United States intervention on behalf of an independent South Vietnam than they were over French efforts, up until 1954, to preserve a nineteenth-century imperial position in the same part of Southeast Asia.

CHAPTER 3. THE DEFENSE OF ATLANTIC FRONTIERS

1. F. O. Miksche, "The Case for Nuclear Sharing," *Orbis*, Fall, 1961, p. 297.

2. The "conventional" school often argues as if tactical atomic weapons had become passé. As Alastair Buchan expressed it:

. . . the European debate on these questions now moves more sluggishly than the American, and European professional and political thought has not assimilated the reasons, based on war games, staff studies, RAND papers, why American military thought has become sceptical about the deterrent value of a heavy concentration of tactical nuclear weapons and alarmed about its implications. European generals are still faithfully repeating the arguments in their favor which they learned from General Gruenther and Admiral Radford, only six or seven years ago.

"Refashioning NATO: A Partnership Puzzle," Washington *Post*, August 12, 1962, Section E, p. 1.

3. *New York Times*, March 29, 1961.

4. Professor Lincoln Gordon (now U.S. Ambassador to Brazil), writing in 1959, offered this highly pertinent conclusion:

The debate on this issue has been confused by a false dichotomy, which conceives of deterrence only in relation to strategic retaliatory power and regards local forces as designed to "fight and win" local contests. Such forces must, of course, be able to fight and win certain types of local contests, but their critical function is to deter those forms of limited aggression which, under thermonuclear parity, strategic retaliation alone cannot deter. They can do this by raising the price of entry to the enemy to a point where, to do anything at all, he must deliberately invite strategic retaliation.

"NATO in the Nuclear Age," *Yale Review*, Spring, 1959, p. 325.

5. Speech by U.S.S.R. Minister of Defense Malinovsky to the October 23 session of the Twenty-second CPSU Congress.

6. In September, 1962, Soviet military strategists published a textbook recommending that Russia prepare for war in outer space. This recommendation was referred to in a review of the new textbook published by the Soviet military newspaper *Red Star*. According to Army General Pavel Kurochkin's review, one of the text's chapters was devoted to the use of outer space for military purposes. Furthermore, the reviewer noted that the United States is already engaged in such activity. The textbook, written under the direction of Marshal V. D. Sokolovsky, appears to be the first serious work on military strategy openly published in Russia since 1926. The following quotations from the book are of particular interest:

The Soviet people are engaged in the peaceful conquest of space. But it is perfectly clear that if the imperialists continue to conduct research for means of using cosmic space for military goals, then the interests of guaranteeing the security of the Soviet state demand definite measures from our side. . . . The strategists demanded larger ground forces than ever before for atomic-age warfare. (This appeared to differ from American strategic concepts calling for smaller and highly mobile tactical units.) . . . all-out nuclear strikes against the enemy homeland, including government and industrial centers. (This appeared to run counter to some Western strategists' theories that the Soviets might confine themselves to attacks on purely military objectives.)

See the Washington *Post*, September 23, 1962.

7. S. S. Varentsov, "On the Field of Battle," *Krasnaya Zvezda*, November 18, 1961, p. 2.

8. V. Lapinov, "Imprisoned in Old Ideas," *Krasnaya Zvezda*, August 13, 1960, p. 2.

9. A. Kazaryan and D. Reznik, "Why a Counterattack Failed," *Krasnaya Zvezda*, August 8, 1961, p. 3. The time consideration has important implications to the military utility of the pause concept.

10. Secretary of Defense McNamara, in a speech on U.S. military policy given at Ann Arbor, Michigan, June 16, 1962, seemed to imply that the U.S. possessed a counterforce capability. Alastair Buchan, in his article "Refashioning NATO: A Partnership Puzzle," *cit. supra,* commented as follows:

> In order to discourage the proliferation of independent nuclear deterrents in Europe, he [McNamara] appears to have thought it advisable not only to remind Europe of the size of the American strategic armory, but somewhat to exaggerate its counterforce capabilities and also to revive the older doctrine of "active deterrence," that is of an American nuclear first strike in response to "a major attack on the alliance," without defining what that means.

11. In a speech before the Conference of the NATO Parliamentarians, given in Paris. Text of speech is reprinted in *Survival,* January–February, 1961, p. 30.

12. John Strachey, "NATO and the Bomb," *Encounter,* April, 1962, p. 14.

13. The operational portion of the Nassau communiqué follows:

> After careful review, the President and the Prime Minister agreed that a decision on Polaris must be considered in the widest context both of the future defenses of the Atlantic Alliance and of the safety of the whole Free World.
>
> They reached the conclusion that this issue created an opportunity for the development of new and closer arrangements for the organization and control of strategic Western defense and that such arrangements in turn could make a major contribution to political cohesion among the nations of the alliance.
>
> (6) The Prime Minister suggested, and the President agreed, that for the immediate future a start could be made by subscribing to NATO some part of the forces already in existence.
>
> This could include allocations from United States strategic forces, from the United Kingdom bomber command and from tactical nuclear forces now held in Europe. Such forces would be assigned as part of a NATO nuclear force and targeted in accordance with NATO plans.
>
> (7) Returning to Polaris, the President and the Prime Minister agreed that the purpose of their two governments with respect to the provision of the Polaris missiles must be the development of a multilateral NATO nuclear force in the closest consultation with other NATO allies. They will use their best endeavors to this end.
>
> (8) Accordingly, the President and the Prime Minister agreed that the U.S. will make available on a continuing basis Polaris missiles (less warheads) for British submarines. The U.S. will also study the feasibility of making available certain support facilities for such submarines.
>
> The U.K. Government will construct the submarines in which these weapons will be placed and they will also provide the nuclear warheads for the Polaris missiles.

British forces developed under this plan will be assigned and targeted in the same way as the forces described in Paragraph 6. These forces, and at least equal U.S. forces, would be made available for inclusion in a NATO multilateral nuclear force.

The Prime Minister made it clear that except where Her Majesty's Government may decide that supreme national interests are at stake, these British forces will be used for the purposes of international defense of the Western alliance in all circumstances.

(9) The President and the Prime Minister are convinced that this new plan will strengthen the nuclear defense of the Western alliance. In strategic terms this defense is indivisible and it is their conviction that in all ordinary circumstances of crisis or danger, it is this very unity which is the best protection of the West.

(10) The President and the Prime Minister agreed that in addition to having a nuclear shield it is important to have a non-nuclear sword. For this purpose they agreed on the importance of increasing the effectiveness of their conventional forces on a world-wide basis.

The Philadelphia *Inquirer,* December 22, 1962, p. 3.

14. Strachey, *op. cit.,* p. 12.

15. As a supplement to mobile land-based missiles, the U.S. and its NATO Allies might develop technologically feasible nuclear ram-jet propulsion craft for high-speed (Mach 3—three times the speed of sound), low-level (several hundred feet) penetration into Soviet-held territory. This highly mobile, relatively small weapon would increase Allied offensive flexibility.

16. Strachey, *op. cit.,* p. 14.

17. *Ibid.*

18. Frederick M. Stern wrote:

The superiority of the Soviet forces is even greater than the numbers of formations in active service may indicate. For they are backed by very large reserve and territorial formations—mostly army—many of which can be thrown into combat in a matter of days or weeks. Moreover, the Soviets are strengthening these reserves in order to make up for the reduction of their active formations. As long as the ground forces of the free nations are vastly outnumbered by those of the communist states, disarmament of atomic weapons, missiles and air forces, even if effectively controlled and fully implemented, would leave the world at the mercy of the Communist Dictators.

To prevent this, large effective reserve forces standing ready at any time can be created at a fraction of the cost of conventional-type forces, and in a way that eliminates all political and psychological fears. The type that fulfills these demands is the "citizen army."

This system can furnish the ready, full-strength reserve formations needed to back up the active first-line divisions. In addition, it provides the forces needed for territorial, anti-air, and civil defense. If sound principles for recruitment, classification, training, and advancement are applied, the quality of the leadership and specialist personnel is of the highest caliber; for a citizen army, air force, or navy, with its short training periods, can draft the candidates for these positions from the vast reservoir of talent of the entire nation, whereas a professional or cadre-conscript army, recruiting such personnel for many years of service on a professional or volunteer basis, must be satisfied with what it can get—some able men, but many who are less so.

"Disarmament and a Citizen Army," *Army*, October, 1960, pp. 41–43.

19. The danger of national nuclear forces is manifest, as is the desideratum of a single nuclear command for the West. Lord Boothby stated the issue succinctly:

> The United States do not ask or wish for a monopoly of nuclear power. What they rightly claim is a general recognition, within the Western Alliance, of their preponderant power; and, therefore, that the ultimate weapon will never be used without their consent. This involves the creation of international organs of political consultation and decision which we do not at present possess. . . . The concept of Atlantic Union is on the march, and cannot now be stayed. But if we are to do it in time, it will require more coherent strategic thinking, less national selfishness, fewer illusions of grandeur, and far more unity of purpose within the Western Alliance as a whole than have been vouchsafed to us in recent years.

"Deterrent Fact and Folly," *Daily Telegram*, London, August 6, 1962.

20. Herman Kahn did much to clarify and categorize the various possible kinds of deterrent posture. See *On Thermonuclear War*, Princeton: Princeton University Press, 1960, p. 126 and following.

21. "It would be almost incredibly rash of the Russians to start a general war by means of an invasion of Western Europe with conventional arms. For by so doing they would hand the opportunity for a thermo-nuclear first strike to S.A.C. on a platter." Strachey, *op. cit.*, p. 15.

22. From speech reprinted in *Survival, op. cit.*

23. New York *Herald Tribune*, May 15, 1962, p. 1.

24. Text of communiqué in *Department of State Bulletin*, Vol. XXXVIII, January 6, 1957. This was the first step toward "nuclear sharing," but because of control arrangements, there was as yet no real sharing. General Lauris Norstad, Supreme Allied Commander, addressing the Sixth Annual NATO Parliamentarians' Conference, asked how a growing desire for a broader sharing in the control of nuclear weapons might be met so that the Alliance could be sure that the weapons would be available to it in all reasonable circumstances for the defense of Europe. He made it clear that he was speaking not of delivery systems, but of committing to the Alliance "the nuclear components which are retained in the strictest custody," thereby making NATO a "fourth atomic

power." He concluded by urging that "consideration should be given to guaranteeing to the Alliance the availability of a basic pool of atomic weapons, those essential to the direct defense of Europe, and to giving to all nations of the Alliance an essentially equal voice in the control of these particular weapons." Text in *NATO Letter,* January 9, 1961, pp. 15–17.

At the Council meeting in Paris in December, 1960, Secretary of State Christian A. Herter put forth a "concept" under which the United States would give NATO five submarines armed with eighty Polaris missiles by 1963, provided that the Allies could agree on a multilateral system of political control. The "concept" also included the purchase by the Alliance from the United States of one hundred mid-range missiles, apparently for deployment at sea, at about one million dollars apiece. *New York Times,* December 17, 1960. The Council reacted with caution in the face of an impending change of Administration in Washington. Its closing communiqué declared that it "took note of the United States suggestion with great interest and instructed the permanent representatives to study the suggestion and related matters in detail." *Department of State Bulletin,* January 9, 1961.

President Kennedy, addressing the Canadian Parliament in Ottawa on May 17, 1961, said that "the United States will commit to the NATO command five—and subsequently still more—Polaris atomic-missile submarines which are defensive weapons, subject to any agreed NATO guidelines on their control and use and responsive to the needs of all members but still credible in an emergency. Beyond this we look to the possibility of eventually establishing a NATO seaborne force, which would be truly multilateral in ownership and control, if this should be desired and found feasible by our allies, once NATO's non-nuclear goals have been achieved." *New York Times,* May 18, 1962.

Up to the time of the NATO Defense and Foreign Ministers Meeting at Athens in May, 1962, the Allies were unable to reach agreement on a scheme for joint control. Therefore the United States at the Athens meeting announced that it would assign five submarines to NATO. This involves essentially a transaction on paper. The submarines were transferred from Admiral Robert Lee Dennison as Commander of the United States Atlantic Fleet to Admiral Dennison as NATO's Supreme Allied Commander, Atlantic (SACLANT). The submarines continue to be manned entirely by American crews; the responsibility for firing the nuclear warhead continues to depend upon an order from the President of the United States.

The implications of various proposals for a NATO deterrent are discussed in Henry A. Kissinger, *The Necessity for Choice,* for the Council on Foreign Relations, New York: Harper & Brothers, 1960, pp. 113–132; Alastair Buchan, *NATO in the 1960's,* London: Weidenfield and Nicholson, 1960; Glenn H. Snyder, *Deterrence and Defense*, Princeton: Princeton University Press, 1961, pp. 174–192; General Pierre Gallois, *The Balance of Terror*, Boston: Houghton Mifflin, 1961; A. L. Burns, "NATO and Nuclear Sharing," in Klaus Knorr, ed., *NATO and American Security*, Princeton: Princeton University Press, 1959; Malcolm Hoag, "What Interdependence for NATO?" *Survival*, May–June 1960 (reprinted from *World Politics*); Albert Wohlstetter, "Nuclear Sharing: NATO and the N plus 1 Country," *Foreign Affairs*, Vol. XXXIX, April, 1961, especially pages 372–377; Robert Endicott Osgood, *NATO: The Entangling Alliance*, Chicago: University of Chicago Press, 1962, Chapters 8 and 9; Henry A. Kissinger, "The Unsolved Problems of European Defense," *Foreign Affairs*, Vol. XL, July, 1962.

25. Osgood, *op. cit.*, pp. 259–260.

26. Discussions of the arguments *contra* can be found in "The Future of Western Deterrent Power," a symposium by Raymond Aron, Klaus Knorr and Alastair Buchan, *Bulletin of the Atomic Scientists*, Vol. XVI, September, 1960; Paul M. Doty, "The Role of the Smaller Powers," in Donald G. Brennan, ed., *Arms Control, Disarmament and National Security*, with the sponsorship of the American Academy of Arts and Sciences, New York: George Braziller, 1961; Wohlstetter, *op. cit.*; Osgood, *op. cit.*, pp. 260–274.

27. Wohlstetter, *op. cit.*, pp. 361–362.

28. Raymond Aron, "De Gaulle and Kennedy," *The Atlantic Monthly*, August, 1962, p. 37.

29. *Ibid.*, p. 38.

30. George A. Kelly, "The Political Background of the French A-Bomb," *Orbis*, Fall, 1960, pp. 284–306.

31. Pierre Messmer, "The French Military Establishment of Tomorrow," *Orbis*, Summer, 1962, pp. 205–216.

32. Richard B. Foster, "Unilateral Arms Control Measures and Disarmament Negotiations," *Orbis*, Summer, 1962, p. 259.

33. C. B. Marshall, *Two Communist Manifestos*, a publication of the Washington Center of Foreign Policy Research, March, 1961, pp. 3 and 4.

34. Foster, *op. cit.*, p. 260.

35. *Evening Bulletin*, Philadelphia, November 21, 1962, p. 11.

36. "The Soviet Defense Minister, Marshal Rodion Malinovsky, declared today that the space flights of Maj. Andiran G. Nikolayev and Lieut. Col. Pavel R. Popovich should serve as a warning to the enemies of the Soviet Union. In a message to the two astronauts, who yesterday completed their epic 'group flight' around the earth, Marshal Malinovsky said: 'Let our enemies know what techniques and what soldiers our Soviet power disposes of.'" *New York Times*, August 17, 1962, p. 1.

37. G. Pokrovosky, Major General, Soviet Army, *Science and Technology in Contemporary War*, New York: Praeger, 1959, p. 66. Translated and annotated by R. I. Garthoff.

38. *New York Times*, August 1, 1961.

39. Composite Report of the President's Committee to Study the United States Military Assistance Program ("Draper Committee"), Volume 1, August 17, 1959, p. 159.

The work accomplished by the NATO Advisory Group for Aeronautical Research and Development is most illustrative. AGARD was created in 1957. An idea of the success of this organization under Dr. von Karman's leadership may be obtained from comparing figures representative of the numbers of scientists working within the organizational framework in 1953 with those of 1962. In 1953 there were some 150 people meeting in three groups twice a year, whereas in 1962 there were some 600.

The following specific achievements can be credited to AGARD:

a) The school on experimental aerodynamics at Rhode St. Genese, Belgium.

b) The NATO Guided Weapons School in Greece.

c) The specification of and assistance in selection of the first true NATO weapon—the G 91 fighter.

d) The full-scale NATO study of operational research facilities in NATO.

e) A very large number of scientific and technical publications, reference to which will soon be available in an index of some 2,000 items.

I find that I had also made mention of the U.S. unilateral efforts in the field: not only has the MWDP taken steps toward bilateral resolution of security problems in specific fields; all of the U.S. forces, Army, Navy and Air Force, have established offices in Europe to encourage and exploit European competence.

From an unpublished letter written by G. H. Cooper, Executive AGARD Structures and Materials Panel, November 28, 1962, to the Foreign Policy Research Institute.

40. Aron, *op. cit.*, p. 37.

41. Robert Strausz-Hupé, William R. Kintner, Stefan T. Possony, *A Forward Strategy for America*, New York: Harper & Brothers, 1961, p. 70.

42. *Increasing the Effectiveness of Western Science*, Fondation Universitaire, Brussels, 1960. The members of the Study Group, who served in their individual capacities, were: M. Louis Armand, Chairman, former President of French Railways, former President of EURATOM, President of the Council of the École Polytechnique; Professor Dr. Med. Wolfgang Bargmann, Kiel; Professor Paul Bourgeosis, Director of the Royal Observatory of Belgium; Professor H. B. G. Casmir, Director of the Research Laboratories, N. V. Philips Gloelampenfabrik, Eindhoven; Sir John Cockcroft, Master of Churchill College, Cambridge, and part-time Member of

the United Kingdom Atomic Energy Authority; Professor André Denjon, Director of the Observatory of Paris; Professor Dr. Gerhard Hess, Bad Godesberg/Heidelberg; Professor G. Puppi, Director of Institute of Physics, University of Bologna; Professor I. I. Rabi, Columbia University; Professor Frederick Seitz, University of Illinois; Professor Sir Solly Zuckerman, University of Birmingham; M. Jean Willems, First Vice-President and Director, Fondation Universitaire, Acting Chairman of the Study Group in April and May, 1960.

The Study Group first convened in Paris on the 14th of September, 1959, and met together periodically. There have also been many smaller meetings of individual members.

43. Dr. J. R. Killian, Jr., former Scientific Adviser to President Eisenhower and Chairman of the Study Group, explained that the new Institute would help close the gap between our accomplishments and our potential in science by partially fulfilling the need for greater cooperation among Atlantic nations and the need for new institutions to demonstrate Atlantic unity. He also stressed the rapidly changing character of scientific research as its instruments become more expensive and the fields more interrelated, the ever more demanding intellectual requirements of higher education and the need for training greater numbers of scientists and engineers. *NATO Letter,* Vol. X, No. 4, April, 1962.

44. *United States Foreign Policy: Western Europe, op. cit.*

45. J. S. Parker, "Impact in Economic Life," in the issue, "Man's Opportunities in Space," *The General Electric Forum,* Vol. V, No. 3, July–September, 1962, p. 20.

46. In the twentieth century there has emerged a new kind of strategy which may be called the "Strategy of Means." It encompasses logistics but is more than this, for it embraces the development and manufacture of weapons, their disposition, their emplacement and their readiness as well as their maintenance. In 1944, when General Eisenhower launched the assault forces across the Channel, he was far more the capable administrator of a powerful "strategy of means" than a military strategist in the traditional sense of the word. The means assembled under his command were so overwhelming that to a considerable extent they could have compensated for any tactical errors committed. . . .

Five years later, however, either the lesson had been forgotten or it had not been properly understood. When the Western governments sought to form a defense system in keeping with the atomic age, they sacrificed everything to the strategy of operations. . . . But at the same time it was left to each nation to train, arm and equip the forces which were its contribution to collective defense. Not only did logistics remain a national concern, but also planning, research and development, production and allocation. Thus while the strategy of operations was jointly conceived, the strategy of means remained, in effect, a purely national responsibility.

Pierre M. Gallois, "New Teeth for NATO," *Foreign Affairs*, Vol. XLI, October, 1962, pp. 78–79.

47. The nuclear club could be widened speedily were the U.S. Congress convinced it would be to the benefit of the United States to change the current laws governing nuclear weapons. Such legislation with respect to NATO could be adopted rapidly. Here, our situation is not symmetrical with that of the Soviet Union. It is probable that Khrushchev cannot trust the East European satellite nations to the extent of giving them nuclear weapons. The power they might give the satellites to throw off the Soviet imperialist yoke must haunt Khrushchev, especially in view of the 1956 Hungarian revolt and uprisings in East Germany and Poland. We, on the other hand, need not fear that the nuclear weapons we might share with our NATO Allies would be turned against us. The Soviets have consistently inveighed against the nuclear arming of our European Allies. There are good reasons to believe that Soviet fears of a Western Europe armed with nuclear weapons are real. They seem deeply rooted in the objective circumstances of the present confrontation in Central Europe.

Foster, *op. cit.*, p. 279.

48. *New York Times*, November 4, 1962, p. 1.

49. Herman Kahn, *Thinking About the Unthinkable*, New York: Horizon Press, 1962, p. 247.

50. According to Paul M. Doty, *op. cit.*, and Harold Simons, "World Wide Capabilities for Production and Control of Nuclear Weapons," *Daedalus*, Vol. 88, pp. 385–409, who both cite the National Planning Association Pamphlet No. 108 (Washington, D.C.: NPA, 1959), twelve nations (Belgium, Canada, China, Czechoslovakia, France, East Germany, West Germany, India, Italy, Japan, Sweden, Switzerland) are technically capable of launching a successful weapons program; eight other countries (Australia, Austria, Denmark, Finland, Hungary, the Netherlands, Poland, Yugoslavia) are capable economically but somewhat limited in the necessary technical manpower; and six other nations (Argentina, Brazil, Mexico, Norway, Spain, Union of South Africa) are five years away, possessing most probably the economic capability but lacking in industrial resources and scientific manpower.

51. Joseph Kraft, *The Grand Design*, New York: Harper & Brothers, 1962, p. 63.

52. *New York Times*, May 30, 1962, p. 18.

53. Nikita Khrushchev, "On Peaceful Coexistence," *Foreign Affairs*, Vol. XXXVIII, October, 1959, p. 5.

CHAPTER 4. THE ECONOMIC BASE OF ATLANTIC POWER

1. In furtherance of this end the communists seek: "(1) to insulate the socialist system against all forms of capitalist interference; (2) to attain complete socialist self-sufficiency, i.e., to eliminate the dependence of the bloc upon Western technology; (3) to employ the resources of a state trading monopoly to carry out economic transactions with non-bloc nations on favorable terms; (4) to employ political conflict methods to retard Western economic programs which might serve to strengthen free nations; (5) to carry on the "forced march" of socialist industrial development, beginning with the inner core—i.e., the U.S.S.R.—and working outward through the other members of the bloc, whose individual economic interests are made subsidiary to those of the U.S.S.R.; (6) to integrate the bloc economy and assign specialized tasks according to a central communist blueprint; and (7) to depress forcibly consumption levels through the centralized pricing system, concentrating the maximum proportion of total resources on programs which promote Soviet strategic power." Strausz-Hupé, Kintner and Possony, *A Forward Strategy for America, cit. supra*, p. 166.

2. Comparable data for the Soviet Union and for the Eastern European satellites are not available.

3. *Department of State Bulletin*, Vol. XVI, p. 1159.

4. Due to the limitations of space, our discussion of the events of 1945–1952 (the Period of "Cooperation") must be limited to the high spots. The reader interested further in this possibly "most critical" period of postwar economic developments will find extended discussion of the period in two classic works—William Diebold, Jr., *Trade and Payments in Western Europe*, New York: Harper & Brothers, 1952, and Robert Triffin, *Europe and the Money Muddle*, New Haven: Yale University Press, 1957.

5. The movement from EPU to full convertibility in the framework of the European Monetary Fund involved a serious conflict of British interest aimed at protecting sterling and Continental interests which wished to move more slowly toward full convertibility. This struggle, which shows in fine relief the conflicts of British financial commitments to both the Commonwealth and the Continent, foreshadowed the broader conflicts of contemporary British policy. For an extended discussion of the transition from EPU to EMF, see Randall Hinshaw, "Toward European Convertibility," *Princeton Essays in International Finance*, No. 31. Princeton: Princeton University Press, 1958.

6. "I want to say in all seriousness that if anyone had asked me years ago to predict what would happen in the postwar period, and if I tried to predict, the most surprising event to me would, I think, not be that the

Russians are growing fast, that at the moment we're not growing fast, but it's the fact that the less than most affluent countries in the world, France, Italy, Western Germany, Japan—these countries have shown a rate of growth that nobody between the wars could possibly have predicted." Dr. Paul Samuelson, speaking on "The World Strategy of the United States as a Great Power," CBS Television, February 19, 1961.

7. The summary refusal of Great Britain to consider membership in ECSC is best summed up by Ernest Haas:

The ruling Labour Party position in 1950 permitted of no doubt. . . . It was argued that close economic cooperation with Europe was unnecessary because the economies concerned are not complementary. Further, the very logic of the Common Market was challenged: Far from leading to a more rational distribution of the factors of production, it was likely to result in chaos. . . . The opposition Conservative Party did not basically challenge the Labour position; in fact, it shared the essence of it.

The Uniting of Europe, Stanford, California: Stanford University Press, 1958, p. 159.

8. Émile Benoit, *Europe at Sixes and Sevens*, New York: Columbia University Press, 1961, p. 91.

9. Walter Hallstein, Speech before the NATO Parliamentarians' Conference, November 12, 1962, p. 2. Max Lerner has compared this political role of the institutions of economic integration to the military concept of "escalation."

If there is an escalation principle in modern warfare, as I have noted earlier, there may also be an escalation principle as applied to European unity. The European leaders, like Jean Monnet, were careful to start with very specific projects like the Coal and Steel Community. They escalated this into a Common Market, and they are in process of overcoming the Six's and Seven's. . . . The next logical step is that of a United States of Europe, which is already being discussed.

Max Lerner, *The Age of Overkill: A Preface to World Politics*, New York: Simon and Schuster, 1961, p. 276.

10. This decision brought about these changes in the EEC schedule for abolition of trade restrictions: (1) the rate of internal tariff reduction was increased 10%; (2) all quotas on industrial goods were abolished at the end of 1961; (3) the deadline for the first percentage movement to the common external tariff was moved forward a year to December 31, 1960; (4) a 20% cut in the common external tariff was made contingent on receiving reciprocal concessions from other nations of the world at the 1960–1961 GATT negotiations. These four actions effectively removed EFTA pressure on Germany and form the first real concrete decision of

the Council of EEC. For a full analysis of the relationship of this decision to EFTA, see Benoit, *op. cit.*, pp. 86–92.

11. When the negotiations were suspended in January, 1963, the economic points at issue between the EEC and the United Kingdom were still substantial. French Foreign Minister Maurice Couve de Murville, in a speech to the National Assembly on January 24, was at pains to make it clear that there was considerable disagreement over certain critical points. First, he said, was the method of Britain's adopting the EEC external tariff. On this question, the British sought to modify the application of the complete schedule against the EFTA nations and tried to have certain products excluded from the common tariff schedule. Secondly, the British wished to modify the EEC's common agricultural policy with respect to the length of the transitional period, the price support system and the methods of financing the supported price levels. See the text of M. Couve de Murville's speech, Ambassade de France, Service de Presse et d'Information, Speeches and Press Conferences No. 186.

12. The participation of Canada in OECD along with the problems posed by the new economic arrangements of the Community for Canada (beyond the Commonwealth preference issue) have not received the attention they deserve in Western diplomatic and academic circles. A brief but excellent résumé of the Canadian position in community-wide ventures is a collection of three short speeches by Peyton Lyon, Henry Maon and Jan Tupker, which appears in the chapter, "Europe's Challenge to Canada," in *The New Europe—The Proceedings of the 31st Coochiching Conference*, edited by D. L. B. Hamlin, Toronto: University of Toronto Press, 1962, pp. 83–90.

13. Article I of the OECD Convention. Full text in *NATO Letter*, Vol. IX, January, 1961.

14. See Secretary of the Treasury Dillon's comments on the role the OECD could have played in avoiding this episode, in *Organization for Economic Cooperation and Development*, Report of the Committee on Foreign Relations, U.S. Senate on Ex. E, 87th Congress, 1st Session, Executive Report No. 1, dated March, 1960, pp. 9–10. The effect of European discount rates on the flow of U.S. short-term capital is clearly demonstrated in *Economic Survey for Europe in 1960*, Geneva: EEC, 1961, Chart 10, p. 44.

15. Even while the OECD meeting was in session, there was considerable doubt that the United States would be able to live up to its part of the bargain in proposing a 50 percent growth as the Western target for the next decade. This would require an annual average growth rate of from 4 to 4.5 percent on the part of the members. The countries of

Western Europe should encounter little difficulty in maintaining this pace, but it is not at all clear that the United States and the United Kingdom will be able to improve their performances, which have been running at less than 3 percent in recent years. Cf. Harry B. Ellis, "OECD Adopts Growth Plan," *Christian Science Monitor*, November 17, 1961.

16. Subcommittee on Foreign Economic Policy of the Joint Economic Committee, Congress of the United States, Washington: U.S. Government Printing Office, 1961.

17. Simultaneously, Howard Petersen, Special Advisor to the President on Foreign Trade Policy, sought in negotiations with EEC to exhaust the tariff-cutting potential of the expiring Reciprocal Trade Agreements Act.

18. The Act leaves the treatment of these products in a somewhat ambiguous state. Section 213 of the Act, "Tropical Agricultural and Forestry Commodities," reads in part:

a) Section 201 (b) (1) [the 50% Reduction Clause] shall not apply to any Article if, before entering into the Trade Agreement covering such Article, the President determines that—

1) such Article is a Tropical Agricultural or Forestry Commodity;

2) the like Article is not produced in significant quantities in the U.S.; and,

3) the European Economic Community has made a commitment with respect to duties or other import restrictions which is likely to assure access for such Article to the markets of the European Economic Community which

a) is comparable to the access which such Article will have to the markets of the U.S.;

b) will be afforded substantially without different treatment as among Free-World countries of origin.

19. For a contrary view, see Edwin L. Dale in Financial Section of the *New York Times,* October 14, 1962, p. 1: "Wages everywhere [in Europe] have been rising far faster than productivity, but competition has kept price increases, at least in the industrial sector, extremely modest. The loser has been profit margins."

20. The best discussion of the theoretical and practical aspects of the effect of larger markets upon the structure of European production (within the EEC) appears in Tibor Scitovsky, *Economic Theory and Western European Integration,* Stanford: Stanford University Press, 1958, especially Chapters 1 and 3.

21. The allocations to national military power by the state-oriented Soviet economy are generally thought to be a considerably higher proportion of GNP than in the United States. However, analysis of the economic costs to the Soviet Union, taking account of the relative cheapness of

manpower and of the output of the defense industries to which the Soviet planners have over many years allocated their best technology—their best engineers and their best machines—indicates that in Soviet terms the current percentage allocation of GNP to military purposes, however menacing, is very little larger than that of the United States. The allocation to consumers is lower than that in the United States or Western Europe, because of the high level of investment and the emphasis on investment for promoting the power-directed heavy industries rather than the consumer-directed light industries and housing.

22. Defense Expenditures by NATO Countries, 1950–1960, in Billions of Dollars at 1959 Prices and Exchange Rates

	1950		1955		1960	
	Dollars	Index	Dollars	Index	Dollars	Index
Total NATO	27.3	100	57.7	221	59.5	218
United States	18.1	100	44.5	246	44.3	245
"Big 4" Europe	7.4	100	9.4	127	12.0	162
Other Europe	1.0	100	1.6	160	1.5	150
Canada	0.8	100	2.2	275	1.7	213

SOURCE: OEEC, *General Statistics*, Paris.

23. OECD, *General Statistics*, January, 1962.

24. Strausz-Hupé, Kintner and Possony, *A Forward Strategy for America, op. cit.*, Chapter 10 and Appendix A.

25. See OECD, *General Statistics*, January, 1962, and *Comparisons of the United States and Soviet Economies*, Joint Economic Committee, 86th Congress, 2nd Session, November, 1959, and Supplemental Statement, June, 1960.

26. Unique problems of association will be posed by Spain due to its political isolation from the rest of Western Europe in the post-World War II era. For an extended discussion of this problem, see Benjamin Welles, "Thunderclouds Over Franco's Spain," *New York Times Magazine*, July 1, 1962, pp. 8–9.

27. The view of TEA as a very radical measure has been set forth by the Administration and by a writer close to the Administration, i.e., Joseph Kraft, *The Grand Design, op. cit.* A more balanced and historical view would consider TEA as the short-run solution to the policy stalemate which emerged in the successive renewals of the Reciprocal Trade Expansion Act in the 1950's. This stalemate is best described in Raymond Vernon, "Trade Policy in Crisis," *Princeton Essays in International Finance*, No. 29, Princeton: Princeton University Press, 1958.

28. The significant differences between the tax structures of the

United States and the rest of the Community are pointed out most strikingly in the following chart.

Out of every $1 of tax revenues of central governments:

	Taxes on Income Produce	Taxes on Capital Produce	Taxes on Sales Produce
United States	83.4¢	1.8¢	14.8¢
Canada	65.0¢	1.6¢	33.4¢
Japan	64.9¢	.6¢	34.4¢
Netherlands	64.6¢	3.4¢	32.1¢
Germany	60.2¢	1.6¢	38.2¢
Australia	58.1¢	1.3¢	40.6¢
Britain	55.3¢	3.7¢	41.0¢
France	51.7¢	1.9¢	46.4¢
Belgium	51.4¢	1.5¢	42.1¢
Sweden	50.6¢	1.5¢	47.8¢
Italy	49.7¢	1.7¢	48.6¢
Denmark	40.0¢	5.3¢	54.7¢
Norway	37.5¢	2.2¢	60.3¢

SOURCE: *U.S. News and World Report,* November 12, 1962, p. 87.

29. Of particular significance in this area is the landmark decision of the Council of the EEC of December 19, 1961. Under this first implementing regulation aimed at a community antitrust policy, the Commission of the EEC was vested with the power of enforcing the Anti-Trust Provisions of the Rome Treaty, Articles 85 and 86. Before this regulation, the Anti-Trust Provisions of the Treaty had been largely ineffective. This state of affairs was due to the legal uncertainty resulting from separate national administration of Articles 85 and 86. For a complete résumé of the regulatory powers vested in the Commission, see *Bulletin of the European Economic Community,* February, 1962, pp. 60–65.

30. The nature of the Agricultural Accord of January 16, 1962, has never been adequately explained to lay audiences. First, the agreement calls for the establishment of common prices on all commodities in the Community. The specific steps enumerated to reach this goal are not totally spelled out. All forms of restriction on the movement of agricultural commodities between the nations of the Community were abolished as of July 1, 1962. These restrictions were, in turn, replaced by a system of variable levies, an amount equal to the difference prevailing in the importing nation and the price (generally lower) offered in the exporting nation. In the matter of specifically establishing common prices, the member states are only generally directed gradually to reduce differences in their domestic support prices in order to achieve uniformity at the end of the transition period. The Accord also delays any decisions of the

Council on common price to the harvest of 1964. A detailed procedure involving all the organs of the Community is set up to hammer out the individual price decisions.

To finance the supported prices which are finally agreed upon, the Accord sets up a European Agricultural Guidance and Guarantee Fund. The money for this Fund will come from two sources. First, all receipts from levies on imports of agricultural commodities from nonmember countries, which will equal the difference in world price and the supported community price, will accrue to the Community and be used to finance the buying of surplus production. Secondly, the Fund will be financed out of the budget of the Community. This fact was a significant French concession, particularly to the Germans. The French had first proposed that the financing of supports be tied to national importation of agricultural products. This scheme would have placed the heaviest financial burden upon the Germans, who will be big net importers under a common price level scheme. Under budgetary financing, Germany, France and Italy each bear 28 percent of the cost; Belgium and the Netherlands 7.9 percent, while Luxembourg picks up .2 percent of the Community bill. *Ibid.*, pp. 13.–14.

31. For particularly striking examples see especially, Title III, Chapter 2, Sections 313, 314 and 315, and Chapter 3, particularly Section 324, wherein payment of trade readjustment allowances to an adversely affected worker are limited to 52 weeks with the following exceptions: (a) such payments may be made for not more than 26 additional weeks to an adversely affected worker to assist him to complete training approved by the Secretary of Labor; or (b) such payments shall be made for not more than 13 additional weeks to an adversely affected worker who had realized his sixtieth birthday on or before the date of total or partial separation.

32. Thirty-second Annual Report of the Bank of International Settlements, Basel, 1962.

33. *The NATO Handbook,* Paris: North Atlantic Treaty Organization Information Service, February, 1962, p. 81.

34. To understand the significance of the gold outflow in these three years, one must be familiar with certain pertinent facts about the United States' payments picture in the last decade. From 1950, with the exception of 1957, there has been an annual deficit in the United States' balance-of-payments. The bulk of the deficit to 1957 (approximately three-fourths) was financed through a net increase of foreign balances of dollars in the United States. This country favored the building up of these balances as it added to the reserve position of the European holders of these currencies and allowed them to achieve convertibility of their own currency.

From 1958 to 1961, the division of the financing of our payments deficit seriously changed. From the 1950–1956 average of one-fourth of the deficit being financed by gold losses and three-fourths being financed by net gains in foreign balances, the gold loss financing moved to an average of 40 percent while the increase in net foreign balances decreased to 60 percent of the deficit. Thus of the total, $13.6 billion deficit in its payments run by the United States over the 1958–1961 period, $5.6 of it was financed through gold movements mainly to the nations of Western Europe while $8 billion was financed through an increase in net foreign balances. For extended discussion of the events of the 1958–1961 period see Committee for Economic Development, *The International Position of the Dollar*, New York, 1961.

35. These estimates were made in the winter of 1960–1961 by William D. Dale, then at Stanford Research Institute. Since September, 1961, the Department of Commerce has published in *The Survey of Current Business* quarterly estimates of exports "Financed by Government Grants and Capital"—a series almost identical with that calculated by the Stanford Research Institute.

36. This is the diagnosis of those who advocate sweeping reform of the Community and International Finance System, i.e., Professor Triffin and others. The best statement of the elements of this diagnostic view appears in Robert Triffin, *Gold and the Dollar Crisis*, New Haven: Yale University Press, 1961, Chapter 1.

37. Robert Roosa, "Assuring the Free World's Liquidity," *Business Review Supplement*, Federal Reserve Bank of Philadelphia, September, 1962, p. 5.

38. The Fund, as lender of last resort, is authorized to grant two different types of short-term credits to tide a nation over balance-of-payments difficulties. First, the Fund may make an actual short-term loan. This type of credit is aimed at solving balance-of-payment difficulties of a seasonal or cyclical nature. Second, the Fund may engage itself in a promise of short-term credits or a "stand-by" credit. This latter method has been employed to bolster confidence in the currency of a nation suffering persistent or frequently intermittent deficits. In effect, the IMF "stand-by" credit adds to the monetary reserves of the deficit nation. Very important use was made of the "stand-by" credit arrangement by the United Kingdom in the late fifties.

39. It happens that for the majority of the nations of the Community these monetary reserves consist of dollars and sterling, especially dollars. It is of extreme importance to note at this point that the only nation of the world where significant holdings of gold exist as monetary reserves is the United States. For a complete statement of the problems involved in the Fund's acquisition of large holdings of dollars and sterling and

Triffin's proposed solution, see *International Payments Imbalances,* Report of the Subcommittee on International Exchange and Payments of the Joint Economic Committee, Washington, 1961, p. 17.

40. The difference between these two plans concerns the uses for which the deficit country could employ the surplus nation's currency borrowed from the IMF. Under the Bernstein variant, currency borrowed in this way would be limited to meet the needs arising out of speculative flights of capital rather than to finance trade deficits in a nation's balance of payments. The Jacobsson plan would not so limit the use of borrowings. *Ibid.,* pp. 14–15.

41. Report of the Committee on the Working of the Monetary System, London: Her Majesty's Stationery Office, 1959, pp. 247–248.

42. *International Payments Imbalances, op. cit.,* p. 16.

43. Roosa, *op. cit.,* p. 10.

44. This disproportion is declining, particularly in view of the 1962 cuts in American foreign-aid appropriations. The Europeans have, on occasion, claimed that there is no disproportion at all if one properly weighs the various kinds of investment and loan aid as well as grant aid, but this argument is difficult to prove and, in any event, the total effort is undoubtedly too low.

45. The law of comparative advantage states that under free international trade each country will produce not those things that it can make more cheaply than any other country, but those things it can make relatively most efficiently, i.e., most advantageously.

46. This suggestion has been put forward by the Stanford Research Institute and Mrs. Doris Iklé.

47. EEC, Implementing Convention Relating to the Association with the Overseas Countries and Territories is the enabling instrument for this Fund.

48. *Ibid.,* Article 7 and Annex A.

49. *Ibid.,* Annex B.

50. *Bulletin of the European Economic Community,* February, 1962, p. 16.

51. "Imperial preference, the system of trade discrimination whereby the United Kingdom agreed to impose duties on a considerable range of foreign foodstuffs and raw materials in order to grant preference to empire producers, grew out of the philosophy of The Home Producers First, Empire Producers Second, and Foreign Producers Last." The Ottawa Commonwealth Conference of 1932 finalized this system which had developed gradually in the period before and after World War I. Isaiah Frank, *The European Common Market: An Analysis of Commercial Policy,* New York: Praeger, 1961, p. 126.

52. The best concise treatment of the problems of trade between the

19. The attitude of Britain's two parties toward the decision to enter the EEC was succinctly characterized by the following editorial comment on Labour's effort to amend the government motion: "If as Mr. Michael Foot put it, the Leader of the Opposition was saying that he would join the European football club provided its rules were changed to those of cricket, the Government at times seemed to be saying that the European footballers are really playing cricket without knowing it." *Manchester Guardian Weekly*, August 10, 1961.

20. See, e.g., the editorial, "How Much Less Sovereign?," The *Times*, July 10, 1961.

21. Mr. Hugh Gaitskell, speaking in the House of Commons, challenged the government to answer whether, if Britain should join, binding decisions would be taken by a Council in which Britain would reserve the right of veto, or whether it was expected that the powers of the Commons were to be transferred in any respect to an elected European parliament. *EFTA Reporter*, No. 27, April 25, 1962.

22. "President Kennedy's 'Grand Design': The United States and a United Europe," *The World Today*, September, 1962, p. 387. For an interesting analysis of official U.S. attitudes toward the applications of the neutral countries (Sweden, Switzerland and Austria) for associated status in the EEC, see Gordon Brook-Shepherd, "Does Europe Need Its Neutrals?," *The Reporter*, May 24, 1962.

23. The *Times*, April 11, 1962. Some months earlier, in an address to the Commonwealth Parliamentary Association, Heath had spoken of the important forms of political consultation which had begun on the Continent among the Six. "We believe that, in consultation of this kind, we should play our part. As part of Europe, we should be allowed to influence this consultation and the decisions which may emerge from it. . . . We believe that we are an essential political element in a free, democratic and prosperous Europe." Excerpts in the *EFTA Reporter*, October 9, 1961.

24. Text of President De Gaulle's Sixth Press Conference, May 15, 1962, published by Service de Presse et d'Information, Ambassade de France, New York, pp. 4–5.

25. *Ibid.*, p. 6.

26. De Gaulle's remark about the danger of an outside federator serves to recall the fact that in the late 1940's there were some Europeans who thought that the United States was not applying sufficient pressure toward unification. Paul Reynaud cited the formula enunciated by Jacques Bainville: "In order to build a federation there must be a federating state." He also called attention to the presence of a federating state in Eastern Europe.

Are we in Western Europe incapable . . . of achieving by an act of our own will what, in another part of the world, is imposed by a dictator? I am afraid that the answer must be in the affirmative. . . . But this outside pressure does in fact exist. It is the threat of withdrawal, or substantial reduction, of Marshall Plan credits. I am aware of the scruples which Americans feel at the thought of interfering in the internal affairs of European countries, but a purpose as lofty as this requires that this delicacy be overcome.

"The Unifying Force for Europe," *Foreign Affairs*, Vol. XXVIII, January, 1950, pp. 262–263.

The implications of de Gaulle's reference to le *fédérateur* as a warning to his fellow Europeans "against the dangers of being swallowed up in a lop-sided Atlantic polity dominated by the United States" are discussed by Edmond Taylor, "De Gaulle's Design for Europe," *The Reporter*, June 7, 1962, pp. 15–16. De Gaulle's allegation that certain champions of European integration were serving the interests of the *fédérateur* led to the resignation of MRP leader Pierre Pflimlin from the Ministry. Taylor concludes that the French President was protesting against the errors or inequities of U.S. leadership, but was not turning his back on the Western Alliance.

27. Washington *Post*, November 4, 1961, and the *New York Times*, November 5, 1961. See also Harry B. Ellis, "De Gaulle's Grand Plan," *Christian Science Monitor*, April 16, 1962.

28. De Gaulle clarified his objectives in the following words:

What is it that France is proposing to her five partners? . . . to organize ourselves politically, let us begin at the beginning. Let us organize our cooperation, let our heads of state or government meet periodically to examine our problems together and to make decisions with regard to these problems which will be the decisions of Europe. Let us set up a political commission, a defense commission and a cultural commission, just as we have already formed an economic commission in Brussels which studies common questions and prepares the decisions of the six governments. Naturally, the political commission and the others will proceed, in this regard, in conditions that are appropriate to their political domains. Moreover, the ministers in charge of these various fields will meet whenever necessary to implement in concert the decisions that will be taken by the Council. Finally, we have a European parliamentary assembly that meets in Strasbourg and is composed of delegations from our six national parliaments. Let us enable this assembly to discuss common political questions as it already discusses economic questions. After we have tried it, we shall see, in three years' time, what we can do to strengthen our ties; but at least we shall have begun to acquire the habit of living and acting together. This is what France has proposed. She believes that this is the most practical thing that can be done.

Sixth Press Conference, *op. cit.*, pp. 3–4.

43. Protocol Modifying and Completing the Brussels Treaty, October 23, 1954, Article 4, Clause 3. Text in A. H. Robertson, *op. cit.*, p. 296. The Assembly of the Western European Union, commenting on the Annual Report of the WEU Council for 1959, criticized the Council for not having discussed the 1958 crises in Iraq and Lebanon. *Proceedings,* Fifth Ordinary Session, First Part, June, 1959, Assembly Documents, I, p. 103.

44. "The Council shall decide by unanimous vote questions for which no other voting procedure has been or may be agreed. In the cases provided for in Protocols II, III and IV it will follow the various voting procedures, unanimity, two thirds majority, simple majority, laid down therein. It will decide by simple majority questions submitted to it by the Agency for the Control of Armaments." Protocol, Article 4, Clause 4, *ibid.*, p. 296. Protocols II, III and IV deal with the size of armed forces, the level of internal and police forces, the deployment of British forces on the Continent, the prohibition against West Germany manufacturing certain types of weapons, and the enforcement of the arms control provisions. According to a Report of the WEU Armaments Control Agency of March 31, 1960, the Agency has developed a combined system of documentary controls and field inspections which operates for all existing weapons on the Continent of Europe. The system, says the Report, is "completely adequate for most of the items which may not be produced in Germany, namely guided missiles (except for air defense), heavy warships, medium-sized and large submarines, strategic bombers, and chemical weapons. Study of controls for biological weapons has already reached an advanced stage, but similar controls for atomic weapons still await a decision by the Council of the WEU."

45. See the discussion of this aspect of the question by Glenn H. Snyder, *Deterrence and Defense (cit. supra)*, pp. 176–178.

46. At present the European Launcher Development Organization, whose membership coincides with that of WEU, has only the modest objective of placing a European satellite in orbit by 1966. The project has a budget of 70 million pounds sterling. Britain will be responsible for producing the first stage, which will be based on Blue Streak; France will produce the second stage and Germany the third; Belgium will develop the down-range guidance; the Netherlands will assume the lead in developing the long-range telemetry links and ground equipment; Italy will be responsible for making the test satellites. Manchester *Guardian Weekly*, April 19, 1962.

47. F. W. Mulley, *The Politics of Western Defense*, New York: Praeger, 1962, pp. 26–27. Mr. Mulley, who has been Vice President of the WEU Assembly and Rapporteur of its Defense Committee, submitted a proposal at the WEU Assembly in December, 1959, for a Joint

8. For [...]
Protracted
Dougherty
and follow

9. *Anal[...]*
p. 66.

10. See,
Foreign A[...]
John Sless[...]
101–108.

11. Sovi[...]
consumptio[...]
27 to Sep[...]
Economy a[...]
and the j[...]
European
Arsumanjar[...]
agreed wit[...]
According t[...]
jan stated [...]
economies [...]
nological ar[...]
tion, in the
markets. Fu[...]
the French
evaluations [...]
thesis that t[...]
capitalism a[...]
but an histo[...]

12. Herb[...]
Affairs, Vol.

13. Georg[...]
Affairs, Vol.

14. Willy
Review of V[...]

15. For a
United State
New York:
1961; especi[...]

16. *Analy[...]*
p. 69.

17. Indiag[...]
Quoted in Er[...]

European Strategic Nuclear Force. The proposal received the support of a large majority of the parliamentarians of the WEU countries. Mulley's plan did not call for joint production of nuclear weapons, nor the sharing of atomic secrets, nor the sharing of actual bombs and warheads. It would, he says, "simply have transferred the control of those that existed from national to joint WEU control and direction." *Ibid.,* p. 87. It was, therefore, a more modest proposal than the one under consideration here.

48. President Kennedy hinted at something like this in a press conference the day after his July 4 "interdependence" speech at Independence Hall. Referring to a European nuclear force "not as dependent upon the United States as the present one," he said: "What we have suggested is that this is a matter that Europe should consider carefully; that we would, of course, be responsive to any alternate arrangement that they wish to make. We would examine it. We recognize their problem." *New York Times,* July 6, 1962.

49. Raymond Aron has given the French view on this and warned against "the much too widespread illusion in Washington and in London that the problems posed by General de Gaulle will be resolved when he is no longer there. The special position of Great Britain in the atomic field will never be accepted in Paris, whoever is in power." In *Le Figaro,* May 26, 1962.

50. *New York Times,* July 6, 1962.

51. Glenn Snyder has suggested that a European deterrent force might be placed under the operational control of a single commander who would in turn be responsible to a political authority such as the WEU. In case it would seem doubtful that the political organ would authorize the commander to use nuclear weapons after a single member had been attacked, the authority could be delegated in advance of war and made contingent upon defined circumstances, such as a nuclear attack upon a member, or a ground invasion beyond a certain territorial limit or with a certain size force. The commander might be empowered to retaliate with nuclear weapons at his own discretion unless he received orders to the contrary within a stipulated time after the aggression had begun. *Op. cit.,* pp. 178–179.

CHAPTER 6. THE GRAND DESIGN AND ITS OPPONENTS: A WESTERN RESPONSE

1. *Analysis of the Khrushchev Speech of January 6, 1961,* Washington: U.S. Government Printing Office, 1961, pp. 56–57.

2. President Kennedy urged the senior officials of his Administration to read this speech, and devoted several hours of a meeting with them to its analysis.

ism," in *Neutralism*, Washington: The Washington Center of Foreign Policy Research, 1961, p. 91.

18. *New York Times*, January 6, 1956, quoted in *ibid*.

19. *New York Times*, March 15, 1960, quoted in *ibid*.

20. Indicative of one neutralist attitude toward alliances was President Nkrumah's admonition to Prime Minister Macmillan regarding Britain's decision to extend military assistance to India after the Chinese communist invasion of October, 1962. In a letter, published by the Ghana Government, Nkrumah wrote:

. . . are you sure that by giving support . . . to one side against the other, you will be able to increase the chances of bringing an end to hostilities? . . . Experience has shown that resort to arms and the employment of power politics have been the main cause of mounting tensions in the world. Let us therefore look at the problems that confront the world today with new eyes and in a new spirit of conciliation, mutual understanding, and unflinching respect for the preservation of peace.

He concluded with a statement that he was attempting to mediate between India and Communist China. Manchester *Guardian Weekly*, November 8, 1962.

21. For example, U Thant, Secretary General of the United Nations, declared, in a lecture at Johns Hopkins University, that the "spirit of compromise" that marked negotiations between the United States and the Soviet Union on Cuba should be extended to other outstanding East-West issues. On the Berlin question, he suggested, "it may become imperative to reach solutions on the basis of compromise and the principle of give and take on both sides." Although he did not elaborate, U Thant probably meant, by the "Berlin question," the future status of West Berlin. Yet concessions by the West might easily lead to a further deterioration of the Western position in the communist-surrounded city. *New York Times*, December 3, 1962.

22. K. Krishna Moorthy, "A Brussels at Bangkok?," *Far Eastern Economic Review*, Vol. XXXV, No. 3, January 18, 1962, p. 94.

23. *Analysis of the Khrushchev Speech of January 6, 1961, op. cit.*, p. 71.

24. Bertrand Russell, *Has Man a Future?*, Middlesex: Penguin Books Ltd., 1961, p. 40.

25. The *Daily Mail* (London), October 22, 1962, p. 1.

26. See *United States Foreign Policy: Western Europe, op. cit.*

27. Pietro Nenni, "Where the Italian Socialists Stand," *Foreign Affairs*, Vol. XL, No. 2, January, 1962, p. 221.

28. H. Stuart Hughes, "Disengagement and NATO," *The Liberal*

Papers, James Roosevelt, ed., Garden City, New York: Doubleday and Company, 1962, pp. 309–310.

29. John W. Holmes, "Canada and the United States in World Politics," *Foreign Affairs,* Vol. XL, No. 1, October, 1961, p. 112.

30. *Alliance for Progress Newsletter,* No. 9, July, 1962.

31. José Figueres, "The Alliance and Political Goals," *The Alliance for Progress: Problems and Perspectives,* John C. Dreier, ed., Baltimore: Johns Hopkins Press, 1962, p. 85.

32. Raymond F. Mikesell, "The Movement Toward Regional Trading Groups in Latin America," *Latin American Issues: Essays and Comments,* Albert O. Hirschman, ed., New York: The Twentieth Century Fund, 1961, pp. 127–132.

33. *Ibid.*

34. Jules Monnerot, *The Sociology of Communism,* London: George Allen and Unwin, 1953, p. 11.

35. *New York Times,* January 11, 1958, p. 6.

36. *Ibid.,* January 12, 1958, Section E, p. 10.

37. James P. Warburg, "A Re-examination of American Foreign Policy," *The Liberal Papers, op. cit.,* p. 95.

38. For a fuller examination of the democratic methodology, see Robert Strausz-Hupé, *Power and Community,* New York: Praeger, 1956, p. 38 and following.

39. David Riesman and Michael Maccoby, "The American Crisis," *The Liberal Papers, op. cit.,* p. 30.

40. McGeorge Bundy, "Friends and Allies," *Foreign Affairs,* Vol. XLI, October, 1962, p. 17.

41. Washington *Post,* September 24, 1962.

42. *New York Times,* September 23, 1962, p. 4.

43. For a full examination of the Soviet vulnerabilities which could be the objective of Western political warfare, see *The New Frontier of War,* W. R. Kintner, J. K. Kornfeder, Chicago: Regnery, 1962, Chapter XVI, "Target Vulnerabilities," p. 317.

44. Robert F. Kennedy, *Just Friends and Brave Enemies,* New York: Harper & Row, 1962, pp. 197–198.

45. "Mr. Khrushchev's efforts during the past few weeks to lure Italy away from the Common Market have been heavy-handed. But they have had a considerable degree of success.

"Many Italian firms, and notably the major combines owned wholly or partially by the State, already have extensive commercial relations with Russia. Among them are ENI, the State hydro-carbon combine headed by Signor Mattei, and the Fiat Corporation." Anthony Mann,

"Mr. Khrushchev's Road to Rome," London *Daily Telegraph*, July 3, 1962.

46. Strausz-Hupé, Kintner and Possony, *A Forward Strategy for America, op. cit.*, pp. 171–173.

47. Samuel Pisar, *A New Look at Trade Policy toward the Communist Bloc*, Joint Economic Committee, Subcommittee on Foreign Economic Policy, U.S. Congress, Washington: U.S. Government Printing Office, 1961, p. 5.

48. From an address in Copenhagen before the Atlantic Treaty Association, September 27, 1962.

CHAPTER 7. INSTITUTIONS FOR THE FUTURE ATLANTIC COMMUNITY

1. *Seventh Annual Session, NATO Parliamentarians' Conference, Verbatim Report, First Plenary Session*, November 13, 1961, p. 13.

2. The Parliamentarians' Conference consists of members of the national legislatures of the NATO countries. Although it has no official status defined in the NATO Treaty, it has become an important Atlantic forum. The resolution mentioned above embodied ideas which were first broached at the North Atlantic Community Conference at Bruges in September, 1957, sponsored jointly by the Collège d'Europe and the University of Pennsylvania.

3. Quoted in *Report of the Political Committee on the Atlantic Convention of NATO Nations*, submitted by Mr. Frans J. Goedhart.

4. A full account of the Convention's proceedings is to be found in *Freedom and Union*, Vol. XVII, February–March, 1962, pp. 6–10.

5. The full text of the Declaration of Paris can be found in *ibid.*, pp. 13–16.

6. See the Summary of Recommendations and Part I, "Political and Economic Questions."

7. In sharp contrast to President de Gaulle, who emphasizes the importance of the individual state executive's role in European unification, the WEU Assembly early in June, 1962, called for a democratic European Parliament empowered to vote on foreign policy, defense and currency questions, and for a central European Community political executive independent of the member states but responsible to the Parliament. Manchester *Guardian Weekly*, June 14, 1962.

8. This was one of the central recommendations made by the Foreign Policy Research Institute in its 1959 report to the Senate Foreign Relations Committee on U.S. Foreign Policy Toward Western Europe.

9. "The purpose of this reform would not be to give the Council supranational powers, nor to abandon its essential rule of private discussion, but to increase the authority of its views with governments, electorates and adversaries by appointing men who can interpret its conclusions and

directives to their own people with high authority." "The Reform of NATO," *op. cit.*, p. 175.

10. Address of the Honorable George W. Ball before the Eighth Annual NATO Parliamentarians' Conference, Paris, November 16, 1962.

11. "The Reform of NATO," p. 173.

12. Sir John Slessor, "Reorganization of the Higher Direction of NATO," a paper prepared for the Atlantic Convention, International Conference Center, Paris, January, 1962. Kurt Birrenbach, a member of the West German Bundestag, has sounded a similar warning against "excessive bureaucratization of the civilian NATO management" and the subordination of SACEUR to a deputy secretary general. "The Reorganization of NATO," adapted from *Die Zukunft der Atlantischen Gemeinschaft* for *Orbis*, Vol. VI, Summer, 1962, p. 245.

13. "The Reform of NATO," pp. 177–178.

14. Relatively little attention has been paid by the proponents of NATO reform to the importance of closer cultural, scientific and intellectual cooperation, and of NATO public relations. The proposed fifth deputy secretary general would be responsible for certain functions which are now located in the Division of Political Affairs. Efforts should be made to accelerate the communication of ideas throughout the NATO area, as well as various forms of cultural, scientific and intellectual cooperation. NATO bodies should be encouraged to expand contacts with interested nongovernmental organizations and press media (especially television) to enhance the effectiveness of informational, educational and other public support programs. More funds should be made available for: the translation and distribution of NATO publications; the production and distribution of NATO films; and the conduct of NATO tours for educators, journalists, and civic, business and labor leaders. NATO seminars on various subjects for various groups of influential persons should be expanded, as should teacher-student exchange programs. Universities should be urged to create chairs of Atlantic studies. Plans should be pressed vigorously for the creation of the proposed European University, and for the possible creation of an International Institute of Science and Technology along the lines laid down in the Armand Report. The proposed office of informational, cultural and scientific affairs would be responsible for providing assistance and cooperation to the Atlantic Institute.

15. Address to the Seventh Annual Conference, *Verbatim Report, cit. supra*, p. 12.

16. Gerhard Liebholz, in the Preface to Wolfgang Birke, *European Elections by Direct Suffrage*, Leyden: A. W. Sythoff, 1961, p. 12.

17. Declaration of Paris, Part I, B. *Freedom and Union, op. cit.*, p. 14.

CHAPTER 8. THE ATLANTIC VISION: A QUESTION OF CHOICE

1. An address on the occasion of the dedication of the Hoover Library at Westbranch, Iowa, August 10, 1962, as reported in the *New York Times,* August 11, 1962.

2. J. W. Fulbright, "For a Concert of Free Nations," *Foreign Affairs,* Vol. XL, October, 1961, p. 3.

3. *Ibid.,* pp. 16–17.

4. On the merits of this configuration and its likely costs to the United States, Paul-Henri Spaak wrote as follows:

Then why a united Europe? Would it not be sufficient if each European country agreed to become a form of American satellite? No. America herself is aware of her need to rely for support upon powerful groups. She knows, because she has made the experiment herself, that political integration multiplies a continent's potentials instead of merely adding them. Since she believes in the identity of goals on both sides of the Atlantic, she is ready to encourage European unification. She may pay a rather high economic price for this, but she is willing to countenance powerful competition, provided the competitor be a reliable partner.

"How I See the Unification of Europe," *Realité,* September, 1962, p. 62.

5. In an address given at the Eighth Annual NATO Parliamentarians' Conference in Paris, November 16, 1962, Under Secretary of State George W. Ball said:

From a strictly military standpoint, we do not feel that the Alliance has an urgent need for a European nuclear contribution. But should other NATO nations so desire, we are ready to give serious consideration to the creation of a genuinely multilateral Medium Range Ballistic Missile force *fully* coordinated with the other deterrent forces of the North Atlantic Treaty Organization. [italics added]

6. For a discussion of weighted voting in the NATO Council, see Livingston Hartley, "On the Political Integration of the Atlantic Community," *Orbis,* Winter, 1963, Volume VI, No. 4. See also the interesting idea set forth by Professor Klaus Knorr of Princeton University in a memorandum on the problems of managing the kind of NATO nuclear force envisaged in the Nassau Agreement. Professor Knorr points out that in case the entire NATO Alliance is subjected to a massive nuclear attack, the problem of decision-making does not arise; the response is automatic. The problem arises in acute form when NATO confronts an emergency created by an ambiguous, less-than-total threat. He suggests that all fifteen NATO members consent to an arrangement whereby the authority of the Alliance can be concentrated in times of crisis. If either a qualified majority (two-thirds of the members) or a qualified minority (the major members) decide that a crisis exists, decision-making power

387 NOTES

would devolve upon the Big Five: the United States, the United Kingdom, France, West Germany and Italy. These would take decisions by simple majority. Any disaffected members (either among the Five or the Ten) could drop out of NATO. The authors consider this aspect of the proposal unduly pessimistic, but they find merit in the general notion that the Alliance members should recognize the pre-eminent responsibility of the leading powers. Professor Knorr notes that the proposed system could just as easily be adapted to Four as to Five. *A NATO Nuclear Force: The Problem of Management,* Policy Memorandum No. 26, Center of International Studies, Woodrow Wilson School of Public and International Affairs, Princeton University, February 5, 1963.

7. Fulbright, *op. cit.,* p. 14.

8. See NATO Parliamentarians' Conference, *Reports and Recommendations,* adopted by the Eighth Annual Conference, Paris, November, 1962, Document E. 188.

9. Text of President Kennedy's speech of July 4, 1962, at Independence Hall, Philadelphia, as reported in The Philadelphia *Inquirer,* July 5, 1962.

10. Spaak, *op. cit.,* p. 63.

POSTSCRIPT

1. The British, it is true, never issued any formal acknowledgment that they were either contemplating or negotiating some form of Anglo-French nuclear cooperation. But there was sufficient speculation to this effect in responsible and usually well-informed periodicals to permit such an inference to be drawn. Cf. "Nuclear Sharing and Arms Control," The *Economist,* April 28, 1962; "Not the Fourth," *ibid.,* May 5, 1962; "Living with de Gaulle," *ibid.,* May 12, 1962; "Three Fingers on the Trigger," The *Times* (London), June 24, 1962; The *Times* (London), June 27, 1962; "Independent Deterrents," *The Manchester Guardian Weekly,* June 28, 1962; and *The New York Times,* November 4, 1962. These various reports are discussed *supra,* in Chapter 3, p. 129, and in Chapter 5, pp. 216, 219 and 220. See also Denis Healey, "After the Nassau Meeting," *The New Leader,* January 21, 1963, pp. 14–15.

2. See note 13, pp. 353–354, for operational portions of agreement.

3. Washington *Post,* January 1, 1963.

4. RAND analyst Malcolm W. Hoag writes that America's broad objective is "to arrest the proliferation of nuclear powers, not to speed it. Therefore, we have persisted in one message to would-be aspirants: 'If you go toward independent nuclear capabilities, you go it alone. The road promises to be long and costly. And for what?' The painfulness of the French experience may, we hope, be a forceful example to others." "Nu-

clear Policy and French Intransigence," *Foreign Affairs,* Vol. LXI, January, 1963, p. 286.

5. Text of President de Gaulle's Seventh Press Conference, January 14, 1963, Ambassade de France, Service de Presse et d'Information, Speeches and Press Conferences No. 185, p. 11.

6. Washington *Post,* January 25, 1963.

7. One prevalent American view is that de Gaulle was determined to prevent Britain from entering EEC unless she changed her basic orientation. The French position, however, does not necessarily betoken bad faith. The timing of de Gaulle's January 14, 1963 speech has led American observers to impute such bad faith to de Gaulle and to imply that his intervention was triggered not by the prospect of failure to agree but rather by the prospect of agreement. This interpretation does not hold with the record, which reads somewhat differently. Two weeks after the negotiations opened in 1961, de Gaulle visited Prime Minister Macmillan. The British, as reported by the *New York Times,* "thought de Gaulle encouraging about Britain's proposed entry into the Common Market and sympathetic about her difficulties with the Commonwealth countries arising from that issue." On February 22, 1962, Britain accepted the principles and framework of the common agricultural policy of the Six but asked for significant modifications in its application. Initial French reaction to this British attempt to modify the rules of the Rome Treaty came in a speech by Foreign Minister Maurice Couve de Murville to the European Parliamentary Assembly at Strasbourg on March 29, 1962. M. Couve de Murville said: "For the moment we cannot lay down any hard and fast rules for membership or association: the doctrine of the Community will have to be defined in respect to the progress of the talks with Great Britain." This attitude did not reflect an intention to wreck the negotiations. Nor can this purpose be read into the public communiqué which issued from the Macmillan-de Gaulle meeting of June 2–3, 1962. The communiqué stated that the two leaders had "confirmed their agreement on the community of interests between France and the United Kingdom. They expressed their intention that this spirit would animate them in the consideration of the great problems with which they have to deal, and it is in this same spirit that they embarked upon and intend to continue the negotiations now pending in Brussels." As the negotiations continued throughout 1962, real differences emerged between the British and EEC positions on the application of the common external tariff to the United Kingdom, and British acceptance of the common agricultural policy of the EEC. The extent of these differences was, however, played down in American circles. The British, on the other hand, seem to have recognized the extent of the difficulties. In late October of 1962, Edward Heath, chief British negotiator at Brussels, warned the House of Com-

mons (at the opening of a two-day debate on the Brussels talks) that "immensely difficult problems" lay ahead in the "formidable negotiations" for Britain's entry into EEC. When the negotiations were suspended in January of 1963, the unresolved issues were substantial. In a statement to the French National Assembly on January 24, 1963, Foreign Minister Couve de Murville summed up these differences and, in defense of the French position, added the following commentary on British conduct of the negotiations:

> How is it possible not to be skeptical when one is asked to put off to the future transformations, certainly cruel but inevitable, on the pretext that they will be easier the day after tomorrow than at the time of the psychological shock which would have been Britain's entry into the Common Market?

These words have the ring of an honest judgment on a year of fruitless negotiation, rather than of a contrived excuse for wrecking a near-successful negotiation.

8. Washington *Post*, February 6, 1963.

9. Alastair Buchan argues that the U.S. should present a clear and continuous picture of its strategic policy—then European governments would understand clearly the considerations which must govern their own defense policies. See "The Reform of NATO," *op. cit.*, p. 180.

10. Henry Kissinger, "Strains on the Alliance," *Foreign Affairs*, Vol. XLI, January, 1963, p. 275.

11. Cf. Charles J. V. Murphy, "NATO at a Nuclear Crossroads," *Fortune*, December, 1962.

12. As Alastair Buchan, a consistently friendly supporter of the United States, has observed: "A NATO solution seems to me to require from the United States a greater consistency as to strategic doctrine so that yesterday's orthodoxy, for instance on tactical nuclear weapons, does not become today's heresy. These rapid changes of U.S. policy . . . undermine European confidence and make it hard to accept American pretensions to be the fount of military wisdom."

13. Washington *Post*, February 13, 1963, page A-9 (emphasis supplied).

14. Translated from an article by Jean-Jacques Servan-Schreiber in *L'Express*, January 24, 1963.

INDEX

Abbreviations of organization names, 139
Acheson, Dean, 53
Adams, Henry, 16
Adams, John, 9
Adenauer, Konrad, 140; loyal to NATO, 51–52; and French policy, 214–15, 220; negotiations with Soviets, 240; replacement of, 341
Aeroflot, propaganda arm, 278
Africa, ix, 61, 184, 231, 236, 237, 266; ambivalent policies, 69; UN solution, 204; policy differences over, 204; French community in, 210; vital to Europe, 213; sub-Sahara, 217; Soviet penetration, 217, 278; U.S. policies, 217; problems common to Asia and Africa, see Asia
Afro-Asian attitude toward alliance, 254–55
Agriculture: EEC threat to U.S., 158–60
Aid: American, 2; cooperative, 178–79, 180; to underdeveloped, 184; to offset trade fluctuations, 184
Alaska, 67
Algeria, 64, 191, 209, 210, 332; NATO problem, 54; importance of French stand in, 55; de Gaulle's need of Allied help in, 55; Franco-Algerian accord, 1962, 62; specter of OAS-type organization in Europe, 98
Allais, Maurice, 315
Angel, Sir Norman, 16
Anglo-American partnership, diminishing returns of, 219; and Nassau Agreement, 331
Angola, 56, 62
Anti-trust policies, 158
Anzus, 297
Arab world, 41
Argentina, 263
Aristotle, 11
Armenia, 10
Aron, Raymond, 113–14, 122, 326
Article II, North Atlantic Treaty, 164
Article VI, North Atlantic Treaty, 54
Asia, ix, 231, 236, 237, 266, 269, 324; Allies' failure to coordinate policies on, 41; emerging nations in, 62, 64; U.S. commitments in, 67–68; criticism of British policy, 205; neutralism, 245, 249, 251–55, 310; nationalism, 254, 305;

unity, 254–55; economic stimulation by Japan, 256; passing of nation-state system, 304; population growth in, 308
Athens, 105
Atlantic Alliance: communists oppose, 3; impetus to basic unity of West, 4; toward political unity, 35; regional blocks, 147; reappraisal of concept, 191; form of European-American partnership in, 191–92
Atlantic Charter, 28
Atlantic Community: outstanding event of century, ix; value system, 13; limits not geographical, 14; meaning of, 14–15; development of not directed against other nations, 15; protection to others desiring freedom, 15; guarded by NATO, 28; must master Soviet expansion, 28; security rests on U.S., 77; integrated nuclear force, 99; six categories of economic policy, 155–56; open societies, 155; and uncommitted nations, 156; and communist bloc, 156; concerted economic policies, 156, 184–85; monetary structure, 156; direct development assistance, 177; capital to underdeveloped, 177; trade with underdeveloped, 181–82; group programs, 189; European-American interdependence, 226; transatlantic nuclear partners, 230; ideological pluralism, 284; basic cultural values, 284; collective political performance, 292, 316; tragedy for, 341; plans for health of, 343
Atlantic Congress, London, 1959, 287
Atlantic Convention, 1962, 287
Atlantic Federal Union, 286
Atlantic Institute, 8, 273
Atlantic nuclear cooperation, 132
Atlantic Organization for Cultural, Scientific and Educational Affairs, suggested, 273
Atlantic partnership: de Gaulle's concept of, 333, 334
Atlantic unity, ix; threat to Communist Grand Design, 28; European reservations, 256–60, 264; American criticism of, 260–61; Canadian reservations, 262; Latin-American reservations, 262–63; American policy, 306